I0823718

Staging Intercultural Ireland

New Plays and Practitioner Perspectives

Staging Intercultural Ireland

New Plays and Practitioner Perspectives

Edited by

Charlotte McIvor and
Matthew Spangler

First published in 2014 by
Cork University Press
Youngline Industrial Estate
Pouladuff Road, Togher
Cork, Ireland

British Library Cataloguing in Publication Data
A CIP catalogue record for this book is available from the British Library.

ISBN 978-1-78205-104-6

Typeset by Tower Books, Ballincollig, County Cork
Printed in Malta by Gutenberg Press

www.corkuniversitypress.com

Contents

Acknowledgements

This book represents the work of twenty-three theatre artists and scholars working at the intersection of inward-migration and interculturalism in Ireland during the last two decades. First and foremost, we would like to thank them for their generous contributions to this book. Without their work, this book would not have been possible.

We would also like to thank National University of Ireland, Galway, San José State University and the University of California, Berkeley for a number of grants that supported travel and research for this project. This work has been supported in particular by the National University of Ireland, Galway's Millennium Fund, a California State University Research Grant, and a number of research grants from the College of Social Sciences at San José State University.

The support of our colleagues has also been pivotal especially Patrick Lonergan, Lionel Pilkington, Rebecca Barr, Elizabeth Tilley, Siobhán O'Gorman, Philip Mullen, Emilie Pine, Thomas Conway, and Cari Powers. We would also like to thank our family and friends for their role in this process, especially Jackie and Martin Clarke, Margaret Macardle, Bern Deegan, Weldon Thornton, Eliot Spangler, and most especially our partners, Ramin Haghjoo and Crystal Smith-Spangler.

Finally, we would like to thank the two anonymous reviewers, Cork University Press, and, in particular, Maria O'Donovan for guiding this anthology to completion.

Notes on Contributors

BISI ADIGUN was born and raised in the Yoruba region of southwestern Nigeria. He worked as a performing artist in London for three years before moving to Dublin in 1996, where, in 2003, he founded Arambe Productions, Ireland's first African theatre company (www.arambeproductions.com). To date, Adigun has produced and directed all of Arambe's productions. In 2006, he was commissioned by Arambe to co-write, with Irish writer Roddy Doyle, a modern version of J.M. Synge's *The Playboy of the Western World*, which premiered at the Abbey Theatre during the fiftieth Ulster Dublin Theatre festival in October 2007. In 2009, Adigun wrote *The Playboy of the Sunny South East*, another version of Synge's *Playboy*, which he directed for a Waterford Youth Arts production in Garter Lane, Waterford. For the 2010 Dublin Fringe Festival, Arambe presented Adigun's *The Butcher Babes*, a tragicomedy based on the 2005 gruesome murder and subsequent decapitation of Farah Swaleh Noor, a Kenyan immigrant, by two Irish sisters now infamously known as the Scissor Sisters. Adigun is currently working on a modernisation of Brian Friel's *Philadelphia, Here I Come!* He holds a BA in Dramatic Arts (Obafemi Awolowo University, Ile-Ife, Nigeria), an MA in Drama Studies (University College Dublin), an MA in Film/Television (Dublin City University), and a PhD in Drama Studies (Trinity College Dublin).

ALICJA AYRES is an international actor based in Dublin, Ireland. She started her acting career with Maybe Theatre Company in Gdansk, Poland. After moving to Dublin, Alicja joined Polish Theatre Ireland and performed in their debut play *Scent of Chocolate*. Other credits include *The Maids, A Christmas Carol, Toxic, Chesslaugh Mewash* at Absolut Fringe and, most recently, *Shibari*, an Abbey Theatre Commission, which premiered on the Peacock stage on 10 October 2012. Credits in film include a featured role in *Sanctuary*, a feature directed by Norah McGettigan, which premiered at the Galway Film Fleadh 2012; a television clip for one of Ireland's most renowned comedians, Tommy Tiernan; and Alicja's first lead role in an indie feature, *Death Waits*, written and directed by Redmond Fitzpatrick. Alicja is also a singer and an art model. She loves photography and writes poems, short plays and mini-screenplays. She graduated from the Gaiety School of Acting in June 2011.

Sara Brady is Assistant Professor at Bronx Community College of the City University of New York. She is co-editor with Fintan Walsh of *Crossroads: Performance Studies and Irish Culture* (Palgrave 2009) and the author of *Performance, Politics, and the War on Terror: 'Whatever It Takes'* (Palgrave 2012). She holds a PhD in Performance Studies from New York University.

John Currivan began his career with Clondalkin Youth Theatre, and graduated from the Bachelor in Acting Studies course at Trinity College Dublin in 2009. He is an actor, writer, director, youth theatre facilitator and the founder of Little Room Productions, which creates and produces new works of theatre and graphic media. As an actor, he has worked with companies across Ireland, including Polish Theatre Ireland, devise+conquer, Fíbín Teo, and the Abbey Theatre. He also appeared in series seventeen of TG4's *Ros na Rún*. He has directed for Little Room Productions, Polish Theatre Ireland, and Clondalkin Youth Theatre. For Little Room, he has written and directed, *Behind the Shamrocks* (audio tour, 2009), *One Waiting Room* (2011), directed and devised *future is* ____ (2012), as well as writing the award nominated comic *If Only I Was a Waterproof Watch* (ICN awards 2011) and the *Cynical Saga of Jeremy Geoffries* mini-comics (2013). He has also written the plays *DIVE, Choleric Sausage,* and *The Dust of My House* (shortlisted for the P.J. O'Connor radio drama award, 2012).

Declan Gorman was founding Artistic Director of Upstate Theatre Project from 1997 to 2010. With Upstate, he wrote and directed several plays, and co-facilitated community drama projects. He began his career as founder and performer with Co-Motion Theatre Company, Dublin in the 1980s. He was the Theatre Programme Director at City Arts (1990–95) and Coordinator of the Arts Council's theatre review (1995–96). Throughout his career, he has written and directed extensively including street spectacles for the Dublin St Patrick's Festival and Calypso Theatre Company, as well as public art projects in Monaghan and Louth. He has taught drama programmes with New York University, NUI Galway, and Dundalk Institute of Technology. He is currently completing his first novel and touring his one-man James Joyce show, *The Dubliners Dilemma.*

Charlotte Headrick is a Professor of Theatre Arts at Oregon State University. She was the 1994 Elizabeth P. Ritchie Outstanding Professor for Undergraduate Teaching, the highest teaching award of Oregon State University. She also received the 2003 Excellence Award from the College of Liberal Arts, the highest honour given by the College. She has directed many Irish plays, including the American premieres of several, such as Charabanc's *Lay Up Your Ends*, Gemma O'Connor's *SigNora Joyce*, Elizabeth Kuti's *Treehouses*, Declan Hughes' *Love and a Bottle*, and Nicola McCartney's

Heritage. Among the other Irish plays she has directed are Patricia Burke Brogan's *Eclipsed* at Western Kentucky University and Indiana University (NEH Seminar'100 years of Irish Drama: Widening the Stage', 1999); *Tea in a China Cup* at the University of Central Oklahoma (1999 and 2000); Frank McGuinness' *Observe the Sons of Ulster Marching Towards the Somme* (2006) at Berry College; *The Playboy of the Western World* (2007 and 2012) and Elizabeth Kuti's award-winning *The Sugar Wife* (2012), both at Oregon State. She is widely published in the field of Irish Drama and has presented numerous papers nationally and internationally on Irish women dramatists. She is the recipient of the Kennedy Center Medallion for outstanding service to the Kennedy Center/American College Theatre Festival. As past-president and member of the American Conference for Irish Studies, she planned and coordinated two conferences at Oregon State University. Three times a fellow at the Center for the Humanities, she is the co-editor with Eileen Kearney of *Irish Women Dramatists: 1908-2001,* an anthology of Irish women dramatists forthcoming from Syracuse University Press. She was a Moore Visiting Fellow at NUI, Galway in the spring of 2013.

JOSÉ MIGUEL JIMÉNEZ studied theatre in Universidad de Chile for four years, after which he became founding member of two theatre companies currently active in Santiago. In 2004, he moved to Ireland and completed the Bachelor in Acting Studies in Trinity College. Acting credits in Ireland include *Love's Labour Lost* directed by Tom Creed; *Big Love* directed by Selina Cartmell in the Peacock Theatre; *Everybody Loves Sylvia* by Randolf SD in the Project Arts Centre, directed by Wayne Jordan and the feature film *Kisses* by Fastnet Films. He then formed a new theatre company in Ireland known as The Company, and with it, he debuted as director during Absolute Fringe Festival 2009 with *Who is Fergus Kilpatrick?,* which won the Spirit of the Fringe award that year. After that, he returned to Chile where he designed the sound for *Arturo* and performed in *Ernesto* as part of the *International Theatre Festival Santiago a Mil [FITAM]*. His second show with The Company entitled *As you are now so once were we,* based on James Joyce's *Ulysses,* received the Best Production award as part of Absolut Fringe Festival 2010. *Who is Fergus Kilpatrick?* toured to the twentieth Bucharest National Theatre Festival in Romania in 2010. *As you are now so once were we* was commissioned by the Abbey Theatre, restaged in January 2011 and toured to Los Angeles and Portugal 2011, and in 2012 to Berlin as part of the first Full Irish festival in that city. The Company's fourth production, *Politik,* appeared in the Dublin Theatre Festival in 2012 and was revived at Fast Forward Festival in Braunschweig, Germany. He directed Mark Cantan's *Jezebel* for Rough Magic Theatre Company in 2012. He is currently working on a collaboration with the Visual Arts department at Project Arts Centre, developing an international collaboration between Chilean and Irish artists entitled *Bernardo* and preparing The Company's fifth production, which will be based on Aeschylus' *The Oresteia* to be premiered in 2014. José Miguel is part of Project Catalyst, an initiative of the Project Arts Centre.

JASON KING lectures in English at the University of Limerick. He was also an Assistant Professor in the English Department and Canadian–Irish Studies at Concordia University; a visiting professor at the Université de Montréal; and a Lecturer in English at the National University of Ireland, Maynooth. His publications include a special issue of *The Irish Review* on 'Memoir, Memory, and Migration in Irish Culture' (2012), *Ireland and the Americas: Culture, Politics, History* (2008), a special issue of the *Canadian Journal of Irish Studies* on 'Irish–Canadian Connections' (2005), as well as numerous articles and chapters about Irish theatre and diasporic writing in journals and edited collections on both sides of the Atlantic.

KASIA LECH, co-founder of Polish Theatre Ireland, is a Lecturer in Performing Arts at Canterbury Christ Church University. She holds a doctorate in theatre studies from University College Dublin. Her research on the importance of verse structure in theatrical performance was supported by the Irish Research Council. Kasia trained as an actor and completed her MA in acting at the Ludwik Solski State Drama School in Wrocław (Poland). She started her professional career in theatre in Poland and has been continuing it in Ireland and UK in both theatre and film. Kasia is also a storyteller and worked in voiceover.

DECLAN MALLON is a co-founder and the current Director of Upstate Theatre Project. He has been responsible for the projects under the Local and Learning banners of the Upstate policy. Before joining Upstate Theatre Project, Declan worked as a freelance drama facilitator mainly based in Drogheda. He founded the Droichead Youth Theatre in 1992 while working as the Droichead Arts Centre's Drama Officer. Declan published a biography of the Irish artist Nano Reid in 1995. He completed a Master degree in Theatre Studies in 2009.

NICOLA MCCARTNEY is a Scotland-based playwright, director and dramaturge. Originally from Belfast, she trained as a director at Charabanc Theatre Company (Belfast) and the Citizens Theatre (Glasgow). She was Artistic Director of Glasgow-based new writing theatre company, lookout, from 1992 to 2002. In 1996, she directed the national tour of *Trainspotting* by Irvine Welsh, adapted by Harry Gibson (1996) for the Citizens Theatre/G&J Productions. As a playwright, her work includes: *Laundry, Easy, Home, Cave Dwellers* (7:84 Scotland Theatre Co), *Heritage* (Traverse), *Convictions,* and *1 in 5* (Tinderbox), *Underworld* (Frantic Assembly), *Lifeboat* (New Victory Theatre, New York), which won the TMA/Equity Best New Show For Children & Young People 2002, and *A Sheep Called Skye* (National Theatre of Scotland). Nicola has worked as a dramaturge and on script development for a range of companies, including Playwrights Studio Scotland, Tron Theatre, Theatre Hebrides, Birds of Paradise, Traverse Theatre, NTS, Stellar Quines, and the Edinburgh International Festival 2005 and Vanishing Point. Nicola was one of the inaugural Associate Playwrights of the Playwrights Studio Scotland. She was a recipient of a Creative Scotland Award in 2003 to work on her first novel. Nicola has also written extensively for radio, televison and film. Her current commissions include: National Theatre Scotland, Abbey Theatre, Tinderbox, Traverse Theatre and BBC Radio Drama. She has been Writer in Residence at the University of Ulster and Shetland Arts amongst others and is currently Lecturer in Writing for Performance at the University of Edinburgh.

ROSALEEN MCDONAGH is a Traveller woman with a disability. Originally from Sligo, she is one of twenty siblings. She worked in Pavee Point Travellers' Centre for ten years where she managed the Violence Against Women programme. Her involvement in leading initiatives on Traveller women's issues and Traveller health issues has led her to be regarded as a leading feminist within the Traveller community. McDonagh's plays include *The Baby Doll Project, Stuck, She's Not Mine, Rings, Mainstream* and an adaptation of Colum McCann's novel *Zoli*. *Rings* was performed at VAS in Washington in June 2010. McDonagh was shortlisted for the P.J. O'Connor radio play Awards 2010. In March 2012, *Beat Him Like a Badger* was commissioned by Fishamble to be part of the *Tiny Plays for Ireland* series. She was commissioned for a feature article in *The Irish Times* in 2012 responding to Channel 4's series *My Big Fat Gypsy Wedding*. *Irish Theatre Magazine* also commissioned her to write 'Cripping Up; Copping Out' about Disability Arts in Ireland. She is currently in development with RTÉ on *Unsettled*, a television drama. McDonagh has a Bachelor of Arts in Biblical and Theological Studies, an MPhil in Ethnic and Racial Studies, and an MPhil in Creative Writing, all from Trinity College Dublin.

CHARLOTTE MCIVOR is Lecturer in Drama at the National University of Ireland, Galway where she is the director of Postgraduate Studies in Drama. She received her PhD in Performance Studies from the University of California, Berkeley in 2011 with a designated emphasis on gender, women and sexuality and has also taught at California College of the Arts and Santa Clara University. Her essays have appeared in *Irish University Review, Modern Drama, Public* and *InVisible Culture: An Electronic Journal for Visual Culture* and edited collections including *Crossroads: Performance Studies and Irish Culture, Deviant Acts: Essays on Queer Performance* and *That Was Us: Contemporary Irish Theatre and Performance*. She is currently working on a book entitled *Migration and Performance in Contemporary Ireland: Towards A New*

Interculturalism (Palgrave), which argues that theatre and performance are at the centre of conceptualising interculturalism as social policy and aspiration in contemporary Ireland.

PAUL MEADE is a writer, director, actor and Artistic Director of Gúna Nua Theatre. From Limerick, Paul trained at the Samuel Beckett Centre, Trinity College, and later received an MA in modern drama from UCD. Work as a writer includes *Faith, Meltdown, Scenes From a Water Cooler, Skin Deep* (Stewart Parker Award Winner), *Thesis* and *Trousers* all for Gúna Nua. Paul has also written *Mushroom* for Storytellers Theatre Company, *Light Signals* for Team Theatre and *Begotten Not Made* for The Irish Council for Bioethics. The latter went on to win the Jim McNaughton/Business to Arts Bursary and was broadcast on RTÉ Radio. Most recently, Paul wrote *The Short Biography of Denis O'Rourke* for RTÉ radio drama's 'What is Life?' series. Paul's translation of *Stop The Tempo* by Gianina Carbinariu received its American Premiere in New York produced by Origin Theatre Company. Paul's directing work includes the award winning *Pondling, The Goddess of Liberty, Little Gem* and *Scenes From a Water Cooler* (co-directed with David Parnell), *Chicane, Meltdown, Shay* and *Aisling's Stories, Taste, The Real Thing* and *Trousers* for Gúna Nua. He has also directed *Green Street* for Percolate, *Translations* for Hands Turn Theatre, *Medea* for Threshold, and *Positive Dead People* and *The Shawl* for Bewley's Café Theatre.

Paul teaches classical text at The Lir and Acting at Inchicore College of Further Education.

BAIRBRE NÍ CHAOIMH has worked extensively as an actor on stage, screen, radio and television. Since making her debut at the Abbey Theatre, she has acted with many companies including the Gate, Druid, and the London Stage Co, performing in Ireland, England, the United States, Japan and Australia. She is also a director whose work has toured nationally as well as internationally to London, Edinburgh, Berlin, Pristina, Skopje, New York and Melbourne. She was an Associate Artist at the Abbey Theatre. She received *The Irish Times* Judges' Special Award in 2008 for her work as Artistic Director of Calypso Productions, and she received an Arts and Culture award and a Metro Éireann Media and Multicultural Award (MAMA) for her intercultural work with the Tower of Babel.

DONAL O'KELLY is a writer and actor. His solo shows include *Catalpa, Joyced!, Bat the Father Rabbit the Son, Rabbit,* and *Aililiú Fionnuala.* Other plays he has written include *The Adventures of the Wet Señor, Jimmy Gralton's Dancehall, Vive La, Running Beast, Operation Easter, The Hand, Judas of the Gallarus, Farawayan, Asylum! Asylum!, Trickledown Town, Hughie on The Wires* and *The Dogs*. He tours with his own plays in Ireland and abroad and tries to combine playwriting with social activism through his work with justice and peace organisation Afri. He was elected to Aosdána, the Irish arts academy, from which he resigned in 2010.

CHARLIE O'NEILL hails originally from a travelling fairground family. He has been involved in arts and culture for over twenty-five years as a graphic designer, theatre set designer, clown, street performer, board member, musician, actor and writer. He has written a number of acclaimed plays including *Rosie and Starwars* (Stewart Parker Playwrights Award) for Calypso; *Hupnouse* and *Hurl* for Barabbas (Galway Arts Festival and Dublin Theatre Festival); and, with Donal O'Kelly, he co-wrote and co-performed *Mulletman and Gullier* (Dublin Theatre Festival). He was also commissioned to write a chapter for the book *Yeats is Dead*, a serial novel by fifteen Irish writers, which is now translated into several languages. He is author/editor of a number of arts publications on the power and benefit of children's and young people's participation in long-term, quality arts practice. Charlie wrote the critically acclaimed *Dodgems* for CoisCéim Dance Theatre, which opened the 2008 Dublin Theatre Festival. Recently, he wrote a play entitled *The Valentine's Day Massacre* for a cast of twenty-four teenagers. He was also commissioned to write a script entitled *Night of the Dark Angel*—a major Halloween outdoor night spectacle—which was produced in the Dublin neighbourhood Rialto, in partnership with Macnas, Ireland's leading outdoor theatre spectacle company. Charlie is also Creative Director and co-owner of Persuasion Republic, a communications agency for Irish charities and NGOs.

MIRJANA RENDULIC, from Zagreb, Croatia, started making theatre as a child on Zagreb pavements with her friends. She later became a member of Little Scene Theatre where she trained under Croatian theatre maker, Zvjezdana Ladika. Mirjana's first performance was playing Beatrice in *Much Ado About Nothing*. The events described in *Broken Promise Land* are based on a combination of autobiography and fiction. Mirjana arrived in Ireland in 2003. Since then, she has completed a FETAC (Further Education and Training Awards Council) diploma in Theatre Studies and a two-year Higher National Diploma in Performing Arts at Coláiste Dhúlaigh, Dublin and a FETAC Diploma in Drama Facilitation from the National Association for Youth Drama. Based in Dublin, she now works as an actor, drama facilitator and playwright. As an actor she has appeared in various short films as well as the feature film *Ecstasy of Isobel Mann*. Mirjana has also appeared as Jolanta in the TV series *Amber*. Her theatre roles include Kalena, a Polish nurse, in a play *Anything But Love* by Mary Coll (Belltable Arts Centre), which was also made into a radio production for RTÉ. *Broken Promise Land* premiered at Dublin's Theatre Upstairs and has also been performed in Limerick, Galway, Offaly and at the 2013 Electric Picnic and was adapted as a radio production for RTÉ in 2014. In summer 2013, Rendulic collaborated with *Broken Promise Land* director Aoife Spillane-Hinks, the Abbey Theatre's Outreach Department and Migrant Rights Centre Ireland to develop a collaborative drama piece with undocumented migrants living in Ireland. *Document* had its first showings in the Peacock Theatre and Liberty Hall in August 2013 and was commissioned by the Abbey in conjunction with their production of George Bernard Shaw's *Major Barbara.* She is currently working as a Drama Facilitator in the Gaiety School of Acting's Outreach Department.

URSULA RANI SARMA is an award-winning writer of Irish/Indian descent. Her plays have been published, translated widely and produced internationally. She is also a published poet. Some of her plays include *Yerma* (West Yorkshire Playhouse), *The Dark Things* (Traverse Theatre; Winner of Best New Play and Best Production at Critics Awards for Theatre in Scotland 2010), *RIOT* (American Conservatory Theatre San Francisco/Theatre Royal Bath), *The Exchange* (Eugene O'Neill Theatre Centre), *Birdsong* (The Abbey Theatre), *The Magic Tree* (Edinburgh Festival), *The Spider Men* (Royal National Theatre), *The Parting Glass* (Origin Theatre NYC), *Orpheus Road* (Paines Plough), *Blue* (Cork Opera House and Theatre 503) and *. . . touched . . .* (Edinburgh Festival) amongst many others. For radio, Ursula's plays include *Car Four* and *A Tiny Light in the Darkness* for the BBC and *The Fishermen* for RTÉ. For screen, Ursula's work includes Ecosse film's hit series *RAW*; short films *The Woods* and *Anywhere But Here*; and feature films *Breaking into Houses and Stealing Things* (Grand Pictures) and *The Trial* (Irish Film Board).

JOHN SCOTT is the founding artistic director of the Irish Modern Dance Theatre (1991, now John Scott Dance). Over the last twenty years, he has emerged as one of Ireland's leading figures in avant-garde dance. Born in Dublin and a graduate of University College Dublin, Scott trained at the College of Dance and later performed with Dublin City Ballet. He has studied or worked with many internationally known dancers and companies, including: Andy de Groat, Pablo Vela, the Living Theatre, Anna Sokolow, Yoshiko Chuma, Meredith Monk, Blanca Arrieta Company (Spain) and the Conservatoire Supérieur National pour la Musique et de la Danse (France). Some of his most widely seen dance productions include *Fall and Recover, The White Piece, Close Ups*, and *Rhythmic Space*. His work has been produced at the Dublin Dance Festival and throughout Ireland, as well as in Brazil, France, Israel, Palestine and New York (La MaMa, *Fall and Recover*, 2011; *The White Piece*, 2013). His film choreography includes *Admit One, Buail*, and *Eternal*. Scott is a founding board member of the Dublin Dance Festival and a guest lecturer at University College Dublin. In 2004, he was awarded the Cultural Prize by the African Refugee Network of Ireland for his pioneering work with survivors of torture.

MATTHEW SPANGLER is an Associate Professor of Performance Studies at San José State University in California. His research and teaching are in the fields of twentieth-century and contemporary Irish theatre, intercultural theatre, immigration studies, playwriting, and adaptation. His articles on James Joyce, W.B. Yeats and intercultural theatre in Irish and global contexts have appeared in *The James Joyce Quarterly, The New Hibernia Review, Text and Performance Quarterly, Theatre Journal, Siar: The Western Journal of Irish Studies, The South Atlantic Review, Nineteenth-Century Literature,* and *Performing the Crossroads: Critical Essays in Performance Studies and Irish Culture*. He is also a playwright. His plays have been produced by the Liverpool Playhouse, Nottingham Playhouse, Theatre Calgary, Citadel Theatre (Edmonton), San Diego Repertory Theatre, San Jose Repertory Theatre, Arizona Theatre Company, Actors Theatre of Louisville, Cleveland Playhouse, La Jolla Playhouse (staged reading), New Repertory Theatre (Boston), the National Steinbeck Center, the Edinburgh Fringe Festival, the Brighton Festival, and the Avignon Theatre Festival, among other theatres and festivals. He is the vice-president of the San Francisco Irish Literary and Historical Society and president for the American Conference for Irish Studies, West. He holds degrees from Northwestern University (BS Performance Studies), Trinity College Dublin (MPhil Theatre), and the University of North Carolina at Chapel Hill (PhD Performance Studies).

MAURYA WICKSTROM is the author of *Performance in the Blockades of Neoliberalism: Thinking the Political Anew*, published in 2012 by Palgrave Macmillan in the *Studies in International Performance Series*, edited by Janelle Reinelt and Brian Singleton; and *Performing Consumers: Global Capital and its Theatrical Seductions* (Routledge, 2006). She has an essay, 'Palestine and Political Invention' in *Performance, Identity, and the Neo-Political Subject*, edited by Fintan Walsh and Matthew Causey for the *Routledge Advances in Theatre and Performance Studies Series* (2013). She also has contributed essays in *Changing the Subject: Marvin Carlson and Theatre Studies, 1959–2009*, edited by Joseph Roach; and in *Rethinking Disney: Private Control, Public Dimensions* edited by Mike Budd and Max K. Hirsch. Her articles have been published in *The Drama Review, Theatre Journal, Modern Drama, Theatre Survey, Theatre Annual, Journal of Dramatic Theory and Criticism,* and *PAJ: A Journal of Performance and Art*. She is Professor of Theatre at the College of Staten Island and the Graduate Center at the City University of New York.

ANNA WOLF is a graduate from Adam Mickiewicz University, Pozna (Poland) in the Theatre and Drama Department. Anna is one of the founders of Polish Theatre Ireland (PTI) in Dublin; she directed their first play, *Scent of Chocolate* by Radosław Paczocha (Focus Theatre, 2010. She produced and directed PTI's devised performance of *Chesslaugh Mewash* staged during Absolut Fringe 2011 (The Lir Theatre). Anna also organised and produced stage readings of

Polish and Lithuanian contemporary plays 'Freedom Ltd' as part of PTI's repertoire (Submarine Bar, 2012). She produced PTI's *Delta Phase* by Radosław Paczocha (Theatre Upstairs, 2012). Most recently she produced *Foreign Bodies* (Project Arts Centre, 2013) and *Bubble Revolution* (Theatre Upstairs, 2013) both written by Julia Holewi ska. Her credits as a translator include: Owen McCafferty's *Closing Time* (into Polish, as part of stage readings of Irish plays in Polski Theatre in Poznan, 2007), Radosław Paczocha's *Scent of Chocolate, Be Like Kazimierze Deyna* and *Delta Phase* (co-translated with John Currivan).

Introduction

INWARD MIGRATION AND INTERCULTURALISM IN CONTEMPORARY IRISH THEATRE

CHARLOTTE MCIVOR and MATTHEW SPANGLER

In October 2007, the Abbey Theatre produced a new version of J.M. Synge's *The Playboy of the Western World* in commemoration of the one hundred-year anniversary of the play's original premiere. Co-written by novelist Roddy Doyle and Bisi Adigun, a Nigerian-born actor, playwright and founding artistic director of Ireland's first African–Irish theatre company, Arambe Productions, the play transposes the events of the original to a contemporary, urban setting. Christy Mahon becomes Christopher Malomo, a young Nigerian man on the run after killing his father (or so he believes) back in Nigeria. He winds up in a West Dublin pub rather than in the heart of Mayo but, apart from these adjustments in time and location, the major plot points of Synge's play remained the same. Doyle and Adigun's desire to revisit arguably the most important and influential play of the modern Irish theatre canon and the Abbey's choice to produce this work for the play's one hundred-year anniversary underscores the role that dramatic literature continues to play in re-envisioning the Irish nation in the wake of the Celtic Tiger economic boom and its attendant social change. Moreover, the decision to adapt Synge's play with a black protagonist from Nigeria—who also happens to be an asylum-seeker of sorts—indicates how prominent the themes of inward migration and interculturalism had become in Irish theatre and society.

In December 2008 and January 2009, the Abbey Theatre produced Adigun and Doyle's *The Playboy of the Western World* a second time. A legal suit followed regarding a disagreement over the payment of royalties and whether Adigun had, in fact, authorised the second production.[1] In the January 2013 settlement of the case, Doyle transferred his interest in the work to Adigun and the Abbey gave up production rights to the play, which are now held by Adigun.[2] The Abbey also agreed to pay Adigun's back royalties and legal fees.[3] While

Adigun and Doyle's *The Playboy of the Western World* may be the most high profile and indeed controversial Irish theatre production on the themes of inward migration and interculturalism, it is far from the only one, a fact to which the eight plays and interviews with nine practitioners gathered here seek to attest.

When inward migration numbers began to climb in the early and mid-1990s, Irish-born and immigrant theatre artists began producing theatrical work that addressed the demographic and cultural shifts that were then starting to take place. These performances have been produced at venues ranging from the Abbey Theatre to mid-sized theatre companies to community centres and even refugee accommodation centres. Yet, few of these works have been published[4] and critical discourse on them has been limited. Brian Singleton even argues that 'there have been few representations of other races in mainstream theatre' as 'the white Catholic nation with its twentieth-century repertoire was not constructed for the new races and the notion of color-blind casting remains an alien practice'.[5] The plays and interviews in this volume feature a range of devising strategies, dramaturgical frameworks, literary forms and performance products. Our goal is to make seminal texts available in print for the first time and permit a greater circulation of these plays for classroom study, future productions and scholarship.

The plays collected here have been selected due to their critical impact within the field of Irish theatre, or, in other cases, for the sites of cultural, social or political contestation that they enter into. We have chosen to focus this collection on dramatic literature, though we note that intercultural performance work has been done in many other forms including dance-theatre, street-theatre, performance installation, parade, photography and spectacle.[6] We have also chosen to focus mainly on intercultural theatre as it has been practised in the Republic, though we should point out that Northern Ireland, too, has an active intercultural arts scene, led by companies and individuals, such as Tinderbox Theatre Company, Artsekta and documentary filmmaker and former founding member of Charabanc Theatre Company, Carol Moore. In addition to the plays, we also include interviews with leading practitioners who have worked as actors, directors, choreographers and facilitators. We have done this in order to acknowledge the elements of process and collaboration that are so central to many of these projects, as well as to call attention to the institutional and market practicalities of making plays about ethnic diversity in contemporary Irish theatre.

We seek to document in this collection some of the major theatrical contributions toward inward migration and/or interculturalism in Ireland, though we note that not all of the plays here address immigrant experiences, as the work of Rosaleen McDonagh demonstrates; nor would all of them be considered intercultural as Julie Holledge and Joanne Tompkins define it: 'the meeting in the moment of performance of two or more cultural traditions'.[7] But all the plays archived here speak either to inward migration or interculturalism and frequently both, as these topics relate to the experiences, concerns and aesthetic representations of Ireland's migrant and minority ethnic communities.

This book, then, offers a contribution to transnational migration studies, as well as intercultural theatre research in a global context. We feel this book also offers a contribution to the ever-growing field of performance studies. With its theoretical focus on the constitutive nature of performance—that is, the capacity of performance to constitute the social world, and thereby, individual and collective identities—performance studies has helped articulate how theatre functions as both a metaphor for understanding everyday life, as well as how theatre plays an active role in the formation of culture. Because culture is something we *do* rather than something we *have*, theatre and indeed all forms of live performance—from the theatrical-aesthetic, to the ritual, to the everyday—have the capacity to sound subaltern voices, bring hybrid subject positions into being and give shape to new cultural formations and identities. Insofar as the plays in this collection, thus, contest and extend the standard hallmarks of what it means to be Irish, they are also agents of cultural change at a unique moment of demographic transformation.

While many of these plays focus on the margins of society and diasporic points of view, in this introduction and in the collection as a whole, we work against the idea of transnational migrants and minority ethnic individuals as 'outsiders' who suddenly arrived in a monoethnic Ireland in the mid-1990s. As Ronit Lentin, Robbie McVeigh, Bill Rolston and Michael Shannon point out,[8] Ireland has always been multi-ethnic and has a long history of receiving migrant peoples from abroad. We seek, therefore, to situate these plays within the current trends of transnational migration to Ireland, as well as broader historical contexts. From Donal O'Kelly's *The Cambria* (2005), which dramatises African–American abolitionist Frederick Douglass' journey to seek asylum in Ireland in 1845 to Rosaleen McDonagh's *Rings* (2012), which calls attention to both disability and the Traveller community as sites of longstanding oppression in Irish society at large, the plays and interviews compiled here reference a historical view of the increase in racial and ethnic diversity during and after the Celtic Tiger era.

Inward Migration and Contemporary Irish Theatre

First, a word on terminology. We use the term 'inward migration' in preference to 'immigration' because we find the former term to be more inclusive of a wider range of people. Immigration, generally, refers to a phenomenon driven by those who relocate to a host country with the idea of settling there, often for the long term. Inward migration, on the other hand, describes a phenomenon that includes long-term immigrants, of course, but also refugees and asylum-seekers, temporary and seasonal workers, as well as the undocumented, not all of whom would be considered or would consider themselves immigrants.

That Ireland, over the last twenty years, has received a higher than historically average number of transnational migrants has been well documented.[9] Due to the combined result of the Celtic Tiger economic boom from 1995 to 2007, Ireland's adoption of the Euro, the expansion of the European Union in 2004, relatively low corporate and personal tax rates, a highly regarded educational system and an overall ease in global mobility and communication, Ireland over the last two decades has seen a sharp rise in inward migration. Many recent migrants are the returning sons and daughters of Irish emigrants; others are asylum-seekers hoping to become refugees; others are 'Convention' refugees who have successfully navigated a series of interviews; others are 'Programme' refugees, a certain number of whom are admitted to Ireland on an annual basis; still others have the liminal status known as 'leave to remain'; others arrive from EU member states to work in low- or mid-paying jobs; others arrive on visas that allow them to work in higher paying professional positions; some are students; some are the victims of human trafficking; and still others have overstayed their visas, or are undocumented for a variety of reasons. Add to this differences of ethnicity, race, culture, religion, nationality, regionalisation, economic standing, gender and sexuality and it is easy to see how transnational migrants are one of the most radically diverse (though uniformly labeled) groups of people in Ireland, or indeed, any country.

In the context of recent transnational migration, 1996 is the so-called 'tipping point': the first year in the modern era in which more migrants entered Ireland than emigrants left. While it is true that the total number of migrants is relatively small, especially when compared to the number of migrants entering other countries in Europe or North America, Ireland's immigration *rate*, on the other hand, is quite large. In 1996, for instance, an estimated 5 per cent of the population was foreign born;[10] in 2006, the foreign born population was approximately 10 per cent;[11] and in 2011, it stood at 17 per cent.[12] This represents a 240 per cent increase in just fifteen years. As reported in the 2011 census, the total non-Irish born population of the Republic was 766,770.[13] The most statistically significant groups of foreign born persons living in Ireland are those born in England and Wales, many of whom are of Irish descent, though these individuals are not necessarily of ethnically homogenous backgrounds, and indeed, statistics show that the racial and ethnic diversity of the Irish population has risen sharply over the last two decades. As one might expect, urban areas have the highest rates of non-Irish born residents. Dublin's foreign-born population is approximately 20 per cent of the total population; in Galway, which leads the nation in the share of its population born outside the state, the percentage of foreign born residents is 25 per cent.[14] While statistics on inward migration recorded a drop in migrants from 2006 (93,200) to 2011 (33,674),[15] likely due to the collapse of the economy and the start of the recession, it is worth noting that the overall number of foreign born persons living in Ireland was greater in 2011 than it was in 2006.

This period of increased inward migration has generated a degree of public angst, which was at its most intense during the spring of 2004 in the lead up to the Citizenship Referendum, a proposal to revoke Article Two of the Irish Constitution that guaranteed citizenship to children born in Ireland. The Immigration Control Platform, among others, argued that large numbers of undocumented pregnant women were coming to Ireland to give birth as a strategy to gain Irish, and thereby, EU citizenship. The Justice Minister at the time,

Michael McDowell, helped popularise the derogatory term 'citizenship tourists' to refer to those who came to Ireland for such a purpose. The pro-referendum campaign highlighted the statistical growth in asylum-seekers since the early 1990s, particularly those of West African descent, and, according to Ronit Lentin and Robbie McVeigh, placed 'the blame for overburdened maternity hospitals on migrant mothers allegedly arriving "at the last moment" to have children-citizens in Ireland (even though the figures do not bear this accusation out)'.[16] The referendum, which Lentin and McVeigh call, 'an act of political brutality presented as a "commonsense" measure',[17] and which was opposed by the Labour Party, Sinn Féin, and the Greens, as well as many in Ireland's arts and literary communities, was passed on 11 June 2004 with 79.17 per cent of the vote and became the Twenty-Seventh Amendment to the Irish constitution.

Five days later, a street theatre performance, based on James Joyce's *Ulysses*, sought, in part, to counter the anti-immigrant rhetoric generated by the campaign.[18] The performance, entitled *The Parable of the Plums* and co-directed by Brian Fleming and Bisi Adigun (whose work is anthologised here), took place on 16 June as part of that year's Bloomsday Centenary. In it, nearly 200 actors and dancers, from Dublin's East Asian, East European and West African communities, used stylised movement and dance to dramatise the 'Aeolus' episode of Joyce's novel. Held in front of the GPO on O'Connell Street before an estimated audience of 5,000 spectators, and coming so closely on the heels of the referendum, the performance publically acknowledged and even celebrated the demographic changes ushered in by transnational migration. Moreover, it seemed to say that the Leopold Blooms of today, and perhaps tomorrow's iconic figures of Irish identity, are to be found in Dublin's minority-ethnic and migrant communities.

The Parable of the Plums is just one of many theatre performances that have sought to comment on these demographic changes and public debates. Indeed, Irish theatre is unique among art forms in that it has so closely attended to the public contours and personal experiences of inward migration and interculturalism. As Jason King notes, 'Irish theatre has proven highly receptive to the experiences of immigrants in Ireland, and provided an impetus for expressions of intercultural contact between them and the collective self-image of the Irish as an emigrant people that is enshrined in historical memory.'[19] A partial list of such productions includes: Donal O'Kelly's *Asylum!*

Asylum! (1994), the first play presented at the Abbey Theatre to explore these issues; Paul Mercier's *Native City* (1998); Joe O'Byrne's *It Come Up Sun* (2000); Eithne McGuinness' *Limbo* (2000); Ken Harmon's *Done Up Like A Kipper* (2002); Jim O'Hanlon's *Buddhist of Castleknock* (2002); Charlie O'Neill's *Hurl* (2003); John Scott's modern dance performance *Fall and Recover* (2004; 2011), which was created through a collaboration between the Irish Modern Dance Theatre and the Center for Survivors of Torture in Dublin; Donal O'Kelly's *The Cambria* (2005); Dermot Bolger's *The Townlands of Brazil* (2006); Paul Meade's *Mushroom* (2007); Sebastian Barry's *The Pride of Parnell Street* (2007); Natalia Kostrewza's *More Light* (2007); Brokentalker's *Track* (2008); Charlie O'Neill's dance theatre collaboration with CoisCéim, *Dodgems* (2008);[20] Victoria Fradgely's *Never After* (2009); Michael Collins' *Worlds Apart, Same Difference* (2010); Paul Kennedy's *Put Out the Light* (2010); and much of Calypso Production's work from its founding in 1993 until it closed its doors in 2008, including Charlie O'Neill's *Rosie and Starwars* (1997), O'Kelly's *Farawayan* (1998), Roddy Doyle's *Guess Who's Coming for the Dinner* (2001), and Maeve Ingolsby's *Mixing it on the Mountain* (2003). Bisi Adigun's founding of Arambe Productions in 2003 marked the formation of Ireland's first African–Irish and minority-ethnic-led theatre company. Arambe's work to date includes: *The Gods are Not to Blame* (2003), *Once Upon a Time & Not So Long Ago* (2005/2006), *The Kings of the Kilburn High Road* (2006), *The Playboy of the Western World* (co-written between Adigun and Roddy Doyle and co-produced with the Abbey Theatre) (2007, 2009), *The Dilemma of a Ghost* (2007), *Through a Film Darkly* (2008), *The Trials of Brother Jero* (2009), *The Butcher Babes* (2010), and *The Paddies of Parnell Street* (2013). Kunle Animashaun, another Nigerian–Irish actor and director, founded Camino de Orula Productions in 2007 and has produced Zulu Sofola's *Wedlock of the Gods* (2007) and Athol Fugard's *Sizwe Bansi is Dead* (2008) as well as most recently the original piece *Fragments* (2014). There are also plays produced outside Ireland that are either written by Irish artists about transnational migration, or that feature inward migration to Ireland as their central theme, such as Nicola McCartney's *Cave Dwellers* (2002, produced in various cities in Scotland), Ronan Noone's *The Blowin of Baile Gall* (2005, Boston and New York), and Gianina Cărbunariu's *Kebab* (2007, London). Something of an anomalous work in this regard, though a story that, nonetheless, owes its creation to the phenomenon of contemporary migration to Ireland, is the Broadway musical *Once* (2012; based on the 2006 film of the same name). This list is not meant to be exhaustive; rather it is an indicator of the diversity and prevalence of minority-ethnic, intercultural and migrant-based theatre in Ireland over the last two decades. These productions include traditional plays, one-person and two-person shows, visual- and music-driven performance art, modern dance and even a Broadway musical.

King attributes Irish theatre's receptivity to minority-ethnic voices to the 'fluid nature of the medium' and its ability to 'prise open and expand the ideal of Irish nationality itself'.[21] Indeed, dating back to the end of the nineteenth century at least, theatre in Ireland has a close, symbiotic relationship with questions of national identity. As Nicholas Grene puts it, 'Irish drama since the time of the early Abbey has remained self-consciously aware of its relation to the life of the nation and the state'.[22] This 'mirror up to nation' phenomenon, to use the oft-cited subtitle of Christopher Murray's book on Irish theatre,[23] underscores the creative and constitutive nature of theatre and its capacity to reflect, contest and create national and cultural identity in Ireland.

But this paradigm of reading Irish theatre as a reflection of the nation, which has been the dominant critical paradigm for the last one hundred years, has come under recent revision, most notably by Patrick Lonergan who argues that the relationship between theatre and nation is not so much due to an inherent trait of Irish theatre per se, but rather the way in which theatre has been *articulated* and *positioned* by scholars. In other words, the relationship between theatre and nation is an arbitrary one, generated by those who write and talk about theatre. Lonergan calls for the use of new paradigms that situate Irish plays in global contexts, rather than strictly national ones.[24] He goes on to argue that, due to the ways in which Irish identity has been 'branded' by its producers with a mostly narrow and regressive set of characteristics for the purpose of ready consumption on the international stage, 'representations of Irishness have narrowed as Irish identity has expanded, creating a tension between Irishness as it is presented to the world and Irishness as it is experienced and expressed within the country itself'.[25] Lonergan finds this tension between Irishness on the global stage and Irishness on the local street ironic, given the obvious changes in Irish society:

> At a time of increased multiculturalism, we might have expected Irish theatre to seek to redefine, expand, and transgress the

> boundaries that mark out Irish citizenship—for theatre practitioners to show that Irishness need not be tied to religion (whether Catholic or Protestant, ethnicity, or other essentialised markers of identity). The problem, however, is that the international success of Irish plays appears largely determined by their use of familiar Irish stereotypes. Globalisation has brought multiculturalism to Ireland, but the globalisation of Irish theatre has, regrettably, meant that the most successful Irish plays are those that present Irishness in narrow and indeed restricted ways.[26]

We would note that Lonergan here is focusing on plays selected and, in some cases, designed for export to international audiences (mostly in the United Kingdom and the United States). These plays—the ones guilty of branding Irishness in restrictive ways—have their imaginative source within Ireland and their target audience outside Ireland.

The plays collected in this book, however, are the products of the reverse cultural flow: transnational migrants coming to Ireland and either themselves creating, or in other ways generating intercultural theatre productions that re-present Irish cultural and national identity for a mostly Irish audience. As we think this collection demonstrates, the globalisation of Irish theatre—by which we mean the ways in which Irish theatre has been shaped by a range of recent transnational influences—has indeed led to a reconsideration of the hallmarks of Irish identity, away from regressive and essentialised markers of being Irish, and in directions that, in fact, increasingly do reflect the demographic diversity of the country itself. Ireland has become increasingly global, not just with respect to the ethnic, racial, and religious diversity of the people now living here, but also in terms of its relationship to a large number of global networks including commerce, politics, culture and technology, as Karen Fricker and Ronit Lentin show in their book *Performing Global Networks*.[27] The plays collected here address the changing nature of Irishness in the context of transnational inward migration and interculturalism, both of which are inextricably caught up in global networks of culture and capital.

In addition to King's claim that the receptivity of Irish theatre to minority-ethnic viewpoints is due to the longtime relationship between the theatre in Ireland and public discourses of national and cultural identity, we would offer a second explanation having to do with the 'liminal' nature of the medium of theatre itself. Because theatre audiences are often asked to empathise with subject positions other than their own—subject positions that are rendered through the physical embodiment of live actors—the event of the theatrical performance has the capacity to create contact zones of sympathetic understanding betwixt and between two or more positions of subjectivity. Liminality, as an intrinsic attribute of live performance, therefore makes the theatre exceptionally capable among art forms of exploring multiple points of view, intercultural conflict, nuances of language and other tensions that frequently mark diasporic identities. Of Charlie O'Neill's *Dodgems*, for example, Aoife McGrath writes, '*Dodgems* harnesses the energy of corporeal collisions' through the dances and scenes staged on and alongside a dodgem track 'to allow for the appearance of the silenced and invisible',[28] namely the immigrants who remain on the periphery of Irish society. The subaltern, hybrid and that which might still be antithetical to everyday hegemony can be brought into being through live performance, thus making it possible to contest the habitual and create new practices and forms of cultural identity. As Dwight Conquergood persuasively argued, the extra-theatrical world is not *reflected* through performance so much as it is 'enacted, reconfigured, tested, and engaged'.[29] In other words, theatre is not merely a mirror held up to reality; it is an active site of emergence in which knowledge might be reconfigured, previously fixed identities reimagined and cultural hallmarks transformed, making the theatre a uniquely appropriate venue for exploring topics related to cultural change and interculturalism.

Which is not to say that all theatre performances achieve these heights—indeed, many do not—nor is it to say that other art forms do not have the capacity to affect their creators and audiences in similar ways. Our point is that the theatre has the *potential* to achieve this, which makes it an especially fertile medium for the expression of migrant, diasporic, intercultural and hybrid positionalities. We feel that the plays archived here not only reflect and comment on intercultural change; they also have a hand in shaping it.

Interculturalism as Policy and Performance

We adopt the term 'interculturalism' in an effort to capture the dynamics of cultural change generated by an increase in minority-ethnic and non-Irish born members of society. We suggest through our use of this term that 'culture' itself, Irish or otherwise, must be understood as always already multiple. To speak of new migrants as 'other' to Irish society would imply a previous or ongoing state of homogeneity and obscure longtime differences of not only ethnicity or race, but gender, class and sexuality amongst other identity markers or positions. Perhaps even more importantly, our use of this term follows the practice of state and non-governmental agencies in post-Celtic Tiger Ireland, as well as broader shifts in social diversity rhetoric in the European Union at large. In these instances, 'interculturalism' serves as a semantic alternative to the models of multiculturalism and assimilationism, which offer binary responses to questions raised by increased social diversity within European societies. In a recent report on the place of Muslims in European society for the Centre for European Policy Studies, Michael Emerson writes, 'if this single word [multiculturalism] can identify a failure of society and of the policies of government, then there has to be a better model, concept and policy', and he offers interculturalism as the term to 'represent' it.[30] Specifically, in Ireland, as McIvor has noted elsewhere, interculturalism:

> as used in government and social policy describes practices aimed at using the occasion of inward migration to work towards mainstreaming services for new and pre-existing minority communities; addressing root causes of poverty and exclusion such as racism and environmental factors; increasing awareness of diversity among the Irish population through media, arts, and sport events; and equalizing participation in civic and social activities (Office of the Minister for Integration). Thus, the injunction to change is ideally directed not only at immigrants, but towards Irish society as a whole.[31]

McIvor goes on to argue that this strain of Irish interculturalism rooted in government and social policy be termed 'social interculturalism' to render it as distinct from practices of 'aesthetic interculturalism'.[32] This latter term more precisely refers to the production of artistic objects or events through the conscious blending of two or more cultural traditions.

Lines between 'social' and 'aesthetic' interculturalisms frequently blur, however, as the arts in Ireland have been targeted as sites of possible integration for minority communities as well as contact zones for majority and minority communities by the Arts Council, the Office of the Minister of Integration, the now-defunct National Consultative Committee on Racism and Interculturalism, and the Department of

Justice, Equality and Law Reform.[33] Mary White, TD, then Minister of State for Equality, Integration and Human Rights, proclaimed in September 2010 at the launch of the Arts Council's *Cultural Diversity and Arts* report, 'I strongly believe that intercultural awareness, understanding and interaction can be promoted and positively influenced through the arts—whether it is through creation, participation or appreciation.'[34] The arts feature prominently in the practical application of theories of Irish social interculturalism through the endorsement and support of a range of arts practices by these and other agencies. Through these partnerships, the boundaries between 'social' and 'aesthetic' interculturalism in Ireland frequently collapse. In this volume, for example, we interview Upstate Theatre Project founders Declan Mallon and Declan Gorman, whose intercultural theatre projects include productions derived by multi-ethnic groups of performers like *Steps* (2002), *Journey from Babel* (2009) and *The Mango Tree* (2012), which have been made possible through funding from the Office of the Minister for Integration and the European Union's Programme for Peace and Reconciliation, in addition to funding from arts-based bodies like the Arts Council or CREATE, the national agency for collaborative art.

Ireland's embrace of interculturalism in both social policy and artistic practice coincides with renewed attention to this term in theatre and performance studies discourse. Until recently, 'interculturalism', as a theoretical construct, was used by scholars primarily to describe Western appropriations of non-Western narratives and performance practices, particularly in reference to debates around the ethics of appropriation in the work of such artists as Robert Wilson, Peter Brook, Ariane Mnouchkine, Richard Schechner and Suzuki Tadashi, as well as earlier legacies of European theatrical modernism in the work of Antonin Artaud, Edward Gordon Craig, and W.B. Yeats. As probably the best-known Irish artist to practice a form of theatre that combined cultural influences, Yeats, in plays like, *At the Hawk's Well* (1916), *The Dreaming of the Bones* (1919), *The Only Jealousy of Emer* (1919), *The Cat and the Moon* (1926), *Resurrection* (1931) and *Purgatory* (1939), sought to render what are essentially Irish stories through the combined presentational techniques of Japanese Noh theatre and Western verse dialogue. In this respect, Yeats' Noh plays sit firmly in a tradition of works by Western theatre artists who have appropriated non-Western theatrical forms in the service of rejuvenating Western theatre. Ric Knowles,[35] Rustom Bharucha[36] and Robert Gordon,[37] among others, have criticised this approach, calling it, in Knowles' words, a 'cannibalisation of forms without respect for the cultures that produced them' that effectively served 'the West's colonisation of the world's cultures and peoples'.[38] Daphne P. Lei recently termed this cluster of practice '"hegemonic intercultural theatre" (HIT) . . . a specific artistic genre and state of mind that combines First World capital and brainpower with Third World raw material and labor, and Western classical texts with Eastern performance traditions'.[39] Following these critiques, theatrical interculturalism potentially represents the worst kind of cultural appropriation and plunder.

Despite the largely negative legacy of interculturalism in Western theatre, Lei, Knowles, Diana Looser and Leo Cabranes-Grant have worked recently to recuperate the term as a frame of analysis in order to 'utilise the rubric of the intercultural as both site and method'[40] in historical and contemporary contexts. As Knowles and Penny Farfan observe in an introduction to *Theatre Journal*'s special December 2011 issue entitled 'Rethinking Intercultural Performance', 'there is room for more globally syncretic and historically grounded understandings of intercultural performance as something that did not begin or end with Western modernism and that does not simply involve Western appropriations of the Other'.[41] Moreover, Lei points out in her study of Wilson's work in Taiwan that 'In today's globalised world, the East is no longer a passive participant, as technological journeys often begin in Asia'.[42] When aesthetic intercultural journeys 'begin in Asia,' questions of power, cultural appropriation, who benefits and who is likely to suffer the effects of misrepresentation, indeed, become complicated ones and their answers may have little to do with Western appropriations of non-Western techniques and material, which opens up the theoretical possibilities of interculturalism to consider a range of other phenomena.

Theories of interculturalism have also been used to describe the hybridity of theatrical forms. Probably the most often used definition of intercultural in this regard is Patrice Pavis': 'a more or less conscious and voluntary mixing of performance traditions traceable to distinct cultural areas'.[43] This use of 'intercultural,' too, has come under recent revision. Leo Cabranes-Grant, for instance, argues that rather than seeking to identify the hybrid zones between discrete cultures in performance—if such zones can be accurately identified or even exist at all—intercultural theatre critics should, instead, attend to the 'engines of emergence (sites for new positionalities, bodies and voices) and deconstructive gestures' that 'recall tensions still at work within cultures'.[44] Cabranes-Grant's recasting of the intercultural in this way shifts the focus from a descriptive project to a critical one. Likewise, following this shift, the plays in this book have been selected more for the ways in which they offer critiques and rearticulations of Irish culture and society than for their formal blending of distinct and traceable cultural influences.

The 'new interculturalism' in theatre, as Ric Knowles calls it, should 'not function merely as sites of semiotic intersection, or as postmodern collages, but as politicised sites for the constitution of new, hybrid, and diasporic identities in space'.[45] In taking issue with Pavis' notion that intercultural exchange should happen along a binary axis, Knowles writes that the '"intercultural" evokes the possibility of interaction across a multiplicity of cultural positionings'.[46] His own practical application of the term, in fact, focuses on 'newly global cities',[47] such as Toronto. Ireland, as a whole, certainly fits within Knowles' 'global cities' paradigm due to the accelerated growth of racial and ethnic diversity that has occurred in the nation during and post-Celtic Tiger. Knowles argues that:

> What is happening now in increasingly multicultural urban centres is the development of performance ecologies in which indigenous and immigrant minoritised populations are working performatively to forge diasporic identities in relation not to the dominant culture—or not to the dominant culture alone—but to one another.[48]

Knowles' distinction here between *indigenous minority* and *immigrant minority* communities has contributed to shaping the frame of this anthology. In the case of contemporary Ireland, Travellers represent the primary indigenous minority population, whereas recent immigrants and other minority populations represent the latter group. Indeed, while activism within and alongside the Traveller community long predates the Celtic Tiger, increased awareness of transnational interculturalism and the resulting increase in social diversity have positively impacted the visibility of Traveller issues as well. Knowles imagines a flexible model of interculturalism initiated by and from minoritarian positions, in which minority groups within a majority society might collaborate across difference to create diasporic or minority identities that do not recentralise the dominant culture. Piaras Mac Éinrí takes this idea a step further when he calls for 'a radical multiculturalism' that would entail 'a multi-locational interrogation of the central hegemonic discourses governing Irish society and of its constituent parts, including minority communities themselves'.[49] Neither Knowles' nor Mac Éinrí's vision has come to pass in Ireland but the goal of collectively-forged, culturally-diverse identities with roots in multiple centres of authority echoes the desire of Irish interculturalism as articulated through some forms of state policy and social rhetoric to remake 'Irish' culture in terms of not only identity, but also increase access for all members of society to practical resources and other less tangible forms of belonging.

The Plays and Interviews

We offer this collection as an opportunity to trace the aspirations of Irish interculturalism in theatrical practice. Knowles argues that the field of theatre and performance studies needs:

> A model of scholarship that understands the multiple performances of difference, local and global, as *processes*, circulations of energy, in which previously marginalised cultures are seen to work together, rather than *against*, constructing genuine, rhizomatic and multiple intercultures that respect difference while building solidarities.[50]

As such, this collection provides plays and artist accounts that, taken together, measure the extent to which Irish theatre has generated 'multiple intercultures that respect difference while building solidarities'. The plays and interviews collected here are preceded by critical introductions that serve to situate the artists and their works within cultural, political and historical frameworks of inward migration and interculturalism. These introductions will provide more detail, though we will attempt here to account briefly for each individual or group's inclusion in the volume.

While we take seriously Lonergan's critique that 'it is important not to exaggerate the value of white middle-class writers producing plays for white middle-class audiences about the marginalisation of Ireland's most recent immigrants',[51] we have, nevertheless, included many works by white Irish-born playwrights, specifically, Donal O'Kelly (*The Cambria*), Charlie O'Neill (*Hurl*), Rosaleen McDonagh (*Rings*), Nicola

McCartney (*Cave Dwellers*), and Paul Meade (*Mushroom*). In fact, these contributions represent the bulk of the volume. We believe that the white Irish-born playwrights included here have worked to 'respect difference' while 'building solidarities', and that their plays should be studied through the paradigm of intercultural analysis as process-based that Knowles proposes. By publishing their work, we seek to make this engagement (and potential critique) possible. It should also be recognised that intercultural performance work in contemporary Ireland is still being produced in the context of a white majority Irish-born scene (as it most likely always will) and by white Irish-born artists who must reckon critically with their privilege and positionality, and who also have a shared stake in the future of intercultural Ireland.

Within this group of white Irish-born artists, we have chosen plays by men and women whose social positions, thematic concerns and activist commitments indicate a greater diversity than simply being representative of white majority hegemonic positions of privilege. Donal O'Kelly's *Asylum! Asylum!* (1994), for instance, was the first play to appear in the mainstream Irish theatre that drew attention to institutional racism and discrimination in the asylum system and professed explicitly political aims of consciousness raising. He and Charlie O'Neill were among the founders of Calypso Productions, a theatre company dedicated to producing an awareness of social issues through innovative theatrical productions. Calypso would function from 1993–2008 as the Irish theatre company that most consistently and critically presented work on Ireland and international issues, system injustices (such as within the Irish prison system), and the lives of ethnic-minority communities and immigrants. Their work would eventually expand and include, among other things, a successful multicultural youth theatre initiative called 'Tower of Babel'. Due to the broad scope and importance of Calypso's work, this volume also includes an interview with Bairbre Ní Chaoimh who served as the company's artistic director from 1999 to its funding-related demise in 2008. Calypso co-founder Charlie O'Neill comes from a 'fairgrounds family' and grew up travelling around Ireland 'bringing shows to small towns', a background he associates with being raised as an 'outsider'[52] before settling in West Clare with his family. O'Neill identifies continuity between this background and Traveller culture, such as 'the fairground language . . . used common words and vocabulary with the Traveller language as well'.[53] He has recently been working with the

Fatima Mansions Urban Regeneration Project to address issues of poverty, crime, drug use and community grassroots mobilisation through the arts.[54]

Nicola McCartney's play *Cave Dwellers*, while something of an anomalous contribution to this anthology, is, nonetheless, a valuable one. Though the exact circumstances of the characters in *Cave Dwellers* remain vague (we are never told exactly what country they are fleeing from, nor exactly what country they seek to enter), McCartney's play offers a unique perspective on the topic of immigration to Ireland. *Cave Dwellers* is the only play in this collection that depicts the characters' actual journey, rather than focusing on their situation after arrival. It is also the most experimental and non-representational of the pieces anthologised here. Finally, the play's sympathies for its migrant characters, in some respects, run counter to the currents of sympathy found in the other plays in this collection as well as theatre about immigrants more generally. McCartney, herself, is the only author included here from Northern Ireland. She was born in Belfast and currently resides in Scotland, where she directs the Masters in Writing for Theatre and Performance programme at the University of Edinburgh.

Paul Meade's *Mushroom* forces attention on difference within and amongst Eastern European minority individuals living in Ireland today, as well as depicting the relationship of a first-generation Irish-born man to the legacy of his Romanian-born mother. *Mushroom*'s genesis was made possible by field research with migrant groups and collective devising between the play's director, Liam Halligan, and the play's multiethnic cast in rehearsal,[55] thus, complicating issues of sole or even primary authorship.

We also present in this volume the work of three of the most successful minority-ethnic Irish playwrights: Bisi Adigun (*Once Upon a Time & Not So Long Ago*), Rosaleen McDonagh (*Rings*), and Ursula Rani Sarma (*Orpheus Road*), as well as the work of emerging artist Mirjana Rendulic (*Broken Promise Land*). Adigun was born and educated in the Yoruba region of Nigeria, immigrated to the UK in 1993 and Ireland three years later. He is the founder of Arambe Productions, Ireland's first African–Irish theatre company and the co-author of the recent adaptation of *The Playboy of the Western World* with Roddy Doyle. Rosaleen McDonagh grew up in a Traveller community and is an outspoken activist on issues of gender, sexuality, disability and Traveller rights, in addition to repeatedly exploring these themes in her dramatic works. McDonagh also managed the Violence Against Women programme for ten years at the Pavee Point Travellers' Centre in Dublin.

Ursula Rani Sarma is the daughter of an Indian father and Irish mother. She was born in Canada and immigrated to Ireland with her family as a child. She currently lives in London, having spent most of her early career in Ireland. Her work does not explicitly address themes of immigration, nor the lives of minority ethnic individuals, and her plays illustrate a more subtle interculturalism than is generally attributed to such plays. Her play anthologised here (*Orpheus Road*), for instance, explores an intercultural relationship between a young girl of unspecified religion and a Catholic boy. Of her plays set all or partially in Ireland, like *The Magic Tree, Blue,* and *Touched,* themes of rural alienation and the sometimes limited opportunities presented to Ireland's youth are pronounced. Much of her work has been produced abroad and her plays have yet to receive a mainstage production at any of the major Irish theatres. This is perhaps due to a problem of 'branding', related to the fact that many of her plays do not feature Irish settings or themes commonly associated with canonical Irish theatre.

Mirjana Rendulic was born in Zagreb, Croatia and began her career in theatre there before immigrating to Ireland to work first as an exotic dancer. *Broken Promise Land* tells the story of Rendulic's work in the sex industry through a mix of autobiography and fiction. Her work as a dancer takes her first to Italy and Japan before her arrival in Ireland. The play focuses on her ultimate decision to stop dancing and pursue university education in Ireland. Rendulic's journey through the transnational networks of the sex industry provides a multi-sited account of migrancy that demonstrates how economic need motivates mobility. Her account of the need to keep moving is unique amongst the migration narratives elsewhere in the collection as is her focus on the sex industry and the material conditions of undocumented migrant labour.

For our interviews, we have chosen individuals whose work demonstrates compelling methodologies for future practices of interculturalism in Irish theatre. These interviews add consideration of not only artistry, but also the business and administration of making Irish theatre on themes of inward migration, interculturalism and ethnic diversity. Bairbre Ní Chaoimh, Declan Mallon and Declan Gorman, for instance, work at the intersection of professional and community drama and have focused at various stages in their careers on both. As the first Irish company to devote a great deal of its artistic output to topics related to immigration and diversity, Calypso Productions created 'Tower of Babel,' an intercultural youth drama group, in addition to mounting professional productions on these themes.[56] Founded in 1997 in Drogheda, Upstate Theatre Project initially focused on the legacy of the Troubles in the North through projects like the 'Crossover Project' (2002–2007), which paired cross-border and cross-community groups in the creation of original theatre pieces. This focus was matched in their professional production work, specifically Declan Gorman's trilogy of plays about the politics of the border region: *Hades, Epic,* and *At Peace*. The trilogy received accolades for the company, including a BBC/Stewart Parker playwriting award in 1999 for Gorman. Following the last play of Gorman's trilogy, *At Peace,* which explores the interrelated dynamics between Nigerian, Latvian and Irish communities in the border towns in which the play is set, Upstate increasingly focused its community drama work on issues of interculturalism and diversity. Notable in this regard is a 2002 collaboration with the Droichead Youth Theatre and the nearby Mosney Refugee Accommodation Centre that led to the creation of an original play called *Steps,* devised and performed by the youth participants under Gorman's leadership. Upstate launched the Louth Intercultural Theatre Project in 2007, the goal of which was to offer 'legally resident migrants an opportunity to be involved in the planning and delivery of a community-based drama project' and '[p]rovide a platform for Irish citizens and new migrants to participate hands-on in an imaginative and creative arts process within their local area'.[57] This resulted in workshops in Drogheda and Dundalk and the performance of an original site-specific piece, *Journey from Babel,* from the Drogheda group in June 2009. Their most recent iteration of this ongoing initiative was *The Mango Tree,* an 'intercultural arts participation project', again devised by a group of internationally and racially diverse community participants under the direction of Stephen Murray.

John Scott, founder of the Irish Modern Dance Theatre (now called John Scott Dance), was invited in 2003 to hold dance workshops with individuals who were clients of the Centre for the Care of Survivors of Torture in Dublin. The most notable performances to come out of these workshops are *Fall and Recover* and *The White Piece,* which have been staged many times over the last decade, most recently at La MaMa in New York in March 2011 and March 2013, respectively. Many of the individual performers have since joined Scott's company, despite the fact that most of them did not have prior dance training. Illustrating aesthetic interculturalism—'the meeting in the moment of performance of two or more cultural traditions'[58]—Scott's work in modern dance mixes various European and non-European influences and results in a unique hybrid form that has struggled to find financial support and a sustained audience in Ireland over the years. Whereas the modern Irish theatre developed as an explicitly national project at the beginning of the twentieth century, the modern and contemporary dance scene in Ireland has had a much less commercially successful development and has suffered from a lack of consistent funding and support infrastructure, although the scene has gained in strength since the mid-1990s.[59] Scott's performance work, therefore, is not simply a combination of discrete dance forms amounting to a straightforward encounter between 'Irish' and 'other,' but rather an endeavour that already foregrounds the unstable status of 'Irish' culture as expressed through the practice of dance. While modern dance technique, an arguably European form, is predominant in the aesthetic of *Fall and Recover* and *The White Piece,* the mixed intercultural roots of this genre of technique remain present, specifically through the Orientalist influences of Ruth St Denis and contributions of African–American dancers working with African diasporic forms of dance, such as Katherine Dunham, Pearl Primus and Alvin Ailey. The intercultural reference points in Scott's work are, thus, quite multiple and span a range of international and historical traditions of dance.

Polish Theatre Ireland (PTI) is an ensemble of actors, directors and playwrights of both Polish and Irish descent. The ensemble formed in 2008 'seeing the need for a theatre that represented the Polish diaspora in Ireland and an eventual institution that could merge the qualities of both Polish and Irish theatre culture to create a new cross breed theatre in Dublin'.[60] We interview PTI's artistic director, Anna Wolf; actor and literary manager, Kasia Lech; and actor and director, John Currivan, all of whom have been involved with the company since its origins. PTI has produced Julia Holewińska's *Foreign Bodies,* original translations of Polish playwright and company member Radosław Paczocha's *Scent of Chocolate* and *Delta Phase,* created an original piece on the work of poet Czeslaw Milosz (*Chesslaugh Mewash*) with an intercultural cast including Slovakian, Lithuanian, Polish and Irish actors, and mounted a series of staged readings called 'Freedom Ltd' of Polish and Lithuanian plays in collaboration with Irish–Lithuanian Theatre Company, Alternatyva Alternatyvai. PTI's approach to interculturalism vis-à-vis theatre practice is unique amongst emergent companies working in this area due to their commitment to serving both the Polish community living in Ireland, integrating Polish and Irish theatre audiences, and staging versions of emergent intercultural Irishness. From Irish-born Currivan's Polish-language performance in *Scent in Chocolate* (despite his not speaking Polish prior to the performance) to multiple languages spoken onstage in *Chesslaugh Mewash* to Wolf's transposition of *Delta Phase* from Poland to Ireland with Irish-born actors using local Irish dialects in roles bearing Polish names, PTI pushes at the limits of intercultural theatre practice in post-Celtic Tiger Ireland and beyond.

Finally, through interviews with Alicja Ayres and José Miguel Jimenéz, we attend to the professional dynamics of working in the business of Irish theatre as a minority-ethnic performer. Ayres trained at the Gaiety School of Acting in Dublin and is one of the original company members of PTI. She has appeared in *Scent of Chocolate* (Focus Theatre), *The Maids* (Made-Up Theatre Company), *A Christmas Carol* (Ouroboros Theatre Company), *Toxic* (Project Arts Centre), and *Chesslaugh Mewash* (Absolute Fringe Festival). Her film and television work include *Death Waits* (Redmond Fitzpatrick), *Sanctuary* (Venon Films), *Club Fear* (The Gaiety School of Acting), *Dave's One Night Stand* (UKTV), and *Wander* (mPestka). Jimenéz is a theatre director, performer and sound designer, born and raised in Chile. He studied acting at Trinity College, Dublin, and with several other graduates in 2009, formed The Company. The first show he directed with The Company, *Who is Fergus Kilpatrick?*, received the ABSOLUT Spirit of the Fringe Award in 2009 and his second show, *As you are now so once were we*, received the ABSOLUT Fringe Best Production Award in 2010. *Who is Fergus Kilpatrick?*, a multi-media performance piece, inspired by Jorge Luis Borges' short story 'Theme of the Traitor and the Hero,' explored the line between illusion and reality. *As you are now so once were we* was also inspired by a secondary source, this time Joyce's *Ulysses* (the title is what Leopold Bloom imagines the dead in Glasnevin Cemetery would say to the living if they could). It was commissioned by the Abbey Theatre where it was presented at the Peacock in 2011 and later toured to Portugal and the United States. Jimenéz was shortlisted by the *Sunday Times* as one of the thirty most promising artists of 2011.

The Future of Intercultural Irish Theatre

An anthology such as this is a ritualistic act of definition. The move to include or omit certain plays, the narrative framing that precedes them, and even their order relative to each other function to perform, and thus, define the subject of the book, in this case, intercultural theatre in Ireland during the recent era of inward migration. But like all rituals, the act of anthologising is partial and provisional. It is partial because it is incomplete. The plays and interviews included here hardly represent a comprehensive totality of theatre at the intersection of inward migration and interculturalism in the Irish context. In fact, we acknowledge that they barely scratch the surface. There are many other texts, artists, and types of performance—in the form of street theatre, music and dance, not to mention technologically mediated performances in cinematic, broadcast, or on-line formats—that we have not included here. This is why an anthology is also provisional. As with all acts of definition, the passage of time and the sounding of other critical and artistic voices will inevitably lead to evolution and revision.

What we can say for sure is that the plays and interviews collected here are both products and critiques of inward migration and interculturalism during a unique period in Irish and global history, a period marked by a rapid intensity of transnational phenomena in the form of economics, culture, communications, politics, transportation and human migration. It is also a time in which the age-old hallmarks of Irish cultural identity are moving in two seemingly contradictory directions at once. While these hallmarks are 'branded' as commodities for export to the global stage, which as Lonergan notes, leads to a process of cultural reduction and sedimentation—evidenced by the globally wide popularity of all things 'Irish'—these very same hallmarks are interrogated and in some cases rearticulated at home. Ireland is not the only nation to experience such a contradictory pull of cultural currents between the nativist and the cosmopolitan. But Ireland is unique in that it is one of a small group of nations to have such a close and powerfully charged relationship between the theatre and debates of national and cultural identity. The theatre in Ireland offers something of a looking-glass through which changing culture might be viewed, though as we have argued, the plays collected here do more than simply reflect an extra-theatrical reality; they are also themselves active agents of cultural change.

The interrelated processes of inward migration and interculturalism in Ireland are likely to continue for the foreseeable future. As Ian Goldin, Geoffrey Cameron and Meera Balarajan put it in their encyclopedic book on the history of global human migration:

> Over the last twenty-five years, the total number of international migrants doubled, and we can confidently say that this strong growth trend will be amplified over the next fifty years. . . . Against a backdrop of rapid globalisation, the individual risks and costs of moving internationally will continue to fall with lower transport costs, better connectivity, and growing transnational social and economic networks. By the middle of the twenty-first century, our societies will be more diverse than ever before.[61]

One might reasonably surmise, therefore, that the trends underpinning this collection of plays and interviews—transnational migration, interculturalism and a reconsideration of 'indigenous' hallmarks of identity—could well be defining features of Irish life for the next century. As a result, we should expect plays and other types of live performance from an ever-wider range of transnational subject positions. Even the notion of what constitutes 'theatre' is likely to undergo further revision, a process that has been underway for at least two decades in Ireland, as more and more people arrive and bring an increasing range of performance traditions with them. We feel this anthology of plays and interviews offers a snapshot of a long-term intercultural process in its very early stages.

Notes and References

1 'Dublin Abbey Sued by *Playboy* Writer,' *The Stage*, 20 May 2010. Read online at http://www.thestage.co.uk/news/2010/05/dublin-abbey-sued-by-playboy-writer. 'Dramatist Sues Doyle in *Playboy* Wrangle,' *Herald.ie*, 18 May 2010. Read online at http://www.herald.ie/news/dramatistsues-doyle-in-playboy-wrangle-27951869.html.

2 'Roddy Doyle Gives Up *Playboy* Rights After Court Battle,' *Herald.ie*, 31 January 2013. Read online at http://www.herald.ie/entertainment/around-town/roddy-doyle-gives-up-playboy-rights-after-court-battle-29043964.html. 'Doyle Transfers Rights to Play as He Settles Court Action,' *Independent.ie*, 30 January 2013. Read online at http://www.independent.ie/irish-news/courts/roddy-doyle-transfers-

rights-to-play-as-he-settles-court-action-29024942.html.

3 'Abbey Pays €200K to Playwright over Dispute,' *Irish Examiner*, 2 February 2013. Read online at http://www.irishexaminer.com/archives/2013/0202/world/abbey-pays-200k-to-playwright-over-dispute-221469.html.

4 Published plays on the themes of inward migration, interculturalism and racial/ethnic diversity include Donal O'Kelly, *Asylum! Asylum!*, in Christopher Fitz-Simon and Sanford Sternlicht (eds.), *New Plays from the Abbey Theatre: 1993–1995* (Syracuse: Syracuse University Press, 1996), pp. 113–174; Ken Harmon, *Done Up Like a Kipper* (Dublin: Nick Hern Books, 2003); Jim O'Hanlon, *The Buddhist of Castleknock* (Dublin: New Island Books, 2007); and Dermot Bolger, *Townlands of Brazil*, in *The Ballymun Trilogy* (Dublin: New Island Books, 2010).

5 Brian Singleton, *Masculinities and the Contemporary Irish Theatre*, (Basingstoke: Palgrave Macmillan, 2011), p. 20.

6 For examples of intercultural performances that blend one or more of these theatrical forms see Matthew Spangler, 'Winds of Change: Bloomsday, "Aeolus," and Immigration in Street Theatre', *James Joyce Quarterly*, vol. 45:1, Fall 2007, pp. 47–68; Christie Fox, *Breaking Forms: The Shift to Performance in Late Twentieth Century Irish Drama* (Newcastle: Cambridge Scholars Publishing, 2008); Holly Maples, 'Parading Multicultural Ireland: Identity Politics and National Agendas in the 2007 St Patrick's Festival', in *Crossroads: Performance Studies and Irish Culture* (Basingstroke: Palgrave Macmillan, 2009), pp. 237–248; Charlotte McIvor, 'Essences of Social Change: City Fusion, Interculturalism and the Dublin's St Patrick Day in the "new" Ireland', *Public*, Issue 45: Art and Civic Spectacle, Fall 2012, pp. 180–191. In addition, notable artists working at the intersection of performance, installation, visual art and film on the themes of immigration and cultural diversity include: Anthony Haughey, 'How To Be A Model Citizen' (2008); Jesse Jones, *12 Angry Films* (2006); Susan Gogan and the Domestic Worker's Support Group at the Migrant Rights Centre, 'Opening Doors' (2008); and Pauline Agnew 'Elsewhere' (2006).

7 Julie Holledge and Joanne Tompkins, *Women's Intercultural Performance* (London: Routledge, 2000), p. 7.

8 See Ronit Lentin and Robbie McVeigh, *After Optimism?: Ireland, Racism and Globalisation* (Dublin: Metro Eireann Publications, 2006); Bill Rolston and Michael Shannon, *Encounters: How Racism Came to Ireland* (Belfast: Beyond the Pale, 2002).

9 For discussions on inward migration during the Celtic Tiger era, see Bryan Fanning, *Immigration and Social Change in the Republic of Ireland* (Manchester: Manchester University Press, 2007); Harry Browne and Chinedu Onyejelem, 'Textualising Radio Practice: Sounding Out a Changing Ireland', in *Projecting Migration: Transcultural Documentary Practice* (London: Wallflower Press, 2007); Olutoyin Pamela Akinjobi (ed.), *Herstory: Migration Stories of African Women in Ireland* (Dublin: AkiDwA African Women's Network, 2006); Ronit Lentin and Robbie McVeigh, *After Optimism?: Ireland, Racism and Globalisation* (Dublin: Metro Éireann Publications, 2006); Ronit Lentin and Robbie McVeigh (eds.), *Racism and Anti-Racism in Ireland* (Belfast: Beyond the Pale, 2002); Bill Rolston and Michael Shannon, *Encounters: How Racism Came to Ireland*; Paul Cullen, *Refugees and Asylum-Seekers in Ireland* (Cork: Cork University Press, 2002); Bryan Fanning, *Racism and Social Change in the Republic of Ireland* (Manchester: Manchester University Press, 2002).

10 Miho Taguma, Moonhee Kim, Gregory Wurzburg and Frances Kelly, *OECD Reviews of Migrant Education: Ireland* (Paris: Organisation for Economic Co-operation and Development, December 2009), p. 15.

11 Central Statistics Office, 'Persons Usually Resident and Present in the State on Census Night, Classified by Nationality and Age Group 2006' (Dublin: Central Statistics Office, 2006). Read online at http://www.cso.ie/en/statistics/

population/personsusuallyresidentandpresentinthestateoncensusnightclassified-bynationalityandagegroup.

12 Central Statistics Office, *This is Ireland: Highlights from the Census-Part I* (Dublin: Central Statistics Office, 2011), p. 30.

13 Ibid., p. 30.

14 Central Statistics Office, *Profile 1: Town and Country* (Dublin: Central Statistics Office, April 2012), p. 14.

15 Central Statistics Office, *This is Ireland: Highlights from the Census-Part I* (Dublin: Central Statistics Office, 2011), p. 31.

16 Ronit Lentin and Robbie McVeigh, *After Optimism?*, p. 99.

17 Ibid., p. 55.

18 The four co-directors of *The Parable of the Plums* included Brian Fleming, Bisi Adigun, Raymond Keane and Eddie McGuinness. The performance was produced and conceived by Philip Mullen, Cormac O'Hanrahan and Helen Monaghan (then director of the James Joyce Centre). See Spangler, pp. 47–68.

19 Jason King, 'Interculturalism and Irish Theatre: The Portrayal of Immigrants on the Irish Stage', *Irish Review*, vol. 33, Spring 2005, p. 25.

20 See Aoife McGrath, 'Choreographing Dissensus: Dodgems and Roundabouts,' in *Dance Theatre in Ireland: Revolutionary Moves* (Basingstoke: Palgrave Macmillan, 2013), pp. 147–162.

21 Ibid., p. 37.

22 Nicholas Grene, *The Politics of Irish Drama: Plays in Context from Boucicault to Friel* (Cambridge: Cambridge University Press, 1999), p. 1.

23 Christopher Murray, *Twentieth-Century Irish Drama: Mirror up to Nation* (Manchester: Manchester University Press, 1997).

24 Patrick Lonergan, *Theatre and Globalization: Irish Drama in the Celtic Tiger Era* (London: Palgrave Macmillan, 2010), p. 27.

25 Ibid., p. 188.

26 Ibid., p. 196.

27 Karen Fricker and Ronit Lentin, *Performing Global Networks* (Newcastle: Cambridge Scholars Publishing, 2007).

28 McGrath, p. 162.

29 Dwight Conquergood, 'Storied Worlds and the Work of Teaching', *Communication Education*, vol. 42:4, 1993, p. 337.

30 Michael Emerson, 'Preface', in Michael Emerson (ed.), *Interculturalism: Europe and Its Muslims in Search of Sound Societal Models* (Brussels: Centre for European Policy Studies, 2011), p. ii.

31 Charlotte McIvor, 'Staging the "New Irish": Interculturalism and the Future of the Post-Celtic Tiger Irish Theatre', *Modern Drama*, vol. 54:3, Fall 2011, p. 313.

32 Ibid.

33 The following documents and reports specifically mention the arts as zones of contact and sites of education for minority and majority members of Irish society on issues of interculturalism and diversity: Arts Council / An Chomhairle Ealaíon, *Cultural Diversity and Arts: Language and Meanings* (Dublin: Arts Council and Office of the Minister for Integration, 2010); Arts Council / An Chomhairle Ealaíon, *Cultural Diversity and the Arts: Policy and Strategy* (Dublin: Arts Council and Office of the Minister for Integration, 2010); Department of Justice, Equality and Law Reform, *Planning for Diversity: The National Action Plan Against Racism: 2005–2008* (Dublin: Department for Justice, Equality & Law Reform, 2005); National Consultative Committee on Racism and Interculturalism, 'Special Edition: Ireland's Strategy for the European Year of Intercultural Dialogue,' *Spectrum: The Journal for the National Consultative Committee on Racism and*

Interculturalism, vol. 16, January 2008, p. 15; Office of the Minister for Integration, *Migration Nation: Statement on Integration Strategy and Diversity Management* (Dublin: Office of the Minister for Integration, 2008).

34 Arts Council / An Chomhairle Ealaíon, 'The Arts Council Announces New Policy on Cultural Diversity', 23 September 2010. Read online at http://www.artscouncil.ie/en/media.aspx?page=2&article=ae7543a0-4f02-46cf-a6a3-49f37266e5b6.

35 See Ric Knowles, *Theatre and Interculturalism* (London: Palgrave Macmillan, 2010).

36 See Rustom Bharucha, *The Politics of Cultural Practice: Thinking Through Theatre in an Age of Globalization* (Hanover: Wesleyan University Press, 2000).

37 See Robert Gordon, *The Purpose of Playing: Modern Acting Theories in Perspective* (Ann Arbor: University of Michigan Press, 2006).

38 Knowles, p. 12.

39 Daphne P. Lei, 'Interruption, Intervention, Interculturalism: Robert Wilson's HIT Productions in Taiwan', *Theatre Journal*, vol. 63:4, December 2011, p. 571.

40 Penny Farfan and Ric Knowles, 'Editorial Comment: Special Issue on Rethinking Intercultural Performance', *Theatre Journal*, vol. 63:4, December 2011, p. i–iii.

41 Ibid.

42 Lei, p. 585.

43 Patrice Pavis, *The Intercultural Performance Reader* (London: Routledge, 1996), p. 8.

44 Leo Cabranes-Grant, 'From Scenarios to Networks: Performing the Intercultural in Colonial Mexico', *Theatre Journal*, vol. 63:4, December 2011, p. 501.

45 Knowles, p. 59.

46 Ibid., p. 4.

47 Ibid., p. 2.

48 Ibid., p. 60.

49 Fanning, p. 218.

50 Knowles, p. 61.

51 Patrick Lonergan, 'Half-Hearted: Irish Theatre, 2003', *New Hibernia Review*, vol. 8:2, 2004, p. 150.

52 Charlie O'Neill, unpublished interview with Charlotte McIvor, 23 February 2009.

53 Ibid., p.4.

54 In 1995, a group of residents in Fatima Mansions, a Dublin-area housing estate with high drug use and crime rates, formed Fatima Groups United and began a plan to revitalise the area and address the roots of the social issues plaguing the community. This resulted in a physical rebuilding of the area and ongoing social programming including an extensive arts component. The perceived success of this project has led to several reports detailing its process. See Joe Donohue and Peter Dorman, *Dream/Dare/Do: A Regeneration Learning Manual* (Dublin: Fatima Groups United, 2006) as well as Niall O'Baoill, *A Local Imagine Nation: A Local Arts Plan for Rialto 2012–2016* (Dublin: Fatima Groups United, 2011) for documentation of the arts-based plan for the area.

55 See Helen Meany, 'Mushroom,' *Guardian*, 29 June 2007 and Sara Keating, 'The Immigrants' Inside Story', *The Irish Times*, 5 June 2007.

56 Jason King, 'Black St Patrick Revisited: Calypso's "Tower of Babel" and Culture Ireland as Global Networks,' in Karen Fricker and Ronit Lentin (eds.), *Performing Global Networks* (Newcastle: Cambridge Scholars Publishing, 2007), pp. 38–51.

57 Paul Hayes, *Upstate Theatre Project's Louth International Theatre Project: Office of the Minister of Integration, Application Form for Immigrant Integration Small Grant Scheme* (Drogheda: Upstate Theatre Project, 2006), p. 3, unpublished report.

58 Holledge and Tompkins, p. 7.

59 See Helen Brennan, *The History of Irish Dance* (Boulder, CO: Roberts Rinehart, 2001); Deirdre Mulrooney (ed.), *Irish Moves: An Illustrated History of Dance and*

Physical Theatre in Ireland (Dublin: Liffey Press, 2006); Helena Wulff, *Dancing at the Crossroads: Memory and Mobility in Ireland* (Oxford: Berghahn Books, 2007); Mick Moloney, J'aime Morrison and Colin Quigley (eds.), *From the Boreen to Broadway* (Madison, WI: Macater Press, 2009).

60 Polish Theatre Ireland, 'About.' Accessed 17 January 2013. Read online at http://polishtheatre.wordpress.com/about/

61 Ian Goldin, Geoffrey Cameron and Meera Balarajan, *Exceptional People: How Migration Shaped Our World and Will Define Our Future* (Princeton: Princeton University Press, 2011), p. 213.

INTRODUCTION TO NICOLA MCCARTNEY'S

Cave Dwellers

CHARLOTTE J. HEADRICK

A small group of asylum-seekers flee an unknown country for an unknown country of refuge. They hide in a system of caves by an unnamed body of water while they wait (and wait) for a smuggler to meet them and ferry them safely across. In its use of a featureless and desolate landscape against which its characters wait for a savior that may not come and may not even exit, Nicola McCartney's *Cave Dwellers* resembles *Waiting for Godot*, but unlike Beckett's work, *Cave Dwellers* references a clear and immediate topic: that of transnational, human smuggling. The play powerfully depicts the confusion and fear of such a journey. Because we do not know what country the characters are fleeing, nor what country they are trying to enter—only that a large body of water separates them from their destination—McCartney's play does not address interculturalism as directly as do many of the plays in this volume that explore a specific national context in which majority and minority ethnic members of a society come into contact. But *Cave Dwellers* does offer a meditation on emigration/immigration and specifically the often-torturous journeys of asylum-seekers who have been smuggled into their host countries. During the Celtic Tiger era, the number of asylum-seekers applying for refugee status in Ireland rose dramatically, from a mere thirty-nine applications in 1992 to over 11,000 by 2002.[1] The top five countries of origin for those seeking asylum in Ireland during the mid-1990s and early 2000s were Nigeria, Romania, China, Somalia and Sudan.[2] This rise in asylum-seekers and refugees, a fair number of whom arrived from cultures quite different from the Irish, served to generate many of the then and current debates surrounding interculturalism in Ireland.

The first production of *Cave Dwellers* was directed by Gordon Laird in 2002 as part of a UK touring production that began in Scotland. The production and the written text were dedicated to John McGrath, the founder of 7:84 Scotland Theatre Company, a political theatre until its closing in 2008 and the producing theatre company for the initial production of *Cave Dwellers*. McCartney was mentored by McGrath and this play is very much a part of the political tradition to which McGrath dedicated his life. As Brian Logan, arts correspondent for the *Guardian*, writes, McGrath was 'Britain's Brecht, Scotland's Dario Fo'.[3] McCartney, in many of her plays, carries on McGrath's commitment to political theatre, particularly in her examination of the marginalisation and desperation of the asylum-seekers in *Cave Dwellers*.

At the same time, though, McCartney is also writing about her own sense of identity in *Cave Dwellers*. Having grown up in Belfast, as a child of a 'mixed marriage', McCartney says it is her 'cultural schizophrenia which makes me write about personal and political identity all the time'.[4] Against her family's wishes, McCartney left Belfast to attend Glasgow University and, since graduation has considered Glasgow her home. Today, she is alternately thought of as an Irish dramatist as well as a Scottish dramatist, two identities that are not always easy to reconcile. She has commented that the Scots see her as Irish, and the Irish see her as a Scot. Her self-description, in this regard, provides an excellent account of her work to date. As Michael says in her play *Heritage*: 'You don't have to be born in a country to belong to it.'[5] Appropriately, McCartney's plays reflect a fascination with contested, fragmented language, a doubling of characters, an overlapping of time and space, strong female voices, as well as an examination of memory and its function in creating reality.

Most prominently, her plays reveal a deep interest in marginalised individuals and those who survive daunting odds to create new homes. *Laundry* (1994, revised 1996) depicts the plight of women in the Magdalene Laundries, and several of McCartney's other plays, including *Cave Dwellers*, focus on characters trying to adapt to dramatic changes in circumstance. For example, Sarah, in *Heritage*, is an emigrant from an Ulster-Scot family in Northern Ireland now trying to make a new life in Canada; Jo, in *Home* (2000), is described as having a 'communication disorder'; and in *Hartland* (2011), the central character is a young woman 'held and abused by a couple throughout her teenage years'.[6] Beth and Bess, the teenage heroines of *Lifeboat*, survive nineteen hours in the water after the sinking of the SS City of Benares, a steam passenger ship that was torpedoed by a German submarine in 1940. Taken together, McCartney's plays serve as object lessons in the survival of identity in the midst of torturous, often liminal circumstances. Her plays also offer excellent roles for women. In addition to the characters already mentioned, *Standing Wave* (2004) centres on the life of Delia Derbyshire, who is best known for her work in electronic music and as the composer of the *Dr Who* theme. Her play *Miracle* (2011) is about Einstein's first wife Mileva Maric Einstein. In her most recent work, *Rachel's House*, McCartney has developed a piece of verbatim theatre centered on the stories of the Rachel's House programme in Columbus, Ohio. This programme mentors female ex-offenders in helping them adjust to life outside prison. In developing the play, McCartney interviewed many of the women who participate in Rachel's House, and the play tells their stories using the language of these interiews. She says of this new work: 'My mission is simple, yet enormous: to capture that struggle and their desire to overcome in the hope that it might inspire others to do the same.'[7]

Given her background, and specifically her sense of belonging to two (sometimes opposing) cultures at once, it is perhaps not surprising that McCartney would be drawn to writing about marginalised individuals. As Kathy McKean writes, '[T]he complex and problematic stagings of identity that characterise McCartney's work contain an element of autobiography.'[8] The depiction of the life-threatening journey of the asylum-seekers in *Cave Dwellers* has its roots not just in contemporary headlines and Western debates about interculturalism and immigration, but in McCartney's own background as well. Pushed out of their 'home' country and not yet accepted by a 'host' country, the asylum-seekers in McCartney's play occupy a space where nothing is familiar and everything, down to the most basic human relationships, must be recreated. *Cave Dwellers* is a powerful statement about the perils of immigration and of those immigrants' struggles as they seek to forge new lives in a new country and a new culture. As the character of Man says in the play: 'Doors are shut against me. I will open them. And I will have my place. I will have my name.'

Notes and References

1 The National Consultative Committee on Racism and Interculturalism, 'Refugees and Asylum Seekers' (March 2005). Read online at http://www.nccri.ie/cdsu-refugees.html. The United Nations defines a refugee as:

> Any person who owing to well-founded fear of being persecuted for reasons of race, religion, nationality, membership of a particular social group or political opinion, is outside the country of his nationality and is unable, or owing to such fear, is unwilling to avail himself of the protection of that country; or who,

not having a nationality and being outside the country of his former habitual residence as a result of such events, is unable or, owing to such fear, is unwilling to return to it.

('The Convention Relating to the Status of Refugees,' adopted 28 July 1951, http://unhcr.org.au/unhcr/index.php?option=com_content&view=article&id=179&Itemid=54). An asylum-seeker, on the other hand, is someone who seeks to be recognised as a refugee as defined by the United Nations.

2 The National Consultative Committee on Racism and Interculturalism, 'Refugees and Asylum Seekers' (March 2005). Read online at http://www.nccri.ie/cdsu-refugees.html.

3 Brian Logan, 'What did you do in the class war, Daddy?' *The Guardian*, Wednesday 15 May 2002, 12.24. Read online at http://www.guardian.co.uk/culture/2002/may/15/artsfeatures.

4 Nicola McCartney, electronic communication to C. Headrick, 15 October 2012.

5 McCartney, *Heritage* (London: Faber and Faber, 2001), p. 66.

6 Kathy McKean, 'Listen I will tell the story to you/As I have been told it: Memory and identity in the plays of Nicola McCartney,' *International Journal of Scottish Theatre and Screen*, Vol. 4, No. 1 (2011), p. 1.

7 Lower Lights Ministries, 'Theatre Project' (August 2013). Read online at http://www.lowerlights.org/9-programs/33-theater-project.

8 McKean, p. 1.

Cave Dwellers

Nicola McCartney

For John McGrath

First produced by 7:84 Scotland Theatre Co for a national tour in February 2001 with the following company:

Cast

Man	Liam Brennan
Young Woman	Helen Devon
Boy	Gary Collins
Old Woman	Mary McCusker

Production Team

Director	Gordon Laird
Designer	Evelyn Barbour
Composer	Robert Berlin
Assistant Director	Gordon Barr

Characters

Man
Young Woman
Boy
Old Woman

nothing will change until the people of this country cease to be cave dwellers of the mind

Michael Ondaatje

We cannot speak of freedom because we have not said I am the place where other people are

Edward Bond, 'The Labyrinth'

And now what will become of us without barbarians? They were a kind of solution.

C.P. Cavafy

Beware the tears of the oppressed: they sparkle in the sky like fire flies

Saying of the Prophet Mohammed

Setting

The present. A cave in a cliff face, overlooking an expanse of water, somewhere in Europe.

Act One

Scene 1

Night. An expanse of water.

(*The Boy appears, fully clothed, and swimming against a strong tide.*)

Scene 2

(*Man appears, picked out of the darkness.*)

Man: Why . . . ? Why . . . ? I have never warmed to 'why.' It's such an unspecific question, don't you think? 'Where' is different. Where is easy—'there', you say. Or 'here'. (*he shivers*) A blanket. I need a blanket. The chill hasn't left my bones yet . . . Or 'when?'—that's a good one. You say, 'Today' or 'twenty-first September'. There are only limited possibilities. And everyone remembers the exact date they left. Or 'who?' . . . No. We have the same problem with 'who' . . . I need a blanket . . . I'm sorry. I'm not stalling, it's just . . . (*he shivers*) I need a blanket. The chill has not worn off my bones yet . . . Please . . . ?

May I have a cigarette . . . ?

Why . . .

It is difficult to be specific . . . In English . . . I will try my level best . . . Ok. I am a child of the high places. I lived in a village, in a deep valley cut through the mountains by the Black River. I was a, I suppose you'd call it, a dreamer? Spent all my days climbing. No time for two plus this or the cat sat on that. I knew it all, devoured books kids twice my age wouldn't blow the dust off. Instinct, I suppose you'd call it. I wanted to know. And I wanted to know more. So I climbed. Every day, I scrambled up to a thin ridge on our side of the valley and lay flat as a sniper, amongst the ferns and the red and white rock lilies. I was Robin Hood. Watching and waiting. Watching our village and the other. Two villages less than a mile apart. Two villages that had not spoken, had not traded, had not laid eyes on the other for maybe fifty, a hundred, maybe two hundred years. Maybe not so long.

Why . . . ? Ah . . .

I would lie there all day until dusk until the lights came on in the two villages and all along the metal suspension bridge and the five hydro-electric dams that straddled the Black River. Then it was time. I would draw out the small red torch—a present to my older brother which I had appropriated for my undercover operations—and a piece of broken compact mirror. Then dit da dit dit da into the blackness—just a little trick I'd picked up from the Saturday afternoon war movies me and my brother saw once a month up in the town. Told you I was, I suppose you'd say, a bright spark. The movies had subtitles. In three languages—take your pick. Dit da every night for days, months, years, and then one night on the other side of the valley: dit da dit dit da . . . Marvellous! Don't you think?

. . . Dit da dit dit da. The same idea! The very same . . .

I am going as fast as I can . . .

Me and the boy—we did this for days, months. No one knew. I never saw him, just flashes in the darkness. One year older. His father worked the dams, my father worked the dams. His mother made and mended clothes, my mother was a hairdresser. He had an older brother and a younger brother too, and an older sister who had sex in the graveyard with her boyfriend—except on holy days. And he too was Robin Hood, but we couldn't have two. And we hatched schemes to ambush the Sheriff of Nottingham on the suspension bridge and seize the king's gold. No one knew. Dit dit da. But we both knew of the trouble in the city and he said they were as afraid there as we were here that the rebels were moving in through the mountains to seize the dams. Dit da. And when the town was taken he was just as disappointed as me that we had to miss the one-off showing of the *Sands of Iwo Jima*—which neither of us had seen on the big screen before, but only on channel two with a fuzzy picture because the army had blown up the transmitter at the head of the valley. Dit dit da. No one knew. Me and the boy agreed to meet. Knew the danger. If someone saw then . . . We couldn't just walk over the bridge. No one had ever done that—ever. So one night, I swam the river . . .

Scene 3

At the cave mouth. Dusk.

(*The* OLD WOMAN *wraps herself tighter in a blanket as she lights a candle and mimes lighting a second. She covers her eyes.*)

OLD WOMAN: Barukh atah Adoshem. Elohanynu, melekh ha-olam . . . eh . . . melekh ha-olam . . . Our Father. No. Silly old fool. . . . Barukh atah . . . No. No. It'll come back . . . Amein . . . Let me die! Why won't you? . . . Silly . . . Hurry up! Hurry up! Soon the children will be coming . . .

Hurry up! Late always late, aren't you? . . . Your black suit? . . . Where d'you think? Where it's always hanging . . . There's a surprise! . . . Silly old fool! . . . And the children . . . Are here. (*she looks around her 'table'; pause*) My son . . . My son . . . My daughter . . . My son . . . Six of them. All six are here. What are their names? . . . And my grandson . . . So like his grandfather, isn't he? And my beautiful girls . . . Here! By me. Help me . . . Ah! Don't touch the bread . . . Not yet. Not yet . . . Their names . . . I got all six! (*she stops, in pain*) Tch tch tch . . . Old bones . . . Die. Why don't you let me? . . . No . . . You're right. You're right. I have all six. Here I have them. This is the way it is and this is the way it will always be. Why would it be different? . . .

And now we break bread . . .
ha motzi lechem min ha-aretz . . .

(*She mimes breaking the bread, puts salt on it, and eats a portion. The* YOUNG WOMAN *enters.*)

OLD WOMAN: And now we can talk. Now we can laugh. Now we can remember . . . This is the way it is and this is the way it will always be. Tch tch tch . . .
Silly old fool.

(*pause*)

Who's there? . . . I said who's there? . . .
Is that . . . Is that you?

(*pause*)

YOUNG WOMAN: Joseph.

OLD WOMAN: Who are you?
YOUNG WOMAN: Joseph.
OLD WOMAN: What are you talking about?
YOUNG WOMAN: Joseph! Joseph!
OLD WOMAN: I have a gun.
YOUNG WOMAN: Joseph?
OLD WOMAN: I know no Joseph. You. Who are you?
YOUNG WOMAN: No?
OLD WOMAN: I don't understand you.
YOUNG WOMAN: What? Is he here? Now? Joseph?
OLD WOMAN: No.
YOUNG WOMAN: No.

(*The YOUNG WOMAN sits down.*)

OLD WOMAN: What's the matter? Are you alright? (*She approaches her. Stops in pain.*) . . . It's okay. It's okay. I won't hurt you. How could I hurt you? . . . (*YOUNG WOMAN moves.*) No. Wait. Please. Wait. You are cold. Yes? Cold? . . . Yes . . . I will give you a blanket. A blanket . . . Can't seem to feel the cold anymore. They say that as you grow older the blood grows thinner, but mine is thicker . . . Where are you from? You're not Italian. No . . . French? Francais? . . . Oh dear . . . Dutch, don't know any Dutch . . . Anyway, why would she be Dutch? Silly old fool. Let's see . . . Is she German?

German . . . Come on, come on . . . (*pause*) Wuenschen Sie noch etwas eine decke . . .? Decke . . .? Ya . . . ? No. No. No. (*holds up a blanket*) Yes?

(*YOUNG WOMAN nods.*)

OLD WOMAN: Good.
YOUNG WOMAN: Thanks.
OLD WOMAN: OK.

(*pause*) Good. That's better? Yes. (*pause*) I thought maybe you were . . . But, no . . . I would give you something to eat . . . To eat . . . But I have nothing . . .

YOUNG WOMAN: I have no food.
OLD WOMAN: No trouble. I thought maybe . . . Have you come a long way?
YOUNG WOMAN: No stars.

OLD WOMAN: Yes, it is dark. It's the clouds. Always rains in this country! In my country when summer announced itself, it knew the meaning of its name. Where do you come from?

YOUNG WOMAN: What?

OLD WOMAN: From. You. Where?

YOUNG WOMAN: No.

OLD WOMAN: You don't understand.

YOUNG WOMAN: Understand you.

OLD WOMAN: Good. Oh good. I am from . . .

YOUNG WOMAN: . . . No . . . Day? What day?

OLD WOMAN: Friday.

YOUNG WOMAN: No.

OLD WOMAN: No. Wait a minute.

YOUNG WOMAN: The YOUNG WOMAN is confused. She goes to speak, but says nothing.

OLD WOMAN: Come to think of it, it's Sunday . . . Ha! . . . Yes. Monday, Tuesday . . .

YOUNG WOMAN: No. It must be Saturday. Saturday.

OLD WOMAN: Calm down, love.

YOUNG WOMAN: Must be. Saturday.

OLD WOMAN: No. Sunday.

YOUNG WOMAN: But Joseph said . . .

OLD WOMAN: Joseph . . . Joseph told you to come here? Yes?

YOUNG WOMAN: You know Joseph?

OLD WOMAN: He told you to wait, yes? (*stops in pain*) Joseph told me to wait here too . . .

YOUNG WOMAN: Can't have gone. Not yet.

OLD WOMAN: . . . I have waited—here—nearly a week.

YOUNG WOMAN: A week?

OLD WOMAN: Yes. So you see, we are the same. Same. You and me. So don't be afraid of me, love.

YOUNG WOMAN: Not afraid of you.

OLD WOMAN: No.

YOUNG WOMAN: One week?

OLD WOMAN: I would give you something to eat.

YOUNG WOMAN: And he doesn't come?

OLD WOMAN: I think it's been . . . Let's see five, maybe six . . .

YOUNG WOMAN: . . . He doesn't come. What's happened?

OLD WOMAN: Rest. You're tired.

YOUNG WOMAN: But why does he not come? Why not?

OLD WOMAN: I don't know! I don't know . . . No point shouting at me.

(pause)

OLD WOMAN: You think I want to be here? . . . I don't want to be here. I should never have come. Never. But what else could I do? Except lie down and die? Not yet. So don't you shout at me.

(The YOUNG WOMAN opens her bag, takes out food and begins to eat. She sees the OLD WOMAN looking. She gives a little to the OLD WOMAN.)

OLD WOMAN: Thank you.

YOUNG WOMAN: That's all I have.

OLD WOMAN: I suppose we'd better introduce ourselves . . . My name . . .

YOUNG WOMAN: Eat. Just eat.

OLD WOMAN: Yes.

(they eat)

OLD WOMAN: I lied about the gun.

Scene 4

(The BOY swimmer reappears.)

MAN: The water was so black even the moon did not reflect off it. But I swam the river. I swam because I could hold my breath under water the longest, because I had seen the *Poseidon Adventure* four times, because I was Robin Hood. That night, I stripped, rubbed olive oil all over my body, then wrapped my grey wool sweater and boots in a plastic bag which I tied to my back. I swam. Through the black and the cold . . . You asked me! . . . You want to know why I ended up on that boat? This is why. You want answers to your questions, then listen. Listen . . . I swam. At the place, at the place at the time, he was not there. I waited.
(he shivers) I waited.

Scene 5

At the cave mouth.

(The YOUNG WOMAN and the OLD WOMAN, waiting.)

OLD WOMAN: What can you see?

YOUNG WOMAN: Few boats. A car ferry.

OLD WOMAN: He will not come in daylight . . . Get down from there! Someone will see you!

YOUNG WOMAN: Police only look at night.

OLD WOMAN: I should never have come here . . .

YOUNG WOMAN: Can see all the way along the shore to the ferry port. Busy. Clear day . . .

OLD WOMAN: What are you looking for?

YOUNG WOMAN: Watching.

OLD WOMAN: It's beautiful. For a change. You can see all the way over.

YOUNG WOMAN: Yes . . . (*a beat*) He will not come tonight.

OLD WOMAN: Don't say that. Don't.

YOUNG WOMAN: Maybe—if the fog comes in. Maybe.

OLD WOMAN: More waiting! I think I'll die waiting.

YOUNG WOMAN: Won't. Not you. Not yet.

OLD WOMAN: Oh yes?

YOUNG WOMAN: Yes . . . I know . . .

OLD WOMAN: Of course you do! You know everything!

YOUNG WOMAN: Not everything . . . Can see all the way.

OLD WOMAN: Where are you going when you get there? Over there? What will you do?

YOUNG WOMAN: Surprised you travel alone.

OLD WOMAN: Yes . . . Too old for all this.

YOUNG WOMAN: No. Not that . . . Your kind—they come looking for you . . . Always. In the camps.

OLD WOMAN: You are from the camps?

YOUNG WOMAN: Take you home and feed you.

OLD WOMAN: No one came looking for us . . .

YOUNG WOMAN: Take you back to your land.

OLD WOMAN: My husband, he said to me, 'Live out your last days among the living.' And the living are over there.

(*silence*)

YOUNG WOMAN: Give me your money.

OLD WOMAN: What?

YOUNG WOMAN: Your money. Not all of it. Give it to me.

OLD WOMAN: I knew it. I knew it. You are from the camps . . .

YOUNG WOMAN: No. No. Food. For food.

OLD WOMAN: Here. All I have! There . . .

(*The* OLD WOMAN *gives her money.*)

YOUNG WOMAN: No . . . Food. I will walk to the port and buy food. With your money and my money . . . Yes? . . .

OLD WOMAN: Yes . . . All right . . . Yes . . .

YOUNG WOMAN: Wait here . . . I will come back.

OLD WOMAN: From the camps . . . My God . . . What were you doing in the camps? Why?

YOUNG WOMAN: I waited.

Scene 6

(*The BOY starts to have trouble staying above the water.*)

MAN: I waited for him . . .
I am freezing. A blanket. Please? . . .
He did not come. I cried.
I was ashamed of him, ashamed and angry. He was a coward. (*he shivers*) Please . . . I swam the whole way back across the river, and walked back to the edge of our village, just as the sun was making its first appearance above the mountains . . .
I saw him.
For the first time. Clinging to the signpost. Blood from his two hands pouring over the name of our village. Blood from his mouth pouring over the name 'traitor' pinned to his grey wool sweater. Crucified. He was eleven years old. (*he shivers*) I need a blanket.

(*The BOY begins to drown.*)

Scene 7

Night. Outside the cave mouth.

(*The YOUNG WOMAN, wet from the rescue, throws the BOY's body to the ground. She begins to try to revive him. The OLD WOMAN watches.*)

OLD WOMAN: He's freezing.

YOUNG WOMAN: Come on!

OLD WOMAN: Looks young. How old is he?

YOUNG WOMAN: Breathe!

OLD WOMAN: Is he? . . .

YOUNG WOMAN: No . . . In the bag. His clothes.

(*The OLD WOMAN starts to unpack the bag. The BOY gasps and splutters water from his mouth.*)

YOUNG WOMAN: That's it . . . Cough it all up. Good. That's it . . . (*to* OLD WOMAN) Warm him up . . . Rub! Rub . . .

(*The two women work to revive the* BOY. *The* OLD WOMAN *notices a pendant round his neck.*)

OLD WOMAN: Look.

(*pause*)

YOUNG WOMAN: . . . That's who he is, then . . . God.

OLD WOMAN: What?

YOUNG WOMAN: Leave him.

OLD WOMAN: But, he'll die . . .

YOUNG WOMAN: Fine. Do what you like. I won't touch him.

(*The* OLD WOMAN *puts the blanket over him and holds him.*)

OLD WOMAN: We must build a fire . . . A fire.

YOUNG WOMAN: You want to be seen?

OLD WOMAN: I will get some wood.

YOUNG WOMAN: No. No fire, I said.

OLD WOMAN: All right, all right . . . Hold him. Keep his head up.

YOUNG WOMAN: No. He needs to . . . Put him down. Down.

OLD WOMAN: No.

YOUNG WOMAN: Won't touch him!

OLD WOMAN: He's only a boy . . .

YOUNG WOMAN: Not him. Dangerous.

OLD WOMAN: You are mad! Mad!

YOUNG WOMAN: Mad?

(*The* YOUNG WOMAN *laughs.*)

OLD WOMAN: See? She is crazy! A crazy person!

YOUNG WOMAN: I am not mad.

OLD WOMAN: You are laughing and he is dying.

YOUNG WOMAN: Don't understand.

OLD WOMAN: You will let him die . . . He is a child and you will let him die.

(*The* YOUNG WOMAN *goes to leave.*)

YOUNG WOMAN: He is not a child . . . He will live. (*leaving*) Keep him warm.

OLD WOMAN: Where are you going?

YOUNG WOMAN: To look.

OLD WOMAN: What for?

YOUNG WOMAN: To look. Talk to him. Talk.

OLD WOMAN: But . . . Come back! Hey!

(she exits)

OLD WOMAN: Mad as a coot. See? . . . Talk? . . . What? (*pause*) Hello. (*pause*) My name is . . . No . . . Oh God . . . God help us . . . This is our cave . . . We are waiting here for . . . No! Don't tell him that! You breathing? . . . Keep breathing. Don't stop. Don't . . . Won't let you . . . (*she is in pain*) I won't let you! . . . God is our refuge and strength . . . Therefore we will not fear though the . . . Damn! Can't seem to . . . (*she sings*) . . . *Got un zayn mishpet iz gerekht, Men tor keyn mol nit zogn . . .* I know I talk too much. Talk too much and you understand so little. Like my mother. She could talk. Friday night into the wee small hours. That's why she was always the first to be called out to a wake. She'd lay out the body and then start talking. Tell stories, sing songs, say prayers and keep them all awake. She died when she was ninety-six years old. But that is how you live, you see? This is how you hold on. You must let the life come out of you . . . Don't stop. Don't. (*she sings*) *Got un zayn mishpet iz gerekht, Men tor keyn mol nit zogn, Got is shlekht. Got veyst vos er tit, Umzist shtroft er keynem nit, Got un zayn mishpet iz gerekht . . .*

Scene 8

(*MAN now has a blanket.*)

MAN: Yes, the boat was too full. Yes. But he was trying to help us, our Captain. A tragedy, a disaster, a poorly thought out plan, call it what you will, but what else do you do when desperation grips you by the throat and won't let you breathe? . . . There was a boy and his grandmother. Half a dozen men—Arabs. And a family . . . with two small children. Did you find the children? . . . I see . . . I'd say there were about thirty of us. Too many in a boat made to carry half that number. But we would have made it. We would have. If your boats had not been chasing us so hard it would not have capsized . . .

Names? . . . I don't know names. People don't give

names. Just histories. And futures . . . If your boats had not been chasing . . . Thank you for the blanket . . . You interrupted. You asked me why I am here now and then you interrupted. Permit me to continue?

Scene 9

The cave mouth. Early morning.

(*The* YOUNG WOMAN *sits wrapped around the* BOY*—it's almost an embrace. She examines him, taking his pulse etc. She lays him on the ground and covers him. The* OLD WOMAN *enters.*)

OLD WOMAN: Old bones. Can't get them moving this morning. Used to move. Boy, did I! Like a whippet! . . . Clean the house, top to bottom before breakfast. Full day's work and home again to feed all six of them—all six. Now look at me! What am I good for, eh? . . . What? . . . How is he?

YOUNG WOMAN: Him?

OLD WOMAN: Yes, him. Who else? He's alright?

YOUNG WOMAN: Fine.

(*She checks through his bag.*)

OLD WOMAN: Look at him . . . I wonder where this one's mother is? . . . It's cold. He should be inside.
(*pause*)
Someone might see us . . .

YOUNG WOMAN: Warm in the sun.

OLD WOMAN: But if someone sees us . . .

YOUNG WOMAN: Watching. Leave him . . . No money, no papers.

OLD WOMAN: You have papers?

(*The* YOUNG WOMAN *nods.*)

OLD WOMAN: And over there? You have family?

YOUNG WOMAN: No family.

OLD WOMAN: Where will you go? Where to?

YOUNG WOMAN: Where I can work.

OLD WOMAN: What kind of work?

YOUNG WOMAN: Work is work.

OLD WOMAN: Joseph . . . How much did you pay? . . .

YOUNG WOMAN: Shhh!

OLD WOMAN: He can't hear me, can he?

YOUNG WOMAN: He will come. We must wait.

OLD WOMAN: I have waited and waited.

YOUNG WOMAN: He has to come.

OLD WOMAN: And what then? We can't just leave him.

YOUNG WOMAN: I pay Joseph. You pay. Yes? Who pays for him? . . . You? . . . We do more than he deserves. No pity. He deserves none.

OLD WOMAN: So young.

YOUNG WOMAN: Your youngest grandchild? How old? (*pause*) Take pity? . . . Do they? . . .

OLD WOMAN: My youngest?

YOUNG WOMAN: They have none. And they take every scrap you have.

(*The* OLD WOMAN *produces a well-worn, precious letter.*)

OLD WOMAN: My youngest . . . I have a letter . . . Written by herself. She says she is frightened. But how should she be frightened? She is safe, isn't she? 'I wanted to stay with you, Grandma,' she says. Stay—can you believe this? No food, no water, no heat. Adults squabbled over every crust of bread. She was the only child left. The only one . . . It cost us nearly everything, but we got her out . . . Not used to the language, she says. Goes to school now and everything! . . . Says she wants to come back, to her beautiful home . . . Ha! A village of the dying! Goes to the cinema, she says! And with boys! If her grandfather knew that . . . If he knew that . . . He would . . . That is where I am going . . . Says she hates being there. Hates me . . .

YOUNG WOMAN: Think only about where you are going. Forward. Always forward. Nothing else.

OLD WOMAN: You don't understand.

YOUNG WOMAN: Understand.

OLD WOMAN: No.

YOUNG WOMAN: I have a son.

OLD WOMAN: How old?

YOUNG WOMAN: Three.

OLD WOMAN: Where?

YOUNG WOMAN: I will find him.

OLD WOMAN: Is he lost?

YOUNG WOMAN: But I will find him again.
OLD WOMAN: Why? How did you lose him?
YOUNG WOMAN: His kind.
OLD WOMAN: Didn't you look for him?
YOUNG WOMAN: Of course I looked. I always look.
OLD WOMAN: And his father? Where is he?

(*Silence. The* YOUNG WOMAN *holds water to the boy's lips.*)

OLD WOMAN: He will come, won't he?
YOUNG WOMAN: Told you.
OLD WOMAN: He is a good man?
YOUNG WOMAN: He is a clever man. The best man. Everyone says.
OLD WOMAN: What if he? . . . What I mean is—it's a lot of money. An awful lot.

(*The* BOY *starts to wake up.*)

YOUNG WOMAN: You still hold half, yes?
OLD WOMAN: Until I arrive.
YOUNG WOMAN: You are safe then.
OLD WOMAN: Safe. Maybe Joseph will take him to a hospital?
YOUNG WOMAN: Maybe . . . Shhh! Signs of life . . .

Scene 10

MAN: When it started it was a Tuesday. It was July. Or at least, that's what I remember. It was just after my birthday. I was fifteen—old enough to have sex in the graveyard. Though, I must confess, I didn't heed the unspoken rule about holy days. It was a Tuesday. They seeped through the villages, through each house. 'Put your valuables and car keys on the table and go. You have thirty minutes.' Then they blew up the suspension bridge. They blew up the roads. They blew up the graveyards. They blew up a little brown and black dog in the street. They blew up all the dams except one. I came running, to the house. And they are in the kitchen. My father is not there. My brothers are not there. Only my mother and she is . . . They have . . . I was very young. I did what they wanted . . . I did what was necessary . . . I will not answer that question . . . I told you, I did what was necessary . . .

Scene 11

Inside the cave mouth.

(The OLD WOMAN*, asleep, and the* BOY *awake; the* BOY *crawls towards the* OLD WOMAN*. The* YOUNG WOMAN *watches him from the shadows. The* BOY *tries to say something to the* OLD WOMAN*, but he has no voice. He might touch her.)*

YOUNG WOMAN: Leave her . . . Away.

(He moves away a little. He tries to speak again.)

YOUNG WOMAN: Saved your life, me . . . Should've pushed you under. Left you to the waves, huh? (*laughs*) You don't understand . . . You're hungry? Yes? . . . You want food?

(He nods. The YOUNG WOMAN *goes to her bag and takes out a little food. She holds it out to him. When he goes to take it, she sets it on the floor. The* BOY *eats.)*

YOUNG WOMAN: Careful . . . Slow . . . You want more? . . . More? . . . You are very tired and you are very hungry? . . . No more. Not for you. Saw the marks on you. Know who you are and what you are. Know if you try to harm us, I will kill you.

(She holds up his pendant.)

YOUNG WOMAN: This is who you are.

(The BOY *tries to take it back, but can't. She tosses the pendant to the ground.)*

YOUNG WOMAN: Scum of the earth . . . Go. Leave us alone.

(He picks up the YOUNG WOMAN*'s bag. The* OLD WOMAN *wakes up.)*

YOUNG WOMAN: Give . . .
BOY: Know . . .
Woman: Give!
OLD WOMAN: Ah . . . He's back. In the land of the living . . .
YOUNG WOMAN: Killed your kind before, don't think I haven't.
BOY: Know . . . you are . . .
YOUNG WOMAN: Hands off, bastard!
OLD WOMAN: What's going on? What's happened?

(The YOUNG WOMAN *goes to take the bag from him and they struggle.)*

BOY: Listen! Listen! Listen!
YOUNG WOMAN: Kill you.
OLD WOMAN: No. Stop this.
BOY: Listen!
OLD WOMAN: What?
BOY: (*to YOUNG WOMAN*) Know you . . .
OLD WOMAN: Let him go. Let him . . .

(*The YOUNG WOMAN throws the BOY to the ground.*)

OLD WOMAN: What did you do that for?
YOUNG WOMAN: (*to BOY*) Out of here . . . Now . . .
OLD WOMAN: You are mad . . . Cruel.
YOUNG WOMAN: Me? . . . You don't understand.
OLD WOMAN: He is sick.
BOY: Know you . . .
YOUNG WOMAN: You don't know what you are talking about. What he is . . .
OLD WOMAN: I don't care who he is! Understand! . . . He is a child . . . Now you leave him alone . . . (*to the BOY*) There, there, my son. It's all right.
BOY: Listen!
OLD WOMAN: Shhh! . . . Rest. (*to the YOUNG WOMAN*) More food. He needs more . . . You must give it.
BOY: Know you . . . Joseph . . .
YOUNG WOMAN: What's he saying? What?
BOY: Joseph?
OLD WOMAN: My God . . . He says, 'Joseph'.
YOUNG WOMAN: Speak about that again, I'll gut you.
OLD WOMAN: Shhh! . . . (*to the BOY*) You are waiting for him?
BOY: (*to OLD WOMAN*) You are waiting for him.
YOUNG WOMAN: What's he saying?
BOY: (*to OLD WOMAN*) You don't understand.
OLD WOMAN: (*to BOY*) No. You. I understand . . .
BOY: You are waiting for Joseph . . .
OLD WOMAN: Yes . . . My God.

Scene 12

MAN: And the house is burning and what can I save? I save, not my mother's body. No. I save a radio. No papers. No money, no papers. Papers burned with the house . . .

And then it rained. And still my father didn't return. In my country, good news comes with the rain . . . Only the soles of her feet, still wearing black shoes, and the underwear around her ankles are not burned . . . I am tuning in the radio. I lie chin deep in the mud and listen. 'Federal agencies detained thirty-one people during "cleansing" operations . . .' Only the soles of her feet . . . And my father is not come. Throat deep I lie. I listen. On the radio, Madonna, 'Just like a prayer . . .' I look up at the sky. I remember, 'The Spanish sky is cloudless.' . . . The signal. *For Whom the Bell Tolls*— Anthony Quinn or is it Gregory Peck. I always confuse those two. I am rising. And the mud is no longer my second skin, but pulses in my veins. I turn the dial . . . 'Born in the USA, I was . . .' Open up the lungs . . . 'Ah ah ah ah stayin' alive . . . Stayin' alive . . .' Only the soles of her feet . . . The boat! The boat! All right! I am getting to that. I am getting there! . . . Ok . . . Who-what-where, when-why . . . I nearly died for the ninth time on that boat . . . Nearly. (*He pulls out a pendant and holds it up.*) See this? Swam with it in my fist. See? This is who I am . . . Our boat was too full. I was clinging on to the side and I fell in. The sea was too rough. I was holding on to a ladder. Your boats were chasing. One got in front of us. The Captain turned the boat to avoid it . . . . What? . . . I do not know his name . . . I do not know it. People do not give names. Not real ones, anyway. I fell in. My hands got cold and I lost my grip . . . You pulled me out . . . I am trying to tell you! This is who I am . . . My hands . . .

Scene 13

Inside the cave mouth. Night.

(*The YOUNG WOMAN, OLD WOMAN and the BOY; the BOY plays with the torch.*)

YOUNG WOMAN: (*to the BOY*) Don't.

OLD WOMAN: It is a beautiful night . . . Clear. When I was your age. On nights like this I used to walk, with his arm through mine.

YOUNG WOMAN: Too much light . . .
OLD WOMAN: When the fields, were asleep . . . I liked silence then.
YOUNG WOMAN: I like it now. He may come tonight.

(*The* BOY *plays with the torch on the wall.*)

YOUNG WOMAN: Don't do that! Waste . . . Give it to me!
OLD WOMAN: It is mine. Let him have it . . .

(*silence*)

OLD WOMAN: (*to herself*) . . . Tuesday, Wednesday. Yes, Wednesday!
YOUNG WOMAN: It's Friday.
OLD WOMAN: Are you sure?
YOUNG WOMAN: The wall. I marked it there.

(*The* OLD WOMAN *goes to look. She moves in pain. The* BOY *lights up the wall with his torch.*)

OLD WOMAN: Thank you . . .
YOUNG WOMAN: How long have you been like that?
OLD WOMAN: Long time. Since they took us away in the railway carriages to the grey place. Since then.
YOUNG WOMAN: You don't complain.
OLD WOMAN: I complain . . . Old bones!
YOUNG WOMAN: Not arthritis . . . No. What happened to you there?
OLD WOMAN: Nothing.
YOUNG WOMAN: I have heard of things they did to people. Terrible things . . .
OLD WOMAN: Nothing happened! . . . I survived it.
YOUNG WOMAN: There was a woman in the village of tents. Screamed in pain every night. I wanted to help her. But I didn't. They would have killed me . . . I had my son.
OLD WOMAN: Of course, you had to think of the child first.
YOUNG WOMAN: I wanted to help . . . I had taken my oath. But they would've shot me if they had found out . . . I was a doctor.
OLD WOMAN: You?
YOUNG WOMAN: I had to . . . Doesn't matter. Stories. Just stories . . .
OLD WOMAN: Why would they have killed you?
YOUNG WOMAN: They wanted to kill all of us. Teachers, doctors, everyone who could help, see? . . . I had my son.
OLD WOMAN: Over there, you can work again.

YOUNG WOMAN: No.

OLD WOMAN: But you must . . .

YOUNG WOMAN: You don't understand.

(*The* BOY *moves to the door with his torch.*)

YOUNG WOMAN: Stop that! Stop! . . . Who were you signalling to? . . . Tell me!

OLD WOMAN: Were you signalling? With the torch?

BOY: No.

YOUNG WOMAN: (*trying to take it from him*) He was. Sure of it. Night they look for us.

OLD WOMAN: You mustn't play with that. You want us to be discovered?

YOUNG WOMAN: Tell him to give me the torch.

OLD WOMAN: Give me the torch.

(*The* BOY *hands it over to the* OLD WOMAN.)

YOUNG WOMAN: He was signalling. I am sure.

OLD WOMAN: Don't be silly. To who?!

YOUNG WOMAN: It is a clear night . . . Watch him.

OLD WOMAN: What if they see you? You know it's night they look for us.

(*The* YOUNG WOMAN *exits.*)

OLD WOMAN: Why does she hate you so much? Eh? . . .

(*The* BOY *doesn't answer.*)

OLD WOMAN: Were you signalling to someone? Were you?

BOY: I want to go over there.

OLD WOMAN: You must pay money.

BOY: You must pay money.

MAN: The money? I am glad you asked about the money . . .

OLD WOMAN: I have no money.

BOY: No money. No papers.

OLD WOMAN: Who do you have left?

BOY: Who do you have left?

OLD WOMAN: I have myself. I am left. And a niece.

BOY: Over there? Yes?

OLD WOMAN: Over there. Yes. And you?

BOY: My father.

OLD WOMAN: And where is he?
BOY: My father.
OLD WOMAN: Yes. You need to find him.

BOY:

I wait . . . I lie very still between the ferns and the rock lilies. I sleep with my eyes open. When my father came back to the house he didn't find us. He buried my mother by the Black river. And then he came looking. He knew. He pulled me out from among the ferns and the red and white rock lilies and we went looking for my brothers and then we gave up. We went back to the ruins and started picking through the rubble. My mother had hidden it—under the floor—years of saving. There must have been two maybe three thousand. Maybe more. My father sewed the money into his trousers . . . and then we walked across the valley to a hospital . . .

He said, 'This is a safe place. Wait here until I come back.' He didn't come back. He left us there. He didn't come back.

MAN:

When my father came back to the house he found us, waiting. He buried my mother. I helped him . . . Then he started picking through the rubble. He knew what he was looking for and where to find it. My mother had hidden it—under the floor—years of saving. There must have been two, three thousand American dollars . . . My father sewed half the money into his trousers and half into mine and then we walked across across the mountains.

He said, 'This is a safe place. Wait here until I come back.'

OLD WOMAN: How old are you?
BOY: . . . ?
OLD WOMAN: Your age . . . How old?
BOY: Eleven.
OLD WOMAN: . . . ?
BOY: (*counting on his fingers for her*) Eleven.
OLD WOMAN: No! You. Now. How old. You. Now.
BOY: I don't know . . . Your niece lives over there.
OLD WOMAN: I think so. Yes . . . I think so.
BOY: And you are waiting for Joseph.

OLD WOMAN: And before that a man called Konstantin and before him a man called Abraham and before him a man called Ricardo.

BOY: A lot of waiting.

OLD WOMAN: In the end I will get there.

BOY: I want to go there.

MAN: The Captain is a legend. In fact, it was something of a privilege to be on his boat. They say he is the swiftest, most nimble of all the skafisti—the Smuggler of all smugglers.

BOY: Money. I want to make money—lots and lots of money.

OLD WOMAN: I have no money.

MAN: That is why they call him 'The Captain'. He has never been caught and never will—or so they say . . .

OLD WOMAN: Look . . . Nothing.

BOY: No . . . I will make. Over there.

OLD WOMAN: Oh . . . How?

BOY: I find my way. There, lots of ways.

MAN: He charges high, for he drives himself. Most of these Mafia bosses hire pizza-faced boys to skipper their boats, youngsters who will throw the people over the side to escape the water police . . .

OLD WOMAN: And what will you do with this lots of money? . . . Money. Buy what?

MAN: That is not the Captain's style. He is a good man. Practical man, intelligent man . . .

BOY: Buy!

OLD WOMAN: What?

MAN: You are chasing us. The boat is slow. Anybody else would have just thrown us over the side and bolted.

BOY: Things. I want. I need.

OLD WOMAN: What do you need.

MAN: Then the boat tips.

BOY: Clothes, food, house . . .

MAN: I thought I was dead . . .

OLD WOMAN: Where will you have this house?

MAN: I really thought I was dead.

BOY: Big city.

OLD WOMAN: Which city?

BOY: . . . First one I get to.
OLD WOMAN: What sort of house will you have? Will you have a flat?
BOY: A big house.
OLD WOMAN: A big house?
BOY: Big, big house. Ten bedrooms . . .
MAN: The people are shouting and crying and praying . . .
OLD WOMAN: Swimming pool?
BOY: No swimming pool . . . Field for tennis.
MAN: The Captain starts shouting, 'You want me to try and save you. I am trying to save us but stop screaming.'
OLD WOMAN: You will need 'lots of money'.
MAN: But they keep crying . . .
BOY: I will.
OLD WOMAN: And a football pitch?
MAN: My hands got cold and I lost my grip . . . I really thought I was dead.
BOY: Don't ask me your questions, ok? . . . Fucking stupid questions.
OLD WOMAN: What's wrong?
BOY: Fucking stupid! Where is she? Where is she?
OLD WOMAN: Wait here.
BOY: Hands off! I'm going to look for her.
OLD WOMAN: No stay. Here. Stay. Won't find her. Now too dark.
BOY: Give me the torch. Give it to me.
OLD WOMAN: And leave me here in the dark?
BOY: Sleep.
OLD WOMAN: No.
BOY: Torch, I said.
OLD WOMAN: I don't want to sleep. Leave me the light. Or at least let me come with you.
BOY: Won't ask again.
OLD WOMAN: We should wait. She will find her way back to us.

(*He goes to take the torch from her. They struggle.*)

BOY: Fucking kill you. Kick you til you fucking die.
OLD WOMAN: It is my torch . . .
BOY: Whore. Fucking . . .
OLD WOMAN: It is mine.
BOY: Cunt . . . Fucking . . . Give, bastard. Give.

(*She slaps him. He cries and lies down. The* OLD WOMAN *is shocked. She gathers her breath.*)

OLD WOMAN: Sorry . . . I am . . . Here. Take it. Take it . . . There . . .

(*She soothes him. The* YOUNG WOMAN *enters.*)

YOUNG WOMAN: Off her bastard! Off! (*to* OLD WOMAN) Did he touch you? What did he? . . .

OLD WOMAN: Shh! (*to the* BOY) Don't stop. Don't . . . You will be all right. God help us.

BOY:
Fuck you.

MAN:
I am a strong swimmer.

YOUNG WOMAN: You think you are still a big man here? You are nothing here.

BOY:
I wanted the torch.

MAN:
I really thought I was dead.

YOUNG WOMAN:
You are nothing! Hear me.

MAN:
You pulled me out.

OLD WOMAN: Voices! Voices!

(*The* YOUNG WOMAN *picks up a rock.*)

OLD WOMAN: No.
YOUNG WOMAN: Kill you.
OLD WOMAN: He's sick.
BOY: Go on, then. Throw it.
OLD WOMAN: He's only a boy.
YOUNG WOMAN: Who cares? Who misses him? (*to* OLD WOMAN) Saw him over you night after he come. Saw him look at you. Evil look.
OLD WOMAN: (*to* BOY) How did you look?
YOUNG WOMAN: Look—a killing look. Or worse.
OLD WOMAN: No.
BOY: (*to* YOUNG WOMAN) Throw.
OLD WOMAN: (*to* BOY) What would you do to me?
YOUNG WOMAN: Tell you. Evil.
BOY: Don't understand.
YOUNG WOMAN: Know you and what you do. Since you came I sleep with a knife in my pocket.

BOY: (*to the* YOUNG WOMAN) Fuck you.

YOUNG WOMAN: Hear him now. Can swear in my language, this 'only a boy.'

OLD WOMAN: Get away!

BOY: Fuck you. And you.

(*The* YOUNG WOMAN *throws the stone and picks up another. He picks up a rock and moves towards the* OLD WOMAN.)

BOY: I will kill her and then I will kill you.

(*She is about to throw the stone at him. Then—*)

YOUNG WOMAN: What did you say?

BOY: Joseph comes, he can take me instead.

MAN: Had you not pulled me from the sea that night, had I flown in on a jet plane and passed through the green channel, if I were sweet-smelling, affluent, civilised like you, you would have welcomed me with open arms, yes? My money is welcome anywhere in the world but I, unfortunately am not, yes? . . . I understand . . . I understand very well . . .

YOUNG WOMAN: You will never ever do that to me again! Hear me! Never do that . . . Get down!

MAN: In my country there are no tourists, there are only guests.

YOUNG WOMAN: Hide!

(*She throws him to the ground. Sound of men approaching.*)

MAN: Hospitality is the law of the mountains. This is not your law, is it? . . . I used to never accept anything unless I could give back in return. Now . . . Even saints are depicted with their hands facing towards themselves . . . Why do I come to you? . . . There is this word again. MAN has always listened to the footsteps of other animals. The rhythm of their feet . . .

OLD WOMAN: I told you to be quiet.

MAN: Why do I come to you, sweet smelling, affluent, civilised? . . . You pulled me out . . .

BOY: Joseph comes he takes me there instead.

OLD WOMAN: I said they would hear you.

YOUNG WOMAN: Get down!

BOY: Tell me nothing . . .
YOUNG WOMAN: I said, get down!
MAN: You want a name . . . I have told you, they call him, The Captain . . . Okay . . . Okay . . . There is another name.
OLD WOMAN: Did they see us?
YOUNG WOMAN: I don't know.
MAN: He goes by many different names . . .
OLD WOMAN: I told you!
YOUNG WOMAN: Quiet! They catch you, they catch me. They will not catch me. Move. Slow. Back toward the cave . . . (*to BOY*) Bags.
MAN: But the one I know is Joseph.

(*He fetches them.*)

YOUNG WOMAN: Go. Back into the cave. Hide! Now!
MAN: I paid a man called Joseph five hundred dollars to bring me here in his boat. You pulled me out.

(*A frenzy of activity and sound: dogs barking.*

Blackout.)

Act Two

Scene 1

Inside the caves.

Darkness. Someone is moving in the darkness.

(*In his own space, the MAN speaks to his interrogators.*)

MAN: I have told you! . . . I have told you and you will not listen . . . On the boat I nearly lost my life for the ninth time. But I am a strong swimmer . . . No, we did not meet at the port. Too public. The place—the rendezvous point—was along on the coast . . . I don't know its name, but there were caves. We sheltered and waited for him . . . I told you, he took a thousand dollars . . . Joseph says to me, 'The sea will be kind tonight.' I am glad when I hear this. Those boats tear through the waves. They hit some speeds. You're chilled to the marrow. If the sea is rough and the winds high, the boat bumps about like a tennis ball and I've seen a child's bones fractured or a man knocked senseless by a single thud on the deck . . .

(*The light of the torch finds the* BOY. *He is terrified*.)

BOY: I surrender!

MAN: But the night he came. It was perfect . . .

BOY: I surrender!

MAN: And we would have made it.

YOUNG WOMAN: Ssssh!

MAN: If your boats had not been chasing so hard, we would have made it.

BOY: Don't shoot. I surrender!

YOUNG WOMAN: Shut up!

(*He holds up his pendant*.)

BOY: This is who I am.

YOUNG WOMAN: Shut up! . . . It's me . . . It's me. You are ok now. You are fine now . . . Calm . . . Sssh . . . Yes? (*a beat*) God, I was right. Your kind really are cowards . . .

BOY: No light.

YOUNG WOMAN: Could do it, you know. Here. Now.

BOY: You—she—disappeared.

YOUNG WOMAN: No one would ever know. (*pause*) Come on. Got to get out of here. Back to the beach. But careful. Quiet. Yes? . . . Place is still crawling with police.

BOY: Police . . .

YOUNG WOMAN: Maybe. Careful.

BOY: Wait . . .

YOUNG WOMAN: We came in deep . . . Must go back . . . Retrace our route . . . .

BOY: No. Wait . . . The light.

YOUNG WOMAN: Come on.

BOY: Where is the old woman?

YOUNG WOMAN: This way.

BOY: No. The old woman. Where is she?

YOUNG WOMAN: I don't know.

BOY: Look.

YOUNG WOMAN: I have looked. We will find her on the way out, maybe.

BOY: No. Near me. She was.

YOUNG WOMAN: No time.

BOY: Wait.

OLD WOMAN: (*soft*) Leave me.

BOY: Listen!
YOUNG WOMAN: Fine . . . Do what you like . . .
BOY: . . . Ssh! . . .
OLD WOMAN: Let me die . . .
YOUNG WOMAN: (*to the OLD WOMAN*) Hello . . .
OLD WOMAN: Bloody leave me alone!
YOUNG WOMAN: Where are you?
OLD WOMAN: I should never have come here. Never.
YOUNG WOMAN: I will find you. Coming to you. Hold on.

(*The YOUNG WOMAN moves away from the BOY. He clings onto her.*)

BOY: Wait! Light!

(*He holds onto her.*)

YOUNG WOMAN: Coward!
OLD WOMAN: Let me die . . . Why don't you?
BOY: Here . . .
YOUNG WOMAN: Hello?
OLD WOMAN: Piss off.
BOY: Here.
YOUNG WOMAN: (*to the OLD WOMAN*) I will find you.
BOY: (*to the OLD WOMAN*) Talk.
YOUNG WOMAN: Talk to me. Are you in pain? . . . Hello! . . . You must keep talking . . .
OLD WOMAN: They brought dogs.
BOY: I see her. See?
YOUNG WOMAN: (*to the OLD WOMAN*) I am coming!
BOY: (*to the OLD WOMAN*) You are hurt. Yes?
OLD WOMAN: When they came for us the first time, they brought dogs.
YOUNG WOMAN: Are you hurt?
OLD WOMAN: I couldn't run from them . . .
YOUNG WOMAN: Get to your feet . . . I'll help you.

(*The YOUNG WOMAN locates the OLD WOMAN.*)

OLD WOMAN: No. No more running.
YOUNG WOMAN: They are gone now . . . (*to the BOY*) Let go of me. Trying to help her.
BOY: (*to the OLD WOMAN*) To your feet . . .
OLD WOMAN: They will be back.

YOUNG WOMAN: We will be careful. Must get back to the beach.
OLD WOMAN: They always come back.
YOUNG WOMAN: Joseph is coming. That's it . . . Let's move.
OLD WOMAN: I want to go home.
YOUNG WOMAN: No. Beach.
OLD WOMAN: Take him with you. The boy can go in my place.
YOUNG WOMAN: No. Get up. Won't leave you in this darkness.
OLD WOMAN: Here take this. (*her bag*) Leave me here. No use to anybody.
BOY: Don't let go of me!
YOUNG WOMAN: Oh, for God's sake! (*to the OLD WOMAN*) You have to get up. Get this lunatic off me. You can't walk, I'll help you.
OLD WOMAN: It's not the walking. I am sick of running.
YOUNG WOMAN: Joseph comes and we're not there
OLD WOMAN: Joseph's not coming!
YOUNG WOMAN: Don't you say that again! Don't you ever, ever say that! (*a beat*) Must move. For your granddaughter, yes? She's waiting.
OLD WOMAN: What?
YOUNG WOMAN: The little girl. Do it for her.
OLD WOMAN: I don't have a granddaughter.
YOUNG WOMAN: You do! The letter . . .
OLD WOMAN: No.
BOY: Came in that way. Over here. Look.
YOUNG WOMAN: (*to BOY*) Wait!
OLD WOMAN: No . . . It is not my letter.
YOUNG WOMAN: What?
OLD WOMAN: My sister . . .
YOUNG WOMAN: You are confused. (*she tries to lift her*)
OLD WOMAN: Bastards! Off me! Bloody, bloody bastards! . . . I can walk.
YOUNG WOMAN: Walk then! (*to the BOY*) She is losing her mind . . .
BOY: Come on!
OLD WOMAN: (*in pain*) You don't understand.
BOY: Out of the dark! Come on!
YOUNG WOMAN: (*to the BOY*) Let go.
OLD WOMAN: My sister . . .
YOUNG WOMAN: Walk for your sister then!
OLD WOMAN: My sister's letter.

YOUNG WOMAN: No time for this. No time.

(*The BOY lifts the OLD WOMAN to her feet.*)

BOY: I will walk her, ok? I will.
YOUNG WOMAN: Fine . . . That is fine . . . Come on. This way.
BOY: No. That's not it.
YOUNG WOMAN: I remember.
BOY: I am sure.
YOUNG WOMAN: Way we came . . . I tell you . . . No time for this.
OLD WOMAN: My sister . . .
YOUNG WOMAN: Die in the dark, then.
BOY: No! Wait! Light! . . . Wait!

Scene 2

MAN: I have told you everything I know . . . Describe him? . . . Well, he's about my height, not so tall, maybe. My build . . . But younger than the man you see before you. Yes, younger. He is like . . . he has the bearing of a gangster . . . No, a drug dealer, yes . . . in East Los Angeles, yes? The sort of man younger men look up to, as he cruises the city streets in his stolen Mercedes, even though they know, maybe because they know, how he makes his money . . . But he is not a drug dealer. He is . . . Robin Hood. He gives to the poor what the rich have—freedom. Freedom to go wherever they want to go . . . You think so? . . . I tell you, he is no ordinary smuggler. I should know . . . Let me tell you about smugglers . . . Most smugglers are bastards. They will trade in anything: drugs, cars . . . Listen . . . I am twenty years old. It is spring—the most beautiful time of the year. I am running. A border town. A giant—switchboard—of dope and dynamite and the dispossessed. Dangerous . . . The Smuggler Boss has his feet on the desk, he's drinking a Coke and watching a *National Geographic* programme on Amazonian monkeys. He was once a fighter pilot in the military, but there's more money in this yes? More money, more women—do you think they are always kind to women travelling alone? And less risk . . . He offers me a Coke. It's warm. 'How desperate are you?' he says. And he looks at me, taking possession of me at that moment. I want to go, anywhere, anywhere. 'The richer you are, the safer the route. You have loads of money, you fly. You have some money you go by sea. The ones with nothing by land'. When one route gets cracked, we use another one . . . He says. He tells me he has two others. 'You can say one is your father, one is your uncle. I will get you papers. It will cost you.' I sip my Coke and feel bubbles in my nose. It's warm. At the cinema they put ice in it. I show him my money—not all of it. I go by land—in a bus to the mountains. We have to get off the bus and sneak over the mountain. At nights the only sound you hear in the mountains is the barking of dogs.

Scene 3

In the caves.

(*The* Young Woman, *the* Old Woman *and the* Boy, *crawling*.)

Young Woman: Mind your heads. Mind.

Boy: Don't remember this.

Old Woman: Rest. I've got to.

Young Woman: Can't stop. We stop, we die.

Old Woman: Freezing. I can't go on.

Young Woman: Don't panic.

Boy: Where are we?

Old Woman: We are lost.

Young Woman: No. I remember.

Old Woman: Bones feel like ice.

Boy: Lost. She has lost us.

Young Woman: Lie on your belly. Lie. Rest. Thinking. Came right . . . Left. Right again . . .

Boy: Can't move like this. Can't find the way this way.

Young Woman: I remember. Don't panic.

Boy: I ran.

Old Woman: I am not panicking. (*in pain*) You must go on.

Young Woman: I will not leave you behind.

Boy: In the dark, I ran.

Young Woman: What's he talking about?

Old Woman: I will not let you carry me. No.

YOUNG WOMAN: I cannot leave you.

BOY: Touched my way.

OLD WOMAN: What am I to you? What am I?

BOY: It did not touch like this. I did not crawl.

YOUNG WOMAN: What's he talking about?

OLD WOMAN: I don't know! . . . Listen. For your son.

YOUNG WOMAN: Don't panic. Will get free.

BOY: Chin deep in mud here. Can't breathe.

YOUNG WOMAN: Tell him to be quiet . . . Thinking . . .

BOY: Can't breathe. Can't—

YOUNG WOMAN: They could still be looking for us!

BOY: Need to move. Run. Need to go. This way. This way.

OLD WOMAN: Ssh.

BOY: Go! Go!

YOUNG WOMAN: Don't panic.

OLD WOMAN: You've got to be quiet.

BOY: Chin deep in mud. In my skin.

YOUNG WOMAN: He must stop panicking. He must!

BOY: In my mouth. Out. Get it out. Eating me. I can't breathe.

OLD WOMAN: It is the mud.

YOUNG WOMAN: A soldier afraid of mud?

OLD WOMAN: You must get him out. Back the way.

YOUNG WOMAN: No. Mud needs water. See? We go towards water.

BOY: Breathe. Can't. Up to my chin.

OLD WOMAN: A soldier?

BOY: Only the soles of her feet.

YOUNG WOMAN: Must keep moving.

OLD WOMAN: Whose feet?

BOY: Only the soles of her feet.

OLD WOMAN: Who?

BOY: The underwear round her ankles are not burned.

OLD WOMAN: No.

BOY: I tried to stop them. I tried . . . My father. Where is my father?

YOUNG WOMAN: What's he saying?

OLD WOMAN: Ok. It's ok . . . (*to the YOUNG WOMAN*) He lost his mother. You don't understand.

(*silence*)

YOUNG WOMAN: Everyone loses their mother . . . Come on.

Scene 4

MAN: Have you ever been hunted by a wolf? Wolves have a special hunting technique for farm dogs in the winter when the snow makes them hungry. One wolf lures the farm dog away from the farm and then the pack pounces ripping at the throat. We began climbing at mid-afternoon. It was snowing and very, very cold. After about five hours, the wolves attacked. We saw them in the distance coming across a plateau. There were five of them. The two smugglers with us beat them off with sticks and they ran. We had been walking all night and were crossing when the soldiers started firing at us and the two smugglers lit out of sight into the darkness. We were freezing and had no food so we tried to make our own way down. Some shepherds found us. They beat us and sold us on to another smuggler. But this one wants two hundred dollars more from each of us to take us across the border . . . I give it . . . I think, this time I will get to a safe place. I get neatly packed in the back of a truck with twelve others in between clothes-washing powder and dog biscuits.

YOUNG WOMAN: Water! Hear it?

MAN: There is no light, so we travel by sound and not by sight for a long way.

YOUNG WOMAN: This way!

MAN: At the checkpoint, we cannot hold our breath when they open the doors, because we have none left to hold.

BOY: Why won't she listen!

YOUNG WOMAN: Light. Look!

MAN: But we close our eyes for even the smallest slither of day is blinding . . . I am greedy for air, for . . .

YOUNG WOMAN: (*to the* BOY) Hold my hand, I'll pull you through. Hold my hand.

MAN: We cross the border . . .

Scene 5

A huge cave. A strange quality of light as the beam of the torch hits the water of an underground lake. It is cold here. They stand in silence for a moment.

(*The* Young Woman *lets go of the* Boy*'s hand.*)

Boy: It's beautiful.
Old Woman: Cold.
Young Woman: Light. Where's the light?
Boy: Up there. Sky . . . See?
Young Woman: . . . It is daylight.
Old Woman: Is it morning or evening?
Young Woman: Don't know . . .
Boy: I don't know where we are.
Old Woman: Well, we found water.
Young Woman: Clear. See your face.

(*They all look.*)

Old Woman: Too old for all this.
Boy: I'm covered in mud.
Young Woman: Thirsty.

(*The* Young Woman *drinks some water.*)

Young Woman: Freezing.

(*The* Boy *drinks.*)

Boy: How did it get here?
Old Woman: There must be a river.
Young Woman: No. Water is still. Must be the rain. (*to* Boy) Fancy a swim? Do you? A swim?
Boy: I know what you are saying.
Young Woman: We should rest a while. Not too long. (*to the* Old Woman) You all right?
Old Woman: My feet won't carry me much further.
Young Woman: You must rest. Eat.
Boy: Maybe there's a way up.
Old Woman: You don't know how to get out, do you?
Young Woman: I know.

(*She checks her bag for food.*)

Boy: I will find the way out.

Boy:	Man:
(*louder*)	
There must be a way out.	We cross the border.

YOUNG WOMAN:
Sssh.

MAN:
A safe place. Safe.

OLD WOMAN: She doesn't know.

YOUNG WOMAN: Hear? . . . (*to the* OLD WOMAN) I know, don't panic. My father taught me to swim. It was cold—colder than this, but he made me. He said, 'When you go under the waves, do nothing. Spread your arms wide,' he said. 'Come up like a cork.'

OLD WOMAN: Your father is dead?

YOUNG WOMAN: At home with my mother . . . First time we went over there.

OLD WOMAN: You have been over there?

YOUNG WOMAN: Long time ago. On holiday. (*food*) Here it is. Our last mouthful.

OLD WOMAN: No . . . What's it like?

YOUNG WOMAN: People from all places go there. They welcome all people . . . Now. Food.

OLD WOMAN: I don't want to eat. I don't understand. If you have papers, why didn't you just go there?

YOUNG WOMAN: Keep you strong. Keep you warm.

OLD WOMAN: Stop giving me your orders.

YOUNG WOMAN: Only want you to live.

OLD WOMAN: That is my trouble. I keep asking Him Upstairs, 'Kill me, why don't you?'

MAN: What? . . . Why do you ask that question?

OLD WOMAN: But He just laughs and shrugs His shoulders.

MAN: I don't understand.

OLD WOMAN: Don't you? What is there to live for?

BOY: A cork! Pop!

YOUNG WOMAN:
What?

MAN:
What?

BOY:
Like a cork!

YOUNG WOMAN:
Yes.

MAN:
What?

OLD WOMAN: They took us away in railway carriages. And now, what is there to live for?

BOY: Pop!

YOUNG WOMAN: There is your daughter—niece . . . There is my son. (*the BOY*) There is . . . There is . . .

BOY: What are you looking at?

MAN: How can I answer a question I don't understand?

BOY: Stop looking like that!

YOUNG WOMAN: (*to BOY*) You don't understand.

OLD WOMAN: I have no children or grandchildren.

MAN: I gave you my name . . .

OLD WOMAN: (*to the YOUNG WOMAN*) You don't understand . . .

YOUNG WOMAN: 'You don't understand.'

BOY:	MAN:
I understand. You will not look at me like that.	I don't understand.

YOUNG WOMAN: 'You don't understand.' Always the same thing.

YOUNG WOMAN/BOY:	MAN:
You think I haven't lost everything?	I nearly lost my life on that boat.

BOY:	MAN:
This is all I have.	This (*the pendant*) is all I have to prove to you who I am.

BOY: This and the thoughts in my head. This is who I am.

YOUNG WOMAN: You are a soldier.

BOY: I am running from them.

YOUNG WOMAN: You have blood on your hands.

BOY: You don't understand.

OLD WOMAN: (*to YOUNG WOMAN*) You have your father, your mother, your son. You have a passport.

BOY:	MAN:
I am running.	I am running.

YOUNG WOMAN	MAN:
Papers? . . . If I had papers would I be sitting here?	Papers. If I had papers would I be sitting here before you now?

OLD WOMAN: You said you had papers.

YOUNG WOMAN: You said you had a granddaughter.

BOY: They killed my mother. I watched them. They put a bag

over her head and they . . . They . . . I watched. I was very young. They put a gun in my hands. They said, 'If you cry again, we will kill you.'

YOUNG WOMAN: Come on. Light's fading. (*to BOY*) Getting dark. Move.

BOY: You don't believe me?

MAN: You don't understand. How can you understand when you don't listen.

BOY: Say that you believe me.

YOUNG WOMAN: Ok. I believe you. Help her.

BOY: No. Give me the torch.

YOUNG WOMAN:	MAN:
Don't start this again.	Don't start this again.

BOY:
Give me it.

YOUNG WOMAN:	MAN:
Take it.	Don't.

(*They wrestle. He takes the torch from her easily.*)

BOY: Now you will follow me.

YOUNG WOMAN: The light on the wall.

BOY: You will follow.

YOUNG WOMAN: On the wall. Shine.

BOY: What?

MAN: Describe any events which have happened . . . You want me to write it?

YOUNG WOMAN: There . . . There! . . . Shine it.

OLD WOMAN: What can you see?

MAN: No. No.

YOUNG WOMAN: Writing.

MAN: You're trying to trick me.

OLD WOMAN: A sign. She says there is a sign.

BOY: You will not trick me!

YOUNG WOMAN: You don't believe me—look! Look!

(*The BOY shines the torch at the wall. Some cave paintings become visible.*)

MAN: You are trying to get me to say something I do not want to say. Why would you do that?

BOY: Animals.

YOUNG WOMAN: Pictures.
BOY: Reindeer . . . Elephant. El-eph-ant?
YOUNG WOMAN: Mammoth.
BOY: Mammoth.

YOUNG WOMAN:	MAN:
Just pictures.	Words. It's just words. If you won't listen . . .

OLD WOMAN: What are they for?
YOUNG WOMAN: Nothing . . . Let us know they were here.
BOY: Wolf . . .
OLD WOMAN: Who was here?
YOUNG WOMAN: Come on. We must move.
OLD WOMAN: Who are you talking about? Are they still here?
MAN: No I will not start again. I will not.
BOY: Look. This way. They run this way.

(*She tries to take the torch. The* BOY *holds onto it.*)

YOUNG WOMAN: Ok. Ok. You keep the torch. But we must move.

BOY:	MAN:
Listen.	You will listen to me.

MAN: You will let me finish . . . I will explain. I am trying to explain. How can you ask questions if you don't want answers? . . . It is not that simple. It is not a question of A to B to C or X equals Y. I can only give you pieces of it.
BOY: We must go this way.
YOUNG WOMAN: No. The way of the water. Water.
BOY: Yes. Follow them. Where else would they be going?
OLD WOMAN: Your way brought us nowhere.

YOUNG WOMAN:	MAN:
No.	Little tiny pieces. All I know.

BOY: Listen.
YOUNG WOMAN: No. No.

Scene 6

MAN: No! You will listen to this. You will . . . We cross the border. The doors open and we spill out into a parking lot in another strange city, into the heat and light of the Mediterranean sun. I think, 'You are safe now. You have made it.' . . . Then, everything goes black . . . I wake up in a cellar. This is where I work, with ten other men sewing fur coats for sale on the internet, to pay back my debt to the smugglers for bringing me to freedom. The women have not been so lucky. Their trade is of a different sort . . . So much for my two hundred dollars . . . And this is the way it works always the same, no matter how much you pay . . . And I am thinking, there has to be a better way than this . . . Hijack a plane and fly to London . . . Where? . . . Board a rusting tub in Turkey and be wrecked on the rocks of Italy, or washed up in the waves in France . . . Explain what? Camp in a container for weeks until the ship is unloaded in Canada . . . Who? I told you who? . . . Stride across the Sahara and sail for Spain . . . Who-what-where-when-why? . . . Why did I pick Joseph? Can't you see why? Why did I pick your shore? Your shore? . . . Don't you listen? Who-what-where-when-why? . . . Questions! All these questions . . . And I nearly died . . . I nearly ended my life at your hands and all you can do is . . . This is who I am. This is my story. Why won't you believe me? Why won't you listen? . . . (*a beat*) All right. All right. I will answer your questions. I will answer you.

Scene 7

A high-domed room off which there are many passage ways—a junction room.

(*The* BOY, OLD WOMAN *and* YOUNG WOMAN *enter.*)

BOY: See? This is the way. Told you they would show us.

YOUNG WOMAN: And where are we now?

(*She shines her light around the room.*)

YOUNG WOMAN: Middle of nowhere. So much for your Noah's Ark.

BOY: The stampede. It goes this way.

OLD WOMAN: And this way.

BOY: We go this way.

YOUNG WOMAN: And here . . . And here . . . And here . . . Which herd do we follow?

OLD WOMAN: Which way now?

YOUNG WOMAN: Good question.

(*a beat*)

BOY: We follow the reindeer.

YOUNG WOMAN: Why?

BOY: Brought us here. In a straight line here.

YOUNG WOMAN: No more! No . . . had enough of this.

BOY: Listen. Reindeer lead us towards the water.

YOUNG WOMAN: Need to follow the ground. Ok? Listen to me.

BOY: Your way leads us to where? Mud.

YOUNG WOMAN: Fine. I go this way. Uphill.

BOY: Follow the pictures. The way they come in is the way out.

YOUNG WOMAN: (*to the OLD WOMAN*) This way. Take my hand!

OLD WOMAN: Wait a minute! Wait. Both of you. There is only one torch. We must go together.

MAN: I will answer you. I will explain.

YOUNG WOMAN: It is my torch . . . Must follow the way uphill. Up. Do you know how caves are made? Do you? . . .

MAN: Explain. Explain . . .

YOUNG WOMAN: Water. Rain, snow melt and trickle down, down, down from the surface, through cracks in the earth. More water, makes the tunnels. See? Must follow the water, uphill . . .

MAN: Please explain why you are applying? . . .

BOY: I will not go with you.

MAN: Begin again. All over again.

YOUNG WOMAN: And how will you manage? In the dark? In the mud?

BOY: Give me the torch.

MAN: Please?

YOUNG WOMAN: You want it. Take it.

OLD WOMAN: I should never have come here.

YOUNG WOMAN: You will come this way.

BOY: No! . . . No more . . . I know . . . Ok?

OLD WOMAN: Give him the light . . . Please, Give it to him.

YOUNG WOMAN: . . . No.

BOY: Don't need it. Don't. (*to the OLD WOMAN*) Your bag.

(*He looks through the* OLD WOMAN*'s bag and fishes out the stump of a candle.*)

BOY: This is who I am. I will not go with you.
OLD WOMAN: We must go together.
BOY: Follow me.
YOUNG WOMAN: Follow him, you will die in here.
OLD WOMAN: Come with us, please. Come.
YOUNG WOMAN: You will die in here.
BOY: You will come with me? I will help you.
YOUNG WOMAN: Come.
BOY: Come. It is dark. Please.

(*The* OLD WOMAN *moves to the* BOY.)

OLD WOMAN: We must go with him.
YOUNG WOMAN: I will ask Joseph to wait for you.

(*The* YOUNG WOMAN *separates from them.*)

BOY: Don't let go of me. Hold on tight.
OLD WOMAN: I want to go home.
BOY: Hold on.

(*They move through the caves.*)

MAN: Please explain why you are applying? . . .
YOUNG WOMAN: This way.
MAN: (*laughs*) Please explain.
BOY: This is the way.
OLD WOMAN: We must go back for her!
MAN: Please.
BOY: This way.
MAN: Describe any specific events which have happened. Explain please where possible, giving the date or dates on which each event occurred. Please.
YOUNG WOMAN: Please explain.

OLD WOMAN:	BOY:	YOUNG WOMAN:
Please.	Please.	Please.

MAN: Everyone knows the exact dates . . . If you claim to have suffered ill-treatment or harassment, who was responsible for this?

BOY:
Before the war, I had two brothers. One got killed. The other was taken to fight, like me . . . He is dead . . . I think . . . I saw another boy from our village when I got captured and he told me that . . . my brother had been captured too. When they catch you, they torture you . . . One night I heard screaming and laughing as loud as each other—coming from the guards' mess. They had taken two of us . . . They made them both strip—right down to the skin. They made one kneel in front of the other. They held a gun to the kneeling one's head and made him bite off the standing one's right testicle. The standing one died. Then they shot the kneeling one—a bullet through his left temple . . . I don't know where my sister is. She just disappeared.

MAN:
Before the war, I had an older brother . . . He is dead now, I think he was taken to fight . . . When they captured him, they tortured him . . . One night they made him kneel down, in front of another man . . . The guards were laughing . . .

My brother was crying . . . In floods of tears.

They made my brother kneel down and bite off the standing man's right testicle.

YOUNG WOMAN: Explain. Give names of any group or organisation involved.

BOY:
Please.

YOUNG WOMAN:
Please.

OLD WOMAN: I thought it was over. I thought, I lived through the railway carriages. I survived it. Things will never be the same again. Why would they?

MAN: What religious group do you belong to? Explain. Please.

YOUNG WOMAN:
I am not a religious person.

BOY:
I am not a religious person.

MAN: Have you always been of this religious faith? Please.

YOUNG WOMAN: Which box do I tick?

OLD WOMAN: I believe do unto others as you would be done to.

YOUNG WOMAN: What category is that?

MAN: Do you have any difficulty practising your religion in your home country?

YOUNG WOMAN: I am not a religious person. I have seen enough of what it does to the world. But I do believe. Do unto others . . . Poor is the man whose life shows no good deed. I was brought up that way.

OLD WOMAN: I am a religious person. I believe: do unto others as you would have them do to you . . . I was brought up that way.

MAN: Explain please, explain.

BOY: When you are thirteen, they make you. Before you're thirteen, you have to watch. But after . . .

OLD WOMAN: Explain?

BOY: After you are thirteen, you must take part. The whole time I was thinking about the soles of her feet, still wearing black shoes, and the underwear around her ankles not burned . . .

MAN: Have you ever moved to a different town or village, explain.

OLD WOMAN: The first time we were forced to move. In railway carriages. Long time ago. One night they came when we were out walking underneath the stars. We were just married. They took us all—my sister and her child, her husband, my parents. In railway carriages.

YOUNG WOMAN: Or to another part of your country to avoid the incidents you have described above?

OLD WOMAN: To a place of the dying. But I was young. I was strong.

BOY: Where? Please. Explain.

YOUNG WOMAN: Where?

OLD WOMAN: I survived it. When the war ended, I thought, 'This time it will be over.' I wanted to go home. So I went home.

BOY: Why am I running?

MAN: If not, why not?

YOUNG WOMAN: Why?

BOY: Why?

MAN: Why? Explain why . . .

OLD WOMAN: Because the others from my village were going home. And we thought it was over.

All: I want to go home.

YOUNG WOMAN: If not why not?

BOY: But it was not over.

YOUNG WOMAN:	MAN:
Why?	Why?

BOY: Why?

MAN: Did you report any of the incidents which you have just described to the police or to other state authorities? If not, why not?

OLD WOMAN: But it was not over. In the camp, a vaccination—all the women were to have one. A simple injection. Very simple. An operation. Very simple. And very simply I have no children, or grandchildren. I am on my own. I have to cope without anyone.

BOY: Explain . . . Explain . . .

OLD WOMAN: It starts again. The same, but different. We are burned out of our homes, but this time, by our neighbours. I am old and I am alone, no children or grandchildren and it starts again. They will not let us have a passport. They will not let us own our homes. We have no place. We have no name. We are not people.

All: I thought it was over.

OLD WOMAN: They could not fit us into their category . . .

YOUNG WOMAN: He had arrived in our city as a teenager, come to the University. He got an official permit, he answered his call up papers. He even served his two years in the army. I got pregnant—stupid—we got married. Then they imposed a compulsory re-registration for all those without permanent right of residence . . . We stood in the queue for two days . . . There were hundreds ahead of us . . . The policeman looked at his papers and said, 'You are from the Republic. Go to room four.' . . . I asked if I could go with him. But the policeman just laughed and said, 'There is no place for you there.' . . .

BOY: Explain please where possible, giving the date or dates on which each event occurred.

YOUNG WOMAN: I waited for three hours . . . Then, I asked at the front desk when I could expect to see him again. The officer said, 'In two or three months.' Drugs charge—possession of heroin. 'Not unusual for his sort,' they said. Slipped into his pocket. He got three years . . . And then another three . . . Every time he came out they found some new excuse to put him back in . . . Wouldn't tell us where he was . . . I always sew my pockets up now, just in case anyone tries to slip anything in . . .

MAN:	BOY:
Give dates and times.	Give dates . . .

YOUNG WOMAN: But I have our son.

OLD WOMAN: And I have no children or grandchildren and no home. No people. But my sister . . . My sister . . . And my niece . . . Over there . . . I am trying to get over there.

MAN: If you claim to have suffered ill-treatment or harassment, who was responsible for this?

YOUNG WOMAN: And then, they came for me. They said put your valuables and car keys on the table and come with us. . . . In the village of railway carriages, all the food I brought was used up quickly. There was no more. My son needed food. I stole. I'm not ashamed to say I stole for him—my baby. The guards . . . There were four of them. They said, 'You have to pay. Pay for the food you stole.'

MAN: Give names of any group or organisation involved.

YOUNG WOMAN: I don't know their names. But I saw the marks on them. I still have the marks they left on me.

MAN:	BOY:
Names!	Give dates and times.

ALL: I should never have come here.

YOUNG WOMAN: There were four of them . . . I kept thinking, it will be over soon . . .

ALL: I thought it was over.

YOUNG WOMAN: They took my son, my baby, and gave him to one of the nurses . . . I kept thinking, when this is over, when they have finished . . .

BOY: I thought it was over.

YOUNG WOMAN: I will take my son and we will get out of this fucking dump, this fucking cess pit, this fucking . . . fucking . . . hole . . . .

OLD WOMAN: Did you report any of the incidents which you have just described to the authorities?

BOY: Hello?

YOUNG WOMAN: I woke up in the tent they called the hospital . . . I couldn't move. I couldn't move—to find him . . . I couldn't speak . . . to tell the officials what had happened . . . Then the bombing started and they moved the invalids to a safe place . . . I couldn't find him.

OLD WOMAN: I just want to see my niece.

BOY: Hello!

MAN: You have to do something . . . Anything to reach anywhere better.

YOUNG WOMAN: I want to go home.

BOY: Hello!

OLD WOMAN: I found you!

(*The BOY finds the OLD WOMAN.*)

BOY: Hello.

OLD WOMAN: Get off! Don't hurt me!

BOY: It's me!

OLD WOMAN: Leave me alone . . .

BOY: Listen . . .

OLD WOMAN: I have a gun you know. I . . . I . . .

BOY: Listen . . . Listen . . . It is this way. This way. Follow me. Don't let go of me.

Scene 8

MAN: You think I am telling you all this to stir your pity? . . . I have told you who I am? Can I prove it? . . . You think I am lying to you? . . . What do you think? You pulled me out of the waves. You saw me nearly drown . . . I have nothing to prove myself except this. (*pendant*) You'll forgive me, but witnesses are a bit hard to lay my hands on since most of them are under the waves or under the earth. I know what it is you want. I know.

You want me to help you. You want to find Joseph and lock him up, yes? . . . You think he doesn't care for the lives of the people he carries? That he is wicked, he has broken, you might say, all the laws of decency and honesty . . . Joseph, for all his sinfulness, supplies something that I demand. What is normal. He doesn't have to market, advertise or persuade people to want something they really don't need. They see on TV. They only want what is normal. What is normal in my part of the world, is that just when people are able to put the last war behind them then it starts all over again. And this one . . . This one we will not forget for a good many centuries. Whatever Joseph is, whatever . . . he gives us hope. What do you give us? What? . . . You want me to help you?

Scene 9

A smaller cave filled with paintings of animals and some of men in combat.

(*The* OLD WOMAN *and the* BOY.)

BOY: This way. This is the direction.
OLD WOMAN: Rest. I need to.
BOY: If Joseph comes . . .
OLD WOMAN: Stop. Please . . . Just stop.
BOY: See? . . .
OLD WOMAN: Oh yes . . .
BOY: Hunter.
OLD WOMAN: I think so.
BOY: No mouth.
OLD WOMAN: I see.
BOY: He has no mouth. He must.
OLD WOMAN: Maybe it's been rubbed off.
BOY: No . . . Why?
OLD WOMAN: I don't know.
BOY: No mouth. Why no mouth? . . .
OLD WOMAN: Maybe he's dead.
BOY: Dead?
OLD WOMAN: Maybe. No mouth—can't speak. He has been killed—in the hunt.

BOY: You can't destroy a single idea in someone's head, you can't. Not even if you cut their tongue out. You can't.

OLD WOMAN: No. No, you can't. My name is Anna. What is your name?

BOY: I am . . . I live in a village, in the valley of the Black River. My father works the dams. My mother is a dressmaker. I have an older brother and a younger brother too, and an older sister. My name is . . . I am seventeen years old. When my father sees me he will not recognise me . . . I am not dead.

OLD WOMAN: No.

BOY: You are not dead.

OLD WOMAN: We are not dead.

BOY: We are not dead . . . Come on.

OLD WOMAN: I want to go home. I should never have come here. Silly old fool.

BOY: You will get home. I will help you. Come on . . . That's it . . . Lift your feet they'll drop themselves . . . My father always used to say that . . . Come on. I have got you . . . It is this way. I am sure it is this way. I can see light. See it? Light . . .

OLD WOMAN: Hold onto me. Don't let go of me.

BOY: Sing to me. Come on . . . That's right.

(*The OLD WOMAN sings and the BOY sings with her. They exit.*)

Scene 10

MAN: Will I help you? . . . Why should I help you? Why? I am running, through the park, to work. I am running and I see a child drowning in the lake. Do I jump in and save him? Yes. Do I get wet, dirty, risk being late for work or worse? . . . Of course I save him . . . No question. Because why? Because it is right . . . But what if there are others present just as able as me to jump in but they walk on by? I still jump . . . But what if the child is in another country? Not drowning, but in danger, yes? The cost of a CD, a haircut, a few of these (*makes a drinking action*), huh? . . . We all want things to be fair, don't we? I write my cheque and stick down my self-adhesive envelope . . .

Scene 11

Somewhere in the Caves. Darkness.

(*The* YOUNG WOMAN *hears faint echoes of the* BOY. *She keeps walking.*)

YOUNG WOMAN: This way . . . I will find you! . . . Left . . . I will find a job. I will find you a house . . . This way . . . No . . . I will find you the softest bed and the whitest sheets . . . Left . . . I am coming to you . . . Uphill . . . That's right . . . Do you know how caves are made? Do you? . . . Water. The rain and the snow melt and trickle down, down, down from the surface, seeping into little cracks in the earth. That's one way . . . I am following the cracks . . . See? . . . When I find you, you're going to be all right . . . And I will never leave you alone again . . . And when it is dark . . . Like this, see? You have to feel your way back . . . And . . . When I get back to you, I will never let anyone . . . Which? . . . Take you . . . . No. Back the way . . . Again . . . I will find you . . .

MAN: Will I help you?

YOUNG WOMAN: I will make my way back to you.

MAN: I have one loaf, to feed me and my family today, yes?

YOUNG WOMAN: We will go home . . .

MAN: Walking home I meet a starving child . . .

YOUNG WOMAN: This is the way. Get out of this fucking cess pit . . . this fucking . . . fucking . . . hole . . .

MAN: Walking home I meet a starving child in the street. Do I give him the bread and send my own children to bed hungry? . . . Of course not. I feed my own children. Maybe I throw the starving child the crusts . . . But he'd have to ask. No demand . . . No supply . . . Who is wise, he that learns from all men. In my country now all we know is how to rape and murder and smuggle and loot. You want to know what it is like, huh? To be hungry . . . I cannot tell you, can I? You know all about it. You sip the news every morning with your filter coffee. As it happens reports from the front line? We get free handouts, yeah? Free if the aid can get through. Free, if we are not blacklisted by the authorities. Free, if we can bribe the soldiers . . . But we are free, yes? Stop complaining! The ordinary man—and I count myself one, I come from a very ordinary family—doesn't need freedom. He needs not to be shot at, robbed and killed. He needs a job and wages. Freedom is useless when you can't use it . . . Stop complaining! Stop it! We are safe, after all. We are snug as bugs in rugs. Safe and sound. Safe as houses—or tents at least. Safe from the war-crazy and the shell-shocked who stumble wild and naked through the tent at four a.m. So why complain? Safe from the misfired missiles. Stop. Safe from typhoid, tetanus and TB. Stop. Stop. Safe from the shotgun soldiers who stop you, striking for the safety of the perimeter fence. Stop. Stop. Stop. We are safe and satisfied and free. Nothing to worry about then. Nothing. No soap. No water. No clothing. No home. No work. No self-respect. Nothing to do all day except pace a little, sleep a little, eat a little and talk, talk, talk. And wait, wait, wait, . . . No concern to anybody. You think I am telling you all this to stir your pity? . . . Fuck your pity! . . . Fuck your self-adhesive envelopes! . . . I don't want a sanitised water supply, I want a Coke—with ice. I don't want a handout, I want a job. I don't want to drive a car, I want to drive a Mercedes . . . So fuck who is my neighbour. If I am not for myself who will be for me? And if not now, then when? . . . I am sorry . . . What was the question?

Scene 12

Dusk. The Cave Mouth.

(*The Boy and the Old Woman.*)

Boy: No stars tonight.

Old Woman: It always rains in this country.

Boy: He did not come . . . Maybe . . . Maybe she left without us.

Old Woman: Maybe.

Boy: I hate to sleep on no stars nights. Out in the open. Night like this was the night I ran from them. My friend . . . I couldn't save him. Like I couldn't save my mother, or my brother . . . I cried. And they said, "If you cry again, we will kill you." I ran all night.

OLD WOMAN: Night is the best time to move.

BOY: When you get there, do you know the way to go?

OLD WOMAN: I have a number. I will call the number.

BOY: And if she isn't there? (*Pause*) I will come with you . . .

OLD WOMAN: Don't let go of me.

BOY: I will not.

OLD WOMAN: What is your name?

BOY: Over there, in their language, they will call me John.

OLD WOMAN: And in your own language?

BOY: Forget.

OLD WOMAN: You must never forget. Never. Or you forget your home.

BOY: There is my home now.

OLD WOMAN: And your father?

BOY: If my father is not dead. He may as well be.

OLD WOMAN: But . . .

BOY: Sssh!

OLD WOMAN: What? What is it?

BOY: A man—coming up the beach.

OLD WOMAN: Joseph . . .

(*The MAN enters.*)

BOY: Joseph?

OLD WOMAN: Joseph.

MAN: I had given you up . . .

OLD WOMAN: You had given us up?! We were waiting and waiting. We had to hide in the cave.

MAN: There were complications.

OLD WOMAN: The police came looking.

MAN: Knew they would. That's why I never move on a clear night.

OLD WOMAN: We could have died waiting.

MAN: I'm here now. Stop complaining. (*looks at the BOY*) How many of you?

OLD WOMAN: Two. Me and him.

MAN: I expected a doctor. A woman.

OLD WOMAN: She is coming. She was in the caves with us and . . .

MAN: (*to the BOY*) Who are you?

OLD WOMAN: He is my grandson.
MAN: You said nothing about a grandson.
OLD WOMAN: I decided to bring him at the last minute.
MAN: (*to the BOY*) How old are you?
OLD WOMAN: Seventeen. He is seventeen.
MAN: Is he mute?
OLD WOMAN: Tired. He is tired.
MAN: No.
OLD WOMAN: Please!
MAN: No . . . (*a beat*) It will cost you.
OLD WOMAN: I have paid you all I have.
MAN: (*to the BOY*) Can you work?
OLD WOMAN: Can you work? Work!

(*The BOY nods.*)

MAN: Good. Can you sew?
OLD WOMAN: He can learn.
MAN: Maybe I can get you work . . . Maybe.
OLD WOMAN: Thank you.
MAN: But you will pay me . . . Understand? . . . Does he understand?
BOY: Understand.
MAN: Who are you?

(*The BOY holds up his pendant.*)

MAN: I see . . . I cannot take him. No.
OLD WOMAN: The woman. She said he should take her place.
MAN: Did she? . . . It will cost you double . . .

(*MAN takes the BOY's pendant.*)

MAN: Insurance . . . If the police come after us, he goes over the side . . . Understand? . . . (*laughs, to the BOY*) Can you swim? Eh? . . . Don't worry. The sea will be kind tonight. Let's go.

Scene 13

MAN: I saw the boy wrestle with the waves to save his grandmother. He lifted her high above the tide several times . . . He was breathing life into her, singing to her—I am sure, singing. But she had no voice left. He let her body go to the waves . . . Then he swam, even after all that fight, stronger than before. And I swam and we both swam taking strength from every hand that was pulled under beneath the surface, reaching out into nothing . . . That is when you pulled me out. But you didn't catch the boy. You couldn't seize him. He touched the shore and vanished! . . . You are a seafaring people, it was the sea that gave you an Empire. But you don't seem to understand what it's like: the sea is . . . the sea can never be filled, not even if all the rivers, clouds and streams flowed into it. All life flows into it and it holds all life. Even I who am a child of the high places and first saw the sea as a man know that. It has no frontiers within it, no territories. It has one voice which sounds like a thousand voices. And it never sleeps. By day and night it makes its voice heard through years and decades and centuries, surging towards the safe shore in pain and rage and patience. You cannot and will not contain it. The tide comes in, yes? But it also goes out. No walls you build will ever hold it back. You cannot shut your doors against. Doors are shut against me. I will open them. And I will have my place. I will have my name.

End of Play

Introduction to Charlie O'Neill's *Hurl*

Sara Brady

Irish sport—and specifically Gaelic games—provides an example in which expressive culture inhabits 'Irish' spaces to stage 'identity,' 'ethnicity' and 'place'. In his play, *Hurl,* Charlie O'Neill addresses the relationship between the historical construction of Irish identity and the effects of contemporary Irish social realities through the performance of these games. The Gaelic games of hurling, camogie and Gaelic football developed at the turn of the twentieth century as part of the Irish nationalist project to distinguish Ireland from its British coloniser. These fast sports still enjoy massive popularity on a grassroots level throughout the country's 2,300 clubs.[1] As codified versions of traditional contests played for decades, or, as some argue, centuries before the formation of the GAA, the modern sports have resisted influence—either on or from other games–due in large part to the GAA's protective policies. The GAA self-consciously lays claim to its own version of Irishness. According to the 2007 GAA Official Guide: 'Those who play its games, those who organise its activities and those who control its destinies see in the GAA a means of consolidating our Irish identity.'[2]

Gaelic games appear to offer a unique cultural opportunity; to master the games is to perform something 'Irish'. Hurling, especially, connotes innate Irishness—consider a typical description by a sports commentator of hurler, Eoin Larkin: 'He has those quick wrists most Kilkenny hurlers get at baptism.'[3] In contrast to Gaelic football, which appears somewhat similar to rugby and soccer, hurling remains unique—a game employing an ashwood stick (*camán,* or hurley) and a hard, leather-bound ball (*sliotar*), which players toss and strike (the 'clash of the ash'). Irish mythological figures, such as Cuchulainn and Fionn Mac Cumhaill performed 'impossible feats of strength' with 'bronze hurleys and silver balls', with the game more closely related to violence and death than skill and competition.[4] As a distinctively Irish game, hurling provided the perfect anti-British cultural artifact to cultivate in the development of Irish nationalism in the late nineteenth century.

Today, on the myriad Gaelic fields across Ireland, where young players have for decades learned 'how' to be Irish by performing hurling or camogie and Gaelic football, communities make contact, offering new immigrants and established Irish opportunities to negotiate—through the performance of sport—cultural expression, and to forge 'new' ideas of what it means to be 'Irish'. Charlie O'Neill's 2003 play, *Hurl*, uses the representation of the Gaelic games to re-imagine cultural identities in early twenty-first century Ireland. In *Hurl*, a group of immigrants and asylum-seekers form a hurling team in rural Ireland—and they *win*.

Hurl was produced at the Galway Arts Festival and Dublin Theatre Festival in 2003. Produced by Barabbas, a theatre company known for its conscious de-emphasis on text and exploration of an 'Irish' physical theatre aesthetic,[5] *Hurl* presents an intensive physical engagement with sport and the 'new' Ireland. *Hurl* shows not only the ways in which culture is contained in sport, but also how, as Mike Cronin explains, 'this common feature of our lives has been harnessed to give voice to changing conceptions of identity—personal, regional, national, and gendered'.[6] *Hurl* is multicultural in that O'Neill's characters present a cacophony of nationalities. The play is also intercultural on two distinct levels. First, *Hurl* brings together the two cultures of theatre and sport, exhibited clearly by the many GAA jerseys worn in the audiences in Galway and Dublin. Second, the story and characters depict an exchange of cultures that occurs through the performance of sport.

The play depicts the rise of a non-traditional club hurling team made up of members originally from Nigeria, Cuba, Argentina, Sierra Leone, Bosnia, Vietnam and inner-city Dublin: an unexpected picture of rural Ireland and the GAA. The athletes, some of whom played hurling in their home countries ('Pajani PJ Ndingi. From Nigeria. Corner Forward. Taught by the Christian Brothers!'), are led by an alcoholic priest and a washed-up trainer. With impressive optimism, O'Neill imagines a team that—despite discrimination and bureaucratic obstacles—wins through sheer will, determination and some hard work. In a country such as Ireland, in which 'inward migration [. . .] was not anticipated' and where research indicates that 'racist incidents against non-nationals have increased in recent years',[7] O'Neill challenges audiences to re-think the status quo.

The mixed response to *Hurl*'s premiere at the Galway Arts Festival and subsequent run at the Dublin Theatre Festival suggests not only a lingering hesitance around the subject of inward migration, but also an ineffectiveness on the part of Irish theatre criticism to fully process the play's significance. For example, Susan Conley's review in the *Irish Independent* praised much of the visual aspects of the piece, which had 'all the beauty one expects from a Barabbas production', yet found the play's presentational style lacking: 'What makes the play less fluid', Conley writes, 'is its use of direct address, which tells us far more than it shows us'.[8] Such a critique exposes not simply a long-standing preference in Irish theatre criticism for the comfort zone of literary theatre, but an inability to appreciate fully the creation of sociocultural knowledge through embodied performance. To imply that Barabbas is known for beautiful spectacle is a way to relegate such work to the visual. A bolder move would acknowledge the fact that by placing bodies from different cultures and ethnicities together in a theatre space in an effort to represent what *could* happen within the performance space of the pitch (the Gaelic field), O'Neill—and Barabbas—created a forum for *Hurl*'s potential.

Notes and References

1 See 'About the GAA.' Official GAA website. Accessed 13 August 2013. Read online at http://www.gaa.ie/about-the-gaa/.

2 Gaelic Athletic Association (GAA), 'The Gaelic Athletic Association,' *Official Guide, Part 1*, (Dublin: Central Council of the Association, 2012), p. 4.

3 John Allen, 'Cody cast studded with A-list superstars,' *The Irish Times*, 27 April 2007, p. 23.

4 GAA historian W.F. Mandle documents historical attempts to ban or control hurling: 'The Brehon Laws contain elaborate penalties for death or injury inflicted during hurling, and the English statutes of Kilkenny of the fourteenth century and clerical prohibitions of the game mention its violent and homicidal side.' W.F. Mandle, *The Gaelic Athletic Association and Irish Nationalist Politics (1884–1924)*, (Dublin: Gill and Macmillan, 1987), pp. 15–16.

5 Charlie O'Neill, email to author, 30 May 2007.

6 Mike Cronin, 'Beyond Sectarianism: Sport and Irish Culture,' in *Ireland Beyond Borders*, eds. Liam Harte and Yvonne Whelan. (London: Pluto Press, 2007), pp. 215–38, 216.

7 Piaras MacÉinrí and Paddy Walley, 'Labour Migration into Ireland' (Dublin: Immigrant Council of Ireland, 2003), p. v.

8 Susan Conley, 'Finding a home through sport,' *Irish Independent*, 3 October 2003. Accessed 28 December 2012. Read online at http://www.independent.ie/lifestyle/independent-woman/celebrity-news-gossip/finding-a-home-through-sport-198687.html.

Hurl

CHARLIE O'NEILL

Hurl was first presented at the Black Box, Galway by Barabbas on 13 July 2003.

CAST

Eamonn Hunt
Dystin Johnson
Daniel Kobbina
Eoin Lynch
Anthony Ofoegbu
Diana O'Keefe
Paul Tylak
Alan Wai

PRODUCTION TEAM

Director	Raymond Keane
Set Designer	Robert Ballagh
Light Designer	Robert Comiskey
Costume Designer	Marie Tierney
Producer	Triona Ní Dhuibhir
Sound Designer	Gwenn Frin
Movement Director	David Bolger
Composer	Gwenn Frinn and Brian Fleming
Additional Music	De Jimbé
Production Manager	Marie Tierney
Stage Manager	Stephanie Ryan

CHARACTERS*

LOFTY
YARN-TELLERS**
WOMAN
MAN
BENITO
FATMATA

---

* Cast doubling is possible.
**Played by the ensemble.

MUSA
AHMED
SANTOS
MIROSLAV
RUSTY
ISTVAN
COMMITTEE MEMBER
PA
SCALLION
NDINGI
SYLVIE
DONG
LUIS
SORRY GIRLS
BLACK MAN
CHINESE MAN
MAN 2
FEMALE
MALE
REPORTER 1
REPORTER 2
IMMIGRATION OFFICER 1
GARDA
IMMIGRATION OFFICER 2
CORA
SERGIO
LOU BOLFORD
BALL
HOG HOGAN
SYLVIES MA
DINKI
SCUD'S MA
DAVY

Note on the Playing Style

The actors play out the drama in three ways. They story-tell—rather than narrate—in direct address to the audience. At these times, they are in fact actors playing story-tellers—warm, talented and witty. They employ a natural delivery of spontaneous but confident yarn telling. Other times, they story-tell as a character in the play. This device allows the character to occupy a different theatrical space—more circumspect, poetic, ironic. Thirdly, the actors play characters in the story according to normal theatrical convention. When they're not 'performing', the audience can see them sit or stand around, still very much an active player in a troupe of story-tellers, watching the show, waiting until they're needed.

The Set

Black box. Goalposts. Pitch lines. A large screen forms the back wall. Benches. Various theatrical models, puppets and shadow screens are utilised in the story-telling.

Sequence 1

Lights up. A disheveled priest on a pulpit. He drinks from a bottle of whiskey.

LOFTY: Brothers and sisters. My sermon today is very important. It will help you all negotiate life, keep you on the straight and narrow. So, pay attention.

YARN-TELLER: Introducing returned missionary, Father Bernard Joseph McMahon. Known to his friends—and enemies—as'Lofty'.

YARN-TELLER: Ministering in the arsehole of rural Ireland. The third world but with more clothes on.

LOFTY: Rules for the soul: You may strike the ball on the ground, or in the air. You can pick up the ball with your hurley and carry it for not more than four steps in the hand. Ah . . . but temptation. The temptation is there to pick it up with the hand. This is a sin! Bad sin. Mortaler maybe. After those four steps you may bounce the ball on the hurley and back to the hand, but you are forbidden brothers and sisters to catch the ball more than twice. This is also a sin. To get around this, one of the skills is running with the ball balanced on the hurley. This is like . . . a virtue. Shitloads of indulgences, I'm quite sure for that. Each team consists of fifteen players. A win is heaven, a loss is hell, a draw is purgatory or limbo . . .

YARN-TELLER: Lofty didn't last long in the job after that. But a few evenings later, before the bishop called him in to explain his redundancy package, a funny thing happened.

YARN-TELLER: A confession box . . .

(LOFTY, dying with a hangover, drinks secretly from a naggin. A woman is telling him her sins.)

WOMAN: . . . and then father shur I know he's me husband but the thought of him climbin me all shlimy haired, his gut shlappin against me like his waters was about to break. J, M and Joseph, I jusht couldn't face it. So when I saw the one gamey eyelid shlidin for sex I shlipped the Laxmax along with the seven sugars in his tea. Between that and the shlurry tank a drink, well, he was gushin from both ends. And that's not all father.

LOFTY: Do I really need to hear this?

WOMAN: When he was on his knees in the jax drivin the porcelain bus shur wasn't I in the bubble bath thinking impure thoughts about . . . well . . .

LOFTY: Who? Impure thoughts about who?

WOMAN: One of the Galway forwards.

LOFTY: What? . . . Jesus . . . Football or hurling?

WOMAN: J, M and Joseph, hurling of course father.

LOFTY: Fine. Cloonan or Broderick?

WOMAN: Kevin Broderick . . . oh bless me father—

LOFTY: —Look, you're grand. Go away let you.

WOMAN: What about penance?

LOFTY: Go home. You've plenty of it there.

WOMAN: J, M and Joseph. Oh my God I'm heartily sorry for—

LOFTY: —Just go. Gowan.

(She leaves. A black man steps in. LOFTY slides across the confession hatch. The man sings quietly.)

MAN: On her body's she's tattooed a map of Ireland
And when she has her bath each Christmas day

LOFTY/MAN: As she rubs the sunlight soap around by Claddagh
You can watch the suds go down near Galway Bay

Lofty: Musa!

(LOFTY jumps out of the confession box and opens the 'sinners' door. They embrace.)

Sequence 2

YARN-TELLER: That was the first time they met since Sierra Leone. Then Musa Sesay brought Lofty to his home. The Asylum-Seeker Direct Provision Centre.

LOFTY: Ahmed! I don't believe it. All the way from Sierra Leone. Great to see you!

AHMED: Father. Lofty!

BENITO: Benito 'Che' Ortiz, Cuba.

FATMATA: Fatmata Mansaray, Sierra Leone.

(LOFTY gives her the once over. She enjoys it.)

LOFTY: Hello. Lofty McMahon.

MUSA: (*to LOFTY*) That is Ahmed's mobile home there. That one is Benito's. That one at the end is our community centre.

LOFTY: Jesus Christ, it's . . . all the same . . . it's . . . a caravan park from hell.

FATMATA: The worst thing here father is the boredom. Sergio here has waited—

LOFTY: —Lofty. Just Lofty.

FATMATA: Sergio has waited a year and seven months for his asylum application to be heard. The government will not allow them to work.

MUSA: It's two miles to walk to the town. We live on nineteen euro each week. When it rains . . . well . . .

LOFTY: —Jesus.

MUSA: Anyway, enough of this. So, Lofty, will you join us?

LOFTY: I don't know anything about asylum applications?

MUSA: Not this, with the hurling. Like you taught Ahmed and I in Sierra Leone . . .

LOFTY: The hurling?!

MUSA: Yes.

LOFTY: God no. That was a different time. I can't believe you're still playing hurling. What for, for Christ's sake?

AHMED: . . . We play soccer too of course.

MUSA: We want to join the local club. It will bring some of the emigrant groups together.

LOFTY: Musa you're a good man. To be doing this work. But this is a crazy idea.

MUSA: We've nothing else to do. We're quite good actually. The Irish think it's funny.

LOFTY: I'll bet they do. D'you know what part of the county you're in? The local club doesn't even play hurling. Why don't you just do English classes or legal aid or . . . or something useful? You'll stand out a mile playing hurling.

MUSA: Yes, you are right. Because now of course we merge in perfectly. The nice tan and all that.

LOFTY: Look this—Why hurling?! I mean, Christ—

FATMATA: —Well, in fact it is your fault.

LOFTY: My fault? How?!

FATMATA: You taught Musa and his friends fifteen years ago in

Africa. This was the start. Someone else's cousin we know joined the university team. Let me introduce you please. This man is Santos from Argentina.

LOFTY: Ola Santos. Que tal?

SANTOS: Bueno. Ola.

FATMATA: Santos is descended from hundreds of Irish emigrants who went there in the 1800s. Grew up learning Irish songs and poetry.

SANTOS: I play . . . played hurling with Buenos Aires Shamrock All Stars. Pero . . . but . . . our economy at this moment is destroyed. I try claim Irish citizenship. My parents can—but no me.

MUSA: It's a simple thing—Santos just wants to play hurling—

LOFTY: —Fine, fine, but what has—

AHMED: There's a man from Croatia who works in a telemarketing company full of crazy hurlers. He learned to play with them—

FATMATA: —He's completely useless of course. And there are other foreigners who just think . . . this is a fucking brilliant, muck-savage game.

LOFTY: Muck-savage game. It's a sophisticated game.

FATMATA: Will you help or not?

LOFTY: Look. If it was as simple as . . . OK. Here it is. Most clubs would welcome you with open arms. The Croke Park leadership would just love it. You'd be advertising Guinness within weeks. But this club. This chairman. This is his empire. And it's not just yeer skin colour. Far as he's concerned, anyone outside the townland boundary is Taliban.

AHMED: —You could help us win something for the club then?

LOFTY: I can't. I haven't coached for years.

FATMATA: Look leave it. We'll do it ourselves.

MUSA: Lofty. Will you at least consider it?

LOFTY: I can't. She's right. You don't need me. Good luck. It was good to see you my friend.

(*He leaves heading the wrong way.*)

FATMATA: It's *this* way. Father. You might pick up a passing taxi from the main road.

Sequence 3

YARN-TELLER: Well that was a year and a half ago. Musa, Fatmata and the lads didn't give up the hurling. They kept tipping away.

YARN-TELLER: It was a way of passing the long days and it intrigued the locals. Opened a few conversations. And a few more joined. Mostly foreigners.

MIROSLAV: (*same YARN-TELLER*) Like Miroslav. I am Bosnian, come to this country. In 1994 I live in west. I work—for cash—very dangerous—on building sites. Two boys I work with, they bring me to see All-Ireland final in Croke Park when county wins. I think this game is crazy but beautiful. We wear yellow and blue everywhere. Peuhh! I am county ethnic minority in Dublin, no? Mad, you know. Great craic. Team win first time in many, many years. My friends go crazy. I go crazy too. I drink twenty pints. Peuhh! I have never go to a lap dancing club. But we go. Mad, you know. I couldn't believe. There I see Katerina, dancing. She is from my school in Kumanovo in Bosnia. Peuhh! Crazy. I not see her in ten years. We talk for few minutes. But Katerina and me—is embarrassed you know. Very soon nothing to say. All we say is life is crazy. Us in Dublin. Me in furry hurling hat. Her in furry g-string. She doesn't offer number—and I don't give mine—to meet again. Difficult. The lads are pissed off—they want her number of course. Next morning I don't need wear county colours—I *am* yellow and blue all over. After that, they show me how play hurling. Great craic. Peuhh! Crazy. Perfect game for Bosnian.

YARN-TELLER: The local GAA club was strictly Gaelic football. So, Musa and the lads asked for a meeting so that they could join up and form a hurling team. Enter the local GAA chairman, the formidable Rusty Cox.

RUSTY: Well as I say men, layve it with me, we'll see, yeah, we'll see, definy like. I d'know lads would ye not try the Gaelic football biys at all, at all? No. Yeah?

MUSA: We wish to play hurling.

RUSTY: There's no hurlin this side of the county like, definy like. Jasus lads for yeer own sake now I'm wonderin would ye be happy here at all. Yeah. Like is this yeer scene, y'know like.

MUSA: We wish to play hurling. We wish to represent the club. Others might join if we play.

RUSTY: Well now biys, y'see definy like the club has a hurlin team—but just for tippin around y'know. In fact, we haven't been represented in hurling now for years and years and I'm not sure yeer the biys . . . yeah. Nothin to do now with yeer . . . yeer . . . origin, definy like . . . like. Would ye not do the runnin biys? Yeer good at that.

FATMATA: I thought you said you didn't have a hurling team Mr Cox.

RUSTY: No now yeah—definy like. We have hurlin, we do. Jusht it's not . . . priority . . . these parts yeah. The easht a the county, now that's where ye should try. Plenty a hurlin clubs—

MUSA: —We live *here*. We want to represent this club.

Rusty: I shpose. Yeah. Right so. Layve it with me then. I'll talk to the committee. Definy like.

FATMATA: Can we not join up now? We can pay membership.

RUSTY: Look money isn't the issue here. Ye could join for nathin for all I care. Definy like. An shur you're a woman. Is she intendin ta play with ye as well lads? Oh yeah. I'd say she's a fasht goer lads! What? Definy. We have the comogie. Shur ye could all play that—

FATMATA: —Comogie?

RUSTY: Yeah . . . hurling for the ladies. What *The Irish Times* buv in Dublin there calls 'Chicks with Shticks'. Would ya credit dat? Definy like.

FATMATA: You'll be telling me next they have to wear skirts.

RUSTY: Oh God yeah. Definy like. Tis lovely now. The girls are shtone mad about it. Smashin rig out . . . ah God yeah . . .

MUSA: Please. Tell us. Why can't we join to play hurling?

RUSTY: Well, there's . . . we have procedures . . . forms . . . Definy like.

FATMATA: Forms? These forms here?

RUSTY: Yes. That's them.

FATMATA: And we'll take up your kind offer of free membership.

MUSA: Thank you Mr Cox.

RUSTY: No problem lads. And ladies.

(*FATMATA shakes his hand.*)

FATMATA: Fellow member. Goodbye.

RUSTY: Yeah. Right. Definy. Right so.

Sequence 4

YARN-TELLER: Musa made one more attempt to persuade Lofty. He hadn't spoken with him in the many months since their last meeting. But he had seen him. In bars. Roaring at dusk on the mountain. Being picked out of the gutter at lunchtime. So Musa backed off and waited for his moment.

MUSA: We walk into Lofty's mountain cottage.

FATMATA: The smell is horrible. The place is a pigsty. Irish men? I wonder to myself.

MUSA: Lofty.

(*LOFTY wakes in an armchair and reaches for a bottle.*)

LOFTY: If I knew you were coming, I'd have dusted.

MUSA: What's happening?

LOFTY: I'm meditating.

MUSA: This is bad.

LOFTY: (*to FATMATA*) Hello again.

MUSA: Father, I wish to—

LOFTY: —Don't call me father, Musa. I'm not in the black militia anymore.

MUSA: The what?

LOFTY: The priesthood. Kicked out.

MUSA: Fine. Well before you join the spirits—we need you.

LOFTY: Are you two . . . you know?

MUSA: We've a team of nine lads now who want to play.

LOFTY: So Musa has found a woman? He was very shy you know in Sierra Leone.

MUSA: They are good players. A couple of very skillful athletes. A few more I believe will join. I really need this to work.

LOFTY: Jesus. You're not still on this hurling mission?!

MUSA: The club is trying to stop us. Or at least control us.

LOFTY: Ah! Good old Rusty?

MUSA: Yes.

LOFTY: Prick. I told you not to bother. Here, have a drink.

MUSA: It's too early for me.

LOFTY: This isn't an early drink. This is still last night's after hours. (*to* FATMATA) You?

(*She declines.*)

FATMATA: This makes you feel important, doesn't it? But we just need a manager. Someone who will make it difficult for them to manipulate us. The rest we are quite capable of doing ourselves.

LOFTY: Fantastic. Great speech. But I said no. You know why? These days I mostly sleep in this chair. One day that door blew open and it took me four hours to motivate myself to get up and close it.

MUSA: You've enough motivation to get alcohol.

LOFTY: Ooohh, nasty.

MUSA: We need help to recruit some experienced hurlers for the rest of the team.
We've a public meeting in the GAA club on Sunday to—

LOFTY: —Rusty gave ye the hall?

MUSA: He couldn't refuse. We are members.

LOFTY: You're a dog with a bone. Anyway, I'm tired. Go. I can't do this.

MUSA: You must. You saved me in Sierra Leone. You're still responsible—

LOFTY: —Ah I saved you . . . such bullshit! Go home Musa and don't come back!

(*FATMATA nods at MUSA to go. He leaves reluctantly.*)

LOFTY: What? What? You go as well. Go.

FATMATA: I'm not moving.

LOFTY: Please. Go. Join your boyfriend.

FATMATA: I'm not finished my business.

LOFTY: Oh? Well I've got things to do.

FATMATA: I can see.

LOFTY: So much drink, so little time.

(*She takes the bottle. She laughs.*)

FATMATA: Rusty said you couldn't manage a team of umpires.

LOFTY: He said that?

FATMATA: Yes. And Musa is not my boyfriend.

LOFTY: God help whoever is. Won't get away with much . . .

FATMATA: We're going to talk for a while now.

LOFTY: Oh God.

FATMATA: Lofty, if you don't do this Musa will forgive you. But you will never forgive yourself.

LOFTY: Oh shite . . . you sound like a feckin counsellor.

(*FATMATA smiles.*)

LOFTY: Jesus Christ, you are.

Sequence 5

YARN-TELLER: So they spread the word. 'Hurlers wanted!' They put up a notice about the meeting. Around the Dispersal Centre. And in town. Then the big day arrived.

(*MUSA and FATMATA are nervous. MUSA addresses the theatre audience.*)

MUSA: Thank you all very much for coming here. Maybe some of you know we are members of the local club and we hope to form a hurling team to represent it. Mr Cox, the chairman, has kindly agreed to let us use the hall to recruit some new players tonight. This is important. Because this team will then enter the County Club Championship. We already have nine players—so please put your hands up. Thank you. Please. Have we any more volunteers?

(*no response*)

MUSA: Our plan is—we are going to find a manager. Some of us have played before but if you haven't, that's OK. Because someone will teach us.

FATMATA: It's just a bit of fun. Something to do. And I think it will make good links with the town. So please join us.

(*A very tall puppet puts up his incredibly long arm.*)

MUSA: Great, sir. What is your name?

MAN: Istvan Bolic.

MUSA: Where are you from, Istvan?

ISTVAN: Sarajevo.

MUSA: How tall are you, Istvan?

ISTVAN: Six feet, eleven inches.

MUSA: Jesus Christ.

FATMATA: Anyone else?

(*nothing*)

RUSTY: If I could just come in here. Maybe simplify things a bit. Given the poor response—it's undershtandable like—I think what we should do is get all the names down here tonight, right? And over the year we'll try to get a bit of intrisht goin. A bit a trainin, definy yeah. And maybe come back to it in the next couple a years? What d'ye think? Is that a proposal or what? Yeah?

COMMITTEE MEMBER: G'man, Rushty! I'll second that.

MUSA: Please, this is not a committee meeting. We are trying to form a team here *tonight*.

RUSTY: Well . . . Moosa, is it? . . . Shur ye're in no shape ta go out an' play a game, definy yeah. Ye've no team, no manager, no training programme, only a few a ye has played the small ball game before. I'm ony thinkin a ye—and the club! Now I think its definy besht to let it lie—

(*We hear a hurl banging slowly on the ground.* LOFTY *appears at the back of the theatre and walks slowly towards the stage, banging the hurl every few feet. Silence.*)

LOFTY: Well, I think you're wrong, Rusty.

(*Everyone looks around.* LOFTY *is shaky, dishevelled but sober.*)

RUSTY: Lofty. The club bar doesn't open till after the meeting.

LOFTY: I'm the manager. Musa there is captain.

RUSTY: I'm surprised you didn't take the United job.

LOFTY: We'll sort the rest out later.

RUSTY: Is that the drink talking now?

LOFTY: No, it's a GAA man talkin.

RUSTY: Well haven't we climbed very high on our horse now for someone that's shtill ony wet from the gutter? Look I'm jusht tryin to go about this the right way. Definy yeah. We need to get the officials—

LOFTY: —Now, what about a few local lads? Pa Daly, Pa we need a full back. You were one of the county's best in your day.

PA: I'm a bit long in the tooth, Lofty.

LOFTY: It's a motley crew, Pa—you'll fit in. You could run trainin as well?

PA: Well, if you think so, I'm in for the craic.

LOFTY: Don't get me wrong, Pa. It'll be damn hard work. Anyone else?

(A man puts his hand up.)

MUSA: What's your name, sir?
MAN: Scallion. Scallion McCallion.
LOFTY: Have you played before, son?
SCALLION: No, sir, but I've twelve years playing Shinti over in Scotland for Lochcarron.

(A few more of the asylum-seekers put up their hands.)

LOFTY: Good. A few more there. Have ye played before?

(They look confused. AHMED *talks to two men in his own language.)*

LOFTY: We'll get back to ye. Anyone else?
MUSA: You, sir?
NDINGI: Yes. Thank you, sir. Pajani PJ Ndingi.
LOFTY: Good man. Have you played the stick game before?
NDINGI: Oh, yes, sir. Corner forward. I was taught by the Christian Brothers.
LOFTY: Oh, they'd know all about sticks all right. Are you any good?
NDINGI: They say, sir, that I'm the DJ Carey of Nigeria.
LOFTY: Modest, too. Welcome aboard. You?
SYLVIE: A'rih' yeah. Stick me down. Sylvester . . . ah Sylvie 'The Scud' Scully.
MUSA: Which country are you from?
SYLVIE: Ah from the independent republic of Fatima Mansions in Dublin. Ah . . . on a rural resettlement scheme down here in the bog y'know. *(to* RUSTY*)* Whar're you lookin ah, ya muppeh?!
LOFTY: Rusty, I think we've a team.
RUSTY: Well, I think that's shtill open to question.
YARN-TELLER: And so the meeting ended. With lots of drama still hovering. A sense of unfinished business. They also discovered that their first match against neighbouring parish, Scrobegnocknahooie, was set for just ten weeks away!

Sequence 6

YARN-TELLER: We want to take you now to the training camp. Lofty's mountainside farm.

(The team is gathered around.)

LOFTY: So let's go back to basics. Hurling is a small ball game for men with big balls—

FATMATA: —I don't have any balls.

LOFTY: That's not the rumour I hear. Anyway, hurling: The Facts. The best and fastest game in the world. Most similar to hockey in that it's played with a small ball and a curved wooden stick. But that's where the similarity ends, thank Christ. It is Europe's oldest field game. The goalposts are H-shaped, with the crossbar lower than a rugby one and slightly higher than a soccer one. Now! The modern game requires elite levels of fitness and skill. And that's Pa Daly's department. Pa?

(Training sequence of traditional ball and stick work led by PA.)

LOFTY: The Vietnamese guy was bound to get slagged from day one. Shur he hadn't a chance with a name like Dong Phuc.

(DONG PHUC practices a very unconventional form of martial arts.)

DONG: Howsitgoin? I'm Irish. Not only that, I'm a feckin culchie. Parents brought me over as a baby in the '80s. The boat people and all that lark. Of course, they changed my name. Because of the . . . Dong . . . thing y'know. It took them three years before they realised—before a neighbour tipped them off. So they changed my name . . . to Michael. How brilliant is that? Such an improvement. At school they called me Mickey. Mickey? . . . A few years ago I got interested in the Vietnamese thing. Though inside I know I'm a redneck mucksavage Paddy, part of who I am is Vietnamese. So now at University I've started using my real name. Well . . . in fairness now . . . it is a great chat-up line. 'Howsitgoin, girls? My name is Dong Phuc.'

(The team is around LOFTY.)

LOFTY: Lads, the game against Scrobeg would have been a tough enough test for a first game. But now we've something else to cope with.

MUSA: What do you mean?

PA: Rusty.

LOFTY: Scrobegknocknahooie is a bit of an aimless team. Rough and ragged. But the word I'm hearing is—behind the scenes, Rusty has taken them on. All on the quiet. He's had them training flat out. Rusty will stop at nothing. So we've our work cut out. Let's get to it!

(*Group training sequence continues in slow motion. Silence.*)

LOFTY: The hurling always brings back Sierra Leone—green and golden, damaged, spice scented. That day many years back when Bingo Collier arrived exhausted with the jeep of supplies from head office in Freetown. Canned food, medicine, artificial limbs and the shock of the sack, sent in error from Ireland, containing thirty hurleys, helmets and sliotars, a few jerseys. The kids were fascinated. For the laugh I showed them the basics. Ball and stick work. When I came out to check on them later, hurling had been replaced by war games. It was comic and tragic, I should have known; they were all obsessed with fighting just like their older brothers, like their fathers. But I remember other days, when they were playing. And I thought, Jesus it's absurd. Some of them—Musa, Ahmed and a couple of others—they had a kind of a knack for it. They were actually beginning to play. Who would have thought it would lead to this? Here! Now!

Sequence 7

(*The match sequences are tightly choreographed to synchronise with the commentaries—interspersing ensemble movement with individual sequences. The movement is stylised, physical, exciting and powerful.*)

YARN-TELLER: The team's first match!

RUSTY: I could have done with more time but match day arrived like a coldsore on a first date. And by Chrisht I had them psyched up like Ger Loughnane on ecshtacy.

(*The players are lined up centre stage on a bench. Both team talks are intercut using the same cast of players. Between speeches the actors spin around to face the other manager.*)

LOFTY: Poetry will be enough to win the day lads. The only hurling we'll be playing from here on in is hurling that flies. We don't have the physical force to play hard hurling. We don't have the traditional hurling skills to play tight hurling. We don't have the history to play patriotic hurling. But they're not the reasons we won't play it that way. We'll play hurling that flies because it's what hurling was made for. Poetry will be enough to win the day.

RUSTY: They're fired up in there definy now with their blow-ins and black fellas and Bosnians. They've red diesel in their veins. They've curry on their chips. Look out in the crowd there biys. It's a fucking circus out there! They haven't come to experience the passion of GAA. They've come for the novelty. Ah lads! The fuckin *novelty*! Winning isn't enough. I'm talkin *wipe-out*! Definy.

LOFTY: Remember the training ground. Natural skill. Unforced miracles. Let poetry write ye're script today lads. And remember, most of these boys are unfit, one or two are as unskilled as ye are and most of them don't know why they're out there. They won't rhyme like ye.

RUSTY: All they have over ye is that some of them might be a bit fitter. Clippy is reffing and we've already misplaced his contact lenses so do damage from a dishtance. This is not shtrictly a game of hurling lads so definy now interpret the rules liberally. I'm not talking broken bones here Kango but I am talking bruises that you could make jam from. Vicegrips!—the usual—at least wan stretchered off first half. The resht of ye—winning usn't enough lads—I want terrorism!

LOFTY: Another thing, they'll never have met a team like ye. When they're running in on goal and facing a huge pair of white eyes jumpin the fuck out of a mad black face, that'll throw them. And when that black face won't go away, when it sticks to them like cattle brand on a heifer's arse, that'll throw them more. I can smell it burning in the air. It's a day for poetry.

(*The players jump up and take their starting positions.*)

YARN-TELLER: Clippy, the half-blind ref throws in the ball.

YARN-TELLER: Sergio is up against an eighteen-stone muck savage.

YARN-TELLER: They both pull. Sergio makes clean contact with the ball but the mucker makes clean contact with Sergio's jaw.

ALL: Clack!

YARN-TELLER: The ball runs one way but the ref goes the other. Ndingi from Nigeria comes flying out to the ball like a gazelle in zero gravity, bounding poetically—and very poetically . . . leaves it behind.

ALL: Shit!

YARN-TELLER: The Scrobeg corner forward scoops up ball; Pa 'Fresh Loaf' Daly dives to block; the forward fouls the ball; but Clippy the ref is cleaning his specs; the forward loads and . . .

ALL: Shhhooooooooottss! Point!

YARN-TELLER: Look, it's Luis Bolivar!

LUIS: Fuego! From the high dropping puck out Luis rises like an antelope on a trampoline. He picks the ball out of a cloud. Brilliant! He lands . . . turns on a six pesetas and heads for Indian country.

YARN-TELLER: The handle of an enemy hurl stabs into his greyhound Brazilian ribcage.

ALL: Thunk!

LUIS: Huhhhghh!

YARN-TELLER: His mouth throws up his breakfast while his hand throws up the ball.

ALL: No!

SORRY GIRLS: Big Mick Mooney, bricklayer, scaffolder and as a part-time bouncer was nicknamed 'Sorry Girls' . . . picks up off the ground and JCBs his way through the wounded Musa, the shitless Tibor Stankovitch and the totally absent Ndingi. He hits hard and ignorant. The ball floats outside the upright but only one umpire flags it wide.

YARN-TELLER: 'Sorry Girls' 'consults' the ref (*he does*) and Clippy records a score. (*he does*)

YARN-TELLER: The pattern was set. Whenever the lads ran it up the wing . . .

ALL: Trip!

YARN-TELLER: When they collected in midfield . . .

ALL: Thunk!

YARN-TELLER: When they got the target in sight . . .

ALL: Chop!

YARN-TELLER: Oh Jesus his face!

YARN-TELLER: And so it went on like this. Brute force against bad poetry. Every time Scrobegknocknahooie hit hard, Musa and the lads tried to take them on, but it was Samson and the

Lion and the jaw bone of the ass was still in Samson's make-up bag.

YARN-TELLER: Scrobeg had one eleven from play. The lads had five points from frees. They limped, dragged and crawled off the field with bruises, gashes, open wounds and quite low self esteem.

YARN-TELLER: So, back to the dressing rooms!

RUSTY: Jimmy! Noel! John Paul! Yeer playing hurling! Yeer actually playing hurling! The lasht thing ye should be doing is playing fuckin hurling. Definy now. If ye don't come back with a shcalp in the second half, ye're not getting paid.

LOFTY: Second half is all change. Don't compete physically—ye'll lose every time. Compete mentally and ye'll win every time. Poetry! Time to start rhymin. Do the maths lads. There's only nine points in it. That's either nine scores, seven scores, five scores or three scores depending on how we play it. (*they all look confused*) It's a no-choice thing. We need three quick goals.

RUSTY: They'll be trying points from everywhere. Attack lads! We need to shlot over the same again. Concentrate on attack.

LOFTY: Make em defend! Keep passing then break for it. Luis and Sergio, I'm depending on you to feed the forwards cos lads ye've got the beating of those rhinos of backs. They're on their last legs. They only scored two points in the last twenty minutes. Start passing the ball. Get them chasing. They won't have the legs or the stomach for it. Short passes, lads.

RUSTY: Even when their forwards get supply, hit them so hard that when they wake up, they'll think they're in an episode of ER!

LOFTY: Now this is important. I want ye to laugh . . . yes, laugh. Start now . . . come on—a smile first . . . laugh in their faces . . . laugh behind their backs . . . when they hit ye, laugh . . . when they miss, laugh louder . . . when ye score, laugh, if ye miss, laugh harder . . . when ye get the goals, laugh ye'r ethnic holes off. Laugh lads . . . it's massage for the body and poetry for the soul. Laugh.

RUSTY: This is fuckin serious lads. Definy like. If we don't put this threat to bed now, the joke will be on us, on ye, on yeer club. Everyone will be laughing at us.

(*whistle*)

YARN-TELLER: Clippy throws the ball in.

YARN-TELLER: This time Sergio steps back just before they pull.

YARN-TELLER: The eighteen stone Scrobegknocknahooie muck savage wallops thin air.

ALL: FFFwhippp!

YARN-TELLER: . . . and falls over spraining his ankle.

ALL: Fuck him!

YARN-TELLER: Sergio picks up calmly. As the Scrobeg centre field generals close in, Sergio handpasses it over their heads . . . guffaws . . .

ALL: Hah!!!

YARN-TELLER: . . . and, with two lumpy missiles of psychopathic meat screaming in for the kill he . . . basically . . . runs away.

YARN-TELLER: Miroslav collects Sergio's perfect pass with a smile. He taps it to Benito. Scrobeg chase and harrie a multi-coloured manic collection of bruised, bloody but laughing faces.

YARN-TELLER: Benito runs on goal then turns back and runs fifty yards. Scrobeg are stunned. He snorts with laughter (*snort!*) as he passes it all the way back to the centre back.

YARN-TELLER: Same build again. Musa leads with short, accurate passes. Patterns going right across the field. Scrobeg are on their last legs, confused and furious.

YARN-TELLER: Sylvie 'The Scud' Scully is showin off his tattoos to the centre-half back and let's just say his tattoos are not on his arm. Then on a signal from Lofty. . .

YARN-TELLER: . . . the machine clicks. Pa 'Fresh Loaf' Daly to Luis.

YARN-TELLER: Luis cross-field to Benito.

YARN-TELLER: Benito's magic passing sequence with Ndingi and . . . Ndingi! . . . You black beauty, you . . .

ALL: Fffthuck!

YARN-TELLER: Top corner screamer!

ALL: Goooooal!

YARN-TELLER: Ndingi lifts his helmet and smiles like a madman. The crowd cheers.

ALL: Yeuuhhhhh!!!

YARN-TELLER: And so the plan went. Goal!!!

ALL: Yeuuhhhhh!!!

YARN-TELLER: Goal!!!

ALL: Yeuuhhhhh!!!

YARN-TELLER: Goal!!!

ALL: Yeuuhhhhh!!!

YARN-TELLER: Scrobeg were exhausted and humiliated. Rusty's worst nightmare had come true. When Musa and the lads started slotting over points from the sideline, Rusty wet himself with fury.

YARN-TELLER: On the final whistle, the small crowd invaded the pitch. Lofty and the lads were, for the moment at least, heroes.

(*Music, celebration dance.*)

Sequence 8

YARN-TELLER: For the team now everything was different. But at the club everything was different also. It was in shock. Rusty's loyalty was in question. The County Board was on his case. And the townspeople were beginning to come around to the notion that a mad shower of multi-skin-toned bastards could represent them.

YARN-TELLER: In fact, they were getting so popular that local people christened their new exotic team. And . . . the name stuck!

(*On this line the* YARN-SPINNER *turns to reveal the words 'The Freetown Slashers' on his shirt.*)

ALL: The Freetown Slashers!

RUSTY: And a few nights later, after training, they bumped into Rushty at the clubhouse. Well, you know me like definy, I was never short of a few 'conshtructive' suggistions.

LOFTY: But everything's fine as it is. You should be proud of this team.

RUSTY: I am, I am, don't get me wrong on this. But Lofty we need to come to a sensible thing on this definy now. They're representing the club at our own, native game and (*under his breath*) hardly a Paddy among them. I mean fuck it like, haven't they enough without taking our game as well for fuck's sake like definy now?!

LOFTY: But y'see Rusty, it isn't really our game.

RUSTY: What?

LOFTY: In one sense, anyway.

RUSTY: What are you on about now?

LOFTY: Well Rusty, as the last ice age was receding on this green land of ours, the Celts caused immigration havoc. When they made their unannounced social call to our modest little island they brought with them their unique culture, language, music. And Rusty, I'm sorry to say that under the 'other interests and hobbies' section of their temporary visas they listed a game called iománaíocht, now called hurling. It's an immigrant game, Rusty.

RUSTY: Ah Jesus.

LOFTY: Fact.

RUSTY: Look that was fuckin ages ago! What about this? What about now?

LOFTY: So you want a more 'mixed' team. That's a good one. A panel of selectors I don't know—apart from you. Pa who's been training gets the chop and I do his job while someone else manages? The benefits are stacking up all right.

RUSTY: Pa is a good man—but he's no qualifications. And he's too banjaxed to play.

LOFTY: Who'll manage?

RUSTY: Rinco here handled the under-twenty-one footballers for three years and now he's kindly offered to take on the hurlers. Definy now.

LOFTY: Hurling is a different universe to football.

RUSTY: He knows players from three different parishes.

LOFTY: And I know players from three different continents.

MUSA: Look this seems very simple. It's clear you don't like us Mr Cox, so we can't agree to you being selector. We want Lofty to manage. Pa to train. Anyone can join us. These are our terms.

RUSTY: Terms? I wouldn't shtart using that language lad jusht yet. Definy now. The County Board's eyes are all over this. This is the way of it. Take it or leave it.

FATMATA: We'll leave it.

LOFTY: The County Board won't stop fellas who want to hurl.

YARN-TELLER: And yes, the County Board didn't take long to sort it out. They'd had enough of Rusty and his antics. Musa and Lofty's team was confirmed as the official club team.

YARN-TELLER: Fate dictated that there were two paths to the County Final. And being from the weak hurling side of the county, the Slashers took the scenic route. The first few matches proved to be non-events. The first team turned up with only twelve players and were never in contention. The second team didn't show at all and they got a bye. The third lot turned up, but shouldn't have bothered.

LOFTY: This wasn't good. We had hardly been tested. And now fate had us in a County Final! In a month's time we'd be up against Killinaclash—the best hurlers from the best club from the best side of the county. And I was beginning to feel the pressure.

YARN-TELLER: Lofty realised that training had to be 'adjusted' to play to the strengths and skills of this exotic team. So Fatmata and Dong began to develop the most unconventional training programme the GAA had ever seen.

Sequence 9

(*A movement sequence calling up the multicultural spirit of the team.*)

Sequence 10

YARN-TELLER: Match day arrived on a bouncy, sunny Sunday. Cars, vans, tractors—even a chipper van—pulled into the ground. And there was something different, apart from the lovely weather—there was an extra bit of colour in the crowd, a slight sense of madness.

YARN-TELLER: And also when you looked around the crowd you could see, here and there, the odd black or brown or sallow face. Looking nervous. Taking it all in. Some were even chatting to the fans beside them.

MAN: Well, fine day for it.

BLACK MAN: Yes, it is lovely.

MAN: Have you travelled far—I don't mean like—y'know today?

Black MAN: Just a few miles. And you?

MAN: Oh, I'm a local. Born and bred, says you.

BLACK MAN: Hurling fan?

MAN: Well we're all Gaelic football round here. But this should be interesting. It should so. I hear ye're handy enough hurlers?

BLACK MAN: Sorry.

MAN: Your team.

BLACK MAN: The Freetown Slashers? Yes, so I hear. But they're your team aren't they?

MAN: Oh yeah, I spose. Absolutely. No, I just thought with the—you being—y'know.

BLACK MAN: I know what you mean. No, I'm supporting Killinaclash.

MAN: Oh, I see . . . Right then. Come on the Slashers! Get stuck into them!

CHINESE MAN: Lovely day for the game.

MAN 2: Begod it is. The finesht.

(*pause*)

MAN 2: Chinese?

CHINESE MAN: Well . . . yyyes.

MAN 2: That was an awful aul' dose hah?

CHINESE MAN: What?

MAN 2: Ah, that aul' SARS thing, y'know.

CHINESE MAN: Oh yes, terrible.

MAN 2: Shur I spose there's draughts in China too.

CHINESE MAN: Yes. I suppose there are.

MAN 2: D'you mind me ashkin . . . are you one of them . . . refugees?

CHINESE MAN: No, I am not. I'm a teacher.

MAN 2: A teacher no less. What do you teach?

CHINESE MAN: Irish.

YARN-TELLER: The County Club Hurling Final! Freetown Slashers versus Killinaclash!

(*A whistle blows. The game's story is told through a stirring and stylish combat dance of two halves. The Slashers dance the opposition into submission. Huge celebration. Jerseys exchanged.*)

Sequence 11

(*two relentlessly jolly TV journalists*)

FEMALE: Good evening. What a fablus game of hurley Traolach?!

MALE: Yes, we've new county champions Gubnet. It seems the

hurling sensation of the year—and maybe the decade—is coming from a hurling backwater, in the west of the county. There, a remarkable drama has unfolded. An exotic team of Africans, eastern Europeans, Asians, Latin Americans with a few natives thrown in, has made GAA history and national news.

FEMALE: Fablus. A multi-ethnic hurling team comes out of nowhere to win the County Hurling Final. We introduce you to the players. We lift the lid on how they took over a small local club. We go behind the scenes. Because certainly around here, everyone is asking questions. Who are these foreign nationals? Where did they learn their hurling? Who is behind them? I'm Gubnet Ní Ghiolla Snoidaigh.

MALE: And I'm Traolach O Tiernaigh. Goodnight.

Sequence 12

(*LOFTY and FATMATA drive back from training.*)

FATMATA: We've got to do something. It's getting to them. Some of the lads are afraid to come to training in case they have to face a line of press. Others are lapping it up, giving interviews—

LOFTY: —Jesus they'll be opening shopping centres soon.

FATMATA: Listen. You know some of them are facing immigration difficulties.

LOFTY: What? Who?

FATMATA: Well, some of them are waiting for their appeal dates. Others are just a long way down the queue before they get processed.

LOFTY: Jesus. What a way to have to live your life.

FATMATA: I think a few of them are secretly hoping that by playing hurling, they can stay.

LOFTY: Oh God. We can't raise their expectations like that.

FATMATA: I've explained that. But now—they feel they have nothing to lose.

LOFTY: And we've come so far. I wish we could do something.

FATMATA: But it's not just that. The most important game we've to play and the whole team—they're beginning to believe that they're . . . well, better than they are.

LOFTY: We'll sort that out fast.

FATMATA: You noticed Tibor wasn't at training tonight?
LOFTY: Yeah. They said he's a cold.
FATMATA: He was modelling underwear in the community centre for Stray Katz manshop.
LOFTY: What?! Christ! Hurlers don't do that kind of thing. Even the Tipp lads—and they're right show-offs. Jesus what an image.
FATMATA: Oh I don't know.
LOFTY: What?
FATMATA: Would you not be tempted yourself?
LOFTY: Oh very funny.
FATMATA: You are well able to shake that big Afro-Celtic boodie.
LOFTY: Oh, shut up. Right from tomorrow. I'll have them focused. On hurling. You too.

Sequence 13

(*training*)

SYLVIE: C'mere boys and I'll show yis lads what we do on our days off in Fatima Mansions.

(*SYLVIE karate chops a pile of hurleys.*)

DONG: Ok. Watch. Where I come from, we do it the hard way.

(*Then DONG steps forward and using mind over matter splits a hurley on its length.*)

YARN-TELLER: Now that they're out of the county, the Slashers are about to meet the cream of not just the province's hurlers, but some of the country's finest. Real GAA men. Elite athletes. Casanovas of the Camán. Some of the players they'll meet in their next match are—
ALL: —Living fucking legends.
YARN-TELLER: They had a quarter final and semi-final to play to get to the grassy theatre of dreams. Massive games. Clubs with huge pride and long traditions. But ask anyone, it was the semifinal against Knockswellin that everyone remembers.

(*The proud and fierce Knockswellin players parade in front of the audience.*)

YARN-TELLER: Knockswellin! The Provincial finalists for three years running. Men who had reached out to grasp the holy

Gaah grail only to have it snatched from their hurl tips. Now they were pissed-off.

YARN-TELLER: For the Slashers, everything had changed. They couldn't get out of the public eye. Everyone wanted a piece of them. Everyone, including one bitter club chairman.

RUSTY: Get me the file on every single one of them. Criminal records, work permits, immigration status, the works. Definy yeah. They'll rue the day they ever upset this lovely little country that we've built for ourselves.

YARN-TELLER: The Provincial Semi-Final! Freetown Slashers versus Knockswellin!!!

(*LOFTY is on the pitch firing them up.*)

LOFTY: Think distribution lads. Distribution is the cardiovascular system of hurling success. And lads—love bomb the bastards. Talk! Talk to them like they're in care and you're their therapist. Talk Nigerian. Talk Roma. Talk Spanish. Tell them stuff lads they've never heard on a hurling pitch. Talk intimate. Talk dirty. That's the job today. Talk them into losing.

YARN-TELLER: Game on!

YARN-TELLER: Come on Knockswellin!

YARN-TELLER: Come on the Slashers, let's get shtuck in now. Gwannn!

YARN-TELLER: Gehhuppp ye biys yah! Put it up to them biys!

YARN-TELLER: Drive int'it now lads! Take no prisoners!

YARN-TELLER: Hhuppp! Gwann!

YARN-TELLER: Go on Knockswellin!

(*A whistle blows.*)

MUSA: You see, Paddy, I'm from Sierra Leone in West Africa. I was a child soldier. They would drug us and beat us and force us to do terrible things. In a way, Paddy, hurling is like a therapy to help me get over that lost childhood. We used have these long machetes and they would make us do amputations. Sometimes the legs or feet but most often the hands or arms. A long sleeve or a short sleeve we used to call it. I remember a few years later, after I was demobbed, I met one of my victims in a special school. I didn't remember him—he was a double short sleeve—but he remembered *me*. He told me that for four years he needed help with everything. He couldn't go the toilet on his own. When I met him he had metal hands. He was carving figures from wood. We drank some Coca Cola together. Oh my God! Ref! Ref! Man down over here!

NDINGI: Hello, sir. Pajani PJ Ndingi. From Ogoniland in Nigeria. You know, where the oil companies took our land? I used to blow up the pipelines. Ever since then I don't like people taking over my place. Like you are now. But don't worry—I like you, Ginger. My God you're a big boy for a midfielder. You're lovely, you know that? The red hair. That tight little bottom. In fact, I think I love you, Ginger. What're you doing after the match?

PA: Pa Daly collects a low ball coming in, skips, and solos forward, ball on hurl. It was one of those handful of times in my life when I rhymed. When the cut teeth gear wheels of brain and body and beauty locked perfectly and made me a dancer. The sliotar stuck to the boss like oil paint on my palette. I shimmied and dipped and turned the backs inside out. I lived my score in slow motion. The dummy. The attempted block. The sidestep. The turn on my right. The one ton gun salute. The ball's blurry ballistics. The goal net's erection.

YARN-TELLER: G'man Pa Daly biy you're some man for wan man!

ALL: Yeeeehuuuuh!

YARN-TELLER: Slashers one point ahead. Nothing left on the clock and a high dropping ball into the war zone of the half forward line pulling in the players. It's falling like a grenade on a helipad. Hurls and hearts rise to claim or clear.

YARN-TELLER: RSJ, the Knockswellin centre half comes late and at pace suspended in that aerial orgasm between rising and falling. Four bodies are thrown sideways as RSJ takes cleanly with impossible grace for his size and violence.

YARN-TELLER: RSJ winds up for the clearance of the game—ball hovering, eyes locked on target, hurl wrapped back. It's going to be big, very big.

YARN-TELLER: He anticipates the ferociously clean impact of explosive completeness. But in the same instant Ndingi fly-dives from twelve feet, hurl stretched, eyes on sliotar. RSJ's swing—

ALL: —Whooosh!

YARN-TELLER: —RSJ's contact—

ALL: Theukk!

YARN-TELLER: Ndingi's acrobatic block—

YARN-TELLER: Clack!

YARN-TELLER: RSJ bewildered, humiliated, robbed of his act of completion. Ndingi picking ball, computing distance, understanding troop movements in a glance. Ndingi in the flylight zone.

ALL: Watch out!

YARN-TELLER: RSJ, a wounded hippo, charges to take him out. Ndingi taps ball on hurl this side, then that, then over RSJ's battering ram head. RSJ slipping, slapping, lost. Ndingi arming and firing on the diagonal, curling, cutting the posts in half.

ALL: Point!

YARN-TELLER: Slashers stretch lead to two! Ndingi, watch out!

ALL: Watch out!!

YARN-TELLER: RSJ thundering late and loose and lethal.

ALL: Watch the fuck out!!

YARN-TELLER: Chopping Ndingi's fine artist's hand. Black skin bursting. Sinews snapping. Bones crushing. Pain searing. Ref blind. Crowd rabid. Ndingi stretchered off.

ALL: Oh my good shite!!!

(*Crowd sounds come from a miniature model stadium. We see the sliotar rising over the wall. We see it flying between the posts for a point as the crowd cheers and horns sound. A loud sharp whistle. The match ends. The cheers are deafening. The stadium spews fireworks in the Slashers colours.*)

Sequence 14

REPORTER 1: In a sensational result today the exotic Freetown Slashers have reached the Provincial Final. In a thrilling if unconventional encounter, a single point separated the sides at the final whistle.

REPORTER 2: Five of the Slashers team were warned by an exasperated referee for over-talking, but it seems this is not covered as an offence in the rulebook. I'm Traolach O Tiernaigh.

REPORTER 1: And I'm Gubnet Ni Ghiolla Snoidaigh.

REPORTER 2: We leave you now with a look at tomorrow's papers, which are full of the shock result in the hurling.

(A photo flash. Performed live, 3 stunning action stills from tomorrow's papers.)

Sequence 15

(The team exercises in the dressing room. NDINGI, *one arm behind his back does a hand exercise repeatedly squeezing a sliotar. He takes his other hand from behind his back. It is in a plaster cast. He tries to exercise it. The pain is too much.* MUSA *goes to* LOFTY.*)*

LOFTY: It's confirmed. The doctor said Ndingi won't play again this summer.

MUSA: We'll have to keep morale up.

LOFTY: See what you started?

MUSA: It's mad isn't it?

LOFTY: I really didn't think.

MUSA: We're into the Provincial Final?

LOFTY: Now what?

MUSA: What do you mean?

LOFTY: Well, we didn't war-game for this.

MUSA: It's frightening but it's a bit exciting too.

LOFTY: I honestly don't think I can handle any more of this. I mean I thought one game, maybe two. Some training. It'd peter out.

MUSA: There's a reason for all this.

LOFTY: Oh, here we go.

MUSA: I always knew I was meant to make my humble mark. I think this is it.

LOFTY: Oh. And what about me Musa?! What if I can't keep going?!

MUSA: We can't stop now. If I don't—

LOFTY: —I'm wrecked!! This is the first time I've been in a pub since I got sober and I swear to Christ, I would give an All-Ireland for a small one right now.

MUSA: You are finding it really tough, aren't you?

LOFTY: Musa, it's killing me. But it's the only thing that's keeping me alive. Pa!

PA: Right girls. This Provincial Final. St John Bosco isn't just a step up. It's a moon shot.

BENITO: This team? They are bery good?

PA: Good? These guys are fast, accurate, unsentimental,

vicious, skillful, ruthless, unpredictable, fit, gymnastic, focused, hungry, adept, tricky, knackey, creative and fine hurlers.

ALL: Holy shit.

LOFTY: But look, lads, we've four days to go and maybe they'll beat us on Sunday. But I'll tell you something true now—we won't beat ourselves. (*Their meeting is interrupted.*) We've made our point. We've . . .

(*IMMIGRATION GARDAÍ enter.*)

IMMIGRATION OFFICER 1: Musa Sesay Fofonah? Musa Sesay?

LOFTY: What the hell is going on here?

IMMIGRATION OFFICER 1: Mr Fofonah, under a request for extradition by the sovereign government of Sierra Leone, I hereby arrest you under Section 3 (9)(a)(1) of the Immigration Act 1999 as inserted by the Illegal—

LOFTY: —Just stop this right now!

GARDA: We've to take him in, I'm afraid.

LOFTY: For what?! He's on the club team. He's playing a Provincial Final on Sunday. You can't arrest him! Musa why . . . why didn't you say?—

IMMIGRATION OFFICER 1: I'm really very sorry but his appeal has been denied. He's an illegal alien.

LOFTY: An illegal alien! Watch who you're talking about sonny! He's our captain! He's a . . . hurler!

IMMIGRATION OFFICER 2: I know. I saw him against Knockswellin. Look, it's the Department.

LOFTY: Ah Jesus. Musa, you knew . . . didn't you?

MUSA: I got the letter a month ago. I knew then I had nothing to lose.

LOFTY: We'll get to work on it right away-

MUSA: It's over Lofty.

IMMIGRATION OFFICER 1: I'm afraid this is the last time you'll see him. He's flying back to Sierra Leone tonight.

LOFTY: This can't be right. Will you be safe, Musa?

MUSA: You know what it's like. I don't know. They will put me in prison. Prison is not safe.

IMMIGRATION OFFICER 1: I'm really very sorry. We have to go.

LOFTY: Musa. Jesus Musa. My good friend.

(The team gathers around. LOFTY and MUSA hug. They take him away. RUSTY is on his way in.)

RUSTY: God lads what's goin on at all lads? Terrible bizhness hah?

LOFTY: You really don't know when to stop Rusty do you?

RUSTY: Well now nathing to do with me now biys definy yeah. But in all fairness now like, if the man is breaking the law I mean definy now, they have to do their jobs like—

(LOFTY makes to go for him. The others pull him back.)

Sequence 16

(Flanked by two officers, MUSA waits handcuffed at the airport.)

MUSA: The last time I was in an airport—the day I arrived here—I met her. I helped carry her buggy on to the bus. I felt it right away. The red hair gets me every time. Cora. From Cork. That sexy accent. And I've always thought that freckled skin is the perfect compromise between black and white. But I could tell she was troubled. Whatever was happening that day. But she still had a dangerous smile. A few weeks later I walked into a corner shop in town. I had cut my hand opening a tin. I was buying some plasters and when I looked up, it was her behind the counter.

CORA: Did damage, did we?

MUSA: Yes, I need a plaster or they'll amputate.

CORA: Sh'God love ya. I've said it to the boss y'know—to get band aid in yeer colour. D'ya know like?

MUSA: What?

CORA: Plasters like. They're always in our colour like. Mind you, who have you ever seen with skin as pink as that?

MUSA: Michael Jackson maybe?

CORA: Oh yeah, right . . . D'ye hear he's gettin back together?

(silence)

CORA: Jesus never mind. Tell you what, we'll compromise. There. Bart Simpson plasters. Perfect match.

MUSA: She was so beautiful. I would go forty minutes out of my way to her shop for unique things I couldn't possibly get anywhere else—like milk.

CORA: Then he asked me out. He obviously had rehearsed it for weeks like. 'Would you like to come out to the cinema and for a drink on Thursday evening next week at 7.30?' So I says I would. Like he was a lasher. But not to the pictures. And not for a drink. And not on Thursday. Oh and not at 7.30 either. Are you busy tonight like?

MUSA: She couldn't get a babysitter for Jessie so we went out, in, in her flat. I cooked. After a few weeks she said she was my 'old doll'. She had to sneak me in whenever I visited. Her landlord is a referee. A small man with a big moustache. Lou Bolford. He didn't like darkies coming around he had told her. From then on I had to sneak in and leave at 6.00 a.m. Two adults behaving like teenagers.

CORA: I couldn't believe it. My new fella was a black fella. The girls were goin to be fuckin ragin like. Jessie adored him.

MUSA: She knew it was illegal for him to do this. But the flat meant security for her and Jessie. Then one day he put up her rent. We knew why. She had to leave. Go back to Cork. Now I'm going back. To hell.

(*The guards lead him away.*)

Sequence 17

(*LOFTY walks home. He takes out a large bottle of whiskey. He gulps it down by the neck.*)

Sequence 18

(*Team meeting. Everyone is sitting around waiting.*)

NDINGI: The final is tomorrow and he's not here.

SERGIO: Where could he be? He neber miss a tactics session.

PA: Something's up. It's not like him.

FATMATA: I have a bad feeling.

NDINGI: Well, here comes trouble now.

(*RUSTY slinks in.*)

RUSTY: G'night gents. And ladies. Sorry ta dishturb ye now, but I've a bit a bad news ah yeah now definy lads. Shame altogether.

PA: Say your piece Rusty and get out.

RUSTY: Aisy, aisy now! Ah no now it's sad like. It's Lofty. Back on the bottle biys I'm afraid definy yeah. He's been ravin all round town. Shame. Look I'll twaddle off here lads. Jusht thought ye'd like ta know . . . By the way . . . don't let it get ta ye tamorrow now lads. We're depindin on ye. Definy. Yeah. G'luck now.

(They are all in shock.)

PA: Right lads. We'll deal with this, right. We're on our own now, fine. Gwon away home now. An early night, right? We'll work something out tomorrow.

Sequence 19

*(*LOFTY *drunk on the mountain. He falls to the ground. He hallucinates. Shadow screen of the hurls arriving in Sierra Leone. He sits up, head in hands. He staggers off.)*

Sequence 20

(A burger van drives across the downstage playing area. Horns and cheers.)

YARN-TELLER: Ladies and gentlemen! The Provincial Club Final!!!

YARN-TELLER: St John Bosco vs The Freetown Slashers!

YARN-TELLER: Yes, St John Bosco's are on the field first to a manic reception.

(Boom. Ecstatic crowd sounds. On the shadow screen, they look huge and fit and confident.)

YARN-TELLER: But in the dressing room, facing into the battle of their lives, with their manager back on the jungle juice, the Slashers are . . . shitless!

(We see them from behind, shaking with terror.)

YARN-TELLER: Five minutes late and the Freetown Slashers are still not on the pitch. The ref fumes on the sideline. Looks at his watch. He is storming towards the dressing room. But deep in the bowels of the dressing room, plans are being hatched. Though Musa was now thousands of miles away, the Slashers decided that his spirit would haunt the most important game of their lives.

(The Slashers explode onto the field. All of the team wear identical masks of their deported captain MUSA*. They line up centrefield and stare at their opponents. They remove the masks.)*

YARN-TELLER: There are more surprises.

YARN-TELLER: Hog Hogan, a twenty-two stone retired hurler, is in for the deported Musa and . . .

ISTVAN Bolic, the forty-two year-old, six foot eleven giant from Sarajevo is in instead of the injured Ndingi.

(*All stand to attention for the national anthem.* AHMED *can be heard singing it in Irish.*)

YARN-TELLER: As the anthem finishes they can't believe their eyes. As if things weren't bad enough. The ref. Look at him! It can't be! But it is. The ref is . . .

LOU BOLFORD: Lou Bolford!

ALL: Oh, shite!

RUSTY: No better nor fairer referee will you find in the GAA. One of our own. G'man Lou!

(*whistle!*)

YARN-TELLER: From the start, the Slashers hit the ground running. The giant Bolic is picking everything out of the air and laying it off. Benito takes and wallops it low, skimming it on the flat grass.

BENITO: Before the game start I was berry berry nerbus but the second I start all my nerbes they go whussshhh! I feel berry berry fit. I get ball from Istvan. I feel like a tiger cat. I pass two defenders berry, berry fastly, I put ball in my hand, I strike hard, it travel berry, berry straight like bullet over bar. I score my first point! But the referee say I take too many steps! No point! I know this not true. Ref, that day was berry, berry bad.

YARN-TELLER: But even with the referee against them, the Slashers were doing all right.

YARN-TELLER: The brusied ball from Pa Daly's sideline cut comes in bouncing, bobbling awkwardly.

YARN-TELLER: Somehow, it wriggles in behind the John Bosco defence.

DONG: And so does Dong Phuc. I spin, taking a big shoulder from the full back. When I stop I am front of goal. Ball on ground. Right in front. Staring at me. Pleading . . .

(*A sliotar comes to life.*)

BALL: I'm all yours! Please hit me, oh please.

DONG: So, I pull on the ball. Clean, crisp contact.

ALL: Kehwoosh!!

(*DONG's celebrations are acrobatic and bizarre.*)

YARN-TELLER: Goal!!! John Bosco's are rattled. But John Bosco's are fired. Here they come. Look Jesus, a flying passing sequence from the half-backs out the line. Gathering pace. Midfield moves it in, ready to distribute. The forwards spread and raid on all sides.

HOG HOGAN: It was my first game.

YARN-TELLER: Watch them, Hog, here they come!

HOG HOGAN: I knew I was a little overweight—by about six stone in fact—so I knew I wouldn't stop those nippy little wasps of forwards with my speed.

YARN-TELLER: They're coming right at you, Hog!

HOG HOGAN: This needed guile.

YARN-TELLER: He's going right by you, Hog!

HOG HOGAN: So I just swung around, gave him a wet slap of my gut and . . . poleaxed him.

YARN-TELLER: G'wan the Hog!

HOG HOGAN: It was nothing really.

YARN-TELLER: Hog Hogan somehow clears the sliotar towards the sideline. Crisis suspended. Attack repelled. Hog heaven.

YARN-TELLER: Slashers take it back. On the offensive again. Ahmed flies up the wing like a squad car on a chipper run. Cuts inside. Gives to Sylvie 'The Scud' Scully.

YARN-TELLER: And thanking you. Sylvie turns. Sylvie spins. Sylvie pirouettes. And Sylvie points!

ALL: Gooowanyaboya!!!

SYLVIE'S MA: That'll show them culchie toe-rags, Silvie. You're really fuckin wreckin their buzz now son.

YARN-TELLER: John Bosco's natural talents are suffocating. They leak points.

ALL: Slot! Slot! Slot!

YARN-TELLER: Within twenty frantic minutes the Slashers are five points ahead. They're playing their best game of the year. The machine is well oiled and humming.

(*All sound stops suddenly.*)

ALL: Then . . . catastrophe strikes.

(*Sound starts again.*)

YARN-TELLER: Look, it's a harmless mill on the forty and Pa runs in to separate the players.

ALL: It's handbags at noon.

YARN-TELLER: To everyone's horror, the ref who has been miles behind the play, red cards Pa.

ALL: Blind Bastard!

YARN-TELLER: The team protests but this . . . oh my God . . . as if things aren't bad enough . . . he gives a yellow card to Benito and Sergio.

ALL: Ah, ref!!!

FATMATA: I had seen enough. So while he was writing in his notebook I stormed on to the field. I went right up to him. (*Kisses him full on the mouth*) And, I kicked him in the sliotars.

YARN-TELLER: The dream was turning into a nightmare. We leaked points.

ALL: Slot! . . . slot! . . . slot!

YARN-TELLER: So that was it. Half time. The team is in disarray without their captain and with their manager AWOL. We're really missing Ndingi out there. Istvan Bolic has so many bruises, cuts and muscle strains he is medium rare. He can't play on. He's fit only for the treatment table.

PA: I was acting captain but I'd been sent off. We were tacticless. By half time we've only scored one more and John Bosco's are four points ahead. In the dressing room—for the first time ever in the history of the team—the lads are broken. And I didn't know what the fuck to say or do.

Sequence 21

(*Dressing room. Footsteps.* LOFTY *limps in, pale but determined. They are dumbfounded.*)

LOFTY: How ye, lads?

PA: Jesus Christ, Lofty. You all right?

LOFTY: D'mind me. I just . . . I want to say I'm sorry, lads. I let ye down. I let Musa down—

AHMED: —This is not true. We—

BENITO: —You let nobody down—

LOFTY: —Look, anyway. Enough of that. We've work to do.

SYLVIE: Lofty. Brother. You're like the bleedin apparition at Fatima!

(*A rhythm builds through* LOFTY*'s team talk building to an inspiring climax.*)

LOFTY: You're all thinking this is the worst disaster. That it's somehow special. Well it's damn well not. It's ordinary. So hear this and hear it good.

Dare, lads. But don't ye dare look me in the eye unless ye're prepared to break yeer hearts. Down here (*punches stomach*) ye've got nerves. Up here (*head*) ye've got doubt. Down here ye've got weakness (*legs*). That's a whole slurry load of feeling. Use it! Use. It. Welcome those nerves. Chat up those doubts. Seduce that weakness. Flirt with fate lads until she changes her mind.

Break yeer hearts, lads. They're made for it. They're not there to pump blood. Mundane mechanics too trivial for such an ungovernable organ. In here (*heart*) ye've got the secret of winning. Right here. In this muscular magic. Love. Love of the game. Love of the fight. Love of the dance.

Last thing lads—and the most important. (*boom!*) Do it for Musa. He broke his heart to make something amazing happen here. And by Christ, yeer going to break years to help him finish it! Go to war, lads. (*boom!*) Yeer guerrilla hurlers. (*boom!*) Break hearts. (*boom!*).

(*The spirit is back. Then* NDINGI *steps in togged out wearing a bandage instead of his cast.*)

LOFTY: Ndingi! What's happened?

PA: Jesus Ndingi, your hand—what's the story?!

LOFTY: Tell me you can play?

NDINGI: Yes. I can play. It must be . . . the hand of God.

Sequence 22

YARN-TELLER: Meanwhile John Boscos were out first again swaggering with confidence. But they could never have expected what was to happen next. Out come the Freetown Slashers—solemn, determined, owning the moment.

(*Each team member is wearing war paint. They perform a Hurling Haka. Whistle!*)

YARN-TELLER: The second half begins with the most bizarre tactics. For each puck out the Slashers' complete forward line and centre field suddenly run in and group in a tight huddle on the opposition's sixty-five metre line.

ALL: Move!

YARN-TELLER: Their markers are forced to join them—twelve players in one tiny area leaving acres of green open space to run at.

YARN-TELLER: It happened again . . . and again.

ALL: Go Davy!

DINKI: The little goalie, Davy Dinki Delaney, hurl in one hand, ball velcro in the other, picks up near the end line. He looks into the sun as if he owns this field. He sends a volcanic puck streaking across his sky, which drops, drops, drops, right down on the bunched combatants.

ALL: Ndingi looks like he's flying!

NDINGI: Ndingi is lifted high above the group. Ndingi, too celestial now for temporal action, doesn't deign to catch the sliotar but instead flicks it miraculously out in front of Santos' run.

ALL: Goowannn Santos!

YARN-TELLER: The entire John Bosco defence run in chase not noticing that the Scud and Dong Phuc are on a raid. Santos draws four defenders, pays his respects, and gives just before contact.

DONG: Dong scooping ball, Dong double summersaulting, Dong flicking it over his head.

SYLVIE: And in to the path of the Scud who takes the inner city route to goal, joyriding the John Bosco ramps, ramming the backs, reverse, into third, pedal to metal and . . . blasts to the net!

ALL: Goal!

SCUD'S MA: Good man Silvester love, ye inner city culchie ya! That's my younfla!

YARN-TELLER: Incredible. For each puck out they move the grouping—centre . . . left wing . . . right wing.

ALL: Move!

DINKI: Sometimes Davy dummies to send a long one but on a signal, I'd pass just twenty metres to Benito.

BENITO: Muchas gracias amigo.

YARN-TELLER: Benito sees a defender.

BENITO: Hola.

YARN-TELLER: Benito passes the defender.

BENITO: Adios!

YARN-TELLER: Benito points!

ALL: Well done Benito!

BENITO: De nada.

YARN-TELLER: The ref—having been so blatantly biased and having got a belt of an ice cream cone from a four-year-old girl—has to tone down his decisions.

YARN-TELLER: But as Ndingi's spectacular point from the fifty metre sideline cut splits the posts they all knew they were scaling the sheer face of a nailbreaking cliffhanger.

NDINGI: Score for score, the Slashers stayed one point in front for the last ten minutes. But St Bosco's were relentless. Dangerous. They always looked like scoring.

LOFTY: This was it. Why I was back. Why I was saved again. We were hurling. And John Bosco's were a ferocious beauty to behold. To feel. Their hurling rhymed. Their hurling made you cry. And my lads were staying with the feckers over every blade of grass.

YARN-TELLER: Eight minutes of extra time played, still a point in it, how can the ref pretend there's any more left? Then came breaking point.

YARN-TELLER: Bosco's on the attack. They own the ball. Freetown can't afford to foul. Then a sequence of seven sensuous passes . . . Sylvie has to take one of the two forwards—the wrong one.

ALL: Oh no!

YARN-TELLER: All of the forward's six foot two aerodynamic frame is bearing down on goal. On poor tiny defenceless Davy, our goalie.

DAVY: The size a him like! I was completely in shadow.

SCALLION: He picks his spot in the net. He books by credit card. Expiry date. He signs off.

DAVY: I had to pick a side. I was in the moment. Calm. Total concentration.

LOFTY: This was it. The losing of it. It had to be all over now.

RUSTY: Bury it you big fucking heifer! Put them two-tone ballet dancers away for good!

DINKI: I waited . . . and waited . . . and when he pulled the hurl back I had the exact co-ordinates. My radar locked on. I dived as his hard-drive exploded. I felt that sweet, impossible contact—bunker buster blocked by bog ash.

ALL: Save!

AHMED: You beautiful little white nigger you!

LOFTY: Holy Christ, he saved it!

RUSTY: Ah ya, fuckin eeeejit!

REPORTER: Saaaaave! Oh my God. Dinky blocks from point blank range! Must be the save of the season!

DINKI: . . . Oh, yes, let's see that one again.

(*The sequence is rewound for the slo-mo replay.*)

REPORTER: What a move this was. The forward takes. Beats the defender. Just slow it down here. Oh, yes. Here he is, goal at his mercy, does everything right. And look at Dinki's little face, the concentration, the determination. Here comes that bullet. Sliotar heading perfectly for its place in hurling heaven. And here comes that impossible dive. Majestic. End of the hurl. Split second timing—stunning!

(*During the next speech a slow motion sequence leading to a spectacular Slashers' goal.*)

LOFTY: I was so proud. They were hurling like heaven. The whole pack connected by one surging central nervous system. On the auto pilot of genius. Both teams. From minute one to sixty. From clash of the ash to clash of the ashen. But the difference was . . . the difference. Not the difference in standard. The difference in styles. And I swayed and knotted and roared at two different, mental and magic demonstrations of the small ball game. On one side, the best of what we learned from hundreds of years of passioning on soggy and scorched grass. On the other, a fearless taking of the permission that difference offers. The club hurling match of the year. It was thrilling. It was heart stopping. And I thought the ref would never blow the fuckin thing up.

YARN-TELLER: The Slashers are Provincial Champions!

Sequence 23

(*A prison. Eerie noises.* MUSA *has a letter and match programme. He reads of the victory.*)

MUSA: Ba mhaith liom, an chorn seo a glacadh ar son foireann Na Freetown Slashers.

(*Then he kneels and cries. Curtain.*)

Introduction to Ursula Rani Sarma's

Orpheus Road (2003)

Charlotte McIvor

Ursula Rani Sarma was born in Saskatchewan, Canada in 1978 to an Irish mother and an Indian father. Shortly afterwards the family moved to Ireland to Lahinch, County Clare. She co-founded Djinn Theatre Company in Cork in 1999, and her work has been produced and/or commissioned by the Abbey Theatre, the National Theatre London, the Cross Border Centre Project, Traverse Theatre, Paines Plough, the American Conservatory Theatre, Origin Theatre Company, RTÉ and the BBC. She has received honours and awards in the UK, Ireland, and US including the 2000 Irish Times/ESB Theatre Awards Bursary. She is also a published poet currently at work on her first full-length collection.

Sarma, who now lives in London, is not easily classifiable within the oeuvre of contemporary Irish theatre. Like other playwrights of her generation, including Mark O'Rowe and Conor McPherson, she has explored the monologue form (though far from exclusively), but she has notably pursued themes of Irish youth, gender, sexuality and rural isolation far more aggressively in works including . . . *touched* . . . (1999), *Blue* (2001), *Orpheus Road* (2003; included in this collection), *The Spider Men* (2006), and *The Magic Tree* (2008). As her career has recently evolved largely outside Ireland, she has worked more and more frequently in television and film, making her short film debut in 2011 with *The Woods,* as well as writing multiple radio plays including *A Tiny Light in the Darkness,* set in the aftermath of the 2005 London bombings. Her plays have also moved away from explicitly Irish themes as in 2009's acclaimed *The Dark Things* mounted by Traverse Theatre, Edinburgh, as well as in her translation work which includes a 2003 translation of Luca de Bei's *The Dogs That Face the Hare* for the National Theatre Studio and a 2011 translation of Federico García Lorca's *Yerma* for West Yorkshire Theatre.

Orpheus Road is set in the North and takes up the well-rehearsed Romeo and Juliet trope by pairing Finn and Emma, two teenagers, who come together during a misdirected Loyalist bombing of an art gallery filled with students on a school trip. Sarma herself studied Northern Irish history at University College, Cork but here she places the broad expanse of this history into a more personal register and specifically focuses it within the storm of the first stirrings of adolescent love.

These young lovers go to schools that mark them as from different 'communities'. Yet Sarma's plot purposefully highlights the ways in which 'Catholic' and 'Protestant' may signify both or either religious beliefs and ethnic affiliation, and that an individual's politics may not align according to their religion and/or ethnicity. While Finn comes from a militant Republican household, Emma is not Protestant and does not identify herself as Catholic either. When Finn asks her why she attends a Protestant school, she responds:

> We could have just as well gone to a Catholic school, I mean it made no difference, it's just the Royal was nearer to where the house was and my Mam sent us there . . . she doesn't care about anything to do with anything as regards what goes on around here, she came for the job.

Here Sarma's play takes a subtle shift that marks this work apart from other novels and plays featuring star-crossed lovers across the sectarian divide, such as Bernard MacLaverty's *Cal* and Christina Reid's *Did You Hear The One About the Irishman.* Not only does Emma not identity herself as part of either 'community', her family are economic migrants to the North. She tells Finn that her absentee father is in Manchester, England, but her mother is South African—and white—and her family's ethnicity of origin is never ultimately specified.

Sarma's refusal to establish Emma's own ethnicity or original home and the multiple dislocations present within her family's history (from a former colonial power to South Africa to somewhere to Northern Ireland) leave gaps that point towards overlapping identities. These complex identities cannot obviate the immediate surroundings of the Troubles yet place Emma and other outsiders—whom she represents—trapped within a violence they cannot personally access even as it determines the structure of their daily lives. There is an 'outside' to simplistic binary notions of 'communities' in conflict in Northern Ireland, and this outside is located within the very heart of the violence as experienced by individuals living within its geographical boundaries.

Sarma does not date *Orpheus Road,* which was first produced in 2003 at the Young Vic Theatre in London, but given the intensity of the violence and the number of attacks and assassinations described within it, it seems safe to assume that this play is set sometime before the Good Friday Agreement. The uneasy relationship between the clichés of the Troubles (bombings, forced initiation of a young man into sectarian violence) and the clichés of teenage love (obsession, hyperbole, promises of always and forever) intentionally jar against one another as Sarma paints a picture of youth interrupted by violence, both imposed (vis-à-vis the Troubles) and chosen (as in the pair's repeated acts of self-harm as an outlet for feelings of isolation and abandonment).

The play ends with a suicide inspired by the fatigue of witnessing one too many acts of cruelty and the line between what violence can be considered imposed and what violence is personally chosen by these young lovers becomes too blurred to ultimately recognise. It is through the overlapping cycles of unrelenting self-directed and political violence in Finn and Emma's lives that Sarma asks her audience to question the impact of constant brutality on individual identity and emotional development.

Orpheus Road is a lament for not only innocence as removed through violence, but for outsiders who cannot find an outside to the violence they must live within. Emma may be literally an outsider, but Finn too remains personally divorced from the violence he is ordered to participate in. Their mutual isolation finds brief respite through their earnestly youthful love affair, but the hysterical excesses of their attachment, which Emma insists will last 'forever', can only ever mirror the madness in which they live.

In 2013, Sarma's *Orpheus Road* reads as prescient, as Emma's outsider status (despite her whiteness) mirrors the outsider status of increasing numbers of immigrants to Northern Ireland since the early 2000s, who have met with frequent hostility and occasionally violent attacks on individuals and groups. And despite Northern Ireland's 'post-conflict' status, dissident Republican attacks and Loyalist agitation continue sporadically, calling into question how memories of violence perpetuate cycles of violence which may claim new targets (such as recently arrived immigrants). Furthermore, the recent flag riots, though thought organised by pro-British paramilitary organisations, too raise doubts as to whether today's youth in Northern

Ireland can separate themselves from habits of violence and anti-social behaviour despite the theoretical absence of an active political conflict. *Orpheus Road* does not offer a way out or answers to these questions, but rather demands a harsh and visceral confrontation with violence as carved on the young protagonists' bodies, both by themselves and others in their communities who fail them.

Orpheus Road

URSULA RANI SARMA

Orpheus Road was written while Ursula Rani Sarma was Writer in Residence for Paines Plough Theatre Company. It was first produced at the Young Vic Theatre in London on 10 June 2003 as part of Paines Plough's Wild Lunch programme of short plays.

CAST

Finn	Michael Legg
Emma	Corrina Cunningham

PRODUCTION TEAM

Director	Vicky Featherstone

CHARACTERS

FINN, *sixteen*
EMMA, *sixteen*

Scene 1

Darkness. The Dubliners 'The Sea Around Us' begins to play quietly and as it increases in volume lights up on FINN, *he hums along and then joins in at the chorus.*

FINN: The sea oh the sea is the grá geal mo chroí,
long may it stay between England and me,
it's a sure guarantee that some hour we'll be free,
thank God we're surrounded by water. (*Beat*)
Is that it?
Da?
I learnt it?
Can I go now?
Can I?
Da?

I've done it,
Just then,
I swear I did,
Did you not hear me?
I learnt it all, I can say it all now,
Now?
But I'm gonna miss my bus Da.

(*beat, speaks to the audience*) And beneath the kitchen table with the sharp side of the bread knife I carve a little word there, f-u-c-k-e-r, that's what you are. Fucker. Tiny red letters coming up on the inside of my arm and if he asks me to say it once more I . . . (*deep breath, slowing down*) Upstairs this morning, in the bathroom, feeling the drops of water fall from my hair and on to my shoulders and down the line of my back and drip dripping on to the floor, clean the steam off the mirror and have a good look.

Count the scars, over and over again, touch the three new red lines just above my belly button (*quite excited*), one two three, one—I did those last night, under the covers. (*beat, whispers*) He doesn't know . . . no one knows.

I can do it in the dark now as well, so it's easier, you know, cos' of sharing with Jacki, and it's a small room, but I can handle it in the dark now, know just how far to go without there being any blood on the sheets. (*excited*) I find the cheap yellow razors the best, sharp enough not to pull the skin but shallow enough so as not to make it any depth that would leave a scar, I can do it all without even thinking . . . first hold the skin taught with one hand and then just slide the blade across in one—even—motion.

(*excitement disappears*) I see his face grow redder and redder, watch the purple veins on the side of his neck, I must have fucked it up again, I think about answering him back, but I want to go to school today, I don't want to stay here with him, so I say it all over again

The sea oh the sea is the grá geal mo chroí,
long may it stay between England and me,
it's a sure guarantee that some hour we'll be free,
thank God we're surrounded by water.
Is that it?
Da?
I learnt it?

Can I go now?
Can I?
Da?

(*to us*) By the time I've said it twice more I get out of the house to see the bus turn the corner below and fuck sake Da . . . fuck sake.

Little Jimmy Doyle from next door gives me the finger from the back window, I'll have to run all the way there now or I'll miss the trip and I'll thump Jimmy when I see him . . . his fault Da's like a badger today anyway.

Jimmy and his brother Liam were burning Union Jacks in the back garden after mass yesterday, watching the blue, red and white go up in little bursts of smoke and ashes with their Da lighting the matches for them. Then Da suggested we do it, too, and Mam almost battered him. She's an atheist she says—no, she says there might very well be a god but if there is then he must have some cunt of a sense of humour. It's because of Jacki, two of us in the womb and me coming out all fine and healthy and Jacki (*beat*) they say Jacki'll be six years old for the rest of his life. (*beat*) She told me she took her cross and chain to the pawn shop the day they left her out of the hospital.

(*beat*) I'm running now, trying to catch up with the fucking thing before it turns down Hinter Street and I'm thinking of last night, of every night, Da there between myself and Jacki, sat between our twin beds and whispering . . . know this story by heart, know it by nature, like the way other kids know Rapunzel is how I know this story . . . eight hundred years . . .

(*in Da's voice*) Sons, do you understand the reason for a thirty-two-county nation? (*kids voice*) We do Da—(*own voice*) Me speaking for Jacki cos' of him not being able to . . .

(*as Da etc.*) Sons do you understand the anger? We do Da
The prejudice? We do Da
The constant double standards? We do Da
Good lads, good lads, goodnight so.

(*beat*) I catch up with the bus and give Jimmy Doyle a right thump behind the ear, little fucker. I light up down the back of the bus, kick some first year out of his seat and get down low enough so Considine won't see me from up the front, put on my headphones, lean back, press play—

(*A sudden blast of the rebel song we heard at the top of the play.*)

—ah for fuck sake . . . Da . . . switched my Pearl Jam for the Dubliners, and I'm gonna miss the bus to the gallery I know I am, fuck sake Da, fuck sake.

(*A large explosion sounds, plunging stage into darkness.*)

Scene 2

(*An orange safety light fills the stage slowly.* EMMA *sits on the floor with her hands over her ears,* FINN *approaches limping slightly.*)

FINN: Are you lost? (*She looks at him nervously, then away again.*) Hey, I said are you lost? (*beat*) You know it's really rude not to answer someone when they speak to you . . . (*She looks at him.*) I said are you lost?

EMMA: Yes.

FINN: Me, too.

EMMA: You, too?

FINN: Yeah. I just ran.

EMMA: Me too.

FINN: Everyone was running—

EMMA: In different directions—

FINN: There was smoke.

EMMA: Everywhere.

FINN: Dust.

EMMA: Everywhere—

FINN: I didn't know—

EMMA: Where to go?

FINN: Yeah . . . I didn't know where to go . . . I thought I was going towards the main door, at the front but—

EMMA: It's not there anymore.

FINN: What isn't?

EMMA: The door.

FINN: The big one? With the gold handles?

EMMA: Gone.

FINN: You sure?

EMMA: Sure . . . there are just broken pieces, splinters and rocks and I saw one of the handles with the angels' faces cracked in two, there's dust everywhere and people were screaming . . . I was in the hallway . . . with the others . . . at least I thought there were others with me, and then I turned in this way and I didn't see the steps and I fell, I think I hurt my ankle. (*beat*) I can't stand on it. (*beat*) Where were you?

FINN: Looking for somewhere to have a smoke actually . . . near one of the bigger rooms with the paintings of the fat ugly naked women . . . and then we heard the blast and the lights went out and everyone was running and . . . I ran with them . . . I dunno where everyone is now, do you?

EMMA: (*shakes her head, beat*) Do . . . do you think . . . do you think everyone is dead?

FINN: Ach, no.

EMMA: (*looks at him earnestly*) No?

FINN: I doubt it. (*he sits beside her*) You got anything to eat?

EMMA: No . . . how can you be hungry?

FINN: I'm always hungry. (*pulling up the leg of his trousers*) You want to see my cut? I think a brick or something fell on it, I reckon I'll need stitches and all . . . you ever had stitches?

EMMA: Once, on my head, my sister swung a golf club and split my eye right open, here. (*points to her eye*)

FINN: I can't see it.

EMMA: Just below my eyebrow.

FINN: Nope, can't see a thing.

EMMA: (*unimpressed*) Yeah well . . . it must be too dark in here.

FINN: Yeah.

EMMA: It really hurt.

FINN: (*beat*) Which group are you with?

EMMA: The Royal, and you?

FINN: St Mary's.

EMMA: Oh.

FINN: We shouldn't be talking so.

EMMA: No.

FINN: Do you want me to sit over there?

EMMA: No (*beat*) I'm afraid . . . of the dark . . .

FINN: Okay. (*sits a bit closer*)

EMMA: Didn't say you could sit beside me.

FINN: (*not moving, beat, pulls up the leg of his trousers again*) Which room were you in?

EMMA: I was in the hallway. (*beat, awkward silence*) My favourite one is in the hallway.

FINN: Favourite what?

EMMA: Painting.

FINN: Which one?

EMMA: The one with the girl in the beautiful red dress, and she's trapped beneath the ground, in hell, I think . . . and you can see her lover above the earth and he's trying to get down to where she is to save her but he has to get across this river to get there and . . . I can't remember the rest of the story . . . but she's beautiful . . . has lovely straight blonde hair . . . and blue eyes . . .

FINN: I don't remember it.

EMMA: Weren't you listening to the guide?

FINN: No, was listening to this. (*holds up his walkman*)

EMMA: What is it?

FINN: Well I had a Pearl Jam tape in here but my Da must have switched it when I was having my breakfast.

EMMA: Switched it with what?

FINN: (*opens walkman and reads from tape*) Rebel Songs of Ireland . . . fuck sake . . . third time this week, too.

EMMA: (*beat*) Where is everyone?

FINN: You worried about your friends?

EMMA: (*beat*) Yeah.

FINN: I'm sure they'll be fine . . . they probably found a way out . . . don't worry . . . (*moves closer to her, puts an arm around her shoulder*)
Don't be sad . . . they'll come find us any minute. (*beat*)
Hey, how do know that ET is a Protestant?

EMMA: (*looking at him incredulously*) What?

FINN: How do you know ET is a Protestant?

EMMA: I don't know.

FINN: Cos' he looks like one . . . (*they both laugh*)

EMMA: That's terrible.

FINN: Sure, it's only an old joke.

EMMA: Okay, what's black and brown and looks good on a Catholic?

FINN: I dunno.

EMMA: A Rottweiler. (*EMMA laughs, FINN doesn't, he looks quite put out.*)
What?

FINN: That's not funny.

EMMA: Sure it's only a joke.

FINN: Yeah, but . . . it's a stupid joke.

EMMA: Ach, you're the one who started it. (*beat*) My Ma gave me money to buy a poster of that painting in the gift shop for my wall . . . (*beat*) I don't suppose there even is a gift shop anymore. (*beat*) What do you think happened?

FINN: (*sarcastic*) Fireworks—what you think happened?

EMMA: (*sighs*) Doesn't matter really anyway does it? That's what my Ma says, doesn't matter who does it, which side, all the same.

FINN: That's not what my Da says. (*takes his arm from around her*) Well, this place is full of Brit paintings and statues so . . . you know. (*shaking her head*) My Da will be rightly fucked off, he'll beat the head of someone when he finds out my school were in here.

EMMA: (*beat*) What does your Da do?

FINN: Electrician, yours?

EMMA: Shags waitresses in Manchester . . . I dunno . . . we don't see him anymore.

FINN: That's shit.

EMMA: Not really . . . I don't remember him, I know he had red hair, I know he used to eat pickles from a jar and always forget when the grill was on, I think he burnt the kitchen down five times . . . my sister remembers him . . . she's two years older . . . I think she misses him . . .

FINN: Is your Mam from Belfast?

EMMA: She's South African.

FINN: But . . .

EMMA: What? I'm not black? There are a lot of white people in South Africa you know.

FINN: I knew that.

EMMA: She says South Africa is the most scarred country in the world, she says Ireland's history is a walk in the park compared to South Africa . . .

FINN: They have Protestants in South Africa?

EMMA: I'm not a Protestant.

FINN: Then why are you in school at the Royal?

EMMA: We could have just as well gone to a Catholic school, I mean it made no difference, it's just the Royal was nearer to where the house was and my Mam sent us there . . . she doesn't care about anything to do with anything as regards what goes on around here, she came for the job.

FINN: You look like your Mam?

EMMA: Why?

FINN: No reason.

EMMA: (*beat*) Mam says she sees bits of Da in me but that's all right. (*big smile*) Cos' they're the bits she liked. (*smile vanishes*) I wish we'd never come here sometimes, it doesn't matter to us, it's sad and all, but shit happens, look at all the beautiful things that have been destroyed . . .

FINN: Yeah, but it's not about the paintings and stuff is it? It's about the bigger picture.

EMMA: Yeah, well I don't get the bigger picture . . . girl in my class' brother . . . just walking home one day and had a group of fella's jump on him, spray some stuff in his eyes and he's blind now . . . I mean what does he have to do with the bigger picture? . . . He's just a little boy who can't see now.

FINN: That's nothing, wee boy in Cookstown . . . just some boy, some young fella, minding his own business, they tied him to an electricity pole at the end of his Ma's garden and put nails driven through his feet and knees . . . (*beat*) crucifixion like . . .

EMMA: (*EMMA stares at him*) I know other stories.

FINN: So do I.

EMMA: (*beat, upset*) Yeah, well . . . I hate it . . . I . . . I don't know what it's about . . . I never know what to think.

FINN: About this?

EMMA: About . . . about everything . . .

FINN: Don't you care?

EMMA: Do you?

FINN: (*beat*) We should . . . well, I should.

EMMA: Do you?

FINN: (*uncomfortable, beat*) Maybe you don't have to know . . . exactly what you think about it . . . maybe it's just like the weather . . . when it's raining . . . it's just raining . . . fuck all you can do about it really.

EMMA: You curse a lot.

FINN: Sorry.

EMMA: S'okay, what's your name anyway?

FINN: Finn.

EMMA: Finn, I don't know any other Finns.

FINN: I'm not surprised (*beat*) It's Irish? After Fionn MacChumhail? (*Beat, EMMA looks at him blankly.*) You've never heard of Fionn

MacChumhail? (EMMA *shakes her head.*) Fuck's sake . . . he was . . . he was like an Irish superhero . . . kind of . . . anyway, he was brilliant. (*beat*) What's your name anyway?

EMMA: Emma (*holds out her hand in the darkness*) Well?

FINN: Well what?

EMMA: Aren't you going to shake my hand?

FINN: Oh . . . course . . . (*holds out his hand*) Finn.

EMMA: Emma. (*They shake hands and look at each other, the shake finishes but still hold on to one another's hands, beat.*) Where do you live?

FINN: Derry Lane, and you?

EMMA: Harrow Hill (*beat*) They'll probably take us to different hospitals . . . when they find us . . . they will come looking for us won't they?

FINN: Course they will.

EMMA: (*beat*) Suppose you won't talk to me, if you see me, out and about.

FINN: Course I will.

EMMA: Your Da wouldn't like it . . . your schoolmates wouldn't like it.

FINN: (*beat*) I don't care . . .

EMMA: Yeah right.

FINN: I don't . . . tell you what . . . I'll meet you if you like.

EMMA: Where?

FINN: Amm . . . ammm . . .

EMMA: See?

FINN: Okay . . . you know Kettle Street?

EMMA: Yeah.

FINN: You know the bridge at the end of it?

EMMA: Think so.

FINN: Me and my mates go drinking under it sometimes . . .

EMMA: You want to meet me under a bridge?

FINN: Well it's good enough for me and my mates (*beat*) You scared?

EMMA: Of you? Don't make me laugh.

FINN: So you'll meet me then?

EMMA: When?

FINN: Thursday, after school?

EMMA: I might. (*beat*) No noise for a while . . . you think we should go look for the others?

FINN: I suppose. (*beat*) Or we could stay here for a minute. (*beat*) You want to stay here for a minute? Like this? You're not afraid?

EMMA: No. (*Reaching out she takes his hand.*) No, not anymore.

(*A loud explosion from above startles them. She buries her face in his shoulder. He's frightened, too, but he tries to be the brave man.*)

FINN: (*stroking her hair*) Don't worry, it'll be okay, you're okay.

(*Another explosion, lights down.*)

Scene Three

(*FINN addresses audience.*)

FINN: For all that week,
for the rest of it until the Thursday,
I didn't cut myself once.

I mean my Da was the exact same, no, worse now that I had been inside the gallery when the bomb went off.

Took it as some kind of personal insult, not that he gave a shit about the thirteen stitches in my leg. (*beat*) Pretty big fuck up for them to make, over a hundred killed.

He broke everything in the kitchen and then the Doyle's complained and we even had the police around. Told him he was disturbing the peace, if my Mam didn't have him caught by the shirt he would have probably swung for them too. (*Beat, tries to clear his head.*)

But the point is, even when I was alone, and had the time and the space, I didn't cut.

Had a fresh pack of blades and everything,
just didn't feel like I needed it.

I counted the days instead,
thought maybe she wouldn't be there,
thought maybe she'd told someone and they told her who my Da is, maybe she met someone else, maybe she was just scared that day and wouldn't have looked twice at me otherwise.

But she did, and that morning when I clean the steam from the mirror and look at myself, I'm not looking too bad I think, not so bad.

Then heading out the door that morning he starts, and I don't even argue, take the tape out of the player myself and switch it with his. And I tell him . . . have a good day. (*beat*)

Not even he can ruin this for me.

Scene Four

(*Under the bridge.* FINN *and* EMMA *stand awkwardly.*)

FINN: (*anxious*) I thought you weren't coming.

EMMA: I'm sorry.

FINN: You said half four, it's almost five.

EMMA: I know, I'm sorry.

FINN: I've been here since four, just in case, in case you were early.

EMMA: I'm sorry, I had swim practice.

FINN: (*trying to impress*) Oh, I'm on the football team at school.

EMMA: I can play soccer.

FINN: Not soccer, football.

EMMA: Football . . . soccer . . . same thing.

FINN: Is not.

EMMA: What's the difference?

FINN: The difference is . . . if I played soccer in St Mary's I'd be kicked out.

EMMA: But you just said—

FINN: Gaelic football.

EMMA: But you said the other day you were a Liverpool fan.

FINN: Yeah, but Jesus Christ—it's not like I tell anyone.

EMMA: (*beat*) It's stupid.

FINN: Can't teach old dogs new tricks.

EMMA: No, but you can put them down if they're crazy. (FINN *looks upset.*) Did you hear the bombing was a mistake?

FINN: Yeah.

EMMA: Meant for a government building down the road, there wouldn't have been so many killed if the police hadn't got people off the streets and into the gallery . . . we were lucky.

FINN: I guess.

EMMA: Let's not talk about it anymore. I didn't even know this place was here, I dunno how many times I've walked over this bridge and I've never even looked down here. How did you know about it? Take another girl here did you? Before me?

FINN: I did and my arse.

EMMA: It's beautiful, the water looks so clear, you think it gets very deep when the tide comes in?

FINN: Ach, no . . . not very . . .

EMMA: Not enough to swim in?

FINN: No, not enough to swim in.

EMMA: Are you a good swimmer?

FINN: Brilliant, saved Jacki from drowning once.

EMMA: Really?

FINN: Really, he was on a deck chair beside the pool in Majorca, don't know how he managed it but next thing he was in the water.

EMMA: He jumped in?

FINN: He couldn't, not on his own . . . (*beat*) no . . . not on his own.

EMMA: Would you save me?

FINN: Course I would.

EMMA: Really?

FINN: Really.

EMMA: (*beat, quietly*) Did you tell your Da about me?

FINN: I don't tell my Da anything.

EMMA: I told my Mam all about you.

FINN: Not a lot to tell.

EMMA: I think there's plenty. (*beat*) What happened to your arms?

FINN: (*Self consciously pulling down his sleeves.*) I fell.

EMMA: No, you didn't.

FINN: I did, off my bike.

EMMA: Show me.

FINN: It's nothing.

EMMA: Please. (*FINN reluctantly pulls up his sleeve and shows her the bright red scars on his arm.*) Are these all over? (*FINN nods*) Why?

FINN: Can't explain.

EMMA: Try?

FINN: You wouldn't understand.

EMMA: I want to.

FINN: It's just . . . it's just a thing I do . . . when I'm . . . you know . . . bored or . . . whatever.

EMMA: (*reaches out and holds his hand*) Really, why?

FINN: I dunno . . . (*EMMA hugs him tightly.*) I dunno.

EMMA: Do you love me?

FINN: What? I've just met you.

EMMA: I know . . . but . . . you've been in my head all week . . . I missed you . . . I couldn't sleep some nights . . . I think I might love you a little bit.

FINN: Oh.

EMMA: Do you love me do you think? Even a wee bit?

FINN: I . . . I suppose.
EMMA: How long will you love me for . . . do ya think?
FINN: Jesus . . . .I dunno . . .
EMMA: Ask me then.
FINN: Ask what?
EMMA: Ask how long I'm going to love you for?
FINN: How long?
EMMA: (*beat, takes her face in his hands*) Forever.
FINN: Forever?
EMMA: Forever.

Scene Five

(*Two years later. FINN addresses audience.*)

FINN: It's my eighteenth birthday today. I'm supposed to be spending it with her, but my Da told me he was taking me for a drive and I know by the tone of his voice it won't do any good to argue. I know where we're going but not how to get out of it, my hands are shaking when I tie my laces, and my voice is shaking when I tell my mother we're only going to the pub. She irons my shirt and pushes a five pound note into the pocket, telling me to stay out of the fighting establishments and to buy a nice girl a drink. It's December, cold, I can see the Doyles putting up their Christmas tree, look like a happy family from here . . . you wouldn't think they're as fucked up as they are from here. The car that picks us up at the corner of Deer Street is an old Ford, Frank Molloy at the wheel, I've met him once or twice. Big bear of a man. We don't speak until we stop outside the house. It's in darkness except for the front room. I can see a young boy in an Arsenal shirt ten sizes too big for him sat in front of a telly. There's a man on the couch, a woman at the sink in the kitchen. (*beat*)

I am only the lookout and even though it is over in seconds, there is still blood on my shirt. In the car Frank slaps my back and laughs and I'm sick all over the back seat. Da is mortified, I search my pockets for a tissue to wipe my face but there is only my Mam's fiver, folded neatly into squares. (*beat*) When I meet her a few hours later, I use it to buy her a drink in the bar of a hotel where no one knows us, a glass of cider and a packet of crisps, two red fingerprints of that man's blood over the queen's face.

(*beat, tries to smile*) At least I did that much anyway. (*beat*) I bought a nice girl a drink.

Scene Six

(*Under the bridge. One year later.* EMMA *sits by the river.* FINN *creeps up behind her with a bunch of flowers, places his hands over her eyes.*)

EMMA: You're late. (*pulling his hands from her face*)

FINN: (*presenting the flowers flamboyantly*) For the lovely lady.

EMMA: (*smelling them*) Ach, they're beautiful, really, thanks.

FINN: (*hands her a huge oversized card, she takes it, softening*) Was the biggest one they had . . . Happy anniversary.

EMMA: You shouldn't have bothered.

FINN: Oh, aye I shouldn't have . . . and be skinned alive for not bothering.

EMMA: Aye you would be . . .

FINN: (*hands her a cardboard poster roll*) And this . . .

EMMA: (*takes it, excitedly*) Oh . . . what is it? What is it?

FINN: Open it up.

EMMA: (*She opens the roll and discovers a print of the painting she loves.*) My painting . . . how did you . . . where did you get it?

FINN: Sent away for it, you like it?

EMMA: I love it, thank you. (*kisses him, then she takes a card from her bag along with a small black box, handing it to him*) Here.

FINN: (*taking it*) Thanks. (*opens the box and takes out a gold chain with half a gold heart unsure how to react*) A necklace?

EMMA: (*shows him an identical chain hanging around her own neck*) I have the other half, see?

FINN: Oh, right.

EMMA: You like it?

FINN: Can a boy wear a necklace?

EMMA: (*annoyed*) Of course . . . you'll wear it always?

FINN: Always, (*beat*) except during football. (*EMMA looks upset.*) It might get broken! I'll wear it all of the other time I promise, okay?

EMMA: Okay. (*They hug and kiss.*) Finn.

FINN: Yeah?

EMMA: I called last night.

FINN: You did?

EMMA: They said you weren't there.

FINN: Who said?

EMMA: Your Da said.

FINN: (*annoyed*) I told you to hang up when he answers . . .

EMMA: (*surprised at his anger*) I forgot. (*beat*) I'm sorry . . . I hadn't seen you in a week . . . I just wanted to talk to you . . . I was lonely.

FINN: It's important . . . look . . . never mind . . . you'll know the next time.

EMMA: Where were you?

FINN: Upstairs . . .

EMMA: Oh.

FINN: He was in bad form last night. (*EMMA looks upset, then smells her flowers and smiles, FINN notices marks on her arms, she's shocked.*) What . . . what happened to your arms?

EMMA: Nothing.

FINN: They're all marked, what happened?

EMMA: Nothing . . . I was shaving my legs . . . I slipped . . . it doesn't hurt.

FINN: (*beat*) What did you do?

EMMA: (*beat*) Don't be cross Finn . . . please. (*beat*) They are just like yours look (*pulls up her sleeve*)

FINN: (*upset*) What you go and do that for?

EMMA: (*hurt*) Because I wanted to . . . I thought you'd be happy.

FINN: Why would I be happy that you've hurt yourself?

EMMA: Because . . . I wanted to . . . I wanted to feel what you feel.

FINN: (*beat*) Promise me you won't do this again . . . promise me.

EMMA: But I like it . . . I want to . . . I know what you're talking about now . . . its way better than drink.

FINN: (*passing his hands over the marks*) Promise me you won't do this again.

EMMA: What's the matter with you? Its okay for you but it's not all right for me? I'm not a little girl you know? I like it, I get it now, I didn't understand before but I get it now, I get why you do it.

FINN: You don't.

EMMA: I do . . . I do now . . . I get it now . . .

FINN: I do it because of him. (*beat*) Promise me.

EMMA: Okay . . . Okay . . . No need to get so upset . . . I promise . . . okay? It's all right . . . I just wanted to feel . . . what you do . . . I never get to see you anymore . . . I . . . I—

FINN: I better go . . . He thinks I'm at study.

EMMA: (*disappointed*) But you've only just arrived. (*beat*) My Mam wants to meet you. (*FINN says nothing.*) It's been years she wants to meet you. (*beat*) Don't worry about us, we'll be fine.

FINN: (*shakes his head*) I've promised him now, I've told him I don't see you . . . Look I do want to meet her . . . I do, I would, it's just, it's everything else.

EMMA: Everyone else you mean? (*Beat, FINN looks away.*)

FINN: I better go.

EMMA: See you tomorrow.

FINN: Actually, I can't.

EMMA: But we always—

FINN: I said can't.

EMMA: Alright, Wednesday? (*beat*) Finn? (*beat*) Love?

FINN: Wednesday.

Scene Seven

(*EMMA addresses the audience, tries to keep upbeat, as if it's really not that bad, but it's the worst thing she can imagine.*)

EMMA: Finn, I mean 'Dear Finn', gosh, I've never written you a letter before, feels weird. (*formal*) I hope that you are well . . . (*softening*) you've probably been wondering where I've been . . . well . . . the thing is . . . I have a lot to tell you . . . about Tuesday . . . (*rambling, not wanting to get to story straight away*) Tuesday my Mam made lasagne, I love lasagne, she seemed happy, most evenings she goes to her room early enough and Rachel and I watch MTV, I guess she's sad a lot, but when I got home from school she was singing in the kitchen and that's always a good sign, a sign she's had a good day, and we'll have a good evening . . . while the dinner was in the oven I helped her put a rinse in her hair and Rachel was telling us about a mad lecturer she has at college and we were laughing and she let me have a half glass of wine while we waited to wash it out, and Rachel a full one, says she'd rather us drink in front of her than behind her back, and she smoked those long cigarettes she likes and after we had the lasagne we sat together on the sofa and watched some stupid comedy where some guy was at a party and he kept breaking things and falling over and ordinarily . . . it wouldn't have seemed so funny but we were in great form and maybe the wine had gone to my head but it seemed like the best night in ages . . . (*beat*) in absolutely ages.

(*beat, change of mood*) I was in bed when they came around, knocked on the door real polite, woke me, woke Rachel, she looked across at me.

'I bet you it's about Da', she said, 'I bet you he's dead', but it wasn't about Da. (*beat*) Mam answered the door, there were two of them, and they spoke in a low voice, we sat on the stairs listening . . . when they said your name I tried to go down but Rachel held on to me, they weren't shouting, not threatening, just telling her in calm quiet words how your Da would appreciate it if she kept a closer eye on my after school activities. I wanted to scream, I bit Rachel's hand over my mouth and kicked at her until I heard my Mam, assuring them she would be collecting me from now on, herself, from the school gates.

And then the door closed and Rachel held me until I'd soaked her pyjamas through with crying and Mam walked up the stairs past us, like we weren't even there, didn't say a word, like saying something would be admitting what had just happened, would make it real. And after school the next day she was outside, waiting for me . . . so I couldn't come and meet you . . . so I'm leaving this here hoping you might come down here like I do . . . I don't know what we're going to do now Finn? (*beat*) What are we gonna do?

Scene Eight

(*FINN addresses audience.*)

FINN: She's not here. (*beat*) Every Wednesday for three years she was but now she isn't, and the first thing I feel is a kind of relief. (*beat*) But it doesn't last long, seconds only. And then I'm left with the thought that maybe I won't see her again, maybe she's had enough. And I want to make it stop, but I can't, and I'm sitting there crying like a baby into the dirty water and I want it to stop. I see an empty beer bottle lying among the stones and without even thinking I smash it . . . into tiny brown pieces and pick one up and I begin to cut . . . just enough to make the pain stop . . . just enough to get some relief.

Scene Nine

(*EMMA addresses audience, her arms are covered in deep red welts.*)

EMMA: Dear Finn, I've been checking any time I can to see if you've left anything for me here, (*beat*) but you haven't. I'm hoping that the wind is blowing them away or that the tide is coming in deeper these days and floating it away . . . I'm afraid to think there is another reason. (*beat*) I don't want to think of there being another reason. (*beat*) I'm useless without you. (*beat*) I'm lonely and alone and I hate my family and I swear I'll run away if you still want to, I'll go wherever you want to go.

Please, give me something. Even if you call the house and hang up at least I'll know it's you?

Please?

I've had my birthday, and the flu, and I drank a bottle of my Mam's wine and got sick in the shower . . . I did all these things without you.

Next Friday, it'll be three years since the gallery and . . . and I'll be here.

I'll be here all day.

I'll wait for you here.

All day.

Yours, always,

Emma.

Scene Ten

(*FINN addresses audience.*)

FINN: Things change, when the hospital rang to say that Jacki had been found on the steps of the swimming pool, beaten, badly beaten, I lost all faith in everything. My Da knew in minutes who had done it and then there we were, in the back of some dirty Hi-Ace van heading through the city and I wasn't even afraid. Not even the smallest bit nervous, just high on it all, cutting all the while with a tip of a safety pin I'd found back in the house, onto the side of my arm, f-u-c-k-e-r-s. That's what they are. Fuckers. Biding the time, thriving on the rush to punch the fucking daylights out of whatever monster would do that to a helpless boy, a boy who can hardly walk.

Turns out there are only three of them, they're fourteen at most, I see my Da go for the smallest guy with the bat he's holding and I only hold back for an instant, a microsecond, and then I fall in. (*As he says these words he mimes kicking, and punching and stamping on the boys.*)

The sea, oh, the sea is the grá geal mo chroí, long may it stay between England and me, it's a sure guarantee that some hour we'll be free, thank God we're surrounded by water.

(*out of breath*)

And it's over,
and they look like children's bodies . . . I can't look away.
My Da has to pull me back into the van,
I'm sick all over my boots.
I'm . . . I'm beyond it now . . . I've crossed the line

Scene Eleven

(*Under the bridge,* EMMA *sits cutting her arms slowly with a small penknife.* FINN *arrives, covered in blood and bruised.*)

EMMA: I thought you wouldn't come . . . what happened? Did someone jump you? Oh fuck . . . tell me what to do . . . what can I do?

FINN: Nothing.

EMMA: Did you get my letters?

FINN: Yes.

EMMA: Why didn't you . . . you should have . . .

FINN: I didn't want to get you in trouble . . . in any more trouble.

EMMA: Who did this? Did your Da do this?

FINN: Not this time.

EMMA: What happened?

FINN: They got Jacki . . . they broke his legs.

EMMA: Jesus.

FINN: I don't want to think about it . . . I don't want to . . . it doesn't matter . . . you matter . . . I missed you.

EMMA: I missed you more . . . so much more . . . I . . .

FINN: Your arms . . .

EMMA: Your arms . . .

FINN: (*upset, almost hysterical*) What are we going to do? Look at us . . . what the fuck are we going to do?

EMMA: I meant what I said . . . I'll go anytime you want to go.

FINN: Where?

EMMA: Any fucking where . . . away from here . . . away from this shit . . . don't you want to go away Finn? Haven't you had enough of this . . . this . . . everything?

FINN: Yes.

EMMA: Yes what?

FINN: Yes.
EMMA: When?
FINN: Now . . . let's go now . . .
EMMA: You mean it?
FINN: I do.
EMMA: We need to get a doctor—
FINN: No . . . no . . . just . . . I can't go anywhere in this shirt . . . I'll get picked up . . . you'll have to go and get me a clean one.
EMMA: I don't want to leave you on your own—
FINN: I'm not going anywhere . . . I'll be here.
EMMA: You promise?
FINN: Aye, I promise.
EMMA: I'll get us some cash, too, and some food, you hungry?
FINN: Not really.
EMMA: (*trying to make light of it*) You're always hungry
FINN: Not today.
EMMA: (*covering him with kisses*) I'll be a half hour . . . no longer . . . I promise . . . I love you . . . things are going to get better for us . . . you'll see . . . I promise Finn . . . I promise.

(*Exit* EMMA.)

FINN: I don't think about it,
I sit,
Look around this place,
wash the blood from my hands,
and it builds slowly at first.

All the little pieces that have led to me being in this place at this time,
and it all seems to make sense, mad clear sense.

I pick up her penknife and turn it over in my hands thinking, my head throbbing from the boot of one of those children we've left to bleed into the concrete, and there's suddenly too much, too much to deal with.

And what's the point of starting something new when chances are it will only be ripped from me again?

I press the blade against the skin and push, but it's not like before, not like I can judge how much is just enough. Not like I want to judge it, and I'm suddenly unbelievably tired, I just want to lie down.

On my back, let the water soothe the banging of my head,
on my back,
in the same place where we used to come to love,

only now, now I want to be two feet under, with the river things, and I can't feel my arms or legs . . . I can't feel anything.

And I see your painting with the lover trying to come and save her from the underworld, I wonder if you're far from here now.

I wonder if you're running . . .
and the water rises . . .
and I even hold my breath and think I see you coming,
and the line is running through my mind . . .
thank god we're surrounded by water . . .
(*beat*) and the light from the sky goes out . . .
(*beat*) and I'm in the dark.

I'm waiting to be rescued,
I'm waiting for you.

(*Slow fade to black*)

The End

INTRODUCTION TO DONAL O'KELLY'S

The Cambria (2005)

CHARLOTTE MCIVOR AND MATTHEW SPANGLER

In 2005, actor and playwright Donal O'Kelly premiered his two-person play *The Cambria,* a fictional recreation of Frederick Douglass' 1845 journey to Ireland from Boston Harbour on a ship of the same name. After spending one night in Liverpool, Douglass stayed six months in Ireland, travelling and speaking throughout the country on slavery and temperance. Since its premiere, O'Kelly has performed the play with actress Sorcha Fox at various venues in Ireland, the UK, and the US. In particular, the election of President Barack Obama in 2008 spurred two runs of *The Cambria* in New York at the Irish Arts Center in 2009 in partnership with the Classical Theatre of Harlem. The second run paired O'Kelly with African–American performer Roger Guenveur Smith's *Frederick Douglass Now* in repertory, with the pair winning the Black and Green award from New York-based newspaper, *The Irish Echo,* an award that celebrates connections between African–Americans and Irish America. In summer 2012, O'Kelly and Fox performed the play in Harare, Zimbabwe and Lusaka, Zambia.

In *The Cambria,* O'Kelly and Fox embody the story of Douglass' sea crossing by shifting seamlessly, with the aid of minimal props and costumes, between a large cast of characters, including: Captain Judkins, the British son of a former slave owner; Solomon, a West Indian seaman; Dignam, an Irish sailor; Cecily, a Northern Quaker choir leader; and Dodd, a Southern plantation owner, and his daughter Matilda. O'Kelly plays Douglass throughout, in addition to Dodd, O'Connell and Judkins; Fox plays Dignam, Cecily, Matilda, Solomon and Judkins. The play notably begins and ends with the story of a contemporary Irish secondary school history teacher mourning the deportation of her Nigerian student, Patrick, in Dublin airport in the company of a sympathetic workman. She tells the man the story of Frederick Douglass in Ireland as a gesture of hope and as a possible model for different approaches to the asylum process in Ireland today.

With the 1994 premiere of *Asylum! Asylum!*, O'Kelly became the first playwright in Ireland to tackle themes of immigration, racism and the asylum process not only in the Irish theatre, but within the space of the National Theatre, onstage, at the Peacock. Multiple resonances exist between *Asylum! Asylum!* and *The Cambria*: black male protagonists, a specific focus on asylum as not only a legal, but a political process, and a focus on violence and, more precisely, torture as the consequence of prejudice and ineffective or biased juridical systems. The biggest departure between *Asylum! Asylum!* and *The Cambria* is the temporal jumps made possible by the nesting of Douglass' story within a contemporary scenario. Through this move, O'Kelly forces a recognition of broader histories of asylum and blackness within Ireland, in addition to raising the spectre of the often uneven participation in the abolitionist movement of the Irish and Irish–Americans.

As noted in the introduction, O'Kelly (along with Charlie O'Neill) was one of the co-founders of Calypso Productions, which would later be helmed by Bairbre Ní Chaoimh (also interviewed in this volume). O'Kelly's commitment to social justice animated his founding of Calypso, as well as the writing of plays like *Asylum! Asylum!* and *The Cambria*. To this day, his politics continue to motivate his still evolving body of work and activist practice. He serves, for example, as Associate Director of the peace and justice organisation, Afri, while he continues to write and perform dramatic work that explicitly tackles a range of social justice issues. For Calypso, he also wrote *Trickledown Town* (1994), *The Business of Blood* (1995) and *Farawayan* (1998). While *Farawayan* also dealt with the issue of asylum, *Trickledown Town* and *The Business of Blood* engage with issues of structural inequalities, poverty and corruption in a wider transnational and thematic context. One of O'Kelly's most recent works, *Aillíliú Fionnuala* (2012), juxtaposes allegations about corruption within the Shell Corporation with poignant reflection on Ireland's own national history of systemic abuses through collaborations between the Catholic Church and Irish state, particularly abuses against children.

O'Kelly's other solo plays that have toured internationally include the award-winning *Catalpa* (1996) (Edinburgh Fringe First, London Time Out Critics' Choice, Best Event Melbourne International Festival), *Bat The Father Rabbit The Son* (1988) (Best Writer and Best Actor nominations Irish Theatre Awards), and *Jimmy Joyced!* (2004)

(Best Actor nomination Irish Theatre Awards). He has starred in films including Roddy Doyle's *The Van* (1996) and the bilingual film adaptation (2007) of Jimmy Murphy's play *Kings of the Kilburn High Road* (2000). He has also appeared frequently onstage at both the Abbey and the Peacock, as well as touring internationally to New York's Lincoln Center and Toronto's Winter Gardens. He founded his own production company, Donal O'Kelly Productions, more recently renaming it Benbo Productions. Benbo Productions is now co-directed by O'Kelly and collaborator, Sorcha Fox. O'Kelly's energetic and wide-ranging career as a performer and playwright, but perhaps more importantly, his continuing and unequivocal commitment to producing political theatre affords him a unique position amongst his contemporaries.

The Cambria

FREDERICK DOUGLASS' VOYAGE TO IRELAND 1845

DONAL O'KELLY

The Cambria opened in Liberty Hall Dublin on St Patrick's Day, 17 March 2005.

CAST

Collette	Sorcha Fox
Vincent	Donal O'Kelly

PRODUCTION TEAM

Director	Raymond Keane
Designer	Miriam Duffy
Music and Sound Design	Trevor Knight
Lighting	Nick Anton
Producers	Maria Fleming and Donal O'Kelly

CHARACTERS

The Cambria is performed by two actors, one male, one female.

It starts in present-day Ireland. This is the springboard into the story of Frederick Douglass' voyage to Ireland aboard the Cambria in 1845.

The play is written to facilitate the following role-playing:

Colette plays Dignam, Cecily, Matilda, Solomon and Captain Judkins.

Vincent plays Frederick, Dodd, Daniel O'Connell and Captain Judkins.

Section One

(Airport environment. COLETTE *sits, quietly, deeply upset.* VINCENT, *dressed in painter's overalls, enters with steps and ropes. A couple of glances as he sets up for painting job.*
Bing-bong! The airport PA sounds.)

COLETTE: I said, please.

VINCENT: I'm going to have to move you in a bit.

COLETTE: Patrick's been deported.

VINCENT: Aw, you're looking for immigration. They're all gone. I'm painting it.

COLETTE: 'I know it's hard. But the law is the law. The papers are signed. He's got to go. That's it.'

VINCENT: Sorry?

COLETTE: I had my speech prepared. Angry. Too late. But I gave it to him anyway.

VINCENT: Have you been here a while? . . .

COLETTE: 'Think of where you come from, generations of Irish flung around the globe . . .' But—no use. The plane was gone to Lagos. Nigeria. Chartered direct.

VINCENT: There's no one here to talk to. They're all gone.

COLETTE: And Patrick was on it. On his own, strapped in his seat. Looking out at the lights of Dublin, getting smaller, then the black of the Irish Sea. Patrick's party piece:—Robert Emmet's Speech from the dock. 'When Ireland takes her place, among the nations of the earth, then and only then, let my epitaph be writ-*ten*!' Patrick got a B in Honours History. He played Saint Patrick in the school pageant.

VINCENT: Nigerian? . . .

COLETTE: I'm a history teacher. In O'Connell's Schools. Of all places. Daniel O'Connell laid the stone himself. We walk upon it every day. Somewhere underneath. Patrick walked upon it every day. Swaggered. Vain. A terrible nuisance when he wanted. Like most of the bright ones. He drove me mad sometimes. Because I tried to help him. Tried to steer him through the interviews, gathered letters of support, why he should stay, the potential value of his talents. Got TDs and councillors to inquire about his case. To express concern. To ask for—clemency.

(*pause*)
That's what it's come to. 'Please.' But . . . power concedes nothing without demand. It never did. And it never will. That's what Frederick Douglass said.

VINCENT: Who's Frederick Douglass?

COLETTE: Frederick Douglass came to Ireland. On a ship. Called *The Cambria* . . . if Frederick Douglass . . . came to Ireland NOW . . .

(*COLETTE takes VINCENT's cap and puts it on her head. COLETTE and VINCENT both morph into CAPTAIN JUDKINS of* The Cambria *in Boston Harbour, 1845.*)

COLETTE: Merchant sea-captain Charles Judkins. At. Your. Service. Served ten years on the Boston–Cork–Liverpool line. Commanding the paddle-steamer *Cambria,* one thousand horse-power engines with four masts for sail-power—

JUDDY: (*looking up*) Magnificent!

COLETTE: —one of Mister Cunard's world-famous fleet. It's the sixteenth of August 1845.

Both: Grey skies above. Impending rain.

JUDDY: White horses visible out beyond the shelter of the Boston Docks breakwater.

COLETTE: Seagulls squawk.

VINCENT: Kwaawk! Kwaawk!

COLETTE: Whistle-spin klaxon-parp.

VINCENT: Cu-nard!

COLETTE: Passengers embark . . . passengers embark . . .

VINCENT: Cargo—load . . . cargo—load . . .

COLETTE: Canvas flaps

VINCENT: Seawater splops

COLETTE: Passengers embark gangplank chain shakes chain shakes.

(*VINCENT morphs into FREDERICK.*)

FREDERICK: Captain! Can you show me where my cabin is?
(*pause*)

JUDDY: Black. The fellow's black.
Ticket please . . .
First class, by Jove! Mister Johnson it says. He waves to some gentlemen friends on the dockside—

Well dressed, fashionable frockcoat, smell of starch from his shirt, penetrating eyes . . .

This way sir. Up to the saloon deck.

Not my job to escort passengers—but I'm so taken aback I'm doing it before giving it a second thought.

FREDERICK: A wonderful day for setting sail, Captain.

JUDDY: Wait until we hit the open sea, Mister Johnson.

FREDERICK: I've never been on the open sea. I'm looking forward to it.

JUDDY: Never been at sea!? You must have been mighty contented in your life on land!

(*pause—a look*)

FREDERICK: How long do you think the crossing will take?

JUDDY: The Blue Riband for fastest trans-Atlantic crossing is within our grasp. It belongs with the Cunard Line. And this ship *The Cambria* in particular.

If we take the prize I promise you champagne breakfast in Queenstown Cork! Your cabin, Mister Johnson.

Will you be joining me later at captain's table with the other first-class passengers?

FREDERICK: I think I'll stay in my cabin. But thank you.

JUDDY: Door-clunk. Thank God he's shy.

FREDERICK: I sit in the dim light of my cabin. I open my case. I take out the one and only copy of my book I've taken with me. I hold it up to my face and I press the open pages hard against my cheeks. I close my eyes.

DIGNAM: Door knock.

Your trunk sir. Trunk-edunk-edunk!

He's sitting with his back to me. He turns to take the trunk.

No, no, allow me!

FREDERICK: I have many times lifted heavier weights.

DIGNAM: (*aside*) I've only ever seen blacks in the crew. And certainly never on the saloon deck with all the posh gobshites! How the Hell did he square this!?

(*to* FREDERICK) Dignam's the name, sir; steward's the game, sir! Will you be requiring anything else, sir?

FREDERICK: A little privacy would be agreeable for the present.

DIGNAM: As you please, sir, no sooner said than—door-clunk.

The gangplank is lifted, the ropes are thrown—clunk

they land on the deck—Paarp and the tug-tug tugboat tugga-tug-tugs.

Tug-tug tugga-tugga tug-tug tugga-tugga
Tug-tug tugga-tugga tug-tug tugga-tugga . . .

Section Two

FREDERICK: It's dark in the cabin. I light the gaslamp. Mirror. Hello Mister Johnson! I decide I'm going to go out, damn it, to advance into the God-given light, to leave the darkness behind. I want to look at the coast of America fading away far astern. I want to shout and roar in the sea wind. I want to jump. I want to go and dance on the poopdeck, wherever the poopdeck is.

MATILDA: I push the cabin door. Hello.

FREDERICK: Oh. Hello little girl!

MATILDA: Do you sing and dance?

FREDERICK: Em—not normally.

MATILDA: But you're a minstrel, aren't you?

FREDERICK: Oh, no.

MATILDA: Oh, yes, you are.

FREDERICK: Oh, no, I'm not!

MATILDA: There! I told you so!

FREDERICK: I'm not a minstrel.

MATILDA: You are! Are you going to entertain us on the ship.

FREDERICK: No.

MATILDA: Oh, yes, you will!

FREDERICK: Oh, no, I won't!

MATILDA: Oh, yes, you will! What's in that box?

FREDERICK: . . . What's your name?

MATILDA: Matilda. I'm in the cabin next door. What's that?

FREDERICK: Oh, that! That's just a book.

MATILDA: Can I see it?

FREDERICK: Em . . . no. It's not a children's book.

MATILDA: Can I look at it?

FREDERICK: It's not the kind of book that you'd enjoy.

MATILDA: But can I look at it?

FREDERICK: Oh, alright. Do you read a lot?

MATILDA: Yes. I love reading.

(*pause*)

FREDERICK: I had a friend just like you when I was small. She taught me how to read.

MATILDA: Was she a teacher at my age?

FREDERICK: She didn't know she was a teacher. But she was. I copied her homework every night. When everyone was asleep. And no one ever knew.

MATILDA: Wow. My teacher doesn't let me copy. My daddy says the fairies scattered letters on me when I was a baby in the cradle. That's why I read so well.

FREDERICK: That's a—nice thing your daddy said. He must be a good man.

MATILDA: Of course, he is! He gave me this beautiful music box—for passing the time on the ship, he said. It has a little ballerina in it. And she twirls and dances to the music.

(*music box tinkle-tune*)

MATILDA: Look! There she is. My ballerina Mirabelle. Say hello.

FREDERICK: Hello, Mirabelle.

MATILDA: See! She bowed to you. She has very good manners.

FREDERICK: It's a beautiful music box. Your daddy must love you very much.

MATILDA: Of course, he does. She'll keep dancing until she gets tired. I feel sorry for her stuck in her box. But still. Daddy says that's her world, it's all she knows, so she's happy in there. Because she's never known anything different. Bye, Mirabelle.

(*Lid clunks shut. Music stops.*)

MATILDA: Oh look! The words in your book are easy! 'The Life of Frederick Douglass.' Can I show you how well I can read?

FREDERICK: Alright. Just a little bit.

MATILDA: 'I was born in Tuckahoe, near Easton, in Talbot County, Maryland. I have no accurate—know-ledge—'

FREDERICK: Very good, Matilda!

MATILDA: '—of my age. I never met with a slave who could tell me with any certainty how old he was.'

Oh! Why do the slaves not know what age they are?

FREDERICK: . . . Perhaps, the writer explains—read on . . .

MATILDA: 'Few at that time knew anything of the months of the year, or of the days of the month. They measured the ages of their children by springtime, wintertime, harvest-time, planting-time, and the like. Masters allowed no questions to be put to them by slaves concerning their ages. From certain events, however, the dates of which I have since learned, I suppose myself to have been born in February 1817.'

But that's terrible!

FREDERICK: I'm pleased to hear you say that Matilda!

MATILDA: I mean—what *date* in February!? When does he get his birthday presents!?

FREDERICK: Oh. I don't know. To tell you the truth, I think his presents come whenever he least expects them.

MATILDA: That is so cruel! But slaves are different. My daddy says they don't feel things as much as we do.

(*Silence from* FREDERICK.)

MATILDA: What's in the box behind you?

FREDERICK: Oh! That's—nothing much.

MATILDA: Oh, yes, it is!

FREDERICK: Oh, no—it's not!

MATILDA: It's your tricks box, isn't it!?

FREDERICK: No.

MATILDA: Oh, yes, it is! You've got all your funny things in there. My daddy brought me to see a black minstrel show. So funny! I know all about your box of tricks. Let me see inside!

FREDERICK: NO!

MATILDA: Oh, please! I want to see the tricks things!

FREDERICK: I don't have any tricks! I'm not a minstrel!

MATILDA: Oh, yes, you are!

(*Pause as* FREDERICK *takes a deep breath*.)

FREDERICK: Oh, I give in! What a clever little girl you are!

MATILDA: I knew it! Now show me your tricks box!

FREDERICK: But don't you know, Matilda, that a minstrel NEVER shows what's in his tricks box!?

MATILDA: Ooooo-oh!

(*Enter* HENRY DODD, *forties. Deep south plantation-owner.*)

DODD: What is the meaning of this?

MATILDA: Daddy!

FREDERICK: This little girl Matilda is just making my acquaintance sir.

DODD: What is the meaning of—you being in a cabin on the first class deck!?

FREDERICK: Well that's the result of my possessing a first-class ticket, sir.

MATILDA: Ha-ha! I knew you were funny!

DODD: What's your name?

FREDERICK: My name is Mister Johnson. And you?

DODD: There's something mighty strange about this.

MATILDA: He's my dada and our name is Dodd. I call him Dodda. And he calls me Dodda too—his dodda, his daughter you see? Daughta Dodda, Dodda daughta, daughta Dodda, Dodda daughta . . .

DODD: Ssh! Mister Johnson and I would like to discuss something in private Matilda. Leave Mirabelle back in our cabin!

MATILDA: Is that alright Mirabelle? Do you want to go back to our cabin? You're very lucky Dodda! She says yes.

(*MATILDA goes out the door.*)

DODD: (*quietly*) I don't like to jump to conclusions, but I do call a spade a spade. Where would you get the money to afford a first-class trans-Atlantic ticket!?

FREDERICK: Damned if I know. But a friend gave me the ticket.

DODD: A friend!? Must be quite a well-to-do friend!

FREDERICK: Yes.

DODD: You have been consorting with my daughter without my permission.

FREDERICK: Matilda is a delightful child. She came into my cabin and brightened my day. As I did hers, I think. She speaks very lovingly of you, sir.

DODD: Who do you think you are to talk to me like that?

FREDERICK: Your next door neighbour, it seems.

DODD: You display an arrogance which will be your downfall!

FREDERICK: I speak merely the truth. Arrogance was the furthest thing from my mind.

(*Running footsteps as MATILDA re-enters.*)

MATILDA: Dodda, he's a funny man. He has a tricks box, like the minstrels you brought me to see! He says Oh yes you will! And oh no you don't! You're going to do a show, aren't you Mister Johnson!? You'll do a show on the ship, won't you!? Please say yes!

DODD: Oh! So you're a showman!!

FREDERICK: Well, I'm—(*quietly*) yes. I do . . . shows.

DODD: You're a minstrel! Golly-wolly! (*laughs*) I see!

MATILDA: Look Dodda! I've been showing Mister Johnson how well I can read!

DODD: Good girl! From this book!? Let me see . . . is it a funny book?

FREDERICK: She just picked it up—

DODD: And what is it!? . . . *The Narrative of the Life of Frederick Douglass, an American Slave!*

FREDERICK: Oh, it was just lying here, and Matilda—

DODD: This is the new book of lies being read by naive folk in the Northern States who take it for the truth. You have been indoctrinating my daughter with this!!?

FREDERICK: No, sir! She just picked it up! In fact, I tried to dissuade her!

MATILDA: Yes, but I know how to get my way, don't I Dodda? Slaves don't know their birthdays! Imagine not knowing your birthday!

DODD: You interested in this kind of thing?

FREDERICK: I—don't know much about it. It was given to me. You may read it if you wish.

DODD: I have no such wish!

MATILDA: He was taught to read by a little girl the same age as me, Dodda.

DODD: Frederick Douglass my foot! The vagabond's name is Bailey. Frederick Augustus Washington Bailey!

MATILDA: Fawb!

DODD: What did you say!?

MATILDA: His initials—F-A-W-B. Fawbulous!

DODD: Good girl, go outside, Matilda! (*sotto voce*) He absconded from the property of Mister Hugh Auld, the shipbuilder of Baltimore Maryland!

MATILDA: (*going outside*) 'Water, water, everywhere,
And all the boards did shrink,
Water, water, everywhere . . .'

DODD: Well now he's written a book! He's raised his head. He'll be easy to find. Agents are hunting him down as we speak! A hefty price on his head I hear! Two thousand dollars! Dead or alive!

FREDERICK: Well, thank you for that information, Mister Dodd.

DODD: Matilda!

CREW: (*sing*)
Way, haul away, oh, haul away together,
Way, haul away, we'll haul away, Joe!
Way, haul away, we'll haul for better weather,
Way, haul away, we'll haul away, Joe!
Boston Cork Liverpool . . .
Boston Cork Liverpool . . .
(*shouts*) Foretopsail!
(*faraway*) Foretopsail!
(*shouts*) Maintopsail!
(*faraway*) Maintopsail!

FREDERICK: It's a marvellous sight to behold. Those sails away up there, flapping and unfurling and filling up with wind. I remember a time, on the shores of Chesapeake Bay, when I was a boy, watching the sailships . . . the Baltimore clippers . . . white sails billowing . . . sailing away . . .

CECILY: (*sings to same tune as crew*)
Sail, sail away, oh, sail away together,
Sail, sail away, we'll sail away, Joe!

(*CECILY HUTCHINSON, choirleader, coughs. She's an assertive, deep-voiced, Quaker Boston woman in her thirties.*)

CECILY: Oh, excuse me! Bloody cough! Since I came aboard! Driving me insane! (*cough*)

FREDERICK: Would you care to use my handkerchief?

CECILY: Thank you! My goodness! Who are you and what are you doing here!?

(*cough and nose-blow*)

FREDERICK: (*taken aback*) My name is Mister Johnston. I'm travelling to Ireland.

CECILY: To do what!?

FREDERICK: To—make some money!

CECILY: How noble.

FREDERICK: Indeed. It—makes the world go around, or so I've heard.

CECILY: Mammon rules in so many souls, I find.

FREDERICK: And may I be so bold as to inquire what brings you aboard Ma'am?

CECILY: We're on our way to Ireland to conduct a tour of singing engagements there.

FREDERICK: Your audiences will be well-pleased.

CECILY: Oh, don't flatter! The crew sound better! It's the dust in steerage. I feel like I'm bedding down in drydock. I can't go on like this! I'll have to see the captain!

CREW: (*sing*) Way, haul away, we'll haul away, Joe!

Section Three

(*CAPTAIN's Cabin*)

DODD: Captain Judkins, she's a wonderful ship, and bears out everything my good friend Cunard has told me about her.

JUDDY: You're a friend of Mister Cunard?

DODD: Very close! Look here—a letter he sent to me. 'My dear friend Dodd . . . signed with the greatest respect, Samuel Cunard.'

JUDDY: I'm pleased to meet you, Mister Dodd, and I hope you have a pleasant voyage on *The Cambria*. And a short one. We're chasing the Blue Riband—

DODD: Wonderful. I appreciate, Captain Judkins, you could not possibly have known Mister Johnson's race when you booked him into the cabin next to mine. However, now that it is an indisputable fact, there is clearly no other course of action than to send him to steerage forthwith!

JUDDY: He has a first-class ticket, Mister Dodd. It is an indisputable fact.

DODD: I have a proposal: I'm willing to offer a very generous fee—two hundred dollars—if Mister Johnson will perform his minstrel act on board ship. That should be more than sufficient to take the sting out of his transfer. Will you put it to him!?

JUDDY: It's not my place to—

DODD: I know. But it would spare all our blushes. Besides, the fellow will be happier among the lower orders. Believe me, I own five hundred slaves, and I know what I am talking about.

JUDDY: I'll see what can be done.

DODD: It's the principle, Captain! And I pride myself on being a man of principle. My grandfather built his dynasty on the motto 'Order is paramount'. A well-kept garden must be rigorously tended. With a pitchfork. So, in our social relations, order must be enforced.

JUDDY: No one knows the value of order better than the captain of a trans-Atlantic vessel, Mister Dodd.

DODD: Touché, as they say in New Orleans. We understand each other.

(*cut to* CAPTAIN*'s cabin, later*)

JUDDY: Sit down, Mister Johnson. I'm faced with a problem which I think you can help me solve. I have a passenger in steerage, a Miss Hutchinson, who is suffering a coughing sickness since we set sail. It seems something in the atmosphere below disagrees with her. She has delicate tubes, she says.

FREDERICK: I've met the lady. She's the choir-leader.

JUDDY: Indeed. And her voice is her fortune. She must protect it. What I propose is this—would you be willing to exchange places with her, so that she may reap the benefits of your first class cabin?

FREDERICK: Why me?

JUDDY: In return for agreeing to this exchange, I'm in a position to offer you two hundred dollars to perform your minstrel show before we drop anchor in Cork.

FREDERICK: What!?

JUDDY: Yes. Two hundred dollars!

(*pause*)

FREDERICK: You want me to perform . . . as a minstrel?

JUDDY: Amuse the passengers! Give us all a good laugh! Sometimes I think it's the greatest gift of all—to make people laugh.

FREDERICK: I'm not a! . . . Who's idea is this!?

JUDDY: It's em . . . well, the kind offer has come from Mister Dodd.

FREDERICK: My next door neighbour . . .

JUDDY: He's anxious to provide a show for his little daughter. He's hoping you'll—fit the bill. Will you swap places with

Miss Hutchinson in return for a fat performance fee?

FREDERICK: I will swap places with Miss Hutchinson for the good of her health. I will not perform a—minstrel—show!

(*pause*)

JUDDY: Are you sure, Mister Johnson? It's a very generous purse . . . I'd be tempted to try a song and dance myself for two hundred dollars.

FREDERICK: Well I'm not tempted in the least!

JUDDY: Very well. But you will vacate the cabin.

FREDERICK: Forthwith.

(*cut to:*)

DIGNAM: All the way down to steerage! Let me say, sir, how outraged I am that you're the one being moved. Outraged I am. I mean, the weight of this case! But they never think of the poor gobshite who has to carry it. Oh no I don't come into it! It wouldn't enter their heads when they're making their mighty decisions!

(*shouts*) Make way, make way! Thanking you, thanking you! We have a passenger needing accomodation.

(*to* FREDERICK) What's your name?

FREDERICK: My name is Mister Johnson.

DIGNAM: Here you! You're in steerage now! None of your airs and graces! What's your first name?

FREDERICK: (*through his teeth*) My first name is Frederick.

DIGNAM: Here's Freddie Johnson—

FREDERICK: There's no need to announce my business to every passenger on the ship!

DIGNAM: Oh! Shy, are we! They say the stage is the shy man's revenge. You keep it all bottled up inside, and then let rip once the curtain rises.

FREDERICK: Look—

DIGNAM: (*low voice*) I hear you're holdin' out! Good man!

FREDERICK: What!?

DIGNAM: (*low*) Holdin' out for a higher fee! Your man Dodd is desperate to keep the daughter happy. Hold your nerve! You'll rise him up a good bit!

FREDERICK: I have no intention—

DIGNAM: That's the spirit!

FREDERICK: I have no intention of—

DIGNAM: Spirit of Enterprise! Granny suckin eggs! Say no more! (*slams down trunk*)

There you are now Freddie! What the blazes have you got going clankedy-clank in that damn box!?

FREDERICK: Oh that's em . . . that's just my tricks box.

DIGNAM: Tricks box! Right! Goodnight Freddie! Goodnight all! Codladh samh as we say in the destitute parts of my land. Agus oiche mhaith! Yahoo! Mind the icebergs! If you see one, check it's not your pillow!

(*sings*) O Moon of Massachussetts, look down on us tonight . . .

FREDERICK: Mister Dignam, people are trying to sleep!

DIGNAM: Goodnight Herr Uten! Goodnight Frau Uten! (*whispers*) Hey Freddie! Try and make the Germans laugh! A guinea says I make the Germans laugh first. A guinea! Go on! You've got the edge and all! Mister professional minstrel!

FREDERICK: I am not a—

DIGNAM: Ah go on! Any jokes? Beware the Quaker choir ladies . . .

FREDERICK: My steerage berth is little more than a bunkbed with a curtain. I'm glad I was moved. I feel at home among the mish-mash of nationalities. I lie down. I draw the curtain.

(*at the* CAPTAIN'*s table*)

JUDDY: I'd like to welcome all you first-class passengers not only to my Captain's table, but also to this voyage across the Atlantic aboard the newest Cunard steamship *The Cambria*.

DODD: Thank you so much for inviting me to share your table, Captain Judkins, and to dine in the company of civilised and convivial gentlemen.

CECILY: (*firmly*) Hello!

DODD: Oh—and I'm pleased to make the acquaintance of Miss Hutchinson also.

CECILY: Thank you Captain Judkins for upgrading me to first-class. I feel so much better already.

JUDDY: My pleasure, Miss Hutchinson!

DODD: You're clearly a lady of refined manners. And we look forward to hearing your choir give us a sample of their dulcet tones before we cast anchor in Cork.

CECILY: I'm sure we could oblige, if that's your wish, Mister Dodd.

DIGNAM: Captain, a nice bit of breast or your usual Pope's nose?

JUDDY: A piece of leg and less lip, Dignam!

DIGNAM: Miss Cecily—a tender cutlet for you—ah-ah the plate is hot—allow me no-ow!

CECILY: Thank you.

DODD: Captain Judkins, may I take this opportunity to thank you for your prompt action in relation to the black minstrel scamp.

JUDDY: The matter's closed Mister Dodd—

CECILY: Sorry—?

DODD: It is an undeniable fact that the wealth of our entire nation depends on the preservation of order as enshrined in our God-given laws. Give a Negro an inch and he'll take your entire plantation! And allow me to add—your claret is excellent. May I declare a toast to the wisdom of our captain!

CECILY: Em—excuse me! Could I ask—. . .

DODD: Oh, I'm so sorry! Would Miss Hutchinson prefer to make the toast herself?

CECILY: Don't be stupid! Captain! Explain what action Mister Dodd is referring to!?

JUDDY: A man by the name of Johnston was berthed in what is now your cabin.

DODD: Ye-es—he has a tricks box! And we're all going to get a look at what's inside when he performs his minstrel act for us. My daughter can't wait!

CECILY: Minstrel?

JUDDY: Well, actually, Mister Dodd, he turned down your kind offer on that subject.

DODD: He turned down two hundred dollars!? What kind of minstrel is this!?

JUDDY: He was quite emphatic. Gravy, anyone?

DODD: Yes, please! Just on the duck. Well, that's mighty strange. I always thought these fellows would sing and dance at the drop of a hat, let alone two hundred dollars! Mighty strange! But the upshot of it is:—Miss Hutchinson, a choral performance on board ship garners you a purse of two hundred dollars!

CECILY: Two hundred dollars!? But that's—

DODD: Damn it, three hundred! It would please me greatly to bestow such a cultured occasion on the passengers of the *Cambria*.

CECILY: Captain! Did Mister Johnson move willingly to steerage?

JUDDY: Yes he did.

CECILY: And did he willingly turn down the performance fee?

JUDDY: Yes he did. Quite emphatically!

CECILY: But . . . why!?

JUDDY: He didn't say. Your guess is as good as mine. He mentioned that he met you earlier . . .

CECILY: Yes! On deck! He was . . . wait a minute! What's going on here!?

DODD: An excellent meal for one thing! The duck is superb!

CECILY: Captain! You're rather mute! Why was Mister Johnson the one to be sent to steerage!?

DODD: I get the distinct aroma of broiling Northern liberal . . .

JUDDY: I'm captain of this ship, Miss Hutchinson. I make decisions based on a range of considerations learnt over a lifetime at sea!

CECILY: Woohoo! Something's amiss! The captain's citing his record! Facts, Captain! I find them far more conclusive than posturing!

JUDDY: Excuse me! Posturing is the one thing that I—

DODD: A spade's a spade, Miss Hutchinson! I am an American! I will not tolerate being berthed next to a black in a first class cabin! It is contrary to the laws of our God-given nation!

CECILY: To some of it! Not to me! And I resent greatly, Captain Judkins, that I have been used to dress up your capitulation to slave law!

JUDDY: I did not capitulate to any such thing!

DODD: I fear your performance fee is slipping from your grasp, Miss Hutchinson.

CECILY: Keep your fee! Put it where you think best! I will not sit and dine with people who assume ownership of other human beings.

DODD: For their own good! Quite clearly!

CECILY: Poppycock!

JUDDY: Mister Johnson was not nearly so exercised about the matter as you clearly are. And he, after all, is black!

CECILY: You should be ashamed of yourself! You let yourself be directed by—the Pope's Nose sucker there, who measures his status by the number of people he claims to own!

DODD: Fee gone! Back to Mister Johnson with a higher offer, I fear! You, Miss Hutchinson, have been infected by the worst form of Northern humbug! Like it or not, slavery built your fine cities!

CECILY: No slaveholder will call me a humbug!

DODD: We would all much prefer if you would relax and converse with us in a civilised way. Reconsider your position, Miss Hutchinson, please! Your place is with us! Not the black fellow!

Section Four

CHOIR LADIES: (*singing/lilting*)

Meanwhile . . . down below . . . .
the ladies sing in harmony-oh . . . .
the ladies sing in harmony-oh . . .

FREDERICK: Pleasant as the choirladies' singing is, I have much on my mind, and long to be alone. I climb up to the afterdeck. The sea wind bites. I watch the coast of America fade away far astern. A burning sun sets. I turn to the bow. I face my future. Of freedom. I am racing towards it. Paddles chant my advance in the fastest vessel known to man. *The Cambria*. The paddles seem to mock me . . .

BOWSPRIT: (*carving through waves*) Mister Johnson, Mister Johnson, Johnson, Johnson the minstrel, Johnson the minstrel, the minstrel, the minstrel . . .

SOLOMON: Douglass! Frederick Douglass!

FREDERICK: Suddenly, a voice seems to call me from the clouds!

SOLOMON: Douglass! Frederick Douglass!

FREDERICK: Undoubtedly, it is coming from above!

SOLOMON: I'm in the crow's nest Fred!

FREDERICK: Solomon! What are you doing here!?

SOLOMON: Able seaman Solomon! At your service! What are you doing dressed up like a dog's dinner!? You don't look like the Freddie Douglass I used to know! I'm coming down now Freddie Douglass! Oh, the light shining out of you, Fre—

Sebastiao Mpembele Kamalandua in *Fall and Recover*
Photo by: Chris Nash

The cast of John Scott's *Fall and Recover* (some names altered to protect identity): Nina, Philip Connaughton, Noora, Meh, Ezekiel Bolinarwo, Sebastiao Kamalandua, Ali, Sylvia Achu Bih, Andre Wandji, Julie Chi, Kiribu, Florence Welalo, Saed, Aisling Doyle

Photo by: Mike Walker

The Company's *Politik* with (clockwise from middle) Nyree Yergainharsian, Robert McDermott, Stefanie Preissner and Brian Bennett

Photo by: Volker Beinhorn Fotografie

The Company's *as you are now so once were we with* (from left) Brian Bennett, Tanya Wilson, Nyree Yergainharsian and Robert McDermott

Photo by: Ros Kavanagh

Janusz Sheagall as Andrzej in Paul Meade's *Mushroom*

Photo by: Futoshi Sakauchi

Mazazi Nyapokoto working with Calypso Productions' Tower of Babel

Photo by: Tom Lawlor

Stephane Mbamba performs with the group from Calypso Productions' Tower of Babel
Photo by: Tom Lawlor

Donal O'Kelly and Sorcha Fox in *The Cambria*

Photo by: Susan Helbock Photography

Mirjana Rendulic as Tea in *Broken Promise Land*
Photo by: Matthew Smyth

Kasia Lech as Vica in Julia Holewi ska's *Bubble Revolution* (translated by Artur Zapałowski) for Polish Theatre Ireland

Photo by: Silver Merick

The Freetown Slashers prepare for battle in Charlie O'Neill's *Hurl*

Photo by: Ros Kavanagh

Performers from Upstate Theatre Project's *The Mango Tree*,
directed by Stephen Murray
Left Row (*from front to back*): Denise Geraghty, Mary Oki, Bianca Browne and Robert Carlos Tunde
Middle Row: Michael Duffy and Derek Cummins
Right Row: Sarah Bromley, Beauty Ogbewe and Thomas Segun
Photo by: Matt Dillon

FREDERICK: Good to see you, Solomon!

SOLOMON: Like the good ol' days in New Bedford! Caulking the whaling-ships, remember!? You and me the number one team! You taught me how to read! And you told me who I was and where I came from and how I should be proud! You great orator, you great leader, Fred–

FREDERICK: Solomon!

SOLOMON: What's the matter with you!?

FREDERICK: Stop calling me—Frederick Douglass!

SOLOMON: What's wrong Freddie? It's your name, isn't it? I remember the day you chose it! How you roared it! Like this: Behold F–

FREDERICK: Yes, but—. . . Look: I've written a book, with Frederick Douglass on the cover, and the slaveholders have put a price on my head. Two thousand dollars I'm told. You know the law. If someone points at me and says 'Frederick Douglass escaped slave', I'll be sent back in chains to Maryland! On this ship my name is Mister Johnson. It's a necessary lie. I'm a fugitive, Solomon!

SOLOMON: He-e-e-e-ey! (*louder*) He-e-e-e-ey!

FREDERICK: What!?

SOLOMON: You always said you'd tell your story! Frederick the Orator! Frederick the Author!

You told me one night deep in the hold of an old whaling-ship!

FREDERICK: I did?

SOLOMON: Ye-e-es you did! And you read from that book you had nailed to the beam while you pumped

'Then and only then—'

FREDERICK: 'let my epitaph be written.' Yes—Robert Emmet's Speech from the Dock!

SOLOMON: Your eyes are still the same even if you're dressed like a posh gobshite—

FREDERICK: A what?

SOLOMON: Derogatory term—Dignam the steward uses it a lot. Don't deny your name Frederick Doug–!

FREDERICK: Keep your voice down! Call me Mister Jonson!

SOLOMON: No! You set me on my path! I can't deny you! If I do I deny myself!

FREDERICK: Oh, for God's sake!

(CECILY *approaches*)

CECILY: (*from afar*) Mister Johnson!

FREDERICK: Remember what I said!

SOLOMON: I remember what you said! Back in New Bedford! 'Never forget the line of wronged heroes you are descended from!' That's what you said! I'm going below to my comrades in the hold! Goodnight—Mister Johnson! Aha! We peel da meat. Dey gib us da skin. An dat's de way, dey take us in. You told me that! Oh no—Frederick Douglass told me that!

CECILY: (*arriving*) Mister Johnson! I've heard the whole story! I want you to know I had nothing to do with your transfer to steerage! I find it indefensible, and I have told the Captain so!

FREDERICK: I have no need for your support, requested or otherwise. I am none of your business.

CECILY: I know you're a comic black minstrel, and per se uncommitted to the struggle of your people.

FREDERICK: What!?

CECILY: I have seen one of you perform—perhaps it was you—and I find the mocking of your own race for cheap laughs and a fat purse downright degrading. Be that as it may, you are as entitled as anyone to a first class cabin. You can have it back.

(*pause*)

FREDERICK: (*quietly, intensely*) I—am NOT—a minstrel.

CECILY: There's no need to deny your trade simply to avoid criticism—

FREDERICK: Have you ever heard—of Frederick Douglass?

CECILY: (*titters*) Frederick Douglass! Come now! Everyone who has ears to hear has heard of Frederick Douglass this past week . . .

FREDERICK: For almost thirty years Frederick Douglass lived his life—if such a phrase can be used—under the yoke of slavery, branded as a piece of property, worked as a beast of burden, whipped on the whim of an owner so-decreed by Law!

CECILY: Barbarous! I whole-heartedly a–

FREDERICK: Because of the colour of his skin. I am NOT going to be lectured by some haughty white lady about who I am or what I should do! Why don't you go back to your first class cabin and reflect a little on your sense of superiority that allows you to judge the actions of others you know NOTHING about! Goodnight Miss Hutchinson! I hope you regain your voice before we cast anchor!

(*Cut to: Interior: CAPTAIN's cabin.*)

CECILY: Captain, far from being a banjo-plucking minstrel, he is in fact one of the most inspiring writers of the age! I've read his newly-published book from cover to cover! It is the most potent weapon the abolitionist movement has to pursue the liberation of all slaves.

JUDDY: Miss Hutchinson, can I just say—

CECILY: Listen to this, his own story, expressed as only one who has suffered under the yoke of slavery possibly could:

'The practice of separating mothers from their children and hiring them out at distances too great to admit of their meeting is a marked feature of the cruelty and barbarity of the slave system. (*FREDERICK joins*) My grandmother's five daughters were hired out in this way . . .'

(*fade into:*)

FREDERICK: 'and my only recollections of my own mother, are of a few hasty visits made in the night on foot, when she was under pressure to return in time for the slave-driver's call at dawn. She walked twelve miles to see me, and had the same distance to travel over again before sunrise. These little glimpses of my mother, meagre as they were, are ineffaceably stamped upon my memory. She was tall and finely-proportioned, of dark glossy complexion, with regular features and amongst the slaves was remarkably sedate and dignified. Her death soon ended the little communication that existed between us, and with it, I believe, a life full of weariness and heartfelt sorrow.

Of my father I know nothing. The opinion was whispered that my master was my father; of the correctness of this opinion I know nothing. (*CECILY joins*) Except to state that my skin is a lighter colour than those who were called my brothers and sisters.'

CECILY: Who could remain unmoved Captain!? Surely it is not too much to ask to hear this famous man speak on board ship!?

JUDDY: Miss Hutchinson, as Captain of *The Cambria*—

CECILY: From the hurricane-deck, perhaps? It would be such a feather in the cap of the Cunard line!

JUDDY: The Blue Riband for the fastest crossing is the only—feather in which this particular cap has the slightest interest!

CECILY: You would slay the albatross.

JUDDY: What!?

CECILY: You, the 'Ancient Mariner', would slay the albatross that lands upon your deck.

JUDDY: Oh, spare me your poetics, Miss Hutchinson!

CECILY: Don't you see? You draw the mariner's curse upon yourself. Look! The sinister fog descends.

JUDDY: We're in the North Atlantic. There's always fog.

CECILY: 'And some in dreams assured were
Of the spirit that plagued us so;
Nine fathoms deep he had followed us
From the land of mist and snow.'

(*pause*)

JUDDY: Mister Coleridge's poem—The Ancient Mariner—is a gothic fantasy. Whereas—we are on the mechanical wonder of the age. The furnaces and paddles are fact! Not bloody fantasy!

CECILY: You are afraid.

JUDDY: I fear nothing except the limits of my temper at this moment.

CECILY: Is it heavy?

JUDDY: What!?

CECILY: The albatross you carry around your neck?

JUDDY: Dear God above, what have I done to warrant this torment!?

CECILY: I forgive your blasphemy. (*sotto voce*) You haven't slain it yet, Captain. You can set it free. The albatross may spread its magnificent wings and fly above your decks. Let—him—speak. I know already people are enthusiastic.

JUDDY: Have you spoken to many passengers about your allegation concerning this passenger?

CECILY: It's not an allegation! I know he is Frederick Douglass! I recognise his spirit.

JUDDY: If that were true, Miss Hutchinson, it would fall to me to take punitive action. The passenger gave his name to me as Mister Johnson. That's the name on his ticket.

CECILY: Insignificant tittle-tattle—

JUDDY: Impersonation is a grave offence aboard ship. Punishable by imprisonment! If what you allege were true, I would have no option but to have the man placed in irons immediately.

CECILY: You are clearly in the pocket of that slaveholder Dodd! I can smell his purse off you! Phuh!

JUDDY: You are the most impossible woman!

CECILY: Not the first time I've been called such! And I pray it won't be the last!

JUDDY: Little chance of that!

CECILY: Frederick Douglass has written a book! He has a message to impart! Are you, the captain of *The Cambria*, going to stifle his cry!?

JUDDY: I hear *your* cry! He, if indeed he is among us, is noticeably silent!

CECILY: Will you make history for Cunard as the shipping line that forced a famous writer to travel in disguise!?

JUDDY: Listen to me! If you persist in this business, I will be compelled to do what I have no wish to do! Can't you see Mister Johnson is content to travel quietly to Ireland without fanfare! Why do you insist on throwing the spotlight on him!?

CECILY: The spotlight, Captain, is on YOU. And—your albatross!

(*cut to*:)

FREDERICK: Deep down in the hold below

SOLOMON: Coal coal shovel shovel
coal coal shovel shovel

FREDERICK & SOLOMON: Fur—nace flame . . . fur—nace . . . flame

SOLOMON: Hey working brothers stop and listen! You people lucky to be in the company of this great orator, this stevedore, this roller of oil casks, this toiler of God's tasks.

This here is Frederick Douglass. I met him in New Bedford, I was in a whaleship crew, and brother Freddie came aboard and took our souls off that stinking ship and led us to a new pasture! Tell them Freddie tell them how you were a slave and how you saw your chance! Tell them the way you told me that night in the Seamen's Bethel in New Bedford when we stank to High Heaven of whale blubber and stale blood. How you saw the open sea . . . Go on, Frederick!

(*murmurs of encouragement*)

FREDERICK: Solomon has given me an introduction I don't deserve. But I think of the three millions of my brothers and sisters still lashed to the yoke in the Southern states. And I think of the countless thousands holed up in the Northern states, in fear of being sent back to their owners in chains. And I know that I have no option but to relate some of my memories.

SOLOMON: Hello Frederick Douglass! I say Hello!!

FREDERICK: I was moved to enquire into the origin and nature of slavery at a very early age. Why am I a slave? Why are some people slaves and others masters? These were perplexing questions and very troublesome to my childhood.

I was told by somebody that 'God up in the sky' had made all things, and had made black people to be slaves and white people to be masters.

I was told too, that God was good and that He knew what was best for everybody.

This was less satisfactory than the first statement. It came point blank against all my notions of goodness. The case of Aunt Esther was in my mind.

COLETTE: Es—ther . . . Es—ther . . . Es—ther . . . Es—ther . . . .

(*down as far as 'scarcely stand'*)

FREDERICK: One night I was awakened by the piteous cries of poor Esther. Through the cracks of my rough closet I could see all that was going on. Esther's wrists were firmly tied, and the twisted rope was fastened to a heavy beam near the fireplace. Here she stood on a bench, her arms tightly drawn above her head. Her back and shoulders were bare. Behind her stood the master, with cowhide in hand, pursuing his barbarous work with all manner of harsh curses. Again and again he drew the scourge through his hand, adjusting it to deal the most pain-giving blow he could inflict. Poor Esther had never before been severely whipped. Her piercing cries seemed only to increase his fury.

When let down she could scarcely stand.

Esther was a young woman who possessed that which is a curse to the slave girl—namely, personal beauty. She was tall, well-formed and made a fine appearance. Esther was courted by Ned Roberts, a fine-looking slave. For some reason, the master disapproved of their courtship. He ordered her to quit the company of young Roberts, or he would punish her severely. But it was impossible to keep this couple apart. The scene I have described was often repeated, for Ned and Esther continued to meet, in spite of all efforts to keep them apart.

FIREMEN: Doug . . . lass . . . Frederick Douglass . . . Douglass . . . Frederick Douglass . . .

(*They pass the word along—up the decks—until last utterance, when a hand goes up to cover the mouth on saying the word.*)

DODD: (*greasing palm*) I thank you for your information.

Interval

Section Five

(*CAPTAIN's cabin.*)

DODD: As my friend Samuel Cunard would say, the matter is simple, Captain Judkins! He's an absconded slave. He must be held in detention.

JUDDY: Mister Dodd, American Law is divided on the subject of slavery, north and south! You can't expect me to impose unity when the state itself is split!

DODD: As Justice of the Peace I declare that United States law still holds aboard this ship.

JUDDY: I am captain of *The Cambria*, and I make all decisions with regard to security on this ship.

DODD: Of course. And I am informing you officially that the passenger calling himself Mister Johnson, and posing as a minstrel, also calling himself Frederick Douglass, is in fact Frederick Augustus Washington Bailey, the escaped slave of Hugh Auld, shipbuilder, of Baltimore, Maryland. I charge you with responsibility for putting this vagabond in chains, and ensuring his return to his rightful owner, in accordance with lawful practice.

JUDDY: There are the ship's manacles, Mister Dodd! I am Captain. My father was a captain before me. It's in my blood. My duty I never shirk. As your grandfather said, order is paramount.

(*below decks*)

DIGNAM: Eh—job to do, Fred, sad but fact,
hope no grudge felt, trying to use tact,
a ship at sea—complicated place,
no need to feel—belittled . . .

FREDERICK: I have been many times hauled and spat upon and thrown into the Jim Crow carriages on trains, forced to travel in the luggage-hold. I never neglect to tell the enforcers of such confinement that THEY are belittled by the act. Not I.

DIGNAM: Fair dues. The confinement detail here is just a bit of dressing,—at ease lads, batons away—
you're a gentleman, I know there'll be no messing,
sure you'll step ashore as free as the rest,
but, for the moment, orders is orders, I'm doing my best to keep you out of trouble,
hope you'll see this as your own—private security bubble.

FREDERICK: We are all confined on a clever arrangement of wood and steel in the middle of the Atlantic. Confinement by one degree more is of little consequence. To me. Who am used to it.

DIGNAM: Timber crunch, bolt shunt, lock clock, key clink.

FREDERICK: The captain needs to hear me.

DIGNAM: Captain's not to be disturbed, strict instructions. I'm just a pawn here, turning a crust, apologies personally, but officially well . . . I can imagine you're—pissed off is the phrase we use . . .

FREDERICK: The captain needs to hear me.

DIGNAM: Freddie, something you said—sorry I have to share it with you through the door—have you ever heard of Daniel O'Connell?

FREDERICK: I first heard his name spat from my master's mouth. He cursed him. And his slaveholder friends cursed him! And I thought this is a man I'd like to meet!

DIGNAM: WELL, On That Subject, Did You Know that he has been offered the support of more than forty MPs for the Repeal of the Act of Union—to free Ireland, big thing, you know?—If Only he'll stay quiet about slavery. But NO, not while one drop of slave blood is spilt, or one slave limb is bound, will he stop his opposition to slavery.

FREDERICK: And what about Dignam?

DIGNAM: He's another great orator, of course. Like yourself! A great way with the words! The Voice and the Pen, do you know it!?

(*sings*)

Oh! The orator's voice is a mighty power
As it echoes from shore to shore—
And the fearless pen has more sway o'er men
Than the murderous cannon's roar. (*Pause*)

My brother sings it better than me. I take it you didn't get a laugh out of the Germans?

(*pause*) No luck here either. We're stuck in stalemate Fred.

(*in the brig*)

FREDERICK: The lock, the door, the dark. The totally alone. How? So near to—white sails, at sea . . .

Our house stood within a few rods of Chesapeake Bay, whose broad bosom was ever white with sails from every quarter of the globe.

Those beautiful vessels, robed in white, so delightful to the eyes of freemen, to me—so many shrouded ghosts, to terrify and torment me with thoughts of my wretched condition.

CREW: (*Sing quietly, as if faraway.*) Way, haul away, we'll haul away Joe!

FREDERICK: Often, in the deep still of a summer Sabbath, I stood all alone upon the banks of that noble bay, and traced, with

saddened heart and tearful eye, the countless number of sails moving off to the mighty ocean. There I would pour out my soul's complaint in my rude way to the moving multitude of ships . . .
'You are loosed from your moorings, and free.
I am fast in my chains, and am a slave!
You move merrily before the gentle gale,
and I sadly before the bloody whip.
You are freedom's angels,
that fly around the world;
I am confined in bonds of iron.
O, that I were free!
O, that I were on one of your gallant decks,
and under your protecting wing!
Alas! Betwixt me and you the turbid waters roll.
Go on, go on;
I am left in the Hell of unending slavery.
God, deliver me! Let me be free!
It cannot be that I shall live and die a slave.
I will take to the water.
And when I get to the head of the bay,
I will turn my canoe adrift,
and walk straight through Delaware and into Pennsylvania.
There, I shall not be required to have a pass.
I will travel there without being disturbed.
At the first opportunity, I am off!
Meanwhile, I will bear the yoke.
I am not the only slave in the world.
It may be that my misery in slavery
will only increase my happiness when I get free.
There is a better day coming.'

(*Before end of speech, percussion approaches from afar.*)

Section Six

MATILDA: Hello Moo-cow how are you this fine night? My goodness, you only have room to stand. Have you seen Mr Johnson Misses Moo-cow? He's going to do a show. And Mirabelle and I are going to be his marvellous assistants.

Hello chicky-chickies feathery peep-peep to you in your little coop just like my Mirabelle chicky-chicks. Have you seen Mister Johnson chicky-chicks? (*calls*) Mis-ter John-son! . . . Mis-ter John-son! . . .

JUDDY: Cracking ice makes a noise more penetrative than any other sound. Icebergs whisper their coming like play-house villains before they are seen. I hear it, the iceberg's bells. I see it in the distance, a temple of pearl. Hello Papa. Here I come on *The Cambria*. Fastest paddlesteamer in the—ah, clanking nonsense you called it, the wind in canvas your God.

Your marathon voyages, from Liverpool docks,—bye-bye Papa—to Africa, America, the letters of fond regards, the stiff return with riches and fine things, strange hollow gifts from a hot place, plentiful our lives, without a wish, without a want, but never your head thrown back in a laugh, never your teeth but clenched.

I step on the iceberg. Of fog. I advance. I bring you the albatross. I drag the swinging wings, the flopped head snags my feet. I have muted it. For you. Take it from around my neck Papa. Take the albatross. I pray. I pray.

DIGNAM: I daren't roar at him for fear of alerting Dodd and his mob. So I whistle through the bloody keyhole. Captain! For God's sake, listen to the silence! The engines have stopped. The furnaces are dead. Solomon's leading the men. In some kind of prayer-chant.

Bloody thick fog seeping into the passenger-decks. Coming at me like a—disappointed spirit. Pointing Dignam Dignam it says.

My blasted stomach's rolling and heaving. Rough sea never a cause. But Captain, you're making me sick, I have to say it, sick, whispering keyholes, for crying out loud!

What sort of nonsense course is this!? You can hide in there, but you can't hide from the truth! The fog is onto us. Daniel O'Connell was thrown in jail. For saying what he believed. I stood outside in the rain. Caught my death I did. And now—look at us! Holding the jailer's key! Pontius Pilate Judkins are you washing your dirty hands!?

FREDERICK: The hot summer of Covey. For six months, Covey kept me broken, for nigger-breaker his boasted profession. In body, mind and spirit. I was broken.

Then one day, work, hot, treading-yard, feeding the fan for the wheat-crusher, wheat-crusher, wheat-crusher—crush. I fall, side of the wheat-fan. Suddenly the sky. Covey above me. Hickory slab. Gash. Hot blood floods my face. Struggle up, Covey—rope, slip-knot my legs, to flog me. I—grapple with him. Know not where. Man help thyself—Beethoven's motto once I read. I find I fight, my fingers to the throat of Covey, eye-popped, shocked. 'Are you going to resist, you scoundrel?' Yes, I say. Yes.

Head to head, blood in my eyes, his gaze unsteady, his chin a-quiver, for two full hours hot sun in the scorching yard. Covey lets go of me.

Covey. Lets. Go.

It was the turning point. I would be a free man.

SOLOMON: Frederick Douglass is held in the brig. While he is confined, *The Cambria* is silent. In shame. Solidarity is the key to change. I heard him say it in New Bedford. All for one. And one for all. We are all for Frederick. Our silence will roar. Our stillness will become an unstoppable advance!

DODD: Gentlemen, we here are the representatives of authority in this floating microcosm of society. Order is paramount; it must be preserved. The lowest class of labourer on board—the furnace-stokers—have capitulated Douglass' chaotic influence. This troublemaker must be silenced! This canker must be crushed!

SOLOMON: Douglass . . . Frederick Douglass . . .
Douglass . . . Frederick Douglass . . .

JUDDY: Take the albatross from me, Papa, let me straighten up. The damn bird has me doubled over. Looking at the ice.

Look at me Papa! Let me see your eyes.

The ice moves under my feet, it's becoming snow-like, fluffing up around my feet, it seizes my legs, damn it the albatross is stuck fast, it pulls me down, Papa release me, it embraces me, it's going to smother me—

Papa. Cold. Eyes. Of ice . . .

It is—you, YOU choking me, freezing the freeness in me,

I—will—scream my mutedness into your sno-o-o-ow . . .

The sun beat down. The busty maidenhead grins bows grins bows. As if she knows me. You again, she asks. The smell of hot caulk. Stifling, in the middle of the still Atlantic. I climb down the rope ladder. Stand on deck. The wall-eyed midshipman prays an Ave as I pass. I look into the hold. The air is—hot, broiling hot, absolutely still. All sound stops. A pair of eyes stare at me. I peer. Move to see better. The eyes stare still. More eyes. As my eyes become accustomed. Hundreds of pairs of eyes. Close together. On racks. Dull rusty metal. Scrape of iron chains. A deep sigh beside me. A young girl makes the sound of a dying man.

A death-rattle cry.

I vomit. Step the rungs. Blind light. White sail covering.

Papa. Captained—this. Decided placings. Rations. Punishments.

Shackles. Bonds. The dances I was told about. That day. Slaves taken up on deck. Look at the sun. The sea. Now dance. To keep the muscles exercised. Dance with no music. Clap! Dance! Whipped to dance. (*sings*) Dance for your daddy, lash, sing for your daddy, lash, dance for your daddy, lash, sing for your daddy, lash, til the boat comes in. Dance for your daddy, dance for your daddy, dance . . .

(*musicbox tinkling*)

MATILDA: Mirabelle, I wish I knew what you were thinking. Do you know your birthday? Or do you only know the time—planting-time, or cherry-time, or harvest-time, or winter-time? . . . That lid must drive you crazy! Always pressing on your head.

I'm going to lift the lid completely Mirabelle! I'll do it in a show! With Mister Johnson the minstrel! He likes you! I could tell! He said 'hello-o-oh Mirabelle!' We'll have everybody watching. And you'll be the star performer! Ladies and gentlemen, now from the darkness of her box, put your hands together in wild applause for marvellous Mirabelle, the dancing slave!

(*musicbox stops*)

Section Seven

CECILY: Fog on the deck, confusion inside,
passengers questioning, answers collide,
I seek Mister Douglass, but nowhere to be found,
I call for the captain, not a sound,
I look around, now almost fog bound . . .
a whisper behind, something cold in my hand,
I feel a key, long cold iron wand,
Dignam drawls a low unexpected tune . . .

DIGNAM: Douglass . . . Frederick Douglass . . .

FREDERICK: A key scrapes in the lock. Silence. I hear a—breath. I push the door. It heaves open. To reveal—

CECILY: Frederick—

FREDERICK: —the lady with the faulty tubes.

CECILY: Mister Douglass! You're free.

FREDERICK: I step into the light. The smell of fog . . . Strange silence of the ship. The calm before the—

DIGNAM: I keep watch, I try to warn—hurry up and hide—but—dig of a pistol—in the kidneys—one of Dodd's men—

DODD: That man is a criminal! In the name of the United States government, I declare him an escaped slave. As a Justice of the Peace I arrest him.

CECILY: Over my dead body!

SOLOMON: And mine!

DIGNAM: People sticking their heads in now. All we need is footlights and we could do a show.

DODD: Hand him over! Aiding and abetting an outlaw is a criminal offence. This man is a liar and a thief!

FREDERICK: What lies have I told, Mister Dodd!?

DODD: You have told lies about good upstanding people who have given a life of worth and some prosperity to your heathen race that would otherwise have been savages in Africa!

FREDERICK: I have seen savagery in the eyes of white slaveholders! I have seen savagery in scourging whips! I have seen savagery inflicted on my mother! My aunt! My cousins! My grandmother! I have been whipped myself many times to the point of unconsciousness. But I have risen up and I have defied the savagery of slavery!

DODD: You are a liar and you will be punished for it!

SOLOMON: I slip a load-rope on Freddie's foot, release the catch—

DIGNAM: Up flies Freddie to the load-beam.

SOLOMON: Rise up, Frederick Douglass! Rise up and speak!

FREDERICK: This man calls me a liar! The Laws of the United States of America cannot be lies! Hear them then!

'If more than seven slaves are found together on any road, without a white Person—*twenty lashes* a piece.

For being on horseback without the written permission of his master—*twenty-five lashes.*

For letting loose a boat from where it is made fast—*thirty-nine lashes*; and for the second offence, *shall have his ear cut off*;

It is punishable by *death* for the second attempt *to teach a slave to read.*'

DODD: You have five seconds to give yourself up! Five, four, three . . . may God have mercy on your heathen soul—

(*musicbox tinkles*)

DIGNAM: Take care little girl! You're up very high!

MATILDA: Dodda!

DODD: Matilda! Go back to the cabin!

MATILDA: But I'm going to be in the show too! Isn't that right, Mister Johnson!?

DODD: It's not a show Matilda!

(*Musicbox stops. Tense silence.*)

DIGNAM: Can I make a suggestion? Matilda! Why don't you go backstage and Miss Hutchinson will show you where to get ready for your piece in the show.

MATILDA: Do you think that's a good idea Dodda?

DODD: Yes Matilda. Go!

CECILY: Wait there, Matilda! I'm coming up! We'll get Mister Johnston's tricks box for him, shall we?

MATILDA: Oh, goody! See you in a few minutes, Mister Johnson.

(*Exit MATILDA.*)

DODD: You will all face charges! Seize him!

DIGNAM: Freddie run clamber up a ladder fast through a door across a floor bucket mop (no Freddie!) slippy-dippy slap-decka dive-slide picky-uppy bent-sprint making for the mizzen mast

DODD: Tally-ho tally-ho . . . hunting down the Negro stealthy stealthy listen for breath in the fog

FREDERICK: I breathe . . . I breathe . . .

DODD: Encroach . . . encroach . . .

DIGNAM: Foredeck a flap of canvas swish of cloaks

DODD: Heave him ho . . . overboard he go-o-oes . . .

DIGNAM: Stop I roar I reach to tear their grip away I bite a rumpled fist I twist a finger rip an ear let him go I banshee . . .

DODD: Send him DOWN damn you DOWN!

FREDERICK: I see sea . . . sky . . . sea . . . sky . . .

DIGNAM: The fingers of my hand peeled . . . back . . . the cloth of his trouser leg . . . slips . . . clinging to a stitch . . .

FREDERICK: (*slowly, internally*) Momma's tired surging eyes . . . twelve miles she walked to see me, twelve more to the slave-driver's call at dawn . . . Go now Momma . . .

JUDDY: (*suddenly*) Mister Dodd!

DODD: Captain Judkins! Thanks be to Jehovah! This man has most mendaciously—

JUDDY: Call off your bloodhounds!

FREDERICK: My boots hit the deckboards hard.

DODD: If I had him in New Orleans! . . .

JUDDY: Mister Dodd! I have here the ship's manacles! Implements I know are dear to your heart! I would confine and shackle you NOW were it not for your daughter! You will remain in your cabin for the rest of the voyage!

DODD: Don't be a fool! Mister Cunard is a close friend of mine!

JUDDY: If he is, he has lost himself the services of the captain of his flagship *The Cambria*! Mister Douglass! Come up here beside me!

(*FREDERICK ascends.*)

JUDDY: I give you the Hurricane Deck! Pitch into them like bricks, Douglass!

FREDERICK: That box that Miss Hutchinson is holding—will you open it please?

CECILY: Certainly, Mister Douglass!

FREDERICK: Lift out the first item please!

DIGNAM: She lifts out this thick ring of rusty iron—

FREDERICK: This is an iron collar which was taken from the neck of a young woman who had escaped from Mobile. If you look closely, you can see that it had so worn into her neck that her blood and flesh still clings to it.

DODD: It's a concoction!

DIGNAM: The choir-leader lady passes it to me. It is no concoction.

FREDERICK: Take out the second item please.

These are fetters used in chaining the feet of two slaves together. I was present when they were sawn off the ankles of both screaming men who had run more than thirty miles over rough ground. (*pause*) This is a pair of handcuffs taken from a fugitive slave who escaped from Maryland into so-called free Pennsylvania. I knew the man well.

DODD: If any of you believe this grotesque fantasy, you are a gullible fool!

MATILDA: (*from the hurricane deck*) Hullo-oh!

DODD: !

MATILDA: I'm ready Dodda. And so is Mirabelle! I've decided I'm going to set Mirabelle free. It's not fair that she should spend so much time cooped up in that box. Just to entertain us, Dodda! It's unforgiveable. Here! She's out of her box and the music still plays. See!? She wants to be in the show. As a trapeze girl! Like the PT Barnum girls we saw! They were Fawbulous!

DODD: 'Fawbulous'? . . .

MATILDA: And so is Mirabelle! She can fly now, Dodda. Catch!

DODD: No, Matilda!

(*musicbox tinkles*)

MATILDA: Mirabelle, Mirabelle, revolving above
you're the star of the show, you're the giver-out of Love,

DODD: Matilda, Matilda, you'll cry til you die
if Mirabelle breaks from the fall unless I—

CECILY: Mirabelle, Mirabelle, herald from the skies,
you're the angel of creation, force of Paradise.

DODD: —throw myself across the deck, slide in the mud,
splinters in my chin damn it worth it if I could just—

SOLOMON: Mirabelle, Mirabelle, the siren of the sea,
back to the furnaces, my comrades and me. . . .

JUDDY: Released from Papa's mast, released from my past,
my albatross is soaring, Miss Hutchinson she laughs. . . .

CECILY: Captain Judkins, I knew he had a heart,
men are so eccentric, so prone to fall apart.
Frederick Douglass, the hero of the day,
minstrel most magical, you have performed your play.

MATILDA: Mirabelle is falling, most awfully fast,
I hope she learns the flying thing she's keeping until last . . .

DODD: Stretch my hand, knuckles burn against the wood,
I—catch little Mirabelle! Matilda—she's good!

MATILDA: Good man Dodda! You caught her! Now we can sing! Is it time yet, Mister Johnson!?

FREDERICK: Yes Matilda, There is a better time coming! In fact, it's here right now! And we will all take part! Miss Hutchinson—how's your voice?

CECILY: Much improved, Mister Douglass. Thanks to you. (*conducting choir*) Three, four,

(*starts to sing*)

Halleluia—

CREW: Paddlesteamer paddlesteamer paddlesteamer paddlesteamer
Way, haul away, we'll haul away together,
Way, haul away, we'll haul away Joe,
Way, haul away, for Queenstown Queenstown,
Way, haul away, for Queenstown Cork.

Section Eight

(*CAPTAIN's cabin*)

FREDERICK: You don't need to use me as an excuse for a champagne breakfast.

JUDDY: You haven't forgotten my pledge to you!?

FREDERICK: I fear I cost you your Blue Riband for fastest crossing.

JUDDY: You gained me the real Blue Riband of truth to oneself. To curse my father is to bless my children. With the ability to laugh. Did you see the look on Dodd's face when I told you to pitch into them like bricks!?

FREDERICK: I was busy at the time, as I recall.

JUDDY: And you did. You pitched into them rightly!

FREDERICK: I reckon Mister Dodd owes me a two hundred dollar performance fee.

(*pause*)

JUDDY: Mister Dodd has served me with legal papers. I and the Cunard Line are impelled to hold you and take you back to Boston. As a carrier we are bound by international agreements. You are, in their eyes, stolen goods. We are charged to do all possible to deliver you to your rightful owner. Otherwise, Cunard will lose the mail franchise. And with it, its existence.

FREDERICK: (*pointedly*) What do you suggest?

JUDDY: My father made his living, and therefore gave me my start in life, from the Slave Trade. He was a ship's captain. I followed in his wake. He may have shipped your very ancestors to a life of slavery. Your mother perhaps. The price he received for his work paid for my training in the merchant navy. I would not be here otherwise. (*pause*) Two years ago I saw a slave-ship. I had cause to go aboard. I knew in that horrific instant why my father never smiled.

FREDERICK: We cannot be our father's keeper. Certainly, I could not be mine.

JUDDY: In Queenstown, we walk together. Gallows-companions. I'm proud. If we swing, we swing for freedom.

(*A brass band is heard in the distance.*)

JUDDY: Oh, no! There's a bloody band. On the dockside. Telescope . . . And Cunard himself on the bandstand. He's travelled to claim the Blue Riband. But we've lost it. Aw calamity!

DIGNAM: (*shouts*) There's Daniel O'Connell! Hey Freddie! There's the man you want to meet!? They've got a platform erected! Look!

DODD: (*loud*) Quite a reception Mister Cunard's organised, don't you think, Captain!? Pity that I'll be serving him with the deposition you have brought upon his head!

JUDDY: (*loud*) Do as you think fit, Mister Dodd!

DODD: (*loud*) I do only what is right and proper!

(*band stops*)

JUDDY: Lower the gangplank!
The bandleader stands watching, baton poised in the air. A silence falls. *The Cambria* bleeds its passengers. Finally, Dodd stands at the top of the gangplank. Hand out for Matilda.

MATILDA: Wait Dodda! (*calls*) Mister Douglass—

DODD: Stop that Matilda—

MATILDA: But I have to do something Dodda!
(*close up to FREDERICK*) Here's Mirabelle! Take her please! I want you to take good care of her! I'm never going to put her in that tiny box again.

FREDERICK: I will. I'll teach her how to read. I'll take her out anytime I hear people singing, Matilda.

MATILDA: Especially birthdays. I knew you were a minstrel!

FREDERICK: Oh, no I'm not!

MATILDA: You're the best minstrel ever. Goodbye.

DODD: Matilda! Mister Cunard and the band are waiting! (*wave*) Damn bandleader doesn't recognise me.

DIGNAM: Then Freddie lifts up his tricks box and his luggage case and steps onto the gangplank!

(*Burst of music from the marching band.*)

DIGNAM: And the music bursts forth! And an almighty cheer breaks from the surging crowd! A fountain of hats and caps in the air! And Daniel O'Connell raises his arms above his head and claps his hands in applause. And the noise of clapping and cheering from thousands of Irish is for one man and one man only . . .

FREDERICK: I walk down the gangplank puzzled by all the noise. Then I hear the chant of the crowd.

CHANT: Douglass . . . Frederick Douglass . . .
Douglass . . . Frederick Douglass . . .

JUDDY: I laugh on the capstan as I watch Frederick Douglass shake hands with Mister Cunard, and talk long and earnestly with Daniel O'Connell MP as everyone shouts and cheers.

SOLOMON: Hey Douglass! Frederick Douglass!

FREDERICK: Solomon!

SOLOMON: May you never have reason to deny your name again!

FREDERICK: Daniel O'Connell gives me a hug as bear-like as Solomon's.

O'CONNELL: Ladies and Gentlemen, it gives me the utmost pleasure, tempered with humility in the presence of one who has suffered so much at the hands of a violent system of repressive governance fuelled by slave labour, to introduce to you gathered here in the name of freedom and self-determination, a man who has lived his life in pursuit of those principles—Mister Frederick Douglass, known, may I humbly submit, among the freedom-loving people of the Northern United States as—the Black O'Connell! Frederick Douglass—

(*the crowd roars*)

FREDERICK: I stand beside O'Connell. He holds my hand up high. A howling cheer of unbelievable volume reverberates around the valley. It echoes back from the mountains before us. Then echoes again from the mountains behind until the very land of Ireland seems to roar in welcome for me.

JUDDY: It's the finest sight I've seen in all my years at sea. He holds the assembled in the palm of his hand.

FREDERICK: We want you to speak to those in America and say 'while your hands are red with blood, while the thumb screws and gags and whips are wrapped in the pontifical robes of the Law, we will have no fellowship with you'.

CHANT: Douglass . . . Frederick Douglass . . .
Douglass . . . Frederick Douglass . . .

FREDERICK: We want to encircle America with a girdle of anti-slavery fire, that will reflect light upon the slave institutions, and alarm their guilty upholders.

CHANT/MUSIC: Douglass . . . Frederick Douglass . . .
Douglass . . . Frederick Douglass . . .

JUDDY: There. I didn't do much, did I!? No hero's role. But it changed my life. I got a letter from Frederick a few months later. 'I have travelled from the Hill of Howth to the Giant's Causeway . . .'

FREDERICK: '. . . and from Giant's Causeway to Cape Clear. I can truly say I have spent some of the happiest days of my life since landing in this country.

I seem to have undergone a transformation. I live a new life. The warm co-operation extended to me by the friends of my despised race; the liberal manner in which the Press has rendered me its aid; the spirit of freedom which seems to animate all with whom I come in contact, and the entire absence of prejudice against me, contrasts so strongly with my bitter experience in the United States, that I look with wonder and amazement on the transition.

In the United States I was a slave—thought of and spoken of as property. But now behold the change! Instead of the bright blue sky of America, I am covered in the soft, grey fog of the Emerald Isle. I breathe and lo! The chattel becomes a man! I gaze around in vain for one who will question my equal humanity, claim me as a slave, or offer me an insult. I find myself regarded and treated at every turn with the kindness and deference paid to white people.

I had been in Dublin but a few days when a gentleman of high office offered to conduct me through all the public buildings of that beautiful city. And soon afterwards I was invited by the Lord Mayor to dine with him. The truth is, people here in Ireland measure and esteem men according to their moral and intellectual worth, and not according to the colour of their skin.

JUDDY: From the man Abraham Lincoln called 'the most impressive man I have ever met!' And the man who said:-

VINCENT: 'Power concedes nothing without demand; it never did; and it never will.'

COLETTE: Frederick Douglass, one-time asylum-seeker and refugee.

(Bing-bong. The airport PA sounds again, as at beginning.)

(blackout)

The End.

INTRODUCTION TO BISI ADIGUN'S

Once Upon a Time & Not So Long Ago (2006)

MATTHEW SPANGLER

Brecht's aphorism that 'Art is not a mirror held up to reality, but a *hammer* with which to shape it' is one Bisi Adigun seems to hold dear. A writer, director, actor and the founding artistic director of Dublin's Arambe Productions—Ireland's first African theatre company—Adigun has sought, through his work in the theatre, to re-imagine traditional images of Irish identity in ways that include people of colour and recent transnational migrants. Few theatre companies have been as instrumental and active during the first decade of the twenty-first century as Adigun's Arambe at exploring the intersection between inward migration and interculturalism in Ireland.

Adigun grew up in the Yoruba region of southwest Nigeria and moved to the UK in 1993, before relocating to Ireland in 1996. He began work in Dublin using his skills as a musician and storyteller to create a series of performance-based workshops, which he called 'Africa Alive', intended to educate participants, mainly schoolchildren, about African culture. He later received an MA in Drama Studies from University College Dublin (1999), an MA in Film/Television from Dublin City University (2002), and served as a co-presenter on RTÉ's intercultural television program *Mono* (2000–03). He then founded Arambe Productions in 2003.

The name Arambe is a combination of the Yoruba saying, 'ara m be ti mo fe da' ('there are wonders I will perform') and the Swahili word, 'harambee' ('let us all pull together'). Arambe's primary goal is to provide African–Irish individuals the opportunity to perform in stage productions. In pursuit of this goal, Arambe has focused on producing three types of plays: classic and contemporary works by mostly West African writers; modernisations and reinterpretations of Irish drama that feature black actors; and documentary plays that dramatise specific intercultural moments in contemporary Irish society. A specific hallmark of many of Arambe's performances is the use of West African music and song.

Under the auspices of Arambe, Adigun has written or directed numerous productions over the last ten years, including: Ola Rotimi's *The Gods Are Not To Blame* (2004), Adigun's *Once Upon A Time & Not So Long Ago* (2005), Jimmy Murphy's *The Kings of The Kilburn High Road* (2006), *The Playboy of the Western World* (which Adigun co-wrote with Roddy Doyle), Ama Ata Aidoo's *The Dilemma of a Ghost* (2007), Joseph Coleman De Graft's *Through A Film Darkly* (2008), Derek Walcott's *Pantomime* (2008), *Celeb8Arambe@5* (2009), Wole Soyinka's *The Trials of Brother Jero* (2009), Adigun's *White Bread, Black Skin* (2010), Adigun's *The Butcher Babes* (2010), and *The Paddies of Parnell Street* (2013). As noted in the introduction to this volume, Adigun also co-directed *The Parable of the Plums*, an intercultural dance adaptation of the 'Aeolus' episode of James Joyce's *Ulysses*, which was performed on O'Connell Street on Bloomsday 2004.

Of these productions the two that have received the most acclaim are *The Playboy of the Western World* and *The Kings of the Kilburn High Road*. Adigun and Doyle's *The Playboy of the Western World* was a modernisation of Synge's play set in a contemporary West Dublin pub with a Nigerian asylum-seeker in the role of Christy Mahon. It received its premiere production at the Abbey Theatre in October 2007 during the Dublin Theatre Festival, and again at the Abbey in December 2008 and January 2009. *The Kings of the Kilburn High Road*, by contrast, was Adigun's interpretation of Murphy's original text, which featured black actors in the roles of the play's white Irish characters, who are themselves immigrants living in London. It was produced in October 2006 at the Dublin Fringe Festival, in February 2007 at Andrew's Lane Theatre and in October 2007 at the University of Notre Dame. Both of these productions reframed what have become familiar narratives in public discourse: the narrative of the asylum-seeker in a Western country, on one hand, and the narrative of the Irish immigrant, on the other. At its best, Adigun's work functions to deconstruct and present anew certain calcified discourses and images of identity.

We include here one of Adigun's earlier works—*Once Upon a Time & Not So Long Ago*—because we think it exemplifies Arambe's critical mission to critique the everyday practice of interculturalism in Irish society and to re-imagine Irish identity in new, more inclusive terms. The first act, *Once Upon a Time*, is a dramatisation of several West African folktales. Its tone is breezy, comic and, in light of the second act, even nostalgic. *Not So Long Ago*, on the other hand, features seventeen short scenes based on interviews Adigun conducted with black Africans living in Ireland. It seeks to engage the experiences recounted in these interviews in ways that foster cross-cultural dialogue and understanding. In one scene, for instance, a black shop assistant is wrapping a gift for a white customer, when the customer asks, 'Did you go home for Easter?' The customer's apparently innocent question is heard by the shop assistant as an accusation of sorts because it implies that, due to the shop assistant's dark skin, her 'home' could not possibly be Ireland. As Adigun himself puts it: 'This is not a question reserved for people who are obviously different: white Irish people ask each other this question as well. [. . .] However, when, on a daily basis, as a black person you see black people being portrayed in the media as foreigners or "aliens", it is difficult not to feel that you are being asked where are you from because you do not look like the "natives".'[1] The very question racialises the shop assistant as alien, or 'non-National,' terms that function to constitute migrants as social contaminants.[2] Of course, the customer does not intend to do this; she means her question as nothing more than an innocuous attempt to make conversation. But, as Adigun would point out, the fact that it would seem harmless and even natural to ask a black shop assistant in Dublin whether she went 'home' for Easter indicates the extent to which black skin remains an antithesis to Irish identity, even as the nation becomes increasingly racially diverse.

Not So Long Ago was funded, in part, by the National Action Plan Against Racism and was first produced at the Project Arts Centre on 17 December 2005. It was presented a second time, along with *Once Upon a Time* as the production's first act, at the O'Reilly Theatre in Belvedere College from 23 to 27 May 2006 to coincide with that year's Africa Day.[3] *Once Upon a Time & Not So Long Ago* is an important play within the canon of Irish intercultural theatre because it represents a performative act of social criticism, as well as a record of cultural change, a snapshot of sorts for a particular moment in Irish history.

Notes and References

1 Bisi Adigun, 'Arambe Productions: An African's Response to the Recent Portrayal of the *Fear Gorm* in Irish Drama', in *Performing Global Networks*, eds. Karen Fricker and Ronit Lentin (Newcastle: Cambridge Scholars Publishing, 2007), p. 61.

2 Likewise, Bryan Fanning and Elisa Joy White, separately, discuss how terms, such as 'asylum-seeker' and 'refugee' have functioned to vilify immigrants. See Bryan

Fanning, 'Racism, Rules, and Rights,' in *Immigration and Social Change in the Republic of Ireland*, ed. Bryan Fanning (Manchester: Manchester University Press, 2007), p. 11, and Elisa Joy White, 'The New Irish Storytelling: Media, Representations and Racialised Identities,' in *Racism and Anti-Racism in Ireland*, eds. Ronit Lentin and Robbie McVeigh (Belfast: Beyond the Pale, 2002), p. 107.

3 Africa Day (25 May), originally known as African Freedom Day, is an annual, world-wide commemoration marking the foundation of the Organisation of African Unity in 1963.

Once Upon a Time & Not So Long Ago

Bisi Adigun

Once Upon a Time & Not So Long Ago was first presented as one piece at the O'Reilly Theatre, Dublin, on 13 May 2006 by Arambe Productions.

Cast

(*each performer plays multiple roles*)

Yemi Adenuga
Gabriel Akujobi
Kunle Animasaun
Thomas Farrell
Sinead Hacket
Rilwan Jayeola
Sebastio Mpembele Kamalandua
John Lawlor
Emma Meehan
Merrina Millsap
Donna Nikolaisen
Bola Ogundeji
Larry Ojelade
Adijat Okusanya
Shane O'Neill
Elizabeth Suh
Abiola Tubi

Production Team

Director	Bisi Adigun
Lighting Designer	Cormac Veale
Scenic Designer	Mia Eveling
Sound Designers	Vincent Doherty and Ivan Birthistle
Choreographer	Robert Connor
Costume Designer	Lucy McKenna

Act One: Once Upon a Time

Prologue: 'Why do we tell stories?'[1]

The show opens with all the actors on stage. Some are playing African games, such as tente, ayo, okoto, suwe, and stone throwing. Narrator is playing ayo with another man. Some are learning a dance routine. All these things are happening as the audience members take their seats. When all the audience is seated, lights go down. The actors leave the stage. Moonlight and the sound of crickets. Then from backstage we hear:

Call: Lisa Ponge	Response: Ponge (*and drum roll*)
Call: Alo o	Response: Alo (*and drum roll*)
Call: Koyi Koyi	Response: Ya (*and drum roll*)

(*Then the song 'Alo Alo o' begins with music and the actors come on stage with a dance formation. At the end of the song, the actors start whispering one after the other in various languages 'why do we tell stories?' For instance, in Yoruba, it is, 'Ki lo fa ta fi n palo?' Then Narrator enters.*)

NARRATOR: (*very loud*) Why do we tell stories? (*silence*) I will tell you.

(*Everyone sits to listen to his story. He begins . . .*)

NARRATOR: The divinities waited, nothing happened. No offering, no thanksgiving, no worship, no music, no dance at the shrine! No sacrifice from the humans! Their priests also waited; nothing happened. No human came to the shrine. The gods decided to try a few tricks: earthquakes, storms, war, thunder and lightning. No effect! The gods then came up with a brilliant idea. They whispered the idea to their priest who went into the market place and spoke:

ALL: (*song*) Itan yeee, la n so o o o
Itan yee yee lomo eleti ngbo o

NARRATOR: Two friends. Two friends! Great friends! Best of friends! (*two friends enter*). Oh, they liked one another, did everything together. They enjoyed their friendship and prospered in their friendship. They thought they needed no one, they needed to go to no shrine, they needed to worship no god to keep the flame of their friendship burning. But Esu the trickster god . . .

ALL: (*song*) Esu ma se mi o
Omo elomi ni o se
O ni le o rita o omo elomi ni o se

(*ESU enters and the actors embody what is described in the story.*)

NARRATOR: Esu the god of confusion noticed these two great friends and decided to teach them a lesson. One day, as the two friends were walking down this big road, Esu came from the back with this huge hat; bright red to one side, pure white to the other side. As the two friends were apart just a little bit, Esu walked in between them and waved a big hello as he disappeared into the distance. The friends stopped.

FIRST FRIEND: Who was that fella with a red hat?

SECOND FRIEND: Red? Blind man! His hat was white.

FIRST FRIEND: You idiot, it was red.

SECOND FRIEND: No! You fool it was white!

FIRST FRIEND: Red!

SECOND FRIEND: White!

FIRST FRIEND: Red!

SECOND FRIEND: White!

FIRST FRIEND: Red!

SECOND FRIEND: White!

FIRST FRIEND: Red!

SECOND FRIEND: White!

(*they argue*)

NARRATOR: A big argument ensued between the two good friends. As they were about to start fighting one another, Esu appeared again, (*ESU enters.*) this time, from the opposite direction. The two friends sprang apart and Esu, once again, walked in between them and disappeared into the distance.

FIRST FRIEND: I am sorry, I can see now that his hat was indeed red. You were right.

SECOND FRIEND: No, keep your humour, you were right. His hat was white.

FIRST FRIEND: No, you were right.

SECOND FRIEND: No, you were right.

FIRST FRIEND: You were right, I was wrong.

SECOND FRIEND: No, I was wrong, you were right.

(*They fight.*)

NARRATOR: In no time, the two friends began to fight like two enemies in battle. Bruised and bloodied! Esu, in the meantime, was standing behind the tree nearby watching the friends as they battered one another. Before they killed one another, Esu sent his priest to the friends to ask why two good friends were brawling. (*The* PRIEST *enters.*) The two friends told their ordeal to the priest. And the priest advised the friends . . .

PRIEST: Go to the shrine of Esu, give offering to the priests, give sacrifice to the god of misunderstanding and your friendship will prosper.

(*The* PRIEST *exits.*)

NARRATOR: The two friends went to the shrine, gave offering, paid homage and gave thanks to Esu. And as a result, their friendship went from strength to strength.

ALL: (*song*)

LEAD: Esu ma se mi

CHORUS: Omo elo mi no se

LEAD: Esu ma se mi

CHORUS: Omo a se ni siro so

NARRATOR: The gods realised the success of their ploy and they called it story. So they made up more stories such as this so that we human beings would revere them and do exactly as they wanted. And they employed their special envoys, the storytellers to spread the word. (*All the actors exit.*) Telling moonlight stories is a way of life in many parts of Africa, especially those areas where electricity is still a thing of the future. I am your designated storyteller for this evening and I have a selection of stories for you from the four different corners of Africa: North, East, South and West. Now, in case you have ever wondered how we managed before justice was ever given to us, my first story, 'Justice,' from Ethiopia, will give you an idea.

Scene 1: 'Justice'

(Actors enter, exit, and embody the story as narrated.)

NARRATOR: Once upon a time, a woman went out to look for her goats that had wandered from the herd. She walked back and forth over the fields for a long time without finding them. She came at last to a place by the side of the road where a deaf man sat before a fire, brewing himself a cup of coffee. Not realising he was deaf, the woman approached him.

WOMAN: Have you seen my herd of goats come this way?

NARRATOR: The deaf man thought she was asking for the waterhole, so he pointed vaguely toward the river.

DEAF MAN: Over there.

WOMAN: Thanks for your help.

(*the sound of goats bleating*)

NARRATOR: And there, by coincidence, the woman found her goats. But a young kid had fallen among the rocks and broken its foot. She picked it up, to carry it home. As she passed the place where the deaf man sat drinking his coffee, she stopped to thank him for his help.

WOMAN: Thank you very much.

DEAF MAN: That's alright.

WOMAN: Would you take this injured kid? Perhaps you can look after it better than I can.

DEAF MAN: No, no, it wasn't me.

WOMAN: Of course, it was you. Here, take the kid.

DEAF MAN: But it wasn't me, I never went anywhere near the waterhole.

WOMAN: Still you knew the kids were there.

DEAF MAN: Leave me alone. I had nothing to do with it!

WOMAN: But you pointed the way

DEAF MAN: It happens all the time with goats!

WOMAN: I found them right where you said they would be.

DEAF MAN: Go away and leave me alone, I never saw him before in my life!

(*People, overhearing the commotion, begin to gather.*)

THE PEOPLE: What's the matter? What's going on?

WOMAN: I was looking for the goats and he pointed toward the river. Now I wish to give him this kid as a present.

DEAF MAN: Do not insult me in this way; I am not a leg-breaker

(*The DEAF MAN in his anger strikes the WOMAN.*)

WOMAN: Did you see that? He struck me with his hand! I will take him before the judge!

NARRATOR: So, the woman with the kid in her arms, the deaf man and the spectators went to the house of the judge. The judge came out before his house to listen to their complaint. First, the woman talked. Then the man talked. Then the people in the crowd talked. The judge kept on nodding his head. But that meant very little, for the judge, like the man before him, was very deaf. Moreover, he was also very near-sighted. At last, he put up his hand and the talking stopped. He gave them his judgement.

JUDGE: Such family rows are a disgrace in our community. (*to the DEAF MAN*) From this time forward, stop maltreating your wife. (*to the WOMAN*) As for you, do not be lazy. Hereafter, do not be late with your husband's meals. (*looking at the baby goat*) And as for the beautiful infant, may she have a long life and grow to be joy to you both.

NARRATOR: When they say justice is blind, now you understand what they mean. (*as the WOMAN, the DEAF MAN, and the crowd exit*) Maybe this is why the jury system was invented. As our next story, 'The Jackal's Lawsuit' will show you, sometimes being a juror is not as easy as it seems.

Scene 2: 'The Jackal's Lawsuit'

(*Again, actors enter, exit, and embody the story as described.*)

NARRATOR: Once upon a time, Leopard and Jackal went out together to hunt on the edge of the village, where Man lived. They captured some game. Leopard captured a goat, but Jackal captured a cow. They drove their prizes home and put them in the field to pasture. Leopard was not happy that Jackal's animal was so much larger than his own. In the night, he went again to look at them in the pasture, and he found that Jackal's cow had given birth to a calf. He was overcome with envy. So he took the calf away from the cow and tethered it with his goat. In the morning, he went to Jackal:

LEOPARD: How lucky I am! This morning I went to the field, and what do you think? My goat has given birth to a calf!

JACKAL: That can't be. For a goat can only give birth to a kid.

LEOPARD: Come for the proof.

NARRATOR: Leopard took Jackal to the field where the calf was tethered with his goat.

LEOPARD: Now you can see for yourself. I have spoken the truth.

JACKAL: Since only a cow can give birth to a calf, the calf is mine.

LEOPARD: Do you see the proof and continue to argue? Can't you see the calf with my goat?

JACKAL: Yes, I see her. But even if I saw her standing with an elephant, still she would be mine.

LEOPARD: Let us be judged! Others will recognise that justice is on my side.

NARRATOR: So, they went in search of judges, and they came across the Gazelle, Hyena and Klipspringer. They narrated their stories to them, but they were afraid of Leopard, as were most animals of the bush. It was Gazelle who spoke first.

GAZELLE: Well, when I was young, it was true that only cows had calves. But times have changed. The world moves on. Now, as you can see, it is possible for goats to have calves. This is my judgement, as Heaven is my witness!

NARRATOR: Then the Hyena came forward.

HYENA: I have given this a serious thought, and I have come to the conclusion that, ordinary goats cannot have calves, but goats that are owned by leopards can. That is my judgement, as Heaven is my witness!

NARRATOR: And at last the Klipspringer gave his view.

KLIPSPRINGER: Once, it was the law of all living things that each one should bear only his own kind. Lions bore lions, goats bore goats, and camels bore camels. But the law has been changed. It is now permitted for goats to bear calves. This is the truth, as Heaven is my witness!

LEOPARD: Since there are no more judges, the calf is clearly mine.

JACKAL: There is still Baboon.

NARRATOR: So all of them went together to the rocky place where Baboon lived. They found him turning over stones to get at the ants and grubs that lived there.

LEOPARD: Judge our case.

NARRATOR: Both Leopard and Jackal told their stories. Baboon listened with a far-off look in his eyes. When they were through, they waited for his judgement. But he said nothing. (*silence*) He held a small stone in his hand and plucked at it with his fingers.

LEOPARD: (*impatiently*) Well? You see how it is. What is your verdict?

BABOON: Can't you see I'm busy?

LEOPARD: What are you doing?

BABOON: I have eaten my meal, and now I must play a little music before I judge.

LEOPARD: Music? What music?

BABOON: (*with irritation*) The music I am playing on this instrument!

LEOPARD: Ha! What instrument? A stone! What a stupid person we have asked to judge for us! No music can come from a stone!

BABOON: (*looking at LEOPARD*) If a calf can come from a goat, surely sweet music can come from a stone.

LEOPARD: Wait! I can hear it now. Hmmm! What a lovely music!

(*Lights down. ALL exit.*)

NARRATOR: It is indeed true that 'if a lie runs for a hundred years, truth will catch up with it in a day.' My next story, ladies and gentlemen, is 'The Bitter Pill'.

Scene 3: 'The Bitter Pill'

(Again, actors enter, exit, and embody the story as described.)

NARRATOR: Once upon a time, there was a King, powerful and proud. He ruled his kingdom with the aid of four councillors. He enjoyed flattery and was quick to anger, so that most of his subjects agreed to everything he said. Three of his councillors were yes-men and one alone, had courage to tell the truth. Though the king was arrogant, he was also hardworking and energetic. Each day, he would think out a new law, each one more tiresome than the other. He would then call his council together and ask them what the people thought of his laws.

FIRST COUNCILLOR: Your majesty can do no wrong in the eyes of the people.

SECOND COUNCILLOR: They think your laws are wonderful and are happy and contented.

THIRD COUNCILLOR: The kingdom prospers under your rule.

NARRATOR: And the king was always content until the fourth councillor would say:

FOURTH COUNCILLOR: Your majesty, far be it for me to criticise in any way the wisdom of your actions, but the people complain of the hardness of your laws. They have no heart to work and there is much that needs improving in the kingdom.

(The THREE COUNCILLORS begin to laugh as the FOURTH COUNCILLOR walks out.)

SECOND COUNCILLOR: Kabiyesi, you should not take his remarks seriously, is he not only one out of four?

THIRD COUNCILLOR: My Lord, he is not quite right in the head.

FIRST COUNCILLOR: My Lord, why don't we fire him. I think he is becoming a nuisance, a disturber of our harmony, and above all, an enemy of progress.

KING: I thank you all for your wise words. I would like you

to give me some time to think about it and I will get back to you.

FIRST COUNCILLOR: Kabiyesi o.

SECOND COUNCILLOR: Your Excellency.

THIRD COUNCILLOR: May your reign be long.

(They all exit.)

NARRATOR: That night when the king went to his room he thought over the events of the recent years. He remembered how in his childhood, the people had danced and sung in the streets. (*silhouette of dancers dancing*) He saw in his mind the smiling faces that greeted his uncle who had been King before him. Suddenly, he realised that it was long since he had seen his own people laugh and sing. And for the first time he had doubts.

KING: Is it possible that the three councillors could be wrong and the fourth councillor is right?

NARRATOR: Before the King finally fell asleep, he came up with a plan. Early the second morning, the King's most trusted servant brought him a gourd of fresh palm wine. Every day, the king took the pot of palm wine and stood it in the sun. Every day, the palm wine grew more and more fermented. Finally, on the seventh day, the King tasted it and it was so bitter that he spat it quickly out. The wine was now ready. It was *odae*. The King then sent for his four councillors for an important meeting.

KING: For many years, my friends, you have acted as my councillors with little or no reward. You have shared my anxieties and advised me in time of trouble. Now something wonderful has happened and I wish to share it with you. This morning Oginni, the palm wine tapper, brought me this gourd of fresh palm wine. As soon as I tasted it, I knew it was the best palm wine I had ever tasted. Immediately, I thought of you, my four councillors, and I have asked you here to share it with me. Because this palm wine is so good, I have thought of rewarding the tapper with a title. But first, you must share some of the wine with me and tell me whether it is a good idea to bestow a title on Oginni, or not. Balogun, you first.

FIRST COUNCILLOR: (*almost choking due to the bitterness of the wine*) O king! This is indeed a wonderful drink and the man who made it deserves to be made chief.

KING: Thank you. You see what I mean. Otun, it's your turn

SECOND COUNCILLOR: (*Tears come to his eyes, but he manages to swallow a mouthful.*) Oh, King! This is a wonderful drink and its maker deserves much gold as well as honour.

KING: I know that I can trust you. Thank you very much. It is your turn, Osi.

THIRD COUNCILLOR: (*He drinks and manages to keep a straight face.*) The first and second councillors have spoken well your majesty.

KING: I thank you all for your kind advice. Apena, it is your turn. You have always disagreed with me but I hope that this time you too will enjoy this drink with me.

FOURTH COUNCILLOR: Your Excellency, I appreciate your kindness and I, too, hope that this time I shall be able to agree with all my colleagues.

(*He lifts the calabash to his lips, but as the wine touches his lips, he spits it out and casts the calabash on the floor.*)

FOURTH COUNCILLOR: My Lord, the man who has made this wine and given it to you has committed treason. Do not drink it or you will die. You can fire me if you wish, but I have always kept my oath to advise you to the best of my ability and to speak the truth at all times. If, like my colleagues, I advise you to drink this wine then I advise you to take poison. It is *odae*.

KING: Again you do not agree. Someone is telling a lie. I am tired of lies. What do you suggest we should do to those who disgrace us by bad advice?

THIRD COUNCILLOR: He should be fired.

SECOND COUNCILLOR: No man should lie to the King.

FIRST COUNCILLOR: Your Majesty, I also think he should be fired.

KING: Very well. Apena have you nothing to say?

FOURTH COUNCILLOR: Your majesty, I have served you faithfully for many years. If now you want to fire me, I will go willingly, knowing that I have committed no offence.

KING: For lying to me (*turns to the other three* COUNCILLORS) you and you and you are fired.

(*lights go down*)

NARRATOR: In the original story of the Bitter Pill, the three chiefs were actually executed, but we think we should temper justice with mercy and let them live. Anyway, enough about truth for the moment. My next story is called 'Talk' and it is a proof that wonders shall never end.

Scene 4: 'Talk'

(Again, actors enter, exit and embody the story as described.)

*Song (*ALL*): 'Ise Agbe' song begins and the actors dance onstage. After the short dance piece, the* FARMER *remains on stage.*

NARRATOR: Once upon a time, a farmer went to dig up some yams to take to market. While he was digging, one of the yams said to him:

YAM: Well, at last you are here. You never weeded me, but now you come around with your digging stick. Go away and leave me alone!

NARRATOR: The farmer turned around and looked at his cow in amazement. The cow was chewing her cud and looking at him.

FARMER: Did you say something?

NARRATOR: The cow kept on chewing and said nothing, but the man's dog spoke up.

DOG: It wasn't the cow who spoke to you, it was the yam. The yam says leave him alone.

NARRATOR: The man became angry because his dog had never talked before and besides he didn't like his tone. So he took his knife and cut a branch from a palm tree to whip his dog. Just then the palm tree said:

PALM TREE: Put that branch down!

NARRATOR: The man was getting very upset about the way things were going, and he was about to throw the palm branch away, the palm branch said:

PALM BRANCH: Man, put me down softly!

NARRATOR: He put the branch down gently on a stone, and the stone said:

STONE: Hey, take that thing off me

NARRATOR: The frightened farmer started to run for his village. On the way he met a fisherman going the other way with a fish trap on his head.

FISHERMAN: What's the hurry?

FARMER: My yam said, 'Leave me alone!' Then the dog said, 'Listen to what the yam says!' When I went to whip the dog with palm branch, the tree said, 'Put that branch down!' Then the palm branch said, 'Do it softly!' Then the stone said, 'Take that thing off me!'

FISHERMAN: Is that all? Is that so frightening?

FISH TRAP: Well, did he take the palm branch off the stone?

FISHERMAN: What!

NARRATOR: The fisherman threw the fish trap on the ground and began to run with the farmer. And on the trail they met a weaver with a bundle of cloth on his head.

WEAVER: Where are you going in such a rush?

FARMER: My yam said, 'Leave me alone!' Then the dog said, 'Listen to what the yam says!' When I went to whip the dog with palm branch, the tree said, 'Put that branch down!' Then the palm branch said, 'Do it softly!' And the stone said, 'Take that thing off me!'

FISHERMAN: And then my fish trap said, 'Did it take it off?'

WEAVER: That's nothing to get excited about, no reason at all.

BUNDLE OF CLOTH: Oh, yes, it is, if it happened to you you'd run, too!

WEAVER: What!

NARRATOR: The weaver threw his bundle on the trail and started running with the farmer and the fisherman. They came panting to the ford in the river and found a man bathing.

MAN: Are you chasing a gazelle?

FARMER: (*breathlessly*) My yam talked to me, and it said, 'Leave me alone!' And my dog said, 'Listen to your yams!' And when I cut myself a branch the tree said, 'Put that branch down!' Then the palm branch said, 'Do it softly!' And the stone said, 'Take that thing off me!'

FISHERMAN: And my trap said, 'Did he?'

WEAVER: And my bundle of cloth said, 'You'd run too!'

MAN: And is that why you're running?

RIVER: Well, wouldn't you run if you were in their position?

NARRATOR: The man jumped out of the water and began to run with the others. They ran down the main street of the village to the house of the chief. The chief's servants brought his stool out, and he came and sat on it to listen to their complaints. The men began to recite their troubles.

FARMER: I went out to my garden to dig yams then everything began to talk! My yam said, 'Leave me alone.' My dog said, 'Pay attention to your yam!' The tree said, 'Put that branch down!' The branch said, 'Do it softly.' And the stone said, 'Take it off me!'

FISHERMAN: And my fish trap said, 'Well, did he take it off?'

WEAVER: And my cloth said, 'You'd run too!'

MAN: And the river said, 'Wouldn't you run too?'

CHIEF: Now, this is a wild story. All of you go back to your work now before I punish you for disturbing the peace.

(*The men exit.*)

CHIEF: Nonsense like that upsets the community.

CHIEF'S STOOL: Fantastic, isn't it? Imagine a talking yam.

CHIEF: (*looking at his servant*) What did you say?

SERVANT: (*pointing to the stool*) It was your stool, sir.

(*Lights come down gradually.*)

NARRATOR: Maybe it is because of the mysteries of inanimate things talking, like in our last story, that some Africans are in the habit of worshipping hills, trees, rivers and rocks. But as our next story, 'Moremi: The Goddess,' will show you, some humans, who perform superhuman deeds while alive, can also become deified gods and goddesses that require humans worship.

Scene 5: 'Moremi: The Goddess'

(*Again, actors enter, exit and embody the story as described.*)

(*Song:*)

Lead: Moremi Ajasoro — Chorus: Moremi Ajasoro
Lead: Ewure o fun mi ma ma gba o — Chorus: Moremi aja soro
Lead: Omo o fun mi ma ma gba lowo mi — Chorus: Moremi aja soro
Lead: Ile o fun mi ma ma gba lowo mi — Chorus: Moremi aja soro

NARRATOR: Once upon a time, in the ancient city of Ile Ife lived a woman, Moremi, married to the ruler, Oduduwa. The people of Ile Ife were always being attacked by the people of Igbos, who lived in the neighbouring forests.

(*War song*)

Call: Igbo kwenu, Response: Ye
Call: Kwenu Response: Ye
Call: Isobu Isobu Response: E yi ba eyi

NARRATOR: They would storm out of the forests, burn, loot, capture men and women as slaves and take them to their villages. Ife people would flee in terror, convinced that their attackers were evil spirits. All efforts to rally the defenders went in vain. Moremi was distressed. Distressed to see their land ruined, their warriors killed. She decided she was going to find a method to repel the evil spirits and stop her people from dying. She went to Esinminrin, the goddess of the river, and asked for her help:

LEAD: Esinminrin ye CHORUS: Iya odo o,
Esinminrin ye e e, gba wa a wi
LEAD: Igbo lo gbogun ti wa o CHORUS: Esinminrin ye.
Igbo lo gbogun ti wa
aki gbe ooo

NARRATOR: Esinminrin, the river Goddess, agreed to help Moremi, but only if she was willing to sacrifice her only son to her if her mission was successful. Was she to save her people and sacrifice her only son, or save her son and allow her people perish at the hands of the Igbo warriors? Moremi consented. Following the river goddess' advice, Moremi took her position in the frontline of defence, when the next attack came.

(*War song*)

Call: Igbo kwenu, Response: Ye
Call: Kwenu Response: Ye
Call: Isobu Isobu Response: E yi ba eyi

NARRATOR: Avoiding the enemies' weapons, Moremi allowed herself to be captured and taken as a slave. Upon arriving in the land of the Igbo, her beauty and charm attracted the Igbo king so much that he took her for a wife. Over months and years, Moremi obtained the confidence of the Igbo king and finally convinced him to allow her to watch their military preparations. Moremi discovered that the Igbos were not spirits, they were warriors dressed in intricate and frightening costumes and masks. That night she escaped back to her people. When the next attack came:

(*War song*)

Call: Igbo kwenu, Response: Ye
Call: Kwenu Response: Ye
Call: Isobu Isobu Response: E yi ba eyi

NARRATOR: Moremi had organised the defence herself. As the shout of the enemies pierced the air, the people of Ife met them with fire and torches. They burnt the spirit disguise and sent the Igbos fleeing. Ife was saved. But a promise must be kept. Moremi took her only son, Oluorogbo, to the river.

(*Song*)

Oluorogbo Oluorogbo
Aja laye Aja lorun o
Oluorogbo

NARRATOR: Up till today the people of Ile Ife still give thanks to Moremi during the festival of Edi for sacrificing her only son and saving them from their enemies. Every year, they pay homage to her, and Moremi became a goddess.

(*Song*)

LEAD: Moremi Ajasoro CHORUS: Moremi Ajasoro
LEAD: Ewure o fun mi ma ma gba o CHORUS: Moremi aja soro
LEAD: Omo o fun mi ma ma gba lowo mi CHORUS: Moremi aja soro
LEAD: Ile o fun mi ma ma gba lowo mi CHORUS: Moremi Ajasoro

(One by one, the actors bow in front of Moremi. Music and singing fade out. Silence. Suddenly, loud R&B music is heard. Then a Man *enters. He is dressed in Western clothing and carries a suitcase. He opens the suitcase and hands the actors pieces of Western-style clothing and other objects, such as wrist watches, mobile phones, sunglasses, mirrors . . .*

The Man *then wheels a large TV onto the stage. He switches on the TV and we see a nature programme about an African gazelle trying to cross a river to escape a lion.* Narrator *tries to talk, but he is ignored, as actors are more interested in the documentary on the TV. Eventually,* Narrator *joins the others to watch the programme. Lights fade. The nature programme continues in the dark. Then it, too, fades out . . .)*

Act Two: Not So Long Ago

Scene 1

(The TV set still sits in the centre of the stage. As the audience take their seats, we hear songs about immigration. Lights fade to black. The words 'Several Years Later' come on the TV screen. This is followed by a commercial for air travel. As the advertisement plays, light comes up to reveal a TV studio stage right. The TV Host *of 'The Great Great Show' is seen having his make-up touched up. There are two cameras pointing in converging directions. Two* Cameramen*, a* Producer*, and a* Production Assistant *stand by.)*

Producer: We are coming out of ad break. Roll tape.

Cameraman 1: Tape 1 rolling.

Cameraman 2: Tape 2 rolling.

Producer: Tapes are rolling. Cue audience.

(The Production Assistant *raises a cue card that reads: 'CLAP' in big bold letters.)*

Producer: *(counting down)* 3-2-1 and . . . action.

(As TV Host says the lines below, we see, upstage, a line of dark-skinned people with umbrellas getting their papers stamped by an immigration officer.)

TV Host: Welcome back to the last part of 'The Great Great Show'. Now, it was not so long ago that Ireland, our country known for mass emigration, began to experience unprecedented inward-migration. People from all over the world began to look to Ireland as a safe haven, where the pasture is greener. As a result, Ireland is now a truly multicultural society, and to celebrate this increasing cultural diversity, we are dedicating the last part of tonight's show to discussing some of the experiences of members of Ireland's African community. For them, living in one of the fastest growing economies in the world must be like a dream come true. But does this dream have a darker side? As a way of exploring this topic, we have decided to feature an African-led theatre company which has created a number of performances, based on the real-life experiences of African immigrants to Ireland. To introduce each of the performances and what inspired them, ladies and gentlemen would you please welcome, the Director.

(*Cue card for 'CLAP' is raised. DIRECTOR, who is the NARRATOR in the first act, comes in. She is greeted by TV HOST and takes her seat.*)

TV HOST: Welcome to 'The Great Great Show'.

DIRECTOR: Thanks for having me on the show. It's great to be here.

TV HOST: Can you first tell us briefly a bit about your theatre company, Arambe Productions?

DIRECTOR: Basically, Arambe was set up to introduce Irish audiences to African theatre traditions and to create an avenue through which interested members of Ireland's African community might express themselves through the art of theatre.

TV HOST: The performances you are going to share with us tonight, I understand each of them is based on the real-life experiences of African immigrants in Ireland—how did this idea come about?

DIRECTOR: Well, first, I should point out that it is not only African people's experiences that are dramatised here, we feel it is also important to show some of the encounters that Irish people have had with members of the African community.

TV HOST: Right . . . right, of course. So tell us, where did the inspiration come from?

DIRECTOR: Sometime early last year, Arambe was asked to present a short theatre piece at a multicultural event. After our presentation, as usual, we asked our audience if they had any comments. One man straight away put up his hand:

MAN: (*in the audience*) This excerpt, that you are after doing is from Jimmy Murphy's play *Kings of Kilburn High Road*, isn't it?

DIRECTOR: Yes, it is.

MAN: He's an Irish playwright.

DIRECTOR: He is, yeah . . .

MAN: So tell me, do you think it is right for you people to come into this country, take our jobs, take our houses and now you've started acting our plays as well. Don't you have plays of your own?

TV HOST: Someone actually said that?

DIRECTOR: Yes. For a while, everyone was dumfounded. It was one of the actors who came to the rescue by explaining that we merely sought to present a commentary on what it means to be an alien in a foreign country, irrespective of where you are from. But before we left, we apologised to the man and assured him that next time we are invited to such events, we will present our own material. So, really, it was that day that the seed for *Not So Long Ago*, a dramatisation of personal experiences of African immigrants, was planted.

TV HOST: So what performance are we going to see first?

DIRECTOR: Our first performance is inspired by an experience of a mixed race actor. And it is titled 'Audition Part 1.'

(*light fades on TV Studio*)

Scene 2: 'Audition'[2] Part One

(*As the lights fade on TV HOST and DIRECTOR, they come up centre stage to reveal an audition in progress. PETER and PAUL sit behind a table watching LADY audition.*)

LADY: (*reading from a script*) Who knows, God help you.

PETER: Great! Excellent!!

LADY: Thanks.

PETER: Well . . . like we were saying, the role we are looking to cast is Pegeen Mike.

PAUL: From *The Playboy of the Western World.*

LADY: Yes. I know the play well.

PETER: Great! Well, I must say that your reading was excellent and you certainly look the part. But we have a few more to see. So we'll contact your agent in the next week or so. Is that alright?

LADY: Oh, yes. Thank you for your time and I look forward to hearing from you so.

PETER: You will. And again, well done. Good luck now.

(*LADY exits.*)

PETER: She was good, wasn't she?

PAUL: Perfect. Right age as well.

PETER: Yeah. We'll see. Who's next?

PAUL: Um . . . (*looking down at a list of names*) Sarah Byrne.

PETER: Well, let's have her in and see what Sarah Byrne can do.

(*PAUL pops his head outside the door and calls out for SARAH BYRNE. SARAH comes in after PAUL, who returns to his seat at the table.*)

SARAH: (*smiling*) Hi. How are you?

PAUL: Fine.

PETER: Great. Eh, have a seat.

SARAH: Thanks.

(*PAUL and PETER exchange a glance.*)

PETER: So. Sarah isn't it?

SARAH: Yes. Sarah.

PAUL: Byrne.

SARAH: Yep. That's me. Sarah Byrne.

(*pause*)

PAUL: My great-grandmother was called Byrne.

SARAH: Really?

PETER: Great strong Irish name.

PAUL: Very Irish.

(*pause*)

PETER: So . . . Sarah . . . Tell us a bit about yourself.

PAUL: Like. Where are you from?
SARAH: Cork.
PETER: Have you lived in Ireland long?
SARAH: Better part of my life.
PETER: So when did you move here?
SARAH: I've lived here practically all my life.
PETER: In . . . Cork?
SARAH: Yep. I'm sorry but, is there a problem?
PAUL: No.

(*overlapping*)

PETER: Yes.
PAUL: Well, Sarah, what we mean is, to be honest, this is a quintessential Irish play, so we are casting only, eh, you know . . .
PETER: Irish actors.
SARAH: But I am an Irish actor. Okay, okay, my dad is Nigerian and I do visit Africa regularly but . . .
PAUL: No, no. That's not the problem. I can tell from your CV that you are a very talented and experienced actress. It's just that . . . well . . . (He looks to *PETER for help.*)
PETER: We've a few more to see and we'll let you know through your agent in the next week or so. Thank you for coming in.
SARAH: I see. No problem. Thank you and good luck with the production.

(*SARAH exits. When outside the room, she realises she still has the script she has just read from. She turns round to return it, but as she is about to go in, she overhears the following conversation.*)

PAUL: How can we cast her, for God sakes? She's black!
PETER: Well, she's not black.
PAUL: Well, she's certainly not white.
PETER: She's more sort of a . . . half-caste?
PAUL: Well, whatever she is, whatever you call her, she certainly doesn't look Irish.

(*The lights fade as SARAH leaves the script on the chair outside door and leaves. The light comes up on 'The Great Great Show'.*)

TV HOST: That is amazing. Basically, Sarah sees herself as an Irish actor that can play any Irish part, but the casting people see her as something else.

DIRECTOR: Exactly! The question is, if you are mixed, is your bottle half empty or half full?

TV HOST: Interesting. Now, the next performance is called 'River Islands.'Tell us about that?

Scene 3: 'River Islands'[3]

DIRECTOR: It is inspired by an incident that happened sometime last year. This African man went into River Island on Grafton Street to do some shopping. It was a wet and miserable day, the kind of day that you would ideally not choose for shopping. But he was under pressure and had no choice as he was travelling to his native country and intended, as is expected of an African returning home, to bring something, no matter how small, for all the relations. After buying this and that, the gentleman made his way to the cashier to pay for all the items he had selected:

(The light comes up to reveal SEB and a CASHIER standing beside a cash register at the end of the transaction. A WOMAN stands in line behind SEB.)

CASHIER: *(offering SEB a receipt)* Here's your receipt. Please keep it in case. Thank you. Come again.

(The CASHIER hands over the paper bag full of shopping to SEB who makes his way to the door. The WOMAN who is on the queue behind SEB steps forward to be attended to. SEB stops in his tracks and turns back.)

SEB: Plastic bag?

CASHIER: What do you mean?

SEB: On parle Francais or Swahili?

CASHIER: Excuse me.

SEB: Désolé de vous déranger. Mais je me demandais si vous aviez un sac en plastique parce-qu'il pleut dehors et j'ai encore des courses à faire. Mes affaires seront abimées si je les apporte sous cette pluie.

CASHIER: What?

WOMAN: He is saying in French that he would prefer a plastic bag because it is raining outside.

CASHIER: I see. Please tell him that we don't have plastic bags. (*returns to attending to the* WOMAN) That will be forty-five euro, ma'am.

WOMAN: Il dit qu'il n'a pas de sac en plastique.

SEB: D'accord. Est-ce que je peux poser mon sac ici pour environ une heure?

WOMAN: He is asking if it would be alright for him to leave his bag here for about an hour.

CASHIER: (*to* SEB) You want to leave your bag?

SEB: One hour.

CASHIER: We don't hold bags for customers.

SEB: What?

WOMAN: Il dit qu'il ne garde pas les sacs pour les clients.

CASHIER: It's against the company's policy to hold stuff for people.

WOMAN: Il dit que c'est contre leur politique.

SEB: Allez, que diable . . . je lui demande seulement parce qu'il pleut beaucoup et cette pluie abimera ce sac.

WOMAN: He said he wanted you to keep his bag for him because it is raining.

CASHIER: I'm sorry there's nothing I can do to help him. How are you paying for this?

WOMAN: Credit card.

SEB: C'est injuste.

CASHIER: If he had not paid for them then I could hold them.

WOMAN: Il dit qu'il ne peut pas les garder pour toi parce que tu les as déjà acheté.

SEB: (*to the* CASHIER) Vous me dites que si je n'avais pas encore paye vous les garderez pour moi, mais parce que je les ai déjà acheté vous ne les garderez pas pour moi?

CASHIER: What?

WOMAN: He is just asking if you would have held the stuff for him if he hadn't paid for them.

CASHIER: Definitely. That is our policy.

WOMAN: (*to* SEB) Oui. Si tu n'avais pas encore payé, il les aurait gardé pour toi.

SEB: Vraiment? Alors demande lui s'ils ont une politique d'echange.

WOMAN: He wants to know if you have refund policy.

CASHIER: Yes, we do.

(*WOMAN nods to SEB*)

SEB: Alors je veux rendre ces biens. Je ne les veux plus. (*He hands the bag back to the CASHIER.*)

CASHIER: (*to the WOMAN*) What is he saying?

WOMAN: He wants to return the stuff.

(*collects the bag*)

CASHIER: That'll be no problem. Can I have your receipt please? This is your refund. Right, your bag is going to be kept if you would like to come back for it.

WOMAN: Il a dit que si tu veux acheter ces biens tu peux revenir et les acheter plus tard. Ils seront derrière le comptoir.

SEB: Alors si je reviens acheter ces affaires, je serai obligé de payer à nouveau?

WOMAN: Oui.

SEB: Merci.

(*he exits*)

CASHIER: Thanks for your help madam. That will be forty-five euro.

WOMAN: No problem.

CUSTOMER 2: Thank God it's brother to brother.

CASHIER: He is not my brother. He is a bloody Cameroonian or something

CUSTOMER 2: Oh I see.

CASHIER: Would you sign here please?

(*As the WOMAN signs, light goes down.*)

END

(*Lights come up on 'The Great Great Show'.*)

TV HOST: That is amazing. I think it is a very clever way of reminding people that although we may speak of Ireland's African community, it is important to remember that Africa is a huge continent with many countries and people from diverse cultures.

DIRECTOR: Precisely! It is interesting that when you ask Irish people that if I am an African what are you? Most of the time they still answer that they are Irish.

TV HOST: Instead of saying that they are Europeans.

DIRECTOR: There you go. But you can't really blame them. While you have English, Irish and German writers in Europe, writers from Africa are usually described as African writers.

TV HOST: That's very true. So what is the next sketch about?

DIRECTOR: Our next sketch is inspired by the question: where are you from? It is entitled *A Question of Home.*

(*Lights fade down on 'The Great Great Show' and come up on a pharmacy.*)

Scene 4: The Question of Home[4]

(*A pharmacy shop: A black woman behind the counter is having a conversation with a white man who is on the shop floor, working as a security man.*)

SECURITY: The last time I was at home, I went with Stephan my son.

SHOP ASSISTANT: I bet he enjoyed it.

SECURITY: It is hard to believe but he didn't.

SHOP ASSISTANT: Why didn't he?

SECURITY: Throughout our stay he just kept asking: Daddy, when are we going back home?

SHOP ASSISTANT: That's kind of interesting.

(*A young black customer comes in and goes straight to the counter to pay for a bottle of shampoo. As he is being attended to, an old woman in her sixties walks in and approaches the security man.*)

OLD WOMAN: Please can you tell me where this is? (*showing him a flier*)

SECURITY: I am sorry I don't know. (*pointing to the black girl at the till*) You can ask her, she will know.

OLD WOMAN: Sure she wouldn't know. (*she speaks something in Irish*)

SECURITY: What?

OLD WOMAN: Oh, you don't have Irish no?
SECURITY: Oh, no. I am from South Africa.

(*The black customer leaves.*)

SHOP ASSISTANT: (*comes to the shop floor.*) Can I help you?
SECURITY: She is looking for directions.
OLD WOMAN: You wouldn't know where this is, would you now?
SHOP ASSISTANT: (*looks at the flier.*) Oh, the community centre?Come. Let me show you. Go through those lights and when you come to Slattery's Pub, turn right. The community centre is down that road on the left.
OLD WOMAN: Thank you very much.
SHOP ASSISTANT: It is my pleasure. *Slán go foil.*

(*Light goes down to indicate the passage of time light comes up as* EMILY *comes into the shop.*)

EMILY: Good afternoon.
SECURITY: Can I help you?
EMILY: Please do you do aftershave?
SECURITY: All our men's aftershaves are on this side.
EMILY: Thank you. (*She goes to check the selection. After a while she selects one*) I'll take this. Do you have wrapping paper?
SECURITY: Yes take it to the cashier over there, she will wrap it for you after you've paid for it.

(*The black cashier has just finished attending to the customer in front of her.*)

EMILY: Can I pay for this please?
SHOP ASSISTANT: Sure. That will be thirty-two euro forty-nine cents. Would you want it wrapped?
EMILY: Yes, thank you.

(*Black shop assistant begins to wrap the gift.*)

EMILY: Where are you from?
SHOP ASSISTANT: Zimbabwe.
EMILY: I bet you miss the weather. The blue skies, the warm climate and all. (*silence*) So did you go home for Easter?
SHOP ASSISTANT: What do you mean?
EMILY: I was just asking if you had a chance to go home for Easter.

SHOP ASSISTANT: And what is your business if I went home for Easter or not? What about you, did you go home for Easter?

EMILY: But Ireland is my home. Here.

SHOP ASSISTANT: There you go. Is it because I am black that you think this is not my home?

EMILY: I am sorry, I d-didn't mean that at all.

SHOP ASSISTANT: How did you mean it then? Tell me.

EMILY: Please, forgive me. I did not mean to insult you.

SECURITY: (*tries to calm things down*) It is okay. It is okay, Meg.

(EMILY pays for the aftershave and as she walks out lights fade on stage.)

(Lights come up on 'The Great Great Show'.)

TV HOST: That did not really happen, did it?

DIRECTOR: Absolutely: The point here is that you may say one thing and people, depending on their circumstances at that particular time, may hear it differently.

TV HOST: I am not following? Irish people tend to ask other Irish people where they are from. Are you suggesting that 'where are you from?' takes a new meaning when a black person is asked?

DIRECTOR: I am glad you ask that question. Now imagine this scenario. You are sitting in a pub and someone collides with your seat. Before you look up, you say, 'Are you blind or something?' And when you finally look up, the person is actually blind. In that context you'll agree with me that the question: 'are you blind?' suddenly takes a different meaning. Doesn't it?

TV HOST: Now I get you. That is a very different way of looking at things. Really. Well . . . tell us what is the next sketch about?

DIRECTOR: Our next sketch is inspired by an experience of an African girl who agreed to go to a restaurant with a regular Irish guy. It is titled 'Food for Thought'.

(Light goes down on 'The Great Great Show'.)

Scene 5: Food for Thought (Dinner)[5]

(Lights come up to reveal a restaurant. There are four tables but only three of these are occupied. TRACY, a young black woman, and SEÁN an Irish man are occupying the table SR; they have just finished their meal. In the background

we have a white couple and on the table SL we have KAYUS*, a black man and* RUTH*, a pretty teenager of mixed race background.* WAITER *is attending to* TRACY *and* SEÁN*. Soft music in the background.)*

WAITER: Hope you enjoyed your meal.

SEÁN & TRACY: Thanks.

WAITER: Anything else?

TRACY: A glass of white wine please. (*to Seán*) You don't mind now do you?

SEÁN: Hey you can drink whatever you want. This is a free country.

TRACY: You are a gentleman.

WAITER: And what about you sir?

SEÁN: Another glass of water will do please. Thanks.

WAITER: Sure. (*leaves*)

TRACY: You don't eat much, do you?

SEÁN: No I am watching my waist . . . And tell me how do you keep in shape and eat such healthy meals.

TRACY: The fact is that I don't usually but I'm particularly hungry today.

SEÁN: I see.

WAITER: (WAITER *brings drinks*) Here are your drinks.

SEÁN: Thanks.

TRACY: Thanks.

(WAITER *leaves goes to another table*)

WAITER: Here is your bill sir. (*waits*)

KAYUS: Thanks. Can you come back please?

RUTH: How much is it?

KAYUS: It's €61.50. I think we can make that sixty-five with service charge.

RUTH: Here . . . that's thirty.

KAYUS: What are you doing?

RUTH: That is my share.

KAYUS: Hey, hey please. Take your money and stop embarrassing me.

RUTH: What do you mean embarrassing you?

KAYUS: I know you are loaded but this is on me.

RUTH: No way, I am going to pay for my share.

KAYUS: I said it's on me.

RUTH: And I said no. I insist that I pay for my meal okay.
KAYUS: Okay, okay. I hear you.
RUTH: Good.
KAYUS: But.
RUTH: But what?
KAYUS: Let me pay for the wine okay. So you contribute twenty.
RUTH: On the condition that I pay for the movie tickets.
KAYUS: Okay, I give up. What time is the movie again?
RUTH: 8:45.
KAYUS: (*leaves the money*) Right let's leg it, we have about eight minutes.

(*As they about to leave, the* WAITER *comes to collect their cheque. As they walk out we hear them.*)

RUTH: Thanks for a nice dinner.
KAYUS: You are thanking me for the dinner you paid for?
RUTH: Okay, thanks for the wine then.
KAYUS: Don't mention.

(*lights on* SEÁN *and* TRACY)

SEÁN: How is your wine?
TRACY: Very nice. Would you like a taste?
SEÁN: No, thanks. I don't drink wine.
TRACY: So what do you drink?
SEÁN: Water when I am in a restaurant and juice when I am out with friends.
TRACY: That is unbelievable. You mean you don't drink alcohol at all?
SEÁN: Not at all. I never had and I don't think I ever will.
TRACY: I thought all Irish men drink.
SEÁN: That's what a lot of people think. It is like saying it is all black men who can dance. A considerable number of Irish adults are teetotallers.
TRACY: Meaning?
SEÁN: A large number of Irish men don't drink at all.
TRACY: That's amazing. Wonder what men like that do on Friday nights. Obviously, they are not on Dublin streets.
SEÁN: Watching the 'Late Late' with a cup of tea maybe.

(*The* WAITER *comes in to their table to pack their plates.*)

WAITER: I hope you enjoyed your food.

TRACY: Everything's perfect. The steak is well done. Thank you very much.

WAITER: Good. And you sir?

SEÁN: The food is very nice. Thank you. Can we have our bill please?

(*The* WAITER *leaves.*)

TRACY: Their food is very nice. I think I will come back here another time.

SEÁN: It is quite a nice restaurant. I really like the atmosphere.

WAITER: (*presenting the bill*) Here you go sir. Call me when you are ready.

SEÁN: Thanks. Now let's see. Hun uh. €120. Whoa! Okay. I had water and curry and coffee. That's €18.50. You had oysters, steak, two glasses of Champagne, a glass of wine. Good, I will contribute €40 you can add the rest.

TRACY: You mean my bill is around €100?

SEÁN: Well all you need to add now is €80. Right? Let me quickly use the gents. I'll be back in a minute.

(SEÁN *leaves for the toilet*)

TRACY: (*dials a number*) Hello Mr Donnelly . . . Hello . . . This is Tracy your tenant in Rathmines . . . Mr Donnelly, you know I promised that I was going to leave this week's rent on the table for you. Please I am very sorry. Something very urgent has come up that I need the money for. I promise next week unfailingly . . . (SEÁN *arrives*) Thanks. Bye.

(*As she starts counting the money from an envelope lights go down.*)

END

(*Lights on 'The Great Great Show'.*)

TV HOST: What is the point in that sketch?

DIRECTOR: The thing is up till now in some parts of Africa when a woman is taken out, she is not required to pay for anything. A man takes care of everything to give the impression that he will always take care of the girl. It is really a cultural thing.

TV HOST: Really. But I suppose Ireland was once like that. But things have changed now. You do your share and the woman does hers. Very good. Now you told me a joke before we came on air. Would you like to share it with our audience?

DIRECTOR: Oh the joke. Is it the one about the pastor?

TV HOST: No. The one based on an incident on a flight.

DIRECTOR: Oh. That one. It is not a joke. It was a real event that took place on a British Air flight between Johannesburg and London.

(Lights down on 'The Great Great Show'.)

Scene 6: The Flight: A dramatised joke

(Light up on stage to reveal inside a plane: An AIR HOSTESS *is attending to a* WOMAN *who is obviously disturbed by being seated next to a* BLACK MAN.*)*

AIR HOSTESS: Madam, what is the matter?

WOMAN: You obviously do not see it then? You placed me next to a black man. I do not agree to sit next to someone from such a repugnant group. Give me an alternative seat.

AIR HOSTESS: Be calm please. Almost all the places on this flight are taken. I will go and check if another place is available.

(The HOSTESS *goes away and then comes back a few minutes later.)*

AIR HOSTESS: Madam, just as I thought, there are no other available seats in the economy class. I spoke to the captain and he informed me that there is one seat in the business class. All the same, we also have one seat in the first class. *(The woman is preparing to stand.)* Hang on ma'am. I must add that it is unusual for our company to permit someone from the economy class to sit in the first class. However, given the circumstances, the captain feels that it would be scandalous to make someone sit next to someone so disgusting. (*She then turns to the black guy.*) Therefore, Sir, if you would like to, please collect your hand luggage, a seat awaits you in first class.

(*The other passengers who were shocked by what they had just witnessed stand up and applaud. Lights fade to black.*)

(*Lights come up on 'The Great Great Show'.*)

TV HOST: It is hard to believe that such things still happen in this day and age.

DIRECTOR: They still happen on the buses but rather in a subtle way.

TV HOST: That can't be true. You mean . . .

DIRECTOR: On many occasions I have seen people standing on a bus when the seat next to me is empty.

TV HOST: That is hard to believe.

DIRECTOR: There you go.

TV HOST: But fair play to that pilot. I gather the next sketch is ready, tell us about it.

DIRECTOR: As a society, Ireland is transforming into one that needs to cater for diverse group of people. When people from different parts of the world come into a society like this they come with their religions, traditions and cultures. These are the things that make people unique and different. And Ireland will certainly be better for it if it can accommodate these differences and appreciate the uniqueness of each individual group of people that have recently made this island their home. Our next sketch is 'A Matter of Tradition'. Some of your viewers may find this story a bit distressing.

Scene 7: A Matter of Tradition[6]

(*Light opens on ABIDEMI singing a lullaby trying to rock his son ISAAC to sleep.*)

ABIDEMI: (*Singing*) Omo mi a kuru bete ku be
Omo mi o, a kuru bete ku be
Bi o ku o ma ra so fun e

Bi o ku o ma re gba orun
Egba orun to yomo lorun.

DIRECTOR: Not so long ago . . . Abidemi and Catherine who met and got married in Ireland gave birth to their first child. He was a boy, so they christened him Isaac after Catherine's father who had died two years ago. Isaac was a strong healthy boy and he was the apple of his father's eyes.

ABIDEMI: You are the best boy in the world. I know your mum does not mind what you do but I would like you to study medicine. Dr Isaac Mayowa Agboola. How does that sound? You can go to Africa and cure all their diseases. That will be good won't it? (*Baby starts to cry*) Okay I understand it is too much responsibility. Okay we'll stay in Europe. Good boy.

(*Starts singing Omo mi o a kuru bete again very quietly.* CATHERINE *comes in.* ABIDEMI *makes a sign to her to be quiet so as not to wake him up. He takes* ISAAC *in to lay him down.*)

ABIDEMI: (*comes back in*) You are early.

CATHERINE: Yes. I forgot that Aoife is coming this afternoon.

ABIDEMI: Aoife?

CATHERINE: The midwife. I got a text from her to remind me of the appointment.

ABIDEMI: I see. What time is she coming?

CATHERINE: About 4.00 p.m.

ABIDEMI: Great. I'll just go out for a stroll. I'm sure Isaac will be down for two hours at least.

CATHERINE: How was he?

ABIDEMI: He is in flying form.

CATHERINE: Good.

ABIDEMI: By the way, would you mind asking Aoife about that issue again? Isaac is almost a month old. It is supposed to be done a few days after he was born.

CATHERINE: Don't worry, I will ask her.

(*door bell rings*)

CATHERINE: That must be her.

(ABIDEMI *goes in. At that moment* AOIFE *comes in.*)

CATHERINE: Hello, Aoife. Really good to see you.

MIDWIFE: You look very well. How's the baby?

CATHERINE: He just went to sleep now.

ABIDEMI: (*comes out*) Hi, Aoife.

MIDWIFE: How are you Abidemi?

ABIDEMI: Well, thank God. You are welcome. I am just going down the road. I'll see you again maybe.

CATHERINE: See you later.

MIDWIFE: Bye.

CATHERINE: Sit down, Aoife.

MIDWIFE: Thanks. Just said I should drop by. How is everything? Is he sleeping well?

CATHERINE: Not a bother on him. He sleeps around seven in the evening and the only time he wakes up is to feed. And as soon as he is full he's gone again.

MIDWIFE: That's pretty good. You are lucky.

CATHERINE: I think he takes after his father. His father can sleep for Africa.

MIDWIFE: And what about you, how are you doing?

CATHERINE: I am very well, thank you.

MIDWIFE: Still breastfeeding?

CATHERINE: Oh, yes. We have decided that we will breastfeed Isaac until he is two, at least. We think he is better off that way.

MIDWIFE: I can't agree with you more. Research has shown that kids that are breastfed are much better for it.

CATHERINE: Abidemi says some kids are breastfed until they are four in Africa. But I think two will do for Isaac. I must go back to work.

MIDWIFE: Right, I am happy that mother and child are doing very well. I think I better start going now. I have a couple of more houses to visit. The next time I see you is (*consults her chart*) Monday fortnight. But if you have any queries at all, do not hesitate to call me.

CATHERINE: Please, Aoife, before you go there's something very important I want to ask you.

MIDWIFE: What is it, Catherine?

CATHERINE: It's that thing . . . we mentioned it to you the day Isaac was born actually.

MIDWIFE: Um . . .

CATHERINE: The . . . (*makes a sign of cutting*) . . .

MIDWIFE: Oh that. That's true. I remember you mentioning it alright.

CATHERINE: I don't really mind personally, but Bidemi seems to be determined to have it done. And he seems to be getting impatient every day. In fact, he mentioned it again just now when I told him you were coming.

MIDWIFE: Well . . . as I have already explained to you, it's not something that the maternity hospital has anything to do with but I know that the hospitals do it on religious grounds, so I don't foresee any problem there. All you need to do is to inform your paediatrician. Who is your paediatrician again?

CATHERINE: Dr Mc Sweeney.

MIDWIFE: Even better. You are lucky because he worked for many years in West Africa. So I don't envisage any problem at all.

CATHERINE: Okay. Thanks a lot for coming Aoife.

MIDWIFE: It is always a pleasure seeing you. Give Isaac a big kiss for me when he wakes up.

(*As light goes down on* CATHERINE *and the* MIDWIFE, NARRATOR *continues.*)

DIRECTOR: Abidemi is determined to have his child circumcised according to his African tradition. He has heard of George who lives and works as a circumcisionist in Ireland. But since they have access to doctors and specialists who could perform the procedure in a much safer and more hygienic environment, Abidemi and Catherine decide to do things the Irish way.

(*Lights on* DR MCSWEENEY*'s office. He has just finished testing* ISAAC.)

DR MCSWEENEY: Congratulations! Your little boy is doing very well. He has gained weight and is thriving in every way. We won't need to see him here again now until he's a year old unless, of course, you experience any problems in which case don't hesitate to contact us.

(*He stands up and offers* ABIDEMI *his hand.* ABIDEMI *stands up but then sits down again quickly.*)

ABIDEMI: I'm sorry doctor I have some other business to discuss with you.

(*DR MCSWEENEY sits back down*)

DR MCSWEENEY: What is on your mind Mr Agboola?

ABIDEMI: It is our wish Doctor that Isaac be circumcised.

DR MCSWEENEY: Oh that's no problem.

ABIDEMI: Really? When can we do it?

DR MCSWEENEY: When you bring him back for his check up in a year's time we'll book him in for the procedure . . .

ABIDEMI: But Doctor you don't understand we would like him to have it done this week or next. It's very important to us.

DR MCSWEENEY: Well, I'm very sorry, Mr Agboola, but the hospital policy is that no elective surgery can be carried out on children until they are one year of age. If you want I can put you on the theatre list for April of next year.

(*ABIDEMI sits there and stares at the doctor in disbelief.*)

ABIDEMI: But I am Isaac's father, and I wish for him to have the procedure now. I don't understand really why the hospital decides for us. Surely, this is not correct doctor . . .

DR MCSWEENEY: I'm telling you Mr Agboola, it's not your decision to make. There are reasons for this rule, if we wait a year, it means that Isaac will be better able to cope with the anaesthetics and any infection or complications of the procedure, that's just the way things are done here, I . . .

ABIDEMI: (*visibly getting angry*) That is precisely why we came here so that things can be done properly . . . to avoid complications. And you sit here and tell me that you won't let me make this decision for my son . . . that it's not up to me, its not my decision to make?

(*ABIDEMI is visibly frustrated. CATHERINE who has been sitting very quietly adjusts herself on the seat and addresses the DOCTOR.*)

CATHERINE: Doctor, I heard that you were once working in West Africa. Which means you especially should understand a bit of African culture.

DR MCSWEENEY: I do know a thing or two about African culture but you have to understand that we are living in a country where the beliefs and traditions are different. I must practice medicine within the guidelines and standards laid down by this country.

(ABIDEMI slaps the table in frustration.)

ABIDEMI: I can't believe this.

DR MCSWEENEY: I'll book the procedure provisionally for one year's time, and we'll talk again then.

ABIDEMI: A whole year.

DR MCSWEENEY: It may seem unfair at this moment, but I assure you, we all have Isaac's best interests at heart.

(DR MCSWEENEY begins to write in the chart again. ABIDEMI at this stage begins to cry freely.)

ABIDEMI: Are you saying, Doctor, that I don't have my son's best interest at heart. This is my child we are talking about here you know? I mean . . .

(He stops mid-sentence. DR MCSWEENEY stands to shake ABIDEMI's hand.)

DR MCSWEENEY: I do understand your frustration, but I am terribly sorry Mr Agboola, my hands are tied. Until then I wish you, your wife and your lovely son God's blessing and good health.

(ABIDEMI rises dejectedly. Light goes down as they leave. And simultaneously comes up in their home.)

ABIDEMI: I think it is high time we contacted George.

CATHERINE: George. Who is George?

ABIDEMI: My cousin. The one that I told you about. He is very good.

CATHERINE: No, Abidemi. We have discussed this many times and I still think there is no harm in waiting for a year as Dr Mc Sweeney has suggested. I know you have ascertained George's competency.

ABIDEMI: He is a fourth generation circumcisionist, Catherine.

CATHERINE: Still, I don't think it is a good idea to expose Isaac to any danger because you think it is a matter of tradition.

ABIDEMI: Catherine. The hen fed on something before corn was discovered. I know everything in this part of the world is according to procedure but what happens to our tradition? Back home, the tradition stipulates that a baby boy must be circumcised before his naming ceremony on the eighth day. Isaac is a month old already and we have to wait until he is one year before we can get it done. I don't get it Catherine.

CATHERINE: Abidemi, I know this is very important to you but I will suggest that we do it properly and when the time is right. It is better to be safe than to be sorry. He is almost two months now which means in ten months the procedure will be done and dusted.

(sound of a crying baby)

CATHERINE: He's awake. I'll get him.

(CATHERINE goes inside.)

DIRECTOR: Day after day Abidemi's disappointment changes to anger. He feels he has done all he can as a respectable law-abiding man without getting anywhere. Isaac has to be circumcised just as he, his own father and his father's fathers had. This is not some flighty whim or mumbo jumbo nonsense; it is a tradition steeped in history. He decides that if his new society refuses to understand this and be scathing of his belief he would have to seek support somewhere else. On the next day he calls George and a day and time is agreed. On the appointed day:

ABIDEMI: *(opening the door)* George, good to see you. You are right on time.

GEORGE: Well remember you said you would like this to be a quickie. Do you have everything prepared?

ABIDEMI: Everything is already.

GEORGE: Good. Where is Isaac?

ABIDEMI: I have to wake him up . . . One minute.

(He goes inside and gets ISAAC. GEORGE sets up his equipment on the table. Prayers are said and ISAAC's nappy is removed. ABIDEMI holds his son as GEORGE cleans the baby with cotton wool soaked in warm water. He takes

the foreskin in his left hand and cuts with his right, blood begins to flow from ISAAC*'s groin area.* ABIDEMI *looks away as* ISAAC *begins to cry. George wraps a tight bandage on the bloody area and replaces the nappy. Further prayers are said and he returns* ISAAC *to his father's arms.* ABIDEMI *starts rocking little* ISAAC *in his arms and gives praise to God.*)

GEORGE: That's it. You should keep the bandage on it for twenty-four hours and then have it replaced. If bleeding persists you can apply a little bit of olive oil. I don't think there should be any problem though. You see, he is stopped crying already.

ABIDEMI: Thanks a lot, George. I truly appreciate this. Hold on one minute.

(He takes ISAAC *in and comes back immediately.)*

ABIDEMI: You wouldn't believe he has already gone back to sleep. Thank you very much, George . . . So how much do I owe you?

GEORGE: That will be €200.

ABIDEMI: Do you take Laser?

GEORGE: Not really.

ABIDEMI: It's a joke. I withdrew the money last night.

(both men laugh)

ABIDEMI: Listen, I truly appreciate your kind consideration and I am sure I will see you soon.

(GEORGE *leaves and* ABIDEMI *clears all the stuff. He then picks up his mobile phone and dials a number.*)

ABIDEMI: Hello, can you hear me now? . . . Good. I said it is a fantastic day . . . Isaac got his thing done a few minutes ago? Oh, he is in good shape. He is a real man like his father. What? . . . Oh, he is asleep at the moment.

(CATHERINE *comes in with shopping bags. While on the phone* ABIDEMI *acknowledges her and makes a sign that* ISAAC *is inside asleep.* CATHERINE *goes indoors.*)

ABIDEMI: (*back on the phone*) What? Oh, mummy wants to congratulate me . . . okay, give her the phone. Hello, mummy. I can't stay too long.

(*Suddenly a scream is heard from backstage.*)

Listen, I will call you back.

(*As* ABIDEMI *drops the phone,* CATHERINE *rushes in carrying* ISAAC. *She is sobbing.*)

CATHERINE: Look, Isaac is bleeding.

ABIDEMI: Catherine he will be alright. We don't need to panic. We just need to apply a bit of olive oil.

CATHERINE: Olive oil. Are you crazy or something? What happened to him?

ABIDEMI: George just left about an hour ago. The bleeding is normal.

CATHERINE: You are out of your mind Bidemi. Look at him he is turning blue. If we don't take him to the hospital now he is going to bleed to death. I can't believe you did this to me Bidemi.

(*she starts sobbing*)

ABIDEMI: Hey, bring him here.

CATHERINE: If you don't take your hands off me.

(CATHERINE *with the baby and* ABIDEMI *make their way out and we hear the sound of a car driving off.*)

DIRECTOR: When Abidemi and Catherine carrying Isaac arrive at the door of the Accident and Emergency hospital, a doctor promptly comes to their assistance.

ABIDEMI: Please help me. I had him circumcised earlier this evening and it won't stop bleeding. Please, help us!! It is all my fault.

(*The* DOCTOR *takes* ISAAC *from* ABIDEMI *and rushes the boy through a double door into a theatre. The other nurse leads the distraught parents to a waiting room . . . After what seems like an eternity . . .*)

DOCTOR: (*with teary eyes*) We did all we could . . . but I am very sorry.

(CATHERINE, *who stands when the* DOCTOR *comes in, falls into* ABIDEMI*'s arms and sobs uncontrollably. The* DOCTOR *leaves the room as the couple hold each other sobbing. Light goes down slowly.*)

(*Lights come up on 'The Great Great Show'.*)

TV HOST: I recall that story when it broke in the news; very harrowing indeed. Well . . . You have another joke for us. I think this is a good time to tell it. Or what do you think?

DIRECTOR: You are right . . . A new pastor was visiting the homes of his congregation. At one house it seemed obvious that someone was at home, but no answer came to his repeated knocks at the door. Therefore, he took out a card and wrote 'Revelation 3:20' on the back of it and stuck it in the door. When the offering was processed the following Sunday, he found that his card had been returned. Added to it was this cryptic message, 'Genesis 3:10.' Reaching for his Bible to check out the citation, he broke up in gales of laughter. Revelation 3:20 begins 'Behold, I stand at the door and knock' while Genesis 3:10 reads 'I heard your voice in the garden and I was afraid for I was naked.'

TV HOST: Excellent. The next sketch is the last one. Am I correct?

DIRECTOR: Yes. It is Audition Part 2, the second part of the first audition piece. We feel, as we said at the beginning, that someone who is of mixed race background should be able to enjoy the best of two worlds. But for most, especially here in Ireland, that does not seem to be the case.

Scene 8: 'The Audition' Part Two

(*Two MEN as audition panel. They have just finished auditioning YETUNDE.*)

MAN 1: Well done, Yetunde. So have you acted much here in Ireland?

YETUNDE: No, not really.

MAN 2: But you are in acting school yeah?

YETUNDE: Yes, Bull Alley.

MAN 2: Great. We'll get back to you within the next two weeks.

YETUNDE: Right.
MAN 2: Could you tell the next person to come in please?
YETUNDE: I will.

(*YETUNDE goes out and she sees SARAH and MEG sitting.*)

YETUNDE: Who is next?
SARAH: I am.
YETUNDE: You can go in now.
SARAH: (*stands*) Thanks.

(*SARAH goes in.*)

SARAH: Good afternoon.

(*offers her hand to the MEN*)

MAN 1: Good afternoon. Please sit.
SARAH: Thank you.
MAN 2: You are Sarah.
SARAH: That's right. I am Sarah. Sarah Byrne.
MAN 2: I can see from your CV that you have done quite a lot as an actor.
MAN 1: You have featured in *Fair City* as well. Very impressive. But Sarah do you know the play we are casting for?
SARAH: Yes. I do. It is *Wedlock of the Gods*. I read it long time ago.
MAN 2: Excellent. So you are familiar with the story.
SARAH: It's been a long time since I read it but I recall that it is based loosely on the story of Romeo and Juliet. The two characters are Uloko and Ogwoma. Isn't it?

(*MAN 1 & 2 look at one another. Undoubtedly impressed.*)

MAN 2: That's right. It has the same ending as Romeo and Juliet.
SARAH: I like the work of Zulu Sofola actually. She writes very strong female characters. I've always wondered how challenging playing the part of Ogwoma would be.
MAN 1: Great.
SARAH: So would you like me to do a prepared piece or you have something for me to read?

MAN 2: Yep, would you like to read from here to here please? My colleague here will read Uloko's lines.

(*they read*)

MAN 2: Excellent.

SARAH: Thank you.

MAN 2: But do you know that the play is set in Africa?

SARAH: How do you mean?

MAN 1: What my colleague is trying to say is that it is black actors that we hope to cast for this play.

SARAH: I see.

MAN 2: It is very obvious, looking at your CV and hearing you read, that you are a very talented and experienced actor but it is a pity that the part of Ogwoma is meant to be played by a black actor.

SARAH: You mean I am not black enough to play the role?

MAN 2: I hope you understand. We are very sorry but we definitely have you in mind if something more appropriate comes along.

SARAH: Hold on . . . does the fact that my father is a Nigerian matter here?

MAN 1: Yeah, but Sarah you are not . . . black black. You know what I mean.

MAN 2: You are . . .

SARAH: Yes, I know what you mean. But can I ask you a question?

MAN 2: Of course.

SARAH: If you are doing a play and it requires a blind character. Are you saying to me that it is only a blind person that can play the role?

(*Silence as the two* MEN *once again look at one another.*)

SARAH: Just think about that okay.

(*Light goes down as* SARAH *leaves the two* MEN.)

TV HOST: Whoa!!!

DIRECTOR: It is whoa indeed. You remember what happened when she went to an audition for the part of Pegeen Mike.

TV HOST: Yes. She was told she was not white enough. Now

they say she is not black black. It kind of reminds me of that Michael Jackson song. What is it again?

DIRECTOR: 'Black or White'?

TV HOST: Yep, that's the one. Anyway, I want to thank you very much for coming to the studio. All your sketches are really thought-provoking.

DIRECTOR: Thanks for having us on your show.

(*Cue Michael Jackson's 'Black or White' song.*)

TV HOST: (*turning to the audience*) That's all we have time for. I hope you have enjoyed all our sketches. On behalf of the cast and crew of *Once Upon A Time and Not So Long Ago*, I say good night to you all and God bless.

(*Michael Jackson's 'Black or White' becomes louder as a spotlight reveals SARAH dressed up as MICHAEL JACKSON. She does a solo Michael Jackson dance and as light comes up everyone joins in with a choreographed dance sequence. Lights fade.*)

Notes and References

1 Sometime in 1995, I had the opportunity to participate in a storytelling show entitled *Itan Kahani* (Story of Stories) with London-based Pan Centre for Intercultural Arts, on a UK tour. Nigerian performing artist, Peter Badejo, narrated the story of 'Why Do We Tell Stories?' and the story of 'Moremi: The Goddess,' both of which I have included in the *Once Upon A Time* stories.

2 This was inspired by the experience of Mary Healy, a mixed race actor, a couple of times she answered an audition call.

3 Based on a personal experience contributed by the author.

4 Based on an Irish person's experience contributed by John Lovett.

5 Based on personal experience contributed by Tracy Obasahon.

6 Based on a true-life tragic story that made the news a few months before we began the workshop for *Not So Long Ago* in 2005; Clare Barret also contributed to the story.

Introduction to Paul Meade's *Mushroom* (2007)

Jason King

'When I first came to Ireland I wanted to see the winter solstice', declares Andrezj, a Polish immigrant, on a visit to Newgrange in Paul Meade's *Mushroom*. 'I came here because I wanted to feel something. Some connection', he explains. Yet, if 'the real place is earth and stone and starlight', then Andrezj finds himself 'sitting in a virtual Newgrange. It is all wires and lights and tricks'. His sense of disconnection from his Irish environs, his fellow Polish and Romanian immigrants, and even his family resonates profoundly at the end of the play.

More broadly, Paul Meade develops the spectacle of mushroom picking into a metaphor for the immigrant's estrangement from Irish society and an Irish sense of place. His play is set largely in the iconic and stark landscape of county Monaghan, which has long provided a backdrop for Irish poets and novelists like Patrick Kavanagh and John McGahern. Whether it be the 'frosty fingers' of Patrick Kavanagh's 'farmer-poet' in 'Art McCooey' that work the county's 'stony grey soil', or McGahern's intimate portrayal of rural self-reliance at Great Meadow in *Amongst Women* (1990), each of them represents agricultural labour in order to furnish insight into the national psyche. By contrast, the immigrant's perception of mushroom picking in Monaghan tends to be less enlightening. The Latvian author Laima Muktupavela has previously depicted the plight of immigrant labourers in 'Black Balts Among Celts: A Tale of Itinerant Latvian Workers in Ireland' in *The Mushroom Covenant* (2004). Like Muktupavela, Meade portrays the mushroom tents and chicken farms of rural Monaghan to be grim settings that stifle the imagination of his immigrant cast in depriving them of any meaningful sense of connection with the land. 'I used to pick mushrooms in the forest at home. Isn't that funny?' asks Maria, a Romanian farm worker whose preconceptions are belied by her experience. 'And I thought Ireland was going to be like that. I loved the idea of such a beautiful country', she adds. If her feeling of 'connection to Ireland' was based on her boyfriend's readings of 'Joyce, Beckett, Yeats' and an image of 'a fairy-tale country. Everybody writing and painting', then the reality appears much more mundane and prosaic: 'Here it's sleep, work, eat too. Just with shitty weather.' Her perceptions of Irish people and culture are defined by exploitative relations and the repetitive tasks she performs. Her sense of place is confined to a mushroom tent, an artificial habitat no less than Andrezj's 'virtual Newgrange'.

Their dystopian vision of immigrant life in rural Ireland is shared by other characters in the play. 'Look at me. I'm living in Ireland, I'm working on a mushroom farm, I'm sharing a room with my father, I'm on Prozac', exclaims Ewa, Maria's co-worker and Andrezj's daughter. 'Now I don't know where it's going. Nowhere', she adds. The play's lack of character or plot development and pervading sense of stasis frustrated some reviewers. 'Now that they have got here, these characters are going nowhere', complained Helen Meaney in *The Guardian* (29 June 2007) when *Mushroom* was first produced at the Project, Dublin. Yet it could be argued that this is the point: to make an Irish audience experience the estrangement of the immigrant from mainstream Irish culture. Of all of the immigrant characters, Andrezj is the longest resident and most integrated into Irish society, yet even he finds limited opportunities to make Irish friends. Although he does not like pubs, he socialises in them on occasion 'because, where else is there'? In Ireland, it would seem that there are neither natural places, nor social spaces that allow him to feel at home.

The estrangement of the immigrant appears most pronounced, however, in the play's thwarted intercultural romantic plotlines. Paul Meade eschews dramatic convention in his refusal to allow romantic liaisons to develop between his Irish and immigrant characters. In recent Irish fiction it has become commonplace, as in Roddy Doyle's short story collection, *The Deportees* (2007), to establish an interracial romantic plotline as a symbolic shorthand for the resolution of cultural conflict: and yet, the achievement of romantic fulfilment is often based less on the accommodation of cultural difference than its elision through the ostensible power of mutual attraction. By contrast, there are no on-stage depictions of intercultural romantic encounters in *Mushroom,* and the ones that occur off-stage tend to end badly. 'I fuck you but I think of him', exclaims Maria, comparing her Irish boss and lover Seán with her Romanian boyfriend. 'It's bullshit. No connection', she adds for good measure. Once again, the immigrant's sense of disconnection from mainstream Irish society is emphasised here, rather than the reconciliation of cultural difference through romantic convention.

The one Irish character in the play, Martin, resembles his immigrant counterparts to the extent that he feels estranged from his mother's Romanian homeland and living uncle Radu. Their miscommunications attest to the strain of migration on familial as much as romantic relations once cultural divides are crossed; likewise, Andrezj struggles to comprehend his daughter Ewa after spending several years apart. Her endeavours, in turn, to reconcile with her strayed husband cast the spectacle of Irish intercultural romance in a most unfavourable light. Moreover, it is in this eschewal of romantic convention that the play is at its most humorous and unsettling for an Irish audience: for in the eyes of the immigrant Other, the image of the Irish appears deeply unflattering. Indeed, it could be argued that *Mushroom* is less a play about immigrant estrangement than the self-estrangement of the Irish host society when confronted with an image of itself through immigrant eyes. It does not purport to 'speak for the Other' so much as to provide a de-familiarised vantage point from which members of the audience can imagine how they must appear to immigrant agricultural labourers and mushroom pickers whom they would otherwise never encounter.

Paul Meade was born in Dublin, California of Irish immigrant parents, and later, returned with his family to Ireland. As he put it in the performance programme for *Mushroom*: 'I spent my first eight years in California wondering why no one (including myself) spoke like my parents and the next two (in Limerick) desperately trying to acquire their accent.' Meade's twice-marked immigrant experience gave him a first-hand understanding of the cultural estrangement that is so pronounced in this play. When Liam Halligan, then artistic director of Dublin's Storytellers Theatre Company, approached Meade about writing a play about immigrant mushroom pickers in Ireland, Meade recalled, 'it never occurred to me how closely their stories could resemble that of my own parents and how my experiences of the treacherous nature of language and culture in some ways mirrored that of migrant workers in Ireland'.

In researching the play, Halligan and Meade interviewed migrant workers at mushroom farms and chicken sheds in Monaghan, as well as the members of various immigrant support groups in Clones and Omagh. In May of that year, Storytellers held devising sessions in Dublin with four actors from Ireland, Romania and Poland: Ioanna Calota, Carl Kennedy, Natalia Kostrzewa and Andrzej Sodowski. The eventual play text grew out of a combination of the interviews Halligan and Meade conducted and these subsequent devising sessions. *Mushroom* was commissioned by the Calouste Gulbenkian Foundation and the Irish Arts Council, and was first produced by Storytellers Theatre Company at the Project Arts Centre in Dublin in June 2007. A year later, after twenty-two years in operation, Storytellers lost its Arts Council funding and closed its doors.

Mushroom

Paul Meade

Mushroom was first presented at the Civic Theatre, Tallaght, on 5 June 2007 by Storytellers Theatre Company.

Cast

Andrzej	Janusz Sheagall
Martin	Carl Kennedy
Ewa	Natalia Kostrzewa
Ion	Emmet Kirwan
Maria	Cristina Catalina
Radu	Dan Tudor

Production Team

Director	Liam Halligan
Set and Lighting Design	Marcos Costello
Costume Design	Catherine Fay
Sound Design	Denis Clohessy

Characters

Andrzej, early forties, from Poland, now living in County Monaghan, Ireland;
Martin, twenty-three years old, from County Monaghan, visiting his uncle in Bucharest;
Ewa, nineteen years old, Andrzej's daughter, visiting her father in Ireland;
Ion, twenty-four years old, from Romania, living and working in County Monaghan;
Maria, twenty-five years old, from Romania, living and working in County Monaghan;
Radu, early forties, Martin's uncle from Romania, living in Bucharest.

The play is set in 2007.

Act One

Scene 1

A strange, clinical working space. In the dark corners we see white mushrooms. They appear like stars in some distant galaxy. The actors enter the space, each in their own world. They are working and move slowly and serenely about the space.

Scene 2

A man appears out of the darkness. He looks at the audience closely. He bends down so that he is looking at them upside down. He speaks in a strong Eastern European accent.

ANDRZEJ: Australia. Mmmm. Australia.

(He straightens up.)

ANDRZEJ: A different perspective. Down Under. That's my next one. Visa could be a problem. We'll see. But fuck! The weather! Beautiful. Sunny? Fuck yes! Ireland? Beautiful country. But, the weather? Ahhh. And the stars? Same stars I've been looking at all my life. Same stars that I've been obsessed with all my life. In Poland I used to spend hours in a cornfield outside Lublin. Night after night when I was . . . eight. A whole summer staring at the stars. These same stars. My parents thought I was crazy. They thought I had lost it. (*beat*) They were right! The same stars. But Australia? Now those stars . . . completely different. Different galaxies, different constellations. Think of it. Lying in the desert, on your back, hands behind your head, letting them tell you things. Listening to their stories. I love to listen to them. I don't always hear them. They are a bit mysterious sometimes. Twinkling but not giving much away. I suppose I could meet some Aborigine out there some night and he might explain some of it. Don't tell me they haven't been working on it. The aborigines. Been there so long that they've probably got it all figured out. And I'll tell them how our ancestors built huge monuments to map the stars. How they found out about their stories, unlocked their secrets. But we have forgotten. We have forgotten. We land on the moon but we don't ask it to help us. We send satellites deep into space to listen for sounds but we hear nothing. Nothing. We forget that they keep time for all of us. Their stories make sense of us. Now we are just wandering the planet. We work here we work there. We don't know why. So . . . we don't know. I came here. I came to Ireland. Everybody asks me, 'You come here to work? Things are not so good for you back home? Will you stay? Do you have family?' They look at me they see a Polishman. I look at them and I think, I have worked all over the world, I fixed roofs in Italy, I built saunas in Germany, I sold kebabs by the Black Sea, I saw the Pyramids, I spoke to the oracle at Delphi, I . . . and you say . . . 'Good man yourself'. What do you think I am doing here? A job? Ha, Ha. A job? I can get a job anywhere. I came because . . . but they don't understand. I came . . . I came because of Newgrange.

Scene 3

(*We hear the sound of the PA in an airport.*)

ANNOUNCER: British Midlands flight BM 1435 has just arrived from Gatwick. Flight BM 1435 just arrived from Gatwick.

ANNOUNCER: (*in Romanian*) Flight CSA 1765 from Prague just arrived at Gate 34. CSA 1765 just arrived from Prague.

(*EWA and MARTIN are on mobile phones.*)

EWA: Hello? Hello? Shit.

MARTIN: Hello. Radu? Hello.

EWA: I'm at the airport. Is this your machine?

MARTIN: Yes. Yes. Um . . . da.

EWA: I'm in Ireland and I want to meet you.

MARTIN: This is Martin. Radu? I . . . I . . .

EWA: I . . . thought you could pick me up. I need to talk. We need to talk. I'm at the airport and I don't know how I'm going to get to Monaghan.

MARTIN: I'm at the airport. Aeroport? It's Martin. Martin? Yes. Yes. Your nephew. Nephew. Um . . . Aeroport? Plane?

EWA: I'll wait for you here. If you get this message come and collect me. Please. Okay? I . . . I love you.

MARTIN: Radu? Are you picking me up or can I get a bus or

something? Um . . . a lift? Martin . . . yes. What about a taxi? Taxi? No Taxi. Okay. Me . . . Aeroport. Do you understand? Da. Da. No, wait don't hang up. Are you coming here? Shit.

EWA: I'm going crazy here. I don't know what to do. Be a good husband and give me a lift please. I'll be waiting. Good . . .

(*They hang up.* ION *and* MARIA *are in a call shop in Monaghan.*)

ION: Yes. Good. Good. Yes.

MARIA: Six euro. I earn six euro per hour.

ION: I have worked many jobs. Many jobs.

MARIA: Good? No, it's not good.

ION: Here in Monaghan. Yes.

MARIA: Mushrooms. No, I pick them. Mama, I told you that last time.

ION: No problem. Building, wood jobs, brick jobs, I can do yes.

MARIA: Why would I be speaking English?

ION: Tiling I am expert. Yes plaster a professional.

MARIA: I'm picking mushrooms all day and they don't talk much.

ION: You know Patsy McKenna? No? I work for him. He is a good man.

MARIA: Did you speak to Constantin? About the webcam?

ION: I work hard. Yes, Boss.

MARIA: I told you he can get it. No, I'll e-mail him myself.

ION: I am legal, yes. It's no problems for me here. No problems. I have much uh . . .

MARIA: So we can speak and you won't be so lonely.

ION: God, what is that word in English?

MARIA: Broadband.

ION: Experience!

MARTIN: Dad?

EWA: Dad?

MARTIN: I'm in the airport.

EWA: Hello? It's Ewa.

ION: I have much experience and I work very hard. Very hard. I am a good. Thank you. Yes.

MARIA: No. There is no orthodox church here. In Dublin yes. I can't go to Dublin every week just for church. Mama. No, I can't.

MARTIN: Yeah, I called him. Well, if he doesn't understand what can I do?

EWA: No, he didn't answer his phone. I left a message but I don't think he'll come. I just know.

ION: Clones? Yes. I know. Okay. You call me? Good. Thank you. Thank you.

MARIA: Yes, I want to. Yes. I'm praying all the time. All the time. That's true, not in a church . . .

MARTIN: Get a bus or a taxi I suppose. Because we had a two-hour wait in Prague. Well, that's your opinion. He's mam's brother so . . .

EWA: Yeah. Can you come and get me? Two hours? I'm sorry, I didn't think Clones was so far away. No, I'll wait here. I'm fine. I'm fine.

MARTIN: I'm fine. I'm fine.

ION: Sorry, can I ask one question? Yes. How much is it for one hour? Oh. Okay. Okay.

MARTIN: Listen, my battery's going. I'll just wait. I'll just have to wait.

EWA: I'll just have to wait. I'll just wait. Okay.

MARTIN: Bye, Dad.

EWA: Bye, Dad.

MARIA: Bye, Mama, bye.

ION: Goodbye.

(*They all hang up.*)

Scene 4

(*ANDRZEJ's flat.*)

EWA: And Kashia is fine, but she's worried about global warming or something.

ANDRZEJ: Global warming? What?

EWA: She's a teenager. She discovers global warming and bang! Everything is global warming. I can't flush the toilet and it's 'global warming'.

ANDRZEJ: A teenager . . .

EWA: I have some photographs.

ANDRZEJ: Yes. I'll look at them later. Now, I want to look at you. (*beat*) You're very beautiful. A woman.

(EWA *gives a little laugh or smile.*)

ANDRZEJ: What?

EWA: Your accent. You speak Polish with a funny accent. 'Woman'.

ANDRZEJ: I've been away a long time. You were only what? Fifteen when I saw you last.

EWA: No, I was sixteen. Just.

ANDRZEJ: Sixteen? No.

EWA: Yes. I remember you were going to Egypt and I cried and you said you'd bring me back a present and I stopped because I thought it was going to be the next week or month but three years later and—here I am.

ANDRZEJ: And you got married.

EWA: Yes.

ANDRZEJ: He was supposed to look after you not marry you.

EWA: He did both.

ANDRZEJ: I tried to talk to him, but he won't listen. I pointed out his responsibilities . . .

(EWA *laughs.*)

ANDRZEJ: What?

EWA: You're someone to talk about responsibilities.

ANDRZEJ: I was just trying to help.

EWA: Maybe you should think about helping your own family. Maybe Jacek was just looking at you and thinking . . . I can leave my wife. It's fine.

ANDRZEJ: Maybe . . .

EWA: I didn't miss you too much when you left. Jacek was always there. He took your place. He ate meals with us. Helped with homework. Gave me a lift twice a week to those stupid dance classes. When we got married he wanted to buy a house. He had a big idea about what 'lifestyle' we would have. So, he needed money and you were already here. It was perfect. I had just started college so . . . I didn't come. Big mistake.

ANDRZEJ: It's not your fault.

EWA: When I found out it was so dramatic. I couldn't believe it. It was like a scene from a film, no a really big opera. Lots of crying and falling down and taking to my bed. That's not me. The last time I cried was the last time you left. But now I can't stop. At the airport, in the car on the way here, now, tomorrow . . .

(*pause*)

ANDRZEJ: I have something. It's nothing really but when I was in Egypt, I had just left you and I was thinking about you a lot. I had promised you something and I found this. I thought you might like it.

EWA: What is it?

ANDRZEJ: It's Egyptian. A scarab.

EWA: It looks like a . . . a little beetle.

ANDRZEJ: It is. A scarab is a dung beetle. The Egyptians saw them as sacred. They admired the way the beetle rolls its eggs in little balls of dung and sand to protect them. These balls could be as big as themselves. And it reminded the Egyptians of the movement of the Sun from east to west. Rising and setting.

EWA: Ah. The stars. The stars.

ANDRZEJ: Yes.

EWA: You care more about them than your family?

ANDRZEJ: No. To me it's all one.

EWA: You travel the world. You're never there.

ANDRZEJ: Yes. But . . . now I'm not the only Polish man who does this.

EWA: No. (*beat*) Where can I . . .? I want to lie down.

ANDRZEJ: You can lie on my bed. There's only one room. I'm sorry. I wasn't expecting . . . You can have my bed and I'll sleep on the sofa. If you don't mind.

EWA: No. Thank you. But I want to. . .

ANDRZEJ: Yes. I will go out. Go to the . . . I don't know. The pub.

EWA: Thank you.

ANDRZEJ: You won't mind sharing with your father? It's not so strange. We can be friends?

EWA: Yes.

ANDRZEJ: I'll cook and clean and . . . yes?

EWA: Yes.

ANDRZEJ: Okay. . .

EWA: Thank you. This is beautiful.

ANDRZEJ: It's turquoise. Green stone symbolises resurrection. The inscription says, 'Beloved of Amun'. Beloved of God. The scarab means to become. To change. New life.

EWA: New life.

ANDRZEJ: Yes. New life. May it bring you strength.

(*Exit* ANDRZEJ.)

Scene 5

(*RADU's apartment in Bucharest.*
Enter RADU singing)

RADU: 'I like driving in my car. It's not quite a Jaguar.' (*he repeats*) 'I like driving in my car . . . '

(*Enter MARTIN with a large rucksack.*)

MARTIN: 'It's not . . . quite . . . a . . . Jaguar.'

RADU: 'I like driving in my car . . . '

MARTIN: 'I'm satisfied I've come this far.'

RADU: Yes. Yes. Well done. See we speak a different languages but we can communicate. It's not so hard. Is it?
(*beat*)

MARTIN: What? Sorry?

RADU: (*beat*) Come in. Come in. This is it. Small but this is Bucharest not Sibiu . . . You will have to sleep here. I'll put your bag here.

MARTIN: It's fine. I'll take it. My bag?

RADU: I can put it here. You sleep here. What do you want?

MARTIN: My bag? That. Please. Bag. Please?

RADU: This? You want this? Yes. You want this. Yes.

(*He gives him the bag.*)

RADU: Now. You are probably quite hungry so I have some stuff in the fridge. Let me see . . . what would you like? Sit down. Please, sit down. Sit down. You have to eat something. Please. Eat something. Eat? Eat?

MARTIN: What? Eat? I'm not hungry. I'm grand.

RADU: Yeah. Eat something. Would you like a drink?

MARTIN: I have something in my bag. A present.

RADU: Sit down. I have sausages. Bread. You can have tea or beer or something a bit stronger. A bit more Romanian. Please sit down.

MARTIN: I just need to get something out of my bag. It won't take a sec.

RADU: Oh. Do you need the toilet? Toilet? You need to wash? Shower? Something? Because the water might not be so hot. These apartments were built by morons. They're a mess. You need to throw a switch. You need to . . . I'll show you.

MARTIN: Jesus, I haven't a clue what you're saying.

RADU: Come on. Come on. I'll show you. Wash. Wash.

MARTIN: Where are we going now?

(RADU leads MARTIN to bathroom.)

RADU: So, this is the switch for the shower and you turn that like this. Left for cold. Left? Yeah?

MARTIN: What? I'm really sorry but . . .

RADU: So, pull and twist. And boom. Yes?

(sound of toilet flush)

RADU: These apartments were built by morons!

(They came back to living room.)

MARTIN: Yeah. I went while I was waiting for you at the airport. Aeroport.

RADU: Aeroport, yes, yes. Brrrmmmmmmm.

MARTIN: Yeah. It doesn't really matter. It's fine. Fine. It's grand Radu. Really.

RADU: Radu.

MARTIN: Yes.

RADU: Okay. I'll leave you. Now you can work it out yourself.

(He begins to back away. MARTIN follows him.)

RADU: No. Go on. Go on. Use it. Wash. Wash?

MARTIN: I'm grand. I'm grand. (*beat*) Fine.

RADU: Yes. Good.

(*pause*)

MARTIN: I . . . I have something. In my bag.

RADU: Are you sure you don't want anything to eat.

MARTIN: It's a book. I have it here. Yeah. So, there you go. Little present.

(*He gives him the book.*)

MARTIN: It's on bees. It's the one thing that I remember my mother saying about you. That you liked bees and you used to make a study of them. Bees like. I always thought that was hilarious.

RADU: Thank you.

MARTIN: 'Course what's even more hilarious, and I'm only thinking of it now. It's in English. But Mam . . . um . . . your sister . . . Magdalena . . .

RADU: Yes. Yes. Magdalena. Your mother. Yes?

MARTIN: She said you loved bees.

RADU: It's a lovely book. I have to say and . . . bees. Good pictures of bees. Bees? BZZZZZ? See picture?

MARTIN: Yes. Yes. Bees.

RADU: I used to help your grandfather with his hives when I was a kid but since your mother left for Ireland a lot has changed. I trained to be an architect and when dad died I kind of forgot about bees. I don't really bother with them like I used to but . . . thank you it's really thoughtful. Thank you.

MARTIN: That word I know. Mulsamesk.

RADU: Yes. Thank you. Now I must give you something. (*He finds a book nearby on James Joyce.*) How about James Joyce?

MARTIN: Ah no I'm grand. Really.

RADU: James Joyce. He is Irish . . .

MARTIN: (*taking book*) James Joyce in Romanian. Fantastic! And . . . I have this for you . . . (*He hands Radu a memorial card of his Mother.*)

RADU: Oh. Ah. Magdelana. Thank you. Thank you. She's so beautiful. I'm sorry I didn't go to the . . . It's . . .

(*RADU and MARTIN both get a little emotional and RADU gives MARTIN a little hug.*)

RADU: Now. Drink? Eat? What would you like? Eat? Eat? Some dinner?

MARTIN: Eat is it? I'm not sure what you . . .

RADU: Eat? Eat? Um . . . essen? Essen? Shit that's German.

MARTIN: Yes. Essen. Essen. Ja. Bitte.

RADU: Ja. Ja. Setzen sie sich bitte. Thank fuck he speaks some German. German but no Romanian. Your grandmother would be turning in her grave. Wurst? Trinken? Schnapps.

MARTIN: Ja. Bitte. Alles gut. Bitte.

Scene 6

(In the mushroom tent. MARIA is showing EWA how to pick mushrooms. They are speaking in English and struggling a little.)

MARIA: So, you stand here. Bucket. Here. This knife you use for cutting. Cutting. Yes?

EWA: Yes.

MARIA: This hat. You wear. Hat. Put it on please. Thank you. This coat. This gloves. Put it on please. Thank you. This mushrooms are first flush. You cut here and put in bucket. Do please. Good.

EWA: Excuse me? What is first flush?

MARIA: This bags when it comes with spores. Yes?

EWA: No.

MARIA: Spores. How do you say? You speak Russian?

EWA: No.

MARIA: I don't speak Polish. Polska. No speak. This spores. Grow. Become first. One. Flush. First. One. Yes?

EWA: Yes.

MARIA: Mushroom. (*she points*) Mushroom. Yes?

EWA: Yes.

MARIA: Now. Cut. Yes?

EWA: Yes.

MARIA: Now grow two. Two? Yes?

EWA: Yes.

MARIA: Second. Good?

EWA: Yes.

MARIA: It's bitch this.

EWA: Bitch?

MARIA: Yes bitch. Hurt back. Cut, cut, cut. Bitch.

EWA: Yes.

MARIA: This door? Close. Always close. This computer. For heat. Dark. Okay?

EWA: Okay.
MARIA: You will learn. Easy. Easy.
EWA: Easy bitch.
MARIA: Yes. Yes. Easy bitch.

Scene 7

(*ANDRZEJ is working on a building site. He is cutting tiles. Enter ION.*)

ION: Hello.
ANDRZEJ: Hello.
ION: What are you working? Huh? What do you work on?
ANDRZEJ: Jacuzzi.
ION: Fuck! Fuck! Jacuzzi? Fuck shit. Jacuzzi? Fucking rich Irish motherfucker! I help you? I can help. I help you?
ANDRZEJ: No. It's okay. I will. . .
ION: I will help. What are you doing? You put tiles down? I can do this? You teach me?
ANDRZEJ: Where is Davey?
ION: I don't know. I don't know where Davey is.
ANDRZEJ: Did he give you some work to do?
ION: Yes but I am finished and now I can't find. He . . . he is going somewhere. I don't know where but he . . . he is going so . . . I can help you.
ANDRZEJ: No.
ION: Okay. (*pause*) Nobody speaks to me here. Nobody.
ANDRZEJ: Because they are working. We come to work. Not speak.
ION: Okay. Me . . . I can speak and work.
ANDRZEJ: Good for you.
ION: What are you doing? Why do you write something? You should be working.
ANDRZEJ: I am working. I have to calculate. All these measurements are in feet and inches. I only know metres and centimetres.
ION: Fucking Irish.

(*pause*)

ION: Where are you from? You come from here? You're not Irish?
ANDRZEJ: No. Poland.
ION: Polska! Ha. Ha. Polska. I am Romanian!

ANDRZEJ: Yes?

ION: Romanian, Polska! How little is the world?

ANDRZEJ: It's too little.

ION: Where in Poland are you from?

ANDRZEJ: Lublin. You know it?

ION: No. (*beat*) But Poland, Romania. It's like almost the same country. (*pause*) I'm not stealing. I'm not a Gypsy. I am Romanian. My mother and father they died. It was very sad but my cousins they collect all the money and give it to me. I can make a some money here and I send it back. So, it's good for everybody.

ANDRZEJ: Oh.

ION: I'm good worker. I work hard. I can help you.

ANDRZEJ: I don't think so.

ION: You have a woman? You have family?

ANDRZEJ: In Poland I have. Yes.

ION: How?

ANDRZEJ: How?

ION: How many? How are they?

ANDRZEJ: Good.

ION: Good. Good. You have a woman here? (*beat*) You need pizde? You pizde?

ANDRZEJ: What? Pizde? You fucking shit!

(*ANDRZEJ drops what he is doing and advances towards ION.*)

ION: What? What? Are you angry?

ANDRZEJ: You are cursing me?

ION: No. No. I'm not cursing you. What? I'm not cursing you.

ANDRZEJ: You think I'm a fucking bitch? You think I'm a prostitute?

ION: No. No. Ha. No! Pizde. In Romanian it mean where the sex of a woman. Where they are pissing. No prostitute. Pizde. (*points*)

ANDRZEJ: Me?

ION: No. We have balls. Poola. I say I can find you a woman; a pizde. (*beat*) You want to go back in Poland?

ANDRZEJ: Now, I'm thinking about it.

ION: I know. Fucking Irish. They don't pay. They don't pay when they say. It can be any time. I am waiting two months for Kelly to pay me. Two months. And they pay the Irish more than us you know. Much more. Same job, same work. Less money. Can you believe it? (*beat*) You want to be my friend? You want to get some girls? I can help.

ANDRZEJ: No.

ION: Why won't you be my friend? It's good to have a friend. I like you. We can drink together. Go in pubs.

ANDRZEJ: Pubs? What can you do in pubs?

ION: We can drink beer. Pints.

ANDRZEJ: Beer? What is beer? You should have a strong drink. Polish drink.

ION: Yes. Yes. I would like. (*beat*) You will be my friend?

ANDRZEJ: I have to work.

ION: I can be your friend. We can drink and talk. I will help you.

ANDRZEJ: How can you help me?

ION: I can get you more work. You want some work. Extra money?

ANDRZEJ: What work?

ION: Chickens. Catching chickens.

ANDRZEJ: Chickens?

ION: Yes. McKenna's Chickens. Ten euro for one hour. I know Patsy. He said, 'Bring friend'. You want to come?

(*beat*)

ANDRZEJ: I'll think about it.

Scene 8

(*Outside the mushroom tent.* EWA *joins* MARIA *on her break.* EWA *takes a pill.*)

MARIA: What's that?

EWA: A pill.

MARIA: What kind of pill?

EWA: Headache.

(MARIA *takes the pill box and looks at the label.*)

MARIA: Big headache.

(EWA *shrugs.*)

MARIA: You are sad?

(*Ewa shrugs.*)

Maria: It's normal. You are far from home. Yes? Shitty job? Yes? It's normal.

Ewa: No. (*beat*) I'm away from home, I have a shitty job, and I'm really tired so why? Why . . . I don't sleep?

Maria: I don't know. Who gave you this?

Ewa: Dr Bosak.

Maria: Polish doctor. In Clones. Yes, Fermanagh Street. She is working with Dr Mulcahy.Did you see him? He's cute.

(*Ewa shrugs.*)

Maria: He's very cute. And lots of money. Designer clothes, BMW, big house and he brings over to Ireland sexy Polish assistant doctor. You should see his house. In Romania, I would have to work five jobs to afford this house. It's a mansion. God, that man has everything. (*beat*) What did Bosak say?

Ewa: I don't know. We talked about Poland.

Maria: You miss home?

Ewa: Yes. But . . .

Maria: Why she is giving you this? For depression. You know? You don't sleep you can get something different. Less . . . You know?

Ewa: I need something because I don't sleep but also because I don't get up. I can't work. I can't talk . . . I need this.

Maria: Oh, okay. I have that feeling too sometimes. Mushrooms can make you feel like this.

(*Ewa laughs.*)

Ewa: I will explain. My husband comes to Ireland. And I wait him one year in Poland but he doesn't come home. So . . . I am coming to get him.

Maria: He is here? Monaghan?

Ewa: Yes. But he lives fifteen miles away. In Monaghan town.

Maria: You are not living together?

Ewa: No.

Maria: Oh. I see. (*beat*) I am taking these pills in Romania.

Ewa: Yes?

Maria: Yes, I took them for some months. They are not healthy.

Believe me, I know. You should talk to someone. Therapy. You know?

EWA: Yes. They are speaking Polish?

MARIA: No.

EWA: And money? How can I pay for this? We are picking mushrooms. When there are mushrooms to pick.

MARIA: Yes. It would be expensive. You could talk to Dr Carlota. She is Polish. She's not a therapist but . . .

EWA: What is to talk about? My husband left me for fat Irish bitch. It's that simple.

(*MARIA laughs.*)

EWA: I saw her. I went to his house. I tried to talk to him but he won't answer the door. He is a big coward. So I wait him and out comes this woman and her ass is . . . (*gestures*) Irish women are so fat. Is that sexy?

MARIA: Oh, not all . . .

EWA: Big asses.

MARIA: Some of them. Yes. Quite big.

EWA: (*makes a gesture*) Like this . . . fucking big . . .

(*The two women laugh.*)

MARIA: I think you have it pretty bad. Maybe you need some stronger pills.

(*They laugh again. Pause.*)

EWA: Why does he like a fat ass? Why?

MARIA: You need to forget about this man. He's not for you. If you forget about him then you can sleep and you don't need this Prozac shit.

EWA: How? Tell me how.

MARIA: I don't know. Meet some other man. I think that works. You are young, beautiful. Meet some nice Irish man. Have some sex.

EWA: Irish men are . . .

MARIA: Yes, but . . . what else?

EWA: You have boyfriend? Irish?

MARIA: No.

EWA: Romanian?

MARIA: No. No boyfriend.

EWA: Why not?

MARIA: I don't know. That's not why I am coming to Ireland. I want to make some money here. I have enough problems with men in Romania you know?

EWA: What problems?

MARIA: We have only one minute left. We must go back to work.

EWA: You love somebody in Romania?

MARIA: I have to go back to work.

EWA: Please, I told you.

MARIA: (*beat*) Yes. I loved somebody in Romania. Now, Seán will be angry . . .

EWA: Why did you leave him?

MARIA: Because I had to get away. I wanted to find something. I want to see the world. I want to pick mushrooms.

EWA: Really?

MARIA: Yes, I love mushrooms. I love to come here early in the morning when there are still stars in the sky and pick mushrooms. It's my life work you know? Now we are late.

EWA: Wait. You say, I should meet some man, but you don't need this? That's no deal. Why should I do this and you not?

MARIA: Yes, well. Maybe I will. If I can find one I like.

EWA: That might be difficult.

MARIA: Or one that likes me.

EWA: That's not a problem.

MARIA: Really?

EWA: Yes. I know how to attract a man in Ireland.

MARIA: Yes?

EWA: Yes. I am studying Irish women. I am seeing how they are doing.

MARIA: Yes?

EWA: Yes. Like this . . .

(*EWA gets a large plastic bag and shoves it down the back of her clean trousers so that her bottom looks huge.*)

EWA: Now I am beautiful yes? You are loving me now? Give me a kiss. Go on. Give me a kiss.

MARIA: (*laughing*) Get away. Get away . . . you are late . . . go back . . .

(*EWA leaves.*)

Scene 9

(*ANDRZEJ is standing alone on stage. He is looking through a large telescope.*)

ANDRZEJ: Some people go to Covent Garden. Some people like the Met in New York. Others go to the Kirov. But if you really want to see some dancing look up here. This is not Hip Hop, it's slow, slow procession. It changes a little all the time. But it's so beautiful. So beautiful. This baby (*telescope*) . . . she comes everywhere with me. I had to pawn her many times but I always got her back. She's my connection. I rely on her very much. But sometimes I like to look just with my own eyes. To see the stars like the ancients saw them. They believed so much in them. I want to believe in them too. The Incas believed so much that the heavens were a gate to the land of their ancestors, that there was a kind of bridge here to the underworld, that they sacrificed their children, so they could send a message. They sent their children up there. All over the world people believed the same thing. Here was a bridge, a gate. When the path of the sun crosses the Milky Way, the centre of our galaxy, there where Scorpio and Sagittarius stand guard. That is the gate. The Incas, the Polynesians, the Romans, the Vikings, they all believed the same thing. This gate is where souls go. They pass through to the spirit world. Hades, Helgrind, Heaven, Hell? Did they know something we don't know? Some guy in a grass skirt on an Island in the Pacific? Some astronomer in Rome? A Viking freezing his ass off in Norway? They all thought the same thing? Why? Too many mushrooms maybe. Too many coca leaves. Man those guys knew how to live. Me, I get high just looking. If I see something new, it's like I'm drunk . . . Don't worry. I'm not crazy. I'm not looking for aliens. I just want to feel what they felt. How they saw all of this . . . (*the stars*). And when I see the gate; Scorpio and Sagittarius, wherever I am in the world, I think of my own daughters and I imagine that they are not in Poland or Ireland but up there with all the Inca children. They are looking down on me, they are smiling . . .

Scene 10

(MARTIN and RADU are sitting watching a football match. Simultaneously we see EWA and ANDRZEJ at home after work. In Ireland, EWA is also watching TV. They are all watching the same football match on the same TV but in different countries.)

RADU: (*sings*) Liverpool. Liverpool. Liverpool. Liverpool.

MARTIN: They're useless. Winning the European Cup was the worst thing that ever happened to that team. Gonzalez is a muppet. Did you see how many times he gave the ball away there? Ridiculous.

RADU: Gonzalez?

MARTIN: Yeah.

RADU: Okay. Gonzalez. Okay?

MARTIN: No. No, shit. Cacat.

RADU: (*laughs*) Shit! Yes. Yes. Shit. Gerrard? Good?

MARTIN: Da. Buna.

RADU: Beer?

MARTIN: Da. Bere.

RADU: He's learning. You're good.

(ANDRZEJ enters. He is wearing yellow rubber washing-up gloves.)

ANDRZEJ: Would you like some cake?

EWA: No, thank you.

ANDRZEJ: Tea? Coffee?

EWA: No, thank you.

ANDRZEJ: What are you watching?

EWA: Football but it's all in English.

ANDRZEJ: You like football?

EWA: No, there's nothing on.

ANDRZEJ: Sometimes there's a film on that channel. I suppose I should really get a DVD player.

EWA: I don't mind. I like just watching and maybe it's good for my English. You know, I can learn it without even trying. Subliminal, you know.

ANDRZEJ: Or satellite. Most people buy satellite in Poland and bring it back. Use it here. But . . .

EWA: You haven't been back.

ANDRZEJ: No. And I don't like the idea of all those satellites. They get in the way . . . up there.

EWA: I had an email from Mum.

ANDRZEJ: Yes?

EWA: She says that Kashia wants to come over now. She thinks it's unfair that I have all the fun.

ANDRZEJ: Yes, but maybe she should finish school first.

EWA: She should try picking mushrooms. That would make her think twice.

ANDRZEJ: Why does she want to come so much?

EWA: To see her father.

ANDRZEJ: (*Looking at his washing up gloves.*) Yes, well, I could wash up for her, too. And what does Elina say about you?

EWA: Mum thinks I'm still going to bring back my husband.

ANDRZEJ: What do you think?

EWA: (*Looking at the TV.*) I think Irish people are ugly.

(*RADU enters.*)

RADU: Beer.

MARTIN: Merci.

RADU: Any score?

MARTIN: Sorry?

ANDRZEJ: Sorry?

RADU: Doesn't matter.

EWA: They are all fat in the face and they have big ears. Like this . . . (*she demonstrates*). Their food is so bad. Chips and potatoes with everything and greasy meat with rich sauces. If I had to eat like that I would die. Seriously.

ANDRZEJ: It's lucky we're so perfect.

RADU: Ah, not again. Gonzalez needs to hold the ball up. How many times has he given it away? Or at least make a run. Crouch is flicking the ball on all day and Gonzalez is behind him. It's pointless. I don't think he has a brain in his head. Honestly.

MARTIN: Da. Da. I haven't a clue what you're saying to me but sure I'll talk at you as if I think you can understand everything I say and you'll probably just smile and think I'm talking about the match. It's crazy, I'm sharing a . . . well a bedsit with you and I haven't had the heart to tell you that I support United and not Liverpool. I think it would break your heart. The beer is piss by the way but at least it dulls the senses. I'd love to speak English with you and ask you about my grandparents and my mother. Find out why she left and you stayed. Ask you why you never married. Why I never met you. Ask you about where you came from. Your home in Sibiu . . .

RADU: Sibiu?

MARTIN: Nein. Nein. It's okay.

RADU: I haven't a notion mate.

MARTIN: Jesus. You look so like my mother when you say that. It's like I just got a little glimpse of her there. Like she was still alive.

RADU: I'm just trying to watch the match. Okay?

MARTIN: Okay.

(*ANDRZEJ starts to hang out clothes on a clothes horse. They are clearly his clothes and EWA's.*)

EWA: I'm going to bed.

ANDRZEJ: It's only nine o'clock.

EWA: Yes, but O'Mahony is picking me up at five in the morning.

ANDRZEJ: Oh, okay. Did you speak to him about your money?

EWA: No. I didn't see him.

ANDRZEJ: You should. He's paying you less and all you have to do is ask. O'Mahony will pay you as little as he can but if you ask him he'll put you on the proper rate.

EWA: Okay. (*beat*) Can you post this for me tomorrow please?

(*She hands him a letter.*)

ANDRZEJ: For Jacek?

EWA: Yes.

ANDRZEJ: Okay. Goodnight.

EWA: Goodnight.

(*ANDRZEJ gives EWA a hug and there is an awkward pause.*)

(*MARTIN gets up.*)

MARTIN: I'm going to bed. Okay? Bed. Schlafen?

RADU: Schlafen? Nein. Football. Yes?

MARTIN: Da. Football. Buna. Good. Me . . . schlafen. Okay?

RADU: Okay . . . okay.

(*RADU goes back to watching the match. MARTIN starts to undo a mattress.*)

(*In Ireland, EWA is in bed.*)

RADU: You can use the bed if you want. I'll watch the match and sleep here.

MARTIN: What? Sorry.

RADU: Go . . . (*he gestures*) . . . in there. Schlafen. Die andere zimmer. Da?

MARTIN: Nein. Hier ist gut. Schlafen. TV okay.

RADU: I can't watch the TV while you're . . . fuck's sake.

MARTIN: It's okay. Okay. Buna. You go . . . watch . . . buna.

RADU: Yeah. Yeah.

(*MARTIN gets into bed and turns over. RADU turns the sound down on the TV. ANDRZEJ is reading a book. EWA starts crying softly. RADU clears away the beer bottles. ANDRZEJ stops reading and looks at EWA. He is unsure what to do. RADU stands looking at MARTIN. Both men switch off the TV. ANDRZEJ starts to sing a Polish lullaby. The scene changes to the mushroom tent. ANDRZEJ's singing is taken up by the whole cast. Gradually, the singing fades.*)

Scene 11

(*MARIA is working in the mushroom tunnel. There is a large box of chocolates on her trolley. Enter EWA.*)

EWA: Can I have one?

MARIA: What?

EWA: Chocolate. You are eating all of these?

MARIA: No. No. You can have one. Please.

EWA: Thank you.

MARIA: It's so hot in here they're all melting.

EWA: They are lovely. Where did you get these?

(*MARIA gives her a look.*)

EWA: What? Did you get a present?

MARIA: Quiet!

EWA: What is the secret? Tell me!

MARIA: Seán. He gave them to me.

EWA: (*beat*) Oh! He likes you?

MARIA: I don't know. I think so. He wants me to go for a drink with him.

(*Ewa starts giggling.*)

Maria: What's so funny?
Ewa: He . . . he's so funny.
Maria: Why? Why is he so funny?
Ewa: Chocolate. He's sooo romantic.

(*Maria starts laughing too.*)

Ewa: What did he say? 'You must go for a drink with me. Now, go back to work. We haven't got all day lads!'
Maria: 'What do you like to drink Maria?'
Ewa: 'Come on, we haven't got all day lads!'
Maria: 'Kiss me.'
Ewa: 'We haven't got all day lads!'
Maria: 'Come to bed.'
Ewa: 'We haven't got all day lads.'

(*They are in fits of giggles. Gradually, they recover themselves.*)

Ewa: Are you going to go?
Maria: I don't know. Maybe.
Ewa: Do you like him?
Maria: No. Yes. I don't know. Maybe. He's a man.
Ewa: You must go.
Maria: Why?
Ewa: We agreed. This is therapy.
Maria: We'll see. I don't know.
Ewa: Maria, this is our plan. You told me.
Maria: We'll see.

(*Pause during which Maria starts singing again.*)

Ewa: What are you doing?
Maria: Picking mushrooms. What do you think I am doing?
Ewa: Don't please.
Maria: What?
Ewa: Sing. I can't bear it.
Maria: It's distracting you?
Ewa: Please. In this shithole singing is a good distraction. Believe me. Just sing a different song.
Maria: What's wrong?
Ewa: Nothing.

MARIA: What?

EWA: It's too beautiful. It makes me sad.

MARIA: Oh. Okay. It's not so beautiful when you know what it's saying. It's about a woman who loves a man very much. Very much.

EWA: I see . . . it's a love song.

MARIA: Yes. It's a kind of love song. (*laughs*)

EWA: Well it's either a love song or it's not. Isn't that right?

MARIA: No. This woman. She loves this man so much. She wants him so much that . . . she wants to break him a little bit. You know?

EWA: Break him?

MARIA: Yes. Break him. You know . . . (*She demonstrates on* EWA.)

EWA: What do you mean?

MARIA: Like, you are so crazy, you just can't get what you want, you are so jealous and in love and stupid and nothing is enough so you just have to . . .

EWA: Oh, okay.

MARIA: You feel like that sometimes?

EWA: Yes. Oh, yes.

MARIA: Me too. (*beat*) 'We haven't got all day lads!'

Scene 12

(*MARTIN is in the toilet (off stage). RADU is talking urgently on the phone on his laptop.*)

RADU: So, I told this guy, you can build that shit but you can't live in it! That was here. In Bucharest. Because of all the shit that they're building. No, no, no. Florentina. I refuse to build shit. The capitalists will find ways to punish you too. It's just another form of tyranny. That's not news, everyone I know is getting into property. Bucharest is like . . . I don't know . . . the Klondike. It's crazy.

(*toilet flush*)

So, did I tell you I have a visitor? My nephew. I never saw him before last week. I was thinking . . . He seems lonely. Why don't you come and meet him. Take him off my hands for a few hours. It would be good for him. Wake him up. I know you don't know English. But can't you talk without talking? Yes, the international language of love.

MARTIN: (*off*) Radu?

RADU: Just meet him. See if you like him. Okay? No obligations. Bye.

(*He hangs up. Shouting to* MARTIN *as he exits.*)

Left for cold!

(MARIA *is sitting in front of a computer. There is a small webcam attached to the top of it and a small microphone.*)

MARIA: And have you pressed enter? The key with the arrow. It's complicated I know. Because it's cheaper. And I can see you. And you can see me. It doesn't matter about your hair.

Wait . . . wait, I can see you. Why don't you look in the camera? The camera. Momma, the camera! All I can see is your ear. The camera must be beside you! Yes. Good. I can see you now Momma, you look great.

Mother, I'm travelling, not finding a husband. I can see that! I can see your expression. (*laughing*) You think I'm stupid because I don't have a man but you, you forget you are on camera. Stop laughing! Come on. I want to talk to you. Stop it. That's better. Now, how is everyone . . .

(*She exits with laptop.*)

Scene 13

(*The sound of screaming chickens.* ANDRZEJ *and* ION *enter.* ANDRZEJ *is clutching his wrist. They take off their masks and gear through this scene.*)

ANDRZEJ: Ah. Ah. Ah. That little . . . ah. The last one. Little . . . he bit me!

ION: You should see you!

ANDRZEJ: You little . . . it's your fault!

ION: My fault?

ANDRZEJ: Yes! You said, 'McKenna's Chickens. Good work. You come.' Now I'm bleeding and scratched and those little bastards! I want to kill them myself! Let me go to the factory. Please!

ION: Come on we had fun.

ANDRZEJ: Yes. Yes. Fun. Until that last little bastard bit me. The last one imagine!

ION: He was waiting for you.

ANDRZEJ: Yeah. He was waiting for me. He saw me coming in. He said, 'Here's the new guy.'

ION: Here's a Polish prick. I'm going to get him.

ANDRZEJ: Look at those scratches!

ION: Andrzej, you need to know how to catch them. Practice. It gets easier.

ANDRZEJ: I hope so. I need my hands for building. You know, I couldn't understand what they were telling me to do.

ION: I couldn't understand also. All I hear is 'hellohhowisgo-hahoaoaohohoaoah'. Is it English?

ANDRZEJ: Irish English.

ION: Hohoaaohoahohafffuhooohwwhaa. He gave you money?

ANDRZEJ: Yes. Let me see. (*He take out a payslip.*) Fifty euros. Minus tax is forty-two. Shit.

ION: You Polish are so stupid. What are you working for tax? (*He takes out a €50 note.*) I am illegal and look. Fifty. Cash. No tax.

ANDRZEJ: But you are illegal.

ION: Yes. It's good. I can make more money. When I am legal I can pay tax. Now it's good. I can make money. Build house. Have children.

ANDRZEJ: Is it coming?

ION: What?

ANDRZEJ: Legal?

ION: Yes. Soon. Very soon. Romania is EU now. I thought I could get automatic visa but I have to get work permit €500. Just needs some employer to pay €500 then . . . bang!

ANDRZEJ: Tax.

ION: Yes. Tax. Exactly.

ANDRZEJ: Listen Ion, why don't you come and have dinner in my house?

ION: In your house?

ANDRZEJ: Yes. I have a daughter. She is young like you. You can talk about . . . I don't know.

ION: Sure. Yes. No problem.
ANDRZEJ: Tomorrow night?
ION: Yes. Good.
ANDRZEJ: Eight o'clock? I live on Cara Street. Number three.
ION: In Clones?
ANDRZEJ: Yes.
ION: Good, I live there too.
ANDRZEJ: (*sarcastically*) Great town.
ION: The best.
ANDRZEJ: So, you'll be there?
ION: Yes, yes, I'll be there, but one thing . . .
ANDRZEJ: Yes?
ION: No chicken. Okay?
ANDRZEJ: No chicken.
ION: Oh, one more thing . . .
ANDRZEJ: Yes?
ION: No shit Polish food. Okay?
ANDRZEJ: Kiss my ass.

Scene 14

(*MARIA and EWA are at a bar in Monaghan town. There is Bon Jovi music playing. EWA is answering a text while MARIA is talking on her mobile.*)

MARIA: You'll be here in ten minutes? . . . No, that's fine Seán. I've just arrived myself . . . Yes, completely alone. (*She waves to EWA who is in the background texting.*) See you soon!

(*EWA joins her.*)

MARIA: What time is your father coming?
EWA: Soon. He comes from Clones.
MARIA: Clones? I thought you said he was in Monaghan.
EWA: No, he thought I was going back to Clones so he went home. He didn't think I was coming here.
MARIA: Oh. He knows the 'Squealing Pig'.
EWA: Yes, he knows.
MARIA: Good.
EWA: (*pause*) He plays Bob Dylan in the car. So, it's cool. I didn't know he liked Bob Dylan.
MARIA: No?

EWA: No. I like Polish music. He likes English music. His English is very good.
MARIA: Ah.
EWA: He lived two years in New York.
MARIA: Really?

(MARTIN and RADU are sitting at a bar in Bucharest.)

RADU: Bon Jovi . . .
MARTIN: Da. Romeo is Bleeding!
RADU: Bleeding, bleeding . . . ?
MARTIN: *(Mimes cutting his wrist with blood spurting out.)* Um . . . Johnny Cash?
RADU: Cash. Yes. Superb. Excellent. Bon Jovi . . . .
MARTIN: Nein. Nein. Ugh . . . Nein.
RADU: Okay. *(beat)*
MARTIN: What are we doing here?
RADU: Excuse me?
MARTIN: Warum . . . hier? Warum?
RADU: Ah. Okay. Hier, Fraulein. Ja?
MARTIN: Oh, good Jesus. You mean we're on the pull?
RADU: Nein. Nein. Freund. Mein freund.
MARTIN: Oh. Friend. Freund. Okay.
RADU: Jesus. What's wrong with Bon Jovi. Fuck's sake. No wonder you're depressed. Afraid to enjoy yourself. The Cure, The Smiths, Leonard Cohen. I'd slit my wrists.
EWA: Dad says I should learn the computer in work. I can get better money. What do you think?
MARIA: Maybe.
EWA: It's small computer really. It only does some things and do them the same way over and over. It has sensors tells the machines what to do. Dad says it's very simple.
MARIA: Yes. Sensors. They are picking up signals. Yes?
EWA: Yes.
MARIA: They tell temperature in the room.
EWA: Yes.
MARIA: They know when it increases.
EWA: Yes.
MARIA: They know if it's too cool.
EWA: Uh . . . huh.

MARIA: They know if the mushrooms need something.

EWA: Yes, humidity, light . . .

MARIA: They are intelligent.

EWA: I think so . . . yes.

MARIA: You don't need to tell them. They sense it.

EWA: Yes.

MARIA: So . . .

EWA: What?

MARTIN: Mein Vater. Er trinkt nicht. Keine Bere. Mein Vater.

RADU: Mein Vater. Er trinkt . . . (*He mimes 'a lot'.*)

MARTIN: Ich bin . . . meine mütter. Magdalena. Weißt du?

RADU: Ja.

MARTIN: Er ist . . . um . . . you see my Father . . .

RADU: Vater.

MARTIN: Nein. You are . . . du bist . . .

RADU: Was?

MARTIN: Bere . . . music . . . football . . . weißt du?

RADU: Ja . . . (*He sees Flori in the distance.*) Florina! Come sit here!

EWA: Who?

MARIA: Seán.

EWA: 'We haven't got all day lads?'

MARIA: Yes.

EWA: Oh. You meet him to drink?

MARIA: Yes.

EWA: For . . .

MARIA: Yes.

EWA: You want me to go?

MARIA: Um . . . yes.

EWA: Okay. I wait my father outside.

MARIA: 'We haven't got all day lads . . .'

EWA: Good luck.

MARIA: Thank you.

(*EWA exits.*)

RADU: (*calling*) Flori! (*Introducing the new arrival.*) Florina. Martin. Martin. Florina. Auf Wiedersehen!

(*He leaves. MARTIN and MARIA stand and smile at their new partners . . .*)

Scene 15

(In ANDRZEJ*'s flat.* ANDRZEJ*,* ION *and* EWA *sit around a table. They have just finished dinner.)*

ANDRZEJ: You like Polish food?

ION: Yes. It's very good. Very good. It's like Romanian. It's good. We are the same. I told you. The same. Same food. Same culture.

ANDRZEJ: It's not the same food. It's different.

ION: It's almost the same. It's not Irish. It's European.

ANDRZEJ: It's different.

EWA: Irish food is shit.

ION: Yes, shit. It gives me a pain in my stomach. Seriously. I have a pain in my stomach when I am eating Irish food. That's true. It's good to eat real food. Drink good wine. Thank you.

EWA: Irish women have fat asses.

ION: True. They do. Very fat. Polish women are beautiful. Thin. They don't eat shit.

EWA: I don't know how they keep their men. Seriously. I think they get them then they get fat. Chips. Burgers. Spicy wedges. Fat, fat, fat.

ANDRZEJ: I think Irish women . . .

EWA: What? What do you think about Irish women?

ANDRZEJ: (*beat*) More wine?

ION: Yes. Please.

ANDRZEJ: Ewa?

EWA: No. Thank you.

ANDRZEJ: Okay! So, please leave these dishes. I will wash them when I return. Just sit back and relax. Talk. Be friendly. I won't be long.

EWA: Where are you going?

ANDRZEJ: I am going to the pub. To meet some friends.

EWA: What friends? Polish?

ANDRZEJ: No, Irish. From work.

EWA: You don't like the pub. You don't go there.

ANDRZEJ: Yes. I know. But these friends, they want to meet there so . . . it would be impolite to say . . . 'Oh, I don't like the pub so we should all go somewhere else.' Because, where else is there?

EWA: How long will you be?

ANDRZEJ: Not long. You can talk. Drink some wine. I'll be back. Ion, drink. I won't be long. Goodbye.

(*Exit* ANDRZEJ. *Pause.*)

ION: How are you liking Ireland?

(EWA *shrugs.*)

ION: Yes. It's not so perfect. But you can make money. You are working? Mushrooms, yes?

EWA: Yes.

ION: Shit work. I am doing this when first I came to Ireland. Patsy McKenna is hiring me. You know Patsy?

EWA: No.

ION: He was okay. But hard work. Jesus. Bad money. Bad hour. I will look for job for you. I can get you job.

EWA: Thank you.

(*pause*)

ION: How are you coming to Ireland?

EWA: Aeroplane.

(*pause*)

ION: There is a funny story. How I came to Ireland. I was involved in some government problems. Romania is a very corrupt country. You know, it was the old communists running the country then. Maybe I said some wrong things. I had to run. Or else. I came to Ireland in a little boat. It was crazy. So, I am illegal. It's unbelievable. I can't go home because I am going to prison. And here I am a criminal too.

EWA: (*sarcastically*) Are you a spy?

ION: Something like that. You are married?

EWA: Yes, um, no.

ION: Yes, no. That's good. Yes, I am married, no, I am not. I don't know. That's good. It's like a joke . . . this woman she says, 'my husband he is so faithful, he is the most faithful person in the world'. The other woman says, 'yes neither is mine'.

EWA: It's not a joke.

ION: Oh, okay. (*pause*) You're a beautiful woman. Very pretty.

EWA: Thank you.

ION: Yes, I like you very much.

EWA: Thank you. Would you like some wine?

ION: Please. (*beat*) You are lonely?

EWA: Why do you say that?

ION: I can see it. In your eyes.

EWA: My father didn't tell you?

ION: No, he is telling me nothing.

EWA: I'm sure he wants to help. Bringing a young man here for me to talk to. Stop me from thinking about . . . I don't blame him. He doesn't know what to do with me. I make him sad but he can't help.

ION: You are his daughter.

EWA: Yes, but he likes to live alone. He's so confused . . . the other day he said maybe I should go back to school. I have left school two years already!

ION: Have some wine . . .

EWA: No, thank you. I've had too much.

ION: No, no. It's good. You drink, you forget. Okay?

EWA: Maybe I don't want to forget.

ION: I can't remember.

EWA: What?

ION: What you want to forget. I just forgot.

EWA: I forgot too. (*beat, they laugh*)

ION: Listen, this is good. Here we are, drinking. You are a beautiful woman. You are lonely. I am lonely.

EWA: You are lonely?

ION: Yes. Since I met you I am very lonely. Very sad.

EWA: Ha. Ha. Very funny.

ION: It's true. You are beautiful.

EWA: You said that already.

ION: So . . .

EWA: So, what?

ION: You want to . . .

EWA: What? What?

ION: You want to fuck?

(*beat*)

EWA: No, thank you.

ION: You sure? I would like to. It would be good.

EWA: No, thanks. I . . . ha . . . no. I will clear up. I'm going to take these inside.

(Exit EWA *with plates.)*

ION: Okay.

(Beat. He leaves the apartment. She returns to see that he has left. She picks up her phone and rings her ex-husband.)

EWA: Hello? Is Jacek there? Where is he? Who is this? You are his woman? Irish woman? You are a fucking bitch. That's what I said. I have seen you. You are a fucking fat ass bitch. I don't care. You won't let me see my husband. You have ruined my life. Do you know that?

*(*ANDRZEJ *steps into view and observes the following.)*

EWA: You come along and you don't give a fuck about anybody. You are a cunt. A fucking bitch. You will pay for all of this pain. I don't know how but God is looking at you and he is seeing that you are a fucking . . . *(screams)* Pick up the phone you fucking bitch! You cow! I will fucking kill you if you don't pick up this fucking phone! You will burn in hell you cunt. Cunt, cunt, cunt, cunt, cunt, CUNT!

*(*EWA *collapses in tears.)*

Interval

Act Two

Scene 16

*(*MARTIN *wakes up. There is a sheet over him but he is mostly naked.* RADU *is looking at him and smiling.)*

MARTIN: *(Pause as* MARTIN *takes in his situation.)* Jesus! Oh, Jesus Christ Almighty! You gave me a fright. What the fuck are you doing there? Where is . . .

RADU: Hey, hey. Casanova. Casanova. Nice one. Nice one.

MARTIN: Casanova?

RADU: Yes. Yes. Casanova.

MARTIN: What are you on about? Flori? *(He indicates a large rose-like hair bobbin on the floor.)*

RADU: Yes. Flori. Flori. Nice woman. Very nice. Lovely. How are you feeling? Good? Yeah? Good?

MARTIN: Flori? Where is she?

RADU: Flori gone. Gone. Away. Flori. It's one night. One night only. I think.

MARTIN: Oh. Gone? Okay.

(RADU ruffles MARTIN's hair.)

RADU: Well done mate. Well done. You little beauty. Bet you feel like a million dollars now!

MARTIN: Get off! Jesus! Get off!

RADU: What? What?

MARTIN: Just . . . get off! Relax. Leave me alone. I'm fucking naked here if you don't mind.

RADU: Fine. Fine.

(pause)

RADU: Essen?

MARTIN: Nein. Danke.

RADU: Okay. *(He lifts up the end of MARTIN's sheet so that he looks like a Roman and puts the hair bobbin in his own hair.)*

RADU: Caeser? Cleopatra gone! *(He bursts out laughing.)*

MARTIN: What are you laughing at? Why are you laughing?

(RADU can't stop and waves in answer.)

MARTIN: Fuck's sake.

(MARTIN pulls on his pants. He takes some money from his pocket and gives it to RADU.)

MARTIN: Here. Take it.

RADU: What?

MARTIN: How much was it?

RADU: What are you doing?

MARTIN: Take whatever. Take it.

RADU: Why are you giving me money?

MARTIN: Take it!

RADU: No! No!

MARTIN: Take it!

RADU: Why? Why? Uh . . . warum? Warum?

MARTIN: Warum? Florina! Flo. Money. Yeah?

RADU: What? What? You little shit. What? No. No. (*laughs*) Take back your money and don't insult me.

MARTIN: I don't understand. Did you pay her money? Did you?

RADU: I don't understand you my little friend and I don't want to. You have a beautiful woman here who sleeps with a little shit like you and you think she is a prostitute? Fuck you.

MARTIN: Take the fucking money. Take it!

(*MARTIN tries to shove the money into RADU's hand and they start to wrestle with each other.*)

RADU: Get away from me!

MARTIN: Go on. I'll pay my way. I'm not a fucking charity case! Take the money! Take it!

RADU: Get off you fucking lunatic! Get off me!

MARTIN: I didn't want her! I didn't want her!

RADU: What are you trying to do? What are you saying?

MARTIN: If I wanted a fucking prostitute I would have asked now take the money!

RADU: Get off!!

(*RADU pushes MARTIN off him and they both fall down. Long pause.*)

RADU: You're a mad bastard. I didn't pay that woman any money.

MARTIN: What? (*beat*) Was?

RADU: Kein geld. Ich hab kein geld uh . . . geben.

MARTIN: Oh.

RADU: Oh.

MARTIN: I just . . . I didn't ask for her.

RADU: What?

MARTIN: It doesn't matter. I'm sorry. Es tut mir leid.

RADU: (*laughs*) Don't worry about it.

(*pause*)

MARTIN: Flori . . .

RADU: Yes?

MARTIN: Bine?

RADU: Good.

MARTIN: Da. Da.

RADU: (*laughs*)

MARTIN: (*laughs*) I'm an idiot.
RADU: What?
MARTIN: I'm an . . . ah it doesn't matter.

(*beat*)

RADU: Martin?
MARTIN: Yes?
RADU: You're an idiot.
MARTIN: What?

Scene 17

(*EWA and MARIA are in MARIA's flat in Clones.*)

MARIA: 'Let's do it?'
EWA: Something like that.
MARIA: 'Let's do it?' Jesus. He's very romantic this boy.
EWA: He's okay.
MARIA: So . . . what's the problem?
EWA: I am worried about the pills. I think they are not so good.
MARIA: I told you. These pills are dangerous.
EWA: But they are helping.
MARIA: Really?
EWA: Well, I feel a lot better. I can sleep.
MARIA: That's good.
EWA: I don't mind coming to work so much. Even though it's shit.
MARIA: Thank you, I know, it's because I am so nice.
EWA: No, these pills are so good, so strong I can even listen to you. No problem.
MARIA: So, what is the problem?
EWA: Yes. I should have slept with this man maybe but I don't feel like anything. Just empty. I don't feel anything for any man.
MARIA: Should you?
EWA: I don't know. I think so. We had a deal.
MARIA: Yes, but look, maybe . . .

(*MARIA's phone beeps again and she cancels it.*)

EWA: Maybe, what?
MARIA: Maybe you are still in love with your husband.
EWA: I'm not. I hate him.
MARIA: Well, why did you call him then?

EWA: To tell him how much I hate him. How he has ruined my life.

MARIA: How has he ruined your life?

EWA: Look at me. I'm living in Ireland, I'm working on a mushroom farm, I'm sharing a room with my father, I'm on Prozac . . . I used to see my life through Jacek. Now I don't know where it's going. Nowhere.

MARIA: You're very young. You can go to college.

EWA: Yes.

MARIA: Your English is okay. We can get a better job. You don't have to pick mushrooms all your life.

EWA: I know. (*beat*) You're sure it's not the pills.

MARIA: I don't know. I don't trust them but . . . I think you need some time to get over your husband first. Then you can think about other men.

EWA: (*beat*) You know I was never with another man.

MARIA: Oh.

EWA: Just my husband.

MARIA: I see.

EWA: So, I can't imagine being with anyone else.

MARIA: Yes, that's natural. You are young and you have a broken heart. It's normal.

EWA: You're young . . .

(*MARIA's mobile phone beeps. There is a message.*)

MARIA: Leave me alone!

EWA: What's that?

MARIA: Message.

EWA: Who is it?

MARIA: Seán.

EWA: Oh, yes?

MARIA: He's texting me all the time now.

EWA: And?

MARIA: Ugh!

EWA: We haven't got all day lads!

MARIA: He's so . . . ugh!

EWA: Are you going to reply?

MARIA: No. It's bullshit. No connection.

EWA: No connection?

MARIA: I studied three years art in Bucharest. His favourite colour is magnolia!

EWA: So, he's your broken heart?

MARIA: No. (*beat*) Someone in Bucharest. I left them behind.

EWA: Why? If you love somebody.

MARIA: I don't know. He was older than me. And he had some stupid principle about not working. I know, believe me I was working three jobs just to earn some money. And he was sitting there dreaming about a Romania that used to be. Or could have been. I had to live in the real Romania. Sleep, work, eat. There must be more in life.

EWA: What?

MARIA: I want to explore the world. I am young. It's normal. Love isn't everything.

EWA: It feels like it is.

MARIA: Yes, but there are mountains and trees and music and colours and birds. There are so many things. Languages and dancing and clothes and lakes and rivers and the sea and flowers and rocks and children and boats and . . . and . . .

EWA: Mushrooms?

MARIA: (*laughing*) Yes. Yes. Actually, it's funny. I used to pick mushrooms in the forest at home. Isn't that funny? And I thought Ireland was going to be like that. I loved the idea of such a beautiful country. Actually, my ex-boyfriend had some connection to Ireland. He was obsessed with it for some reason and he read Joyce, Beckett, Yeats. I thought it was a fairytale country. Everybody writing and painting. So, when I had to leave I thought, this is the place for me. But it was just a dream. Here it's sleep, work, eat too. Just with shitty weather. I think it's time to move on.

EWA: Can I come too?

MARIA: Sure. I just don't know where I'm going. Is that okay?

EWA: Yes.

Scene 18

(*RADU and MARTIN are just outside Sibiu. MARTIN is on a mobile phone. RADU is singing a rural folk song.*)

MARTIN: It's only been a month. No. I'm not unhappy. I'm not. We're getting on grand. Fine. He speaks a bit of German. In school. I learnt it in school. For six years. I'm not imposing. I just know Dad, okay? We're in Sibiu at the moment where Mam is from. I know you know. He wanted to show me their farm and things. I don't know. I'm fine. I'm fine. Radu buys the . . . it's dead cheap over here. Well, I'll get a job. Because . . . because . . . if you'd let me . . . because he's like mam that's why! Little things. I don't know. His sense of humour . . . the clicking sound he makes when he reads the paper . . . the towels in the bathroom. Same as Mam. And it's like sometimes, when he does those little things, it's like she's still here and it's brilliant. And it's strange and everything but . . . (*long pause*) Dad, don't. You'll set me off. Yeah. Yeah. Talk to you then. (*MARTIN hangs up. Beat.*) What's that? I know that song.

(*MARTIN sings a bit of the song.*)

RADU: Your mother, Magdalena and I sang that song in a choir. We toured Europe with it.

MARTIN: She used to sing it to me to stop me crying.

(*They sing another snatch of the song. MARTIN gets upset.*)

RADU: Ah. Was? Was? Was?

(*He holds MARTIN for a bit.*)

RADU: So, hier ist Sibiu.

MARTIN: Ja. Da.

RADU: Heim. Magdalena und mich.

MARTIN: Da. This was your farm. We have a farm in Ireland too.

RADU: Feld, bauer, um . . .

MARTIN: Ja. Ja. Feld. Mein Vater er hast . . . bauer auch. Farm. He's doing the lambing now. Um . . . lamb? Baa.

RADU: Martin, es tut mir leid aber du mußt zuruck gehen.

MARTIN: Go back? Nein! Warum?

RADU: Mein Vater . . . um . . . mein Vater. Er was ein Doctor . . . okay? Aber Ceaucescu . . . swartz . . .

MARTIN: Swartz . . . .black . . .

RADU: How do I say blacklisted?

MARTIN: Swartz . . . black. Blacklisted (*He makes a signal 'finish.'*)

RADU: Yes, blacklisted. (*He makes the same gesture.*) So, he became a farmer instead . . . auch, er mußt bzzzzz. Bees und . . .

MARTIN: (*makes animal noise*)

RADU: Genau! (*they laugh*) Magdalena und mich wir gehen ins Deutschland, leider, weißt du?

MARTIN: Ja, ja. You went to Germany together. With the choir.

RADU: Magdalena sie gehen, zum Irland. Ich bleibe . . . warum? Mein Vater. Weißt du?

MARTIN: Ja. You stayed behind? For your father?

RADU: Es war . . . schrechlich aber . . . mein Vater . . . war mein Vater.

MARTIN: Your father is your father, yes.

RADU: I . . . am . . . sorry. I . . . didn't go to the funeral. I was angry. Magdalena. She left me . . . with . . . (*He indicates 'everything around here.'*) I hated her. I'm sorry. I hated her. Mein Vater. Herz . . . (*He indicates that his father's heart was broken.*) Mein Vater war mein Vater. Du mußt zuruck gehen.

(*pause*)

MARTIN: Mein Uncle . . . ist mein Uncle.

RADU: Nein. Nein. Du mußt zuruck gehen.

MARTIN: I don't want to go back.

RADU: Ich bin dein Uncle. Aber nicht deine Vater. Nicht deine mutter. Sie ist tot. She is dead. Sie ist tot.

Scene 19

(*ANDRZEJ enters with a small backpack.*)

ANDRZEJ: Newgrange was built over 5,000 years ago in 3,200 BC. That's 1,000 years before Stonehenge and centuries before the Great Pyramids. Think about that. This little island. 5,000 years ago people were looking at the sky and making sense of it. They lived their lives by it. The sun's power. The moon's grace. A little chamber, a chink above the door. Like I did as a sick child tracing the light travelling across my bedroom. From the wardrobe to the bed, exploding at one point and dying in a corner at the end of the day. That light was my only visitor. Simultaneously my comfort and proof that I was alone. It's motion along the furniture was a reminder that I must survive alone. But this is so much more complex. One day of the year this light hits the back of a long dark tunnel. In the middle of winter, on the shortest day of the year, when the sun gives us the least, on that day darkness is illuminated, literally and symbolically. It's so brilliant. Such a clever concept. There are places so deep and dark that only the winter sun can touch. The summer sun is too bright, too high in the sky. The winter sun is like a torch or a laser beam. It hits the darkness and travels along the womb-like chamber caressing it gently (*He gestures with his hand.*) 'I am here. Even in the bleak mid-winter, I am here.'

Scene 20

(*Enter* ION. *He is carrying a small bunch of flowers.*)

ION: Hello.

MARIA: Hello.

ION: I am looking for a girl.

MARIA: Really?

ION: Her name is Ewa.

MARIA: You are Romanian.

ION: Yes. You are also.

(*The next section in Romanian.*)

MARIA: Where are you from?

ION: Bucharest. You?

MARIA: Yes. How did you come here?

ION: It's a funny story actually. I am a carpenter and I worked for this man in Bucharest. He was Irish, from Monaghan. He was a property developer and I was his head man in Bucharest and he brought me here on a contract and I had one pint of Guinness and I decided to stay. One pint.

MARIA: That's a good story.

ION: Yes. You know Ewa?

MARIA: Yes. She is my friend. We work together.

ION: You like to pick mushrooms?

MARIA: No.

ION: It's not so bad. I picked mushrooms. It's not so bad.

MARIA: You picked mushrooms?

ION: Yes.

MARIA: In Ireland?

ION: Yes.

MARIA: I thought you said you worked with a property developer.

ION: Yes. Before. But then that work ended and I needed some money, so . . . Now I work in construction.

MARIA: Oh. She's over there.

(ION makes his way to where EWA is working.)

ION: Hello.

EWA: Hello.

(ION holds up the bunch of flowers.)

EWA: What are you doing here?

ION: These are for you. Please.

EWA: Um . . . thank you.

ION: You are very beautiful.

EWA: Thank you.

ION: I have very deep thoughts about you.

EWA: I have to work. I'm working now.

ION: I cannot stop thinking about you. You are so beautiful.

EWA: Yes. But I am working now and I will lose my job if I am talking to you.

ION: It's okay. Relax. I know the supervisor. He is a very good friend of mine. This is not a problem.

EWA: Please.

ION: No. Please. I was so wrong the other night. I was bad. Telling you just to fuck. I realise now that you are a woman, a lady, very special. I would like to talk to you and buy you some things when I have some money.

EWA: I have to work. I can't talk to you.

ION: Will you be my friend? Please. I have no friends here. I just want to talk. I would be your friend and maybe we can kiss if that is what you . . . want. I am a peasant yes. My manners are not so good. I can learn. I like you.

EWA: Please leave. Now. It's not . . . just go.

ION: What do you want? I give it to you. What do you want? Money?

EWA: I want you to leave. Now.

ION: Okay. See . . . I am going. You are working. That is good.

I respect you very much. I will see you later. After work maybe. When you are not so busy. I will see you. Yes?

MARIA: (*in Romanian*) Can't you see she's working?

ION: (*in Romanian*) It's okay. You don't need to get involved. (*in English*) So, I will call you?

EWA: I'm working.

MARIA: (*Romanian*) I'm going to call the manager if you don't leave.

ION: (*Romanian*) Fuck off! (*English*) Please?

MARIA: (*Romanian*) Shut the fuck up you asshole. Get the fuck out of here now! Dickhead.

ION: (*Romanian*) Listen geebag, shut your fucking mouth and go back to work, alright?

EWA: What's he saying?

MARIA: Nothing. He's an asshole.

ION: I'm going. I'm going. Goodbye.

MARIA: (*Romanian*) Yeah fuck off like a good boy.

(*ION leaves.*)

EWA: What was all that about?

MARIA: Nothing.

EWA: He's kind of sexy when he shouts isn't he?

MARIA: What?

EWA: I'm joking.

Scene 21

ANDRZEJ: There are stones here with sundials inscribed on them. How to tell the time in 3,200 BC. 3,000 years before Christ they were telling the time here. Right here in Newgrange. And there are lunar images on some of the stones. The phases of the moon. And all these spirals. Curving in and out of each other, dancing along the stone. Not the hard lines of the Egyptians, the Greeks and the Romans but soft, mysterious, disorderly spirals. In this place art and science and religion meet. When I was growing up in Poland they were separate. Religion was the church. Science was the state and art was underground. Here they are all the same thing. They are life. The big star shines in the tomb, (*As he speaks now the sun begins its slow journey across the chamber, across his face.*) the carvings are awoken, they dance, the god is present, he brings this dead place to life. Light and dark, life and death, man (*He gestures to the carving.*) and god. (*He gestures to the light.*)

Scene 22

(*Ewa is at home reading a letter.*)

Andrzej: 'Ewa. I have gone away for a while. I'm sorry that you are feeling so bad. I want to help you but I don't know how. Maybe I will find some help where I am going. Remember I told you about Newgrange. It is a sacred site and full of mysteries. If I find something I will bring it back for you to make you happy. I have left some money, you can pay the rent while I'm away. I don't know when I'll be back. I love you always. Papa.'

(*Ewa lets the note drop onto the table and picks up the money. She begins to cry. She picks up the phone and dials a number. During this phone call Ion enters the room unseen.*)

Ewa: Hello. Hello. I was thinking of you today. I was thinking of our first night together. It was beautiful. So beautiful and exciting. It made me want you again. I can't understand how something so beautiful and right can turn into such shit. It doesn't make any sense. All those secret jokes we had together. We used to laugh so much about them and no one else could understand. How can that be gone? Thinking about that I want you so much. I want your weight on top of me and your breath on my face but I know that's gone now. That's gone now. I won't call you again.

(*Ewa starts to cry.*)

Ion: Ewa.

Ewa: What the fuck!

Ion: Hello.

Ewa: What . . . what are you doing here?

Ion: It's okay. I came to see you, the door was open. I thought maybe you are . . . you are crying?

EWA: I'm okay.
ION: That's bad. Why are you crying?
EWA: It doesn't matter. It's nothing.
ION: I heard. It's okay. Here . . .

(*He goes to hug her.*)

EWA: What are you doing?
ION: It's okay. I understand. I am helping you.
EWA: Leave me alone. Please.
ION: I can help you with this problem.
EWA: What?
ION: I can help you. Here . . .

(*He kisses her.*)

EWA: Get off. Go away!
ION: Please . . . please. You are so beautiful.
EWA: Aaah! Get off.

(*EWA slaps ION and pushes him.*)

EWA: NO!

(*ION springs back.*)

ION: I am sorry. I am so sorry. I am sorry.

(*ION gently hugs EWA like a child hugging a sad adult.*)

(*Pause. Then EWA starts to kiss ION.*)

Scene 23

(*MARTIN and MARIA are packing bags and speaking on the laptops simultaneously. MARIA has a head-set on and can see her mother on the web.*)

MARTIN: Yeah, I can't stay on long because I'm using Radu's computer. I can't get credit here.
MARIA: I'm catching a bus in a few hours. Yes, I have saved a lot of money so I will be okay. Because I was paid a lot of money to pick mushrooms.
MARTIN: Sorry, have you actually met Radu? Look, I can't stay on. I'm coming back home anyway. Yeah. Today.
MARIA: I found that icon that you left in my bag again. In a little side pocket. It's beautiful. No, really I think it's beautiful. I know, Romania is beautiful. Yes, we have trees, mountains,

rivers, lakes . . . I know. I just want to see some other trees, mountains, rivers, lakes . . .

MARTIN: Why? Jesus, you were the one didn't want me to go in the first place. Listen, I don't want to stay on long, I said. Because, I want to get out of here before he comes back. Because I don't want to say goodbye to him. It's too awkward. It's like Mam yeah. Exactly.

MARIA: I'm going with Ewa. She works with me. I told you about her already. I will be safe. I am going to go to Dublin. A Romanian friend . . . we can stay with her. She's going to get us a job . . . she has a gallery there.

MARTIN: Well, I was going to help with lambing first anyway. Sure you were the whole time telling me I was the only one could do it.

MARIA: Ewa's coming over now and then we will leave. I have to go now. So, goodbye. I am taking your ikon. Look, I am putting it in the bag.

MARTIN: I'll see you at the airport so . . . Yeah. I've to go. I don't know, I'll write him a note. In English I suppose. He can get it translated. Okay, that's it, I'm going. See you soon. Bye, Dad. Bye.

MARIA: Bye, Mama, bye.

(MARIA hangs up. She dials another skpe account. RADU's computer starts to alert him that someone is calling. MARTIN answers. Pause as both MARIA's and MARTIN's faces appear on the screens.)

MARTIN: Hello?

MARIA: Radu?

MARTIN: Sorry. Radu isn't here just now . . .

(She hangs up quickly. MARTIN hangs up and the faces disappear.)

Scene 24

ANDRZEJ: I got the bus today from Clones. I didn't tell my daughter that I was going. I didn't tell my employer that I was going. I thought that once I got here, in Newgrange, that is the end of Ireland for me. I'm sick of waiting. I am sitting here watching the mid-winter sun lighting up the chamber and it is summer. That is only a stage-light and these drawings are only a set. I am sitting in a virtual

Newgrange. It's all wires and lights and tricks. The real place is earth and stone and starlight. But I got here too late today and it's booked out already. When I first came to Ireland I wanted to see the winter solstice. But it's so rare and precious that you have to put your name on a list and it's a lottery to get in there. I put my name on this list. Maybe I will wait. Maybe I will stay in Ireland and catch chickens and build houses and wait.

(He sits down on the floor.)

Scene 25

(MARIA is finished packing and sits by her case waiting to leave. She is singing a song. MARTIN is packing. RADU enters. He is singing the same song as MARIA. He looks at her as if she was a distant memory and then exits.)

(EWA enters to hear the end of the song.)

EWA: Hello.
MARIA: Hello.
EWA: You are singing.
MARIA: I am waiting.
EWA: What were you singing about?
MARIA: I was singing about Seán.
EWA: 'We haven't got all day lads.'
MARIA: Yes. I was just thinking about him and our affair.
EWA: What was the song?
MARIA: I suppose you could translate like this: 'I fuck you but I think of him.'

(EWA laughs nervously.)

MARIA: You are not coming?
EWA: No.

(MARTIN is writing a little note. RADU enters. He sees the bag and the note. MARTIN gives him the note.)

RADU: 'Aufwiedersehen mein freund.'

(RADU gives Martin a hug.)

MARIA: Why? I hope it's not because of that stupid Romanian boy.

EWA: Well, no. I want to wait on my father. He has gone away and I can't say goodbye when he's not here.

MARIA: Okay.

(*RADU folds the note and puts it with the book on bees and the memorial card.*)

EWA: I will miss you.

MARIA: Do you have broadband?

EWA: No.

MARIA: You must get this. It's cheaper than phone.

EWA: Okay . . .

MARIA: This is how I talk to my mother.

EWA: Okay . . .

MARIA: This is where I'll be in Dublin.

EWA: Okay . . .

(*RADU takes MARTIN's backpack.*)

RADU: Martin, Radu. Radu, Martin. Brrrrrrr! (*As in a plane.*)

MARTIN: Brrrrrrrrrr!

(*they exit*)

MARIA: This is for you.

(*She gives EWA the icon her Mother gave her.*)

EWA: Thank you. It's beautiful. All different little shiny pieces . . .

MARIA: Yes, but together they all make sense. They make this picture. (*pause*) It's Orthodox but . . .

EWA: No, it's nice thank you.

MARIA: Tell Seán for me . . . tell him . . . tell him . . .

EWA: Yes?

MARIA: 'We haven't got all day lads.'

(*She is crying and they hug.*)

Scene 26

(*ANDRZEJ, in the same position as before.*)

ANDRZEJ: I came here because I wanted to feel something. Some connection. I wanted to connect to the ancestors, to all of our ancestors. Adam and Eve? Or some monkey that decided to take a walk? It doesn't matter. That's all bullshit. This . . . is all bullshit. These wires, this light. It's nothing. I want to look at a light that is millions of years old. I want to look at old light. Stars. When I look at a star I don't want to understand it. I don't care that the universe may be expanding or contracting. I don't give a shit for the mathematics. I love the mystery of it. The beauty. It means everything. It says everything. You are not the centre. You are just a part. But, you are a part. The universe flows through you and you flow through it. We will return through the gate. The Milky Way. We will meet the ancestors and we will understand what they understood.

(RADU returns to the flat with car keys. He looks at one of his architect models and he suddenly throws it in the bin. He goes to the book MARTIN gave him, takes out Magdalena's memorial card and puts it in his pocket.)

RADU: Magdalena . . .

(He then throws the book in the bin also. He disconnects his laptop and puts it under his arm. He looks around the apartment as if for the last time and leaves.)

Scene 27

(Graveyard in Monaghan a few months previously. MARTIN is standing alone by the grave of his mother. Enter ION carrying a shovel.)

ION: Hello.

MARTIN: Hello.

ION: How are you?

MARTIN: Um . . . alright.

ION: *(reads)* 'Magdalena McConville.' Your mother?

MARTIN: Yes.

ION: Very sad. Very sad. Both my parents, they are dead.

MARTIN: I'm sorry.

ION: No . . . please. I am working here. Digging and . . . believe me. I see some sad people. Very sad. And me . . . believe me . . . I'm okay. Some people they give a little . . . you know some . . . and it's nice but . . . not necessary. Not necessary.

MARTIN: Oh. I'm sorry. Did my Dad not sort you out? I'm sorry.

ION: No, no please. It's not necessary to . . . . *(MARTIN gives him some money.)* Thank you very much. My pleasure to help you. *(beat)* Magdalena. This is Irish name?

MARTIN: No. My . . . she was Romanian.

ION: No! You're kidding me. Romanian. Fuck shit! I am Romanian.

MARTIN: Really?

ION: Yes. So, you are Romanian too. Yes?

MARTIN: Ah, I wouldn't say that. I can't even speak Romanian.

ION: But your blood. Your soul. Your ancestors. You are Romanian. You have relative? In Romania?

MARTIN: She has a brother in Bucharest.

ION: Bucharest . . . fuck shit . . . Bucharest. Best place man. Best place.

MARTIN: Yeah, so I wrote to him, like. When Mam was ill. But I heard nothing. I think she was close to him at some stage 'cause every now and again when she wasn't thinking she'd call me 'Radu'.

ION: Radu. Yes. You should go there. You should meet this Radu.

MARTIN: He probably wouldn't want me there . . .

ION: Look around you. This place. Your mother. You think if she could come back would she say, 'No, I don't need this.' You can go. Go. He is your uncle. And your uncle is . . . your uncle.

MARTIN: Yeah, maybe. Yeah.

ION: Look . . .

MARTIN: What?

ION: Is it okay . . . I have to . . . (*fill in the grave*)

MARTIN: Oh, right. I . . . sorry. The others have gone to the pub and I came back . . .

ION: Yes, of course. They wait you now.

MARTIN: Yeah. Thanks.

(*Exit MARTIN. ION looks at the grave.*)

Scene 28

ANDRZEJ: This is a dead place. Here, in this room, where I can't even see the sky, I feel nothing. Nothing. Air conditioning. Spotlights. Fire door. Concrete and steel. There is nothing here. Nothing. This is a dead place. (*beat*) But I can't move. I can't go on and I don't want to go home. I don't want to share a room with my daughter. To see her crying. When she was a baby she cried like . . . like she was posessed. One night I took her out in the fields and walked. I only meant to walk down the road a bit but she wouldn't stop crying and I walked for miles. And miles. I walked and walked. All the way she cried. She cried and cried and I was going crazy. I was talking all the time. Cassiopea, Ursa Minor, Ursa Major, look, look. When I got back the next morning it was twelve o'clock and my wife had called the police. There was a big police officer there he looked tired and pissed off, he had been searching for a long time. But he was a father too and he just shook his head and smiled. But he should have arrested me. My daughter was still crying and I was already planning my escape. I was already planning to abandon her. (*beat*) I should go back but I want to . . . I want to stay here. With my fake sun and my fake stones and my fake sky. I will sit here until they close.

Scene 29

(*ION is finishing a phone call . . .*)

ION: Yes, I can move anywhere. Yes, it's no problem. I have worked many places. Cooking is no problem, I am three years chef in Dublin. You know Patsy McKenna? A Spanish restaurant! I am native Spanish! Yes, my father was Romanian but my mother, yes, yes, you can call . . .

The End

Introduction to Rosaleen McDonagh's

Rings (2012)

Maurya Wickstrom

One of the principle objectives of this volume, articulating the value of inward migration to Ireland, is shadowed, in the case of the Irish Travellers, by something like irony. The situation of contemporary Travellers is such that movement, migration within the Republic of Ireland is no longer possible.

And yet, migration is not exactly the right term. The Travellers are an indigenous ethnic minority and are nomadic. Nomadism is outside/alongside migration. That is, it is a practice conceived not as moving from one place of residence to another, but as a deliberate moving without staying, moving without ever becoming 'settled,' without becoming part of the dominant sedentarist ideology, without becoming a 'buffer'.

Rosaleen McDonagh's play *Rings* is written in the context of an Ireland in which nomadism has become a crime. Nomadism is threatening to capitalist societies in which a 'settled' relationship to private property is the cornerstone of existence, alongside individuality and a person's commitment to wage labour. Travellers have endured years of discrimination and public denunciation and continue to do so. Most egregiously, the Irish state has been attempting to house or settle the Travellers since the 1940s. This long history culminated in the Housing (Traveller Accommodation) Act of 2002, more commonly referred to as the 'Trespass Law'. The law made the traditional means of travelling illegal, thus, effectively, criminalising it.

Throughout the years, various means of 'housing' Travellers have been instituted by the government, including conventional housing projects. But many Travellers are 'housed' on what are known as halting sites, which is where the deaf boxing beoir (girl) who is the central character of *Rings* lives with her family. Halting sites consist of a varying number of trailers gathered together in what is usually a barren and isolated location. Sometimes there are also small concrete structures that may hold a kitchen and bathroom, sometimes not. Sometimes there is a central facility which functions as a kind of community centre, sometimes not. Sometimes there is grass and a space for kids to play, and sometimes not. The sites are overcrowded and ill-planned by the government. Halting sites are small reservations.

And yet, trailers remain the central living space at the sites. Even without travelling, the trailer signifies nomadism. And nomadism has become a referent, not only to actual travel, but to a way of being that continues to insist upon itself. This is why Travellers are still nomads, still Travellers, even when they no longer actually travel. Nomadism is what I have called elsewhere a 'multivalent reference to a collective of practices'.[1] It can and does function, among other things, as the foundation for the Traveller activism that has been gathering strength since the 1960s, particularly in organisations like Pavee Point Travellers' Centre, where Rosaleen McDonagh worked for ten years. This activism is fiercely anti-assimilationist and this is loud and clear in *Rings*.

McDonagh's central character in this two-person play is Norah. By virtue of both her disability—her deafness caused by childhood meningitis—and her devotion to and talent for boxing, Norah is a challenge to her family, the other Travellers on their site, and to an extended Traveller network. Her father refuses to learn to sign, and rejects her boxing, keenly aware of the 'shaming' these would bring. Men his age are enraged by Norah's boxing as she shows up their sons in this explicitly masculinist sport. Norah comments repeatedly on her gendered existence in which everyone expects her domestic skills to be especially good since she is deaf. If this sounds critical of the Traveller community, it is. But what is notable in McDonagh's work, like that of Michael Collins, another Traveller playwright, is that the plays push on the boundaries of Traveller expectations and traditions, while at the same time refusing to let this critique imply that Travellers wish to take on the 'freedoms' of settled people. She refuses the simple modernist narrative in which Travellers would be urged to move from a presumed 'traditional' life to a more realistic modernisation (although there is mention of this movement in the play). It is as if there are serious adjustments to be made to what remains a concretely and specifically Traveller existence.

Thus, McDonagh positions herself within debates about representation that have played out through the years of identity politics by choosing to almost aggressively foreground flaws within Traveller society. She risks, of course, feeding more negative images of Travellers to a settled society in which many such images continue to circulate. She demands something of her fellow Travellers, as is evident not only in *Rings* but also in her play *Stuck* (performed at the Project Arts Centre, Dublin, 2008). McDonagh is disabled herself. She is highly educated, with a Masters from Trinity College in Dublin, and thus, has personally countered deep gender expectations, as well as suspicion of settled education, among some Travellers. In this play, she is simultaneously an activist for gender and disability equality within Traveller life itself *and* a voice for the integrity and validity of the ways in which Travellers continue to construct themselves in an ongoing way as an alternate and nomadic community within a changing Irish society.

Theatre is a relatively new genre for Travellers. While theatrical improvisation and other techniques have been and are often used in Traveller community centres, it has been only recently that plays have been written with a professional context in mind. It is possible that, in the context of the interculturalism this volume is foregrounding, theatre does become one of the means through which it is possible to 'make an appearance', to come, so to speak, onto the stage of human rights discourses, governmental policy, and other forums ostensibly addressing inequality. And yet, so far, the two Traveller playwrights I know of, Collins and McDonagh, have met with little success in getting productions supported. McDonagh's other plays include *The Baby Doll Project, She's Not Mine, Stuck, Mainstream* and an adaptation of Colum McCann's novel *Zoli.* In March 2012, *Beat Him Like a Badger* was commissioned by Fishamble to be part of the *Tiny Plays for Ireland* series. She is currently also in development with RTÉ on *Unsettled,* a television drama. Collins has starred in his own works *It's A Cutural Thing, Or Is It* and *Same Difference, Worlds Apart* produced by the Traveller Wagon Wheel Theatre which 'exists to enhance Traveller potential, ability and skills to address the issues which affect the quality of their lives through the medium of Arts'.[2]

While there is a long history of representations *of* Irish Travellers in theatre—from Lady Gregory and J.M. Synge to Marina Carr—Travellers, like the Roma in Ireland—for whom Travellers, with their history of intercultural activism, fiercely advocate—remain the limit cases for Ireland's tolerance and intercultural openness. Over the course of the Traveller activism that has resulted in adjustments to state policy with regard to Travellers, Travellers have found that assimilation lurks closely under the surface of the state's avowed interculturalism. This is exemplified in the Citizen Traveller poster campaign of 1999. Although a historical example, it is also paradigmatic of state policy toward the Travellers. In it, Travellers, as individual people with socially useful and admired qualities, and with a distinct culture and their own heritage, were trumpeted as Irish citizens like any other. But when Travellers contributed campaign posters alluding to the criminalisation of nomadism, showing a trailer crossed out in a red 'x', the campaign, along with its pictures of thriving Traveller citizens, was abruptly withdrawn.[3]

If theatre itself risks being a 'housing' operation, McDonagh's uncompromising position against assimilation, even as she criticises her fellow Travellers, resists this overtaking. Norah, deaf, refusing to marry the man chosen for her because she is on her way to the Olympics, using her hands as much for fighting as for signing, nevertheless remains very much a Traveller.

Notes and References

1 Maurya Wickstrom, *Performance in the Blockades of Neoliberalism: Thinking the Political Anew* (Hampshire UK and New York: Palgrave Macmillan, 2012).

2 'Traveller Wagon Wheel Theatre,' Irish Theatre Playography. Read online at http://www.irishplayography.com/company.aspx?companyid=427.

3 'Ireland gives a summer welcome to Citizen Traveller – yet again', Indymedia Ireland. Read online at www.indymedia.ie/article/66108. Irish Traveller Movement, 'Citizen Traveller.' Read online at www.itmtrav.com/citizentrav.html.

Rings

ROSALEEN MCDONAGH

Rings was presented originally as a staged reading as part of *Turning Point: A Reading of Four Short Plays by Writers With Disabilities* by Fishamble: The New Play Company and Arts & Disability Ireland on 31 March 2010.

CAST

NORAH	Mary Murray
FATHER	Michael Collins

PRODUCTION TEAM

Director	Jim Culleton
Producer	Orla Flanagan
Project Development	Jim Culleton, & Pádraig Naughton
Sound Technician	Ivan Birthistle
Stage Manager	Clive Welsh
Camera Operator	Jillian Srigley
Captioner	Ruth McCreery
ISL Interpreter	Caroline O'Leary

CHARACTERS

NORAH, seventeen or eighteen
FATHER, early forties

Scene 1

(A man in his early forties is sitting in the corner of a makeshift boxing ring. The scene is dimly lit. There is some gym equipment, weights and two or three old punch bags around the room. They are leaning against the walls. There are hooks hanging from the wall with tracksuits on them. In the far corner of the ring there's a mirror with light bulbs all around the edge. There are make-up bags and a silk boxing dressing gown. Directly over the ring there is a picture of the sacred heart. FATHER *is sitting on a bench and there's a punch bag hanging opposite him at the far end corner. There's a pair of red boxing gloves beside him on the bench and there is also a pair of hand weights. Occasionally, he picks up one of the gloves and rubs his fingers on the outside of the leather. He doesn't try the gloves on but runs his hand across the back of the gloves so that his palm and his fingers are clasping it.*

The scene opens with a light coming through an open door. NORAH *is standing alone in the ring. She is wearing a wedding dress and boots and is holding her headgear.* NORAH *signs throughout, sign language is her only method of communication. This is fundamental to the piece.)*

NORAH: I know what he's doing! This is what he's always done. He goes ahead and listens to other people, but doesn't listen to me! When he gets drunk he starts talking about the guilt of what happened, like it's supposed to be my fucking fault. Meningitis—we were living in Sligo, every child on the site got it, but they got better. I stayed sick. Meningitis, this is how they explained it to me. It doesn't happen to everyone. They all didn't become deaf the way I did. It is some sort of an inflammation to the membrane. This is what they call the outer covering of somebody's brain. (*As she's explaining this, she's examining the headgear in her hands.*) This protects the brain. In my head it got damaged.

FATHER: All the years of trying to understand what was wrong with our only daughter. Doctors, hospital appointments, we drove the length and breadth of the country. (*He stands up and sits down again.*) Half the time I didn't know what they were telling us. I used to get Kate to do all the talking. But deep in my heart I was breaking up inside. Each time they'd start to tell us why she wasn't able to hear us it was like taking another body blow.

NORAH: This is what happened to me. All those visits to the doctor, to the hospital, not knowing what people were saying to me. By the time I was eleven I could hear nothing. In some ways I was glad. In the other normal school they just thought I was a thick knacker sitting in the back of the classroom not knowing what was going on. Mam kept coming to meetings. But sure she was embarrassed. She couldn't explain things. She got no schooling herself. In a way they were kind of saying that I had a mental disability because I was so backward I kept failing every test.

FATHER: All the way through those years we took her everywhere. Every holy well, every holy man or woman, Knock, Lourdes. Her mother Kate wanted her to go to Medjugore, the place in Portugal. Some of the Pavee families from the site were going. We thought. (*he pauses*) That's what Travellers do when they have sick children. She'd kill me if she knew I was calling her sick but that's how we understand it. (*he sits down again*) Anyway, she was fourteen and she wasn't having it up or down, no way was she going. She said she didn't want to be cured, she was happy the way she was. (*he laughs*) She was cheeky enough to tell her mother that we might think of getting cured ourselves, cured of our Traveller shame as she called it. I had said to Kate, 'We're letting her away with too much. That school.' (*he pauses again*) I'm all for getting an education, my generation didn't and someone like needs it but she just knew her own mind. There was no saying anything to her. Being bossed around by my only daughter of fourteen years of age. (*He stands up and walks around the ring inside the ropes.*) To tell you the truth despite the show of disappointment Kate put on, deep down I knew she was proud that her daughter was standing up and doing her own thing. Sometimes me and Kate fell out over the boxing. Kate said it keeps her out of trouble, it keeps her occupied. Kate kept saying, 'To hell with what other families think. She's our daughter. They're not rearing a deaf child.' I made the foolish mistake of not going to her fights. Before I knew it not only did I have the two women in my life doing things their way but me own wife was telling me that our deaf daughter was better than any settled boy boxer in the ring.

Kate was proud of her in the way I'd be proud of my son doing the same thing.

NORAH: Then my Mam suggested, well it was him, me Daddy, he was the one that copped it that I couldn't hear things. He said we better go and see a doctor. He confirmed it all right. After that they sent me to the deaf school. (*She gets visibly frustrated with herself, and throws down the headgear.*) At first I hated it. They knew I was a Pavee. That I wasn't going to sign *their* language. In some ways I felt lost everywhere. At home, in the school and then in the deaf school. That's what it's like for Pavees like me. You don't fit in anywhere. My Mam and my brothers, they know a little bit of sign only because it suits them. (*She walks towards an empty chair that's in the ring.*) My brothers had me for their little slave; well they think I'm their slave. They do all the signs for grub, no problem there. (*she pauses*) Mam, in the beginning she was always crying. As a child I can remember the look on her face when she'd have to touch me to let me know she was trying to tell me something. She was the first one that I was able to lip read. She's always trying. She doesn't give a shit what the other Travellers say. (*She lifts her leg up on the chair and pulls her wedding dress up to her knee. Her boxing boot is visible.*) Mam came to every fight I had. (*Her father walks over and starts tying her lace for her.*) The deaf school from the beginning the teachers, they were just saying I wasn't trying hard enough, that I was embarrassed or ashamed to do sign. They were trying to tell my parents I wouldn't accept things. (*she laughs*) My parents were the ones that wouldn't accept things. (*She swaps legs abruptly.*) Especially him. He couldn't accept how I was. How I am. Anyway, how could I sign in a language that wasn't me own? I don't do Buffer talk. That's a good thing about being deaf.

FATHER: If I'd learned. (*He rubs his hands over his face while he's still trying to tie the lace of her boxing boot.*) If I'd learned . . . it came easy to Kate and to her brothers. I used to pretend I wasn't looking at them but even when she was small the rest of the family found a way of reaching Norah. Her mother begged me, coaxed me to just try. Only at the trailer where no one else could see, nobody would make a laugh of me. See that's what Travellers do. They make a laugh of you if they saw you in public talking with your hands. When stubbornness and shame get mixed up in your head you end up giving in to shame. Kate warned me that I was losing her because I wouldn't learn. I just kept saying I was busy or I don't need to learn. How stupid can a father be? Putting his pride before his daughter instead of having pride for his daughter.

NORAH: Then there were two more Pavees, deaf Pavee lads, they were Joyces. I thought they'd be back-up for me but they were useless. I suppose they were half afraid of the Buffers as well. The three of us were put into the one class. It didn't matter what ages we were or how smart we were. We were all the one to them cos we were Pavees. We started to make our own sign, our own language. (*The laces are tied and the father moves the chair away.*) I've no idea why but the Pavee thing, despite what they say, what he says, well, deep in my heart even as a small child, even when I couldn't be part of what was going on around me, the Pavee thing. I knew where I was and I loved it. Making up our own signs even at eleven or twelve I didn't really give a shit when teachers, including the ones that were deaf, were telling us it wasn't a proper language. We'd never be able to communicate. The teacher called it the outside world but I knew she meant the Buffer world. That was her world not mine. She was saying that she'd read a little bit about Cant Pavee language, but she wasn't convinced it would be any use to us. (*Her father walks towards her and hands her her gloves.*) It nearly drove them fucking mad! Deaf people, deaf teachers, it was us, the three of us. We locked them out of our world, not the other way around. I used to love *that* part of it! Then one day I realised I could use my hands for more than just signing. They were calling me names—well, signing names at me—even though I wouldn't do Irish sign, I still learnt it for back-up. I knew the sign for *knacker* and the sign for *smell* and the sign for *cunt.* They were two young fellas, they'd just started signing in front of me, signing those things about me, like I wasn't even there, like I wasn't supposed to understand. I just lifted my right hand and then the left, and knocked them straight to the ground. Yes, even in special schools, they suspend you for fighting! My mother was raging with me. (*She touches the cross on her neck.*) Getting suspended, Mam was ashamed. My family are strict. It was a big deal to have their only girl go away to school and boxing, I can still see the look on her face. She was telling the teachers that she didn't rear me like that. Anyway, whatever about Mam's reaction, he went crazy. But of course he went crazy for the wrong reasons. He wanted to keep me out of school. Saying he was right all along not to send me there. Him and her, me parents, for the whole week I was suspended, they were arguing. Mam was trying to explain that I did draw blood from the young fella's nose. Paddy, my brother, he'd tell me that Daddy tried to say they must've given me good reason. Mam, wasn't havin any of it. That was a long time ago and I really did break my mother's heart. The one thing she said to me stayed with me. She said, 'Norah, I didn't raise a bully. You might be deaf, you might be a Traveller girl. People are going to do things to you, all sorts of things and it's not fair but you have to learn not to react in front of them.' I was only eleven and Mam was telling me about holding things in. Now I know she meant holding things inside the ring. Not exploding outside of it. (*Her father is helping her lace up her gloves.*)

FATHER: It was her mother's idea, saying she needed to be with people like herself. They said she'd lots of energy, but she was using it the wrong way. I knew what they were getting at—even though I can't read and write I knew they were saying, 'Typical Travellers, they're all rough and ready, always on for a fight.' But it was *my* little girl they were talking about! We tried running, we tried swimming and we tried football. I was kind of glad *that* didn't work out, her being a girl and all that. Little did I know what was to come at me next.

NORAH: (*continues signing*) I was eleven—our Paddy, well, all of them: Paddy, Joseph, Michael and John, they were laughing at what I did to the little Buffer boy and they were always trying spar with me in my bedroom in the trailer. It used to be for a laugh then they'd show me things. Sometimes they'd forget I was a girl. We'd be thumpin each other but they wouldn't hurt me. Sometimes if Paddy thought it was getting too rough he'd tell me to watch my hands. He was always worrying about that, he knew they were needed and not just for cooking his dinner. They all used to go to the gym on a Saturday and in the evening. He'd bring them (*She nods towards her father.*) Making 'men' out of them before their time. I begged and plagued our Paddy to let me go with them, he was next to me in age. I promised him I wouldn't be messing, I was just sick of being stuck in the school and then stuck in the trailer, washing and cleaning all the time. You get sick of that too, even though that's girl's work, they think when you're deaf you can do it better, you're more gifted in that area.

FATHER: (*takes off his tie*) When my back was turned Paddy had hid her in the van, and then snuck her into the ring with him. I remember just looking up and not believing my eyes, that my little girl was in a room full of young fellas, holding the punch bag for her older brother and she was loving it! For a minute I wanted to run up and just pull her out and bring her home, but as I got closer to the ring I realised it was Paddy that was holding the punch bag, and it was she was doing the boxing. After that, I had no real say. (*he shrugs*) Sure, I'm only the father! And the mother was right behind her and still is. I swear to God, that woman of mine, even though I love her she's done too many courses. The day she learned to drive was a bad day for this family. Oh a curse. She plagued me to let take her theory test, saying she needed it and the school was encouraging the girls to be independent. That fucking deaf school interfering with everything in this family.

NORAH: I found something I was good at. Something I could do on my own—I'm not saying people respected me, but I knew our Paddy did, and the coach did. All I'm saying is, I found something that I loved, that I could do better than any boy and that felt so great! It didn't matter in the ring that I was deaf, all I had to do was look at the feet, look at the hands—sure, that's what I do all the time anyway, look at the hands! (*FATHER takes off his suit jacket and removes the flower from the button hole.*)

FATHER: I wanted to be proud of her, but to tell you the truth, I did all in my power to stop her, but sure, what could I do? The brothers, they made it possible: when I said she couldn't go, sure, they found a way of getting her there. Before I knew anything, the coach was up visiting the site. He's a lovely aul man, and for years I used to tell the other men on the site, I used to say he was here to talk about one of the boys. I never let on he was trying to convince me about Norah. Then the other lads in the site—they were in the boxing club too—rumour went flying round the site.

NORAH: (*Starts shadow boxing, dancing back and forth lightly.*) Those fucking aul ones! It drove them mad! A girl like me, a little, deaf Beoir, was a boxer better than any of their sons in or outside the ring. Oh, that went hard on them all right. My brothers used to stick up for me, and my own mother, she was better than *him.* (*She nods at her father.*) But at the same time I knew what was expected of me. I wasn't even sure they were going to find someone for me to marry. Well, you know how Travellers are: if you're not perfect, you won't get a man, and sure that's the most shameful thing of all. The boxing, it set me apart from other Beoirs, like being deaf it gave me freedom that other Beoirs don't have. Travellers, they think they're protecting girls and women. Especially families, but deep down you know the boys and the men have more freedom. In the deaf school they used to ask us about Traveller culture. It was hard to explain the rules and regulations for women. You can't go wild you can't talk to boys. The ones in the deaf school, they couldn't believe about the arranged marriages, the love matches. They used to be slagging me, asking me was I going to get married before I did my Leaving Cert. I never knew what to say. I didn't know whether him and her were going to find me someone. I used to watch me cousins and I was bridesmaid for some of them. I knew my own situation was different. I never talked about it with Mam. I mean she let me wear what I wanted and let me talk to the other young ones but I knew she was a bit like him. Not really wanting me to grow up. See, that's why the boxing took over my whole life, my whole head and my whole heart. I got something for myself. Something that no one could give me or find for me. I did all the right things and I knew, not just in the school but in the site and some of my brother's friends and of course my cousins. I knew they were looking at me and they used to take a good long look but our Paddy would kill anyone if he thought anything was on their minds. I tried to explain, even though I was deaf. My family and my brothers, especially my brothers. They'd be watching all the time. (*She wipes her forehead with the back of her arm.*) Beoirs, despite what the men say, we carry our family.

FATHER: I listened to them, I listened to what other Travellers were saying, warning me, shaming me, making a laugh of me. And all the time the coach would come down and talk to my little girl in a way I couldn't. In a matter of six months he had learned sign, talking with his hands. I'd sit and watch, well that's a lie, she'd tell you herself. I'd make one of her brothers stay and I'd get up and leave them. I couldn't bear it. (*He runs his hand through his hair.*)

NORAH: I explained to the coach—Toby—that's what I call him—that I couldn't get my hair cut, that Traveller Beoirs had to have their hair long, and if I was going to fight I'd have to bring Mam and one of my brothers would have to be there. I explained women of any age, it wouldn't be right, even for my mother to be going places on her own. We'd always need one of my brothers to come with us if it was an overnight fight. Toby didn't laugh at me, or make fun of how things are or tell me that my family were behind the times. He seemed to understand me. After that I did boxing as often as I could. I didn't care what people were saying: 'The only daughter! Bad enough that she's deaf, but she's also a boxer!' And then he turns up. (*FATHER gets up and stands behind her. He talks to the audience over NORAH's shoulder.*)

FATHER: A young fella going deaf after an accident. Other people were saying it could have been worse, but sure, didn't I know . . . (*He pauses and puts his two hands on her shoulders.*) No family would want him for a son-in-law. At night in the trailer I started talking to Kate. Norah was at that age. What were we going to do? Her brothers were all going to be married soon. I'd be happy to have her stay with us for the rest of her life, but sure, that wouldn't be right either. Kate was crying. Well, we both were. That's the thing about it, with a deaf daughter. Every age brings a new worry. The sadness, it never leaves you. You want her to have the same chances as other young ones but you know, well you think you know. It can't be like that. We didn't know what to do, me and Kate, but it turns out we didn't have to do very much. A few of them, they were all enquiring about what age was Norah. That's how Travellers do it. They knew well what age she was but that's how they bring up the subject. They're letting you know they're interested. Kate wasn't happy, but sure, what could I do? I'd have to get her married and I'd try and find someone right. Maybe one of her own. (*He touches the back of her and fixes the helmet.*) The problem is you never expect badness or danger to come from your own. I mean your own family. I mean one of your nephews. Then about a month ago they landed up—Norah's mother had suspicions, she said to me: 'They're not coming up here just looking for small talk or the price of a trailer or a van! Those people have something on their minds.' I was angry and delighted at the same time. My Norah, a woman? Sure I couldn't deal with that. She's deaf. We did all in our power. I warned the young fellas at all times, don't let anyone take advantage. If I said it once I said it a thousand times, I was trying to explain . . . it wasn't just normal family stuff of minding your sister. It was that she was deaf and she had to be minded at all times. (*He takes off a gold cross from around her neck and then takes off her gold hoop earrings.*) When we went to the pub, Kate asked to come too, but of course, she couldn't be found. She was training or something, and Paddy was with her. I got a good look at the young fella, at John-Joseph. He was good and strong, pure good-looking. They came from our own people so there was no problem there.

NORAH: (*Starts trying to pull at her dress with her gloves on.*) Paddy said the Joyces were up. He was falling about the place laughing, that I was going to be asked. For a while I didn't know what he meant—he had to explain to me. *John-Joe* wants to marry you! He's probably asked already! In that second it was like as if I got a jab into the right side of my head. Thank God the gym was empty! I went mad. On top of everything else it was supposed to be the modern way—like a love match. He'd ask *me* and I was supposed to agree. That's a load of shite! A love match? It's just the same as the old days—the families do the organising. Just because he asks me after he asks my father—is that supposed to make it ok? That's supposed to be modern? Our Paddy got me to calm down—he begged and craved me to go home and put on something—suitable. I said, 'Sure. Is my tracksuit all right?' Now even Paddy was falling into the trap. They were all against me.

(FATHER starts to help her take off her wedding dress from around her shoulders. NORAH's boxing vest is visible; the dress drops to her waist, and on her top, the letters spell out 'Pavee Princess'.)

FATHER: I mustn't have been looking at her, but when she walked into the pub with Paddy she was the cut of her mother twenty years ago. He had gotten her out of the tracksuit and she put on a good show. Pure beauty, long dark hair. My little girl was a woman. Part of me felt delighted, but part of me felt I didn't know her and I'd never know her and now she was leaving me. All I could do was shake the young fella's hand and buy him a drink. I couldn't—I couldn't—I couldn't, you know—

NORAH: *(Steps back. Her father helps her out of her dress.)* He wouldn't sign—my aul fella never learnt to sign. It was like he was in denial of me and my life. But John-Joseph, he couldn't believe it. When I saw him, I did like him and he liked me. He was gorgeous and I could feel he couldn't take his eyes off me. Even though we weren't supposed to talk—like, proper talk—apart from my brothers, sure no one knew what we were saying, so we had our freedom. He asked me about the boxing, saying he knew I could fight better than any man.

(Her FATHER is gathering up the dress and hanging it over the ropes of the ring.)

FATHER: I don't know what happened. My sons reassured me he was never alone with her, that he never laid a finger on her. (*He gives a sideways glance.*) Things have changed, not like our day. You wouldn't dare talk . . . but a young fella would chance his arm to see what she was like. Finding out if she is easy or dirty. I had me own suspicions. It doesn't matter that he was deaf. He's still a man and I know he must've said something to her because she kept on saying no. She didn't want to get married to him. Now I was confused. She was asked was she happy about marrying him. 'No' was her answer. I was half afraid to tell the other family. The young fella's family. Breaking a wedding off is a very hard thing to do. Families get insulted. (*He pulls over the punchbag that's hanging near him.*) Her mother tried to talk her round—but she wasn't having any of it. I got her mother to try to explain to her, to get her excited about the wedding, the dress, how she was the only girl and there'd be nothing spared—even trying to get her mixing with her cousins, this was still no good. Then I had a word with Toby, the aul man, the coach. I said I wanted it to stop; I barred her and her brothers from going down to the club. I barred him from the trailer, from having anything to do with her. But sure, she was in all the newspapers, things were happening without me knowing. She had her mind made up, like her mother said, because I never learnt to communicate with her I had no right to stop her doing anything. And then it happened. I found out that young fella wanted to ruin my little girl. Take her name.

(*NORAH holds one side of the punchbag while her FATHER holds the other.*)

NORAH: John-Joseph came up to Dublin twice a month. His mother wasn't too happy with me—it was the boxing. Sometimes with my brothers and him, we'd go to the pictures and stuff. The second time we met my brothers were all around us, the whole family was. The two families! Anyway, I had a fight two days before he came up. I had a cut on my lip. I was asking Mam to try and help me to hide it. Even though we weren't allowed sit near each other, as he was leaving our trailer—(*She takes a tube of lip balm out of her sports bag.*)

I still have it—he ran it over his lips, then left it down on the counter on the way out the door, looking at me. When he went outside his family were getting ready to go back to Sligo. He was standing with all my brothers but he looked in the kitchen window of our trailer. He saw me pick it up. This lipbalm—I rubbed it on my lips the same way he had done on his. After that I couldn't stop thinking about him; on the days he'd come up I'd make sure I had my hair washed and my best clothes on. I'd wear high heels. The parents, his and mine, were talking about setting a date. I remember Toby my coach, the little man, when I told him, he just said, 'Norah, am I going to lose you?' He was talking about the date for the selection for the national team for the Olympics. I said there was no date set for the wedding. But I knew he was looking at me, I knew he was thinking that my head was somewhere else and my heart was being pulled away from the ring.

Then one time, after he bought me the ring, my mother was with me; she understood what he was signing. She got more thick with him than I did. Then his mother stepped in and she made it clear that if the wedding was really going ahead in the next few months, I'd have to put any ideas of boxing or going to the Olympics out of my head. (*Starts punching the bag.*) How could I choose? But they were all making me choose. The family wanted the wedding over the boxing. I was even losing Toby now. (*She sighs and drinks some water from the bottle on the floor.*) That's the thing, you try to explain to a Buffer, you try telling them about Traveller ways. They nod and they don't really understand. The truth is they just don't really understand. I'm sure Toby thought I was being forced to marry him, but I wasn't. I wanted it, too. Until I found out what he was really like. Even though we were engaged, to spite his mother I wouldn't agree to anything, like giving up boxing. I wouldn't agree to it. I'm not saying I wouldn't do it, I'm just saying I never said I would. Anyway, he got it into his head; he used to insult my Daddy in sign so that nobody would know only me. My brothers were there—if they knew what he was saying the family would have killed him. The first time it was just joking but then it got more serious. He'd start saying my Daddy didn't really love me, because if he did he'd learn sign. He was saying my father was throwing me away, had no value set on me because I'm deaf. I knew my Daddy loved me whether he could sign or not, I knew he loved me. The date was coming up to be picked for the Olympic team. Even though getting married and excited, for two weeks beforehand I put in a lot of training. A *lot* of training. Then he got this idea into his head, he asked me to run away with him so that the wedding would go on quicker. Oh, I knew what his reason was. It wasn't just to give me a bad name or my family a bad name, he wanted to get me pregnant so if I did get picked for the Olympics I wouldn't be able to box anyway. To me he was showing what things would be like when were married. He'd be the boss. Having power and control over my body and mind. The men I knew weren't like that. Me Daddy and me brothers, show respect. When I told our Paddy that John-Joseph wanted me to run away with him. Paddy got all serious. He signed you're not going to go with him are you? I shook me head. Then my brother hugged me and signed that he'll fucking kill him if he ever saw him again. John-Joseph's mother put the word out. She said it was the only way to stop me from fighting. She said, 'Any man would do that.' Daddy didn't think so. John-Joseph, he is a Pavee féin. I had feelings for him. But I expected more from him. Him being deaf.

FATHER: My girl got picked. *My* daughter will carry the Irish flag, and I'm so proud of her. We're all going. The whole family. We're going to support her. Toby told me there's every chance she'll get a medal. He also told me any father could have a daughter with a wedding ring, but not many fathers can have a daughter with an Olympic gold medal. If she wants to get married, that's her own business. I want her to be happy, to be good at something, and to be respected and loved the way I love her.

(NORAH is hugging the punchbag while her FATHER is hugging it also. Neither of them can reach each other but they're smiling.)

Introduction to Mirjana Rendulic's

Broken Promise Land (2013)

Charlotte McIvor

Mirjana Rendulic's *Broken Promise Land* combines autobiography and fiction in a one-woman show. The play challenges stereotypes of dancers and sex workers as victims through relating a fictionalised version of Rendulic's experience. She uses transnational networks within the club industry to travel the world in order to gain clarity about her future goals for her education and career. She creates a fictional version of herself named Stefica, and while inspired by her life, the chronology and circumstances of Stefica and Rendulic's lives are not exactly the same. For example, Rendulic worked as an au pair in London for £40 a week and studied computer programming in Croatia. She took up dancing after struggling unsuccessfully to obtain a work permit or student visa for the English-speaking countries she wanted to live in. For Rendulic, *Broken Promise Land* is about 'lap dancing and the immigrant experience, but it's also about a girl growing up. She's not a tragic martyr, she's just a girl with a mission'.[1]

Rendulic is an emerging artist who has lived in Ireland since 2003. While living in Croatia, she was a member of Little Scene Theatre where she trained under Croatian theatre maker, Zvjezdana Ladika. Her professional acting debut in Ireland was in Mary Coll's *Anything But Love* (Belltable Arts Centre) followed by *Sylvia's Quest* (Wonderland Productions). *Broken Promise Land* (in which she also performed) marks the first professional production of her own work, premiering at Dublin's Theatre Upstairs in March 2013. Her training in Ireland includes a FETAC (Further Education and Training Awards Council) diploma in Theatre Studies and a two-year Higher National Diploma in Performing Arts at Coláiste Dhúlaigh, Dublin and another FETAC Diploma in Drama Facilitation from the National Association for Youth Drama. Rendulic's collaboration on *Broken Promise Land* with director Aoife Spillane-Hinks led to a commission from the Abbey Theatre's Outreach Department to develop a collaborative drama piece with undocumented migrants living in Ireland. *Document* had its first showings in the Peacock Theatre and Liberty Hall in August 2013 and was also supported by the Migrant Rights Centre Ireland.

For Rendulic, the 'Broken Promise Land' referenced in her title is not Ireland, but rather the United States. Seduced by the world of American television as a child, Stefica dreams of leaving Croatia and attending college at the University of California, Berkeley 'sitting under a tree . . . and reading literature'. After pursuing a litany of jobs after high school in Croatia, including childcare and door-to-door sales, she finds herself with a permanent position at the local shopping centre in her village. Faced with a future she feels is a dead end, Stefica pursues a friend's suggestion to take up dancing in clubs—a line of work that takes her to Italy, Japan and finally, Ireland. *Broken Promise Land,* perhaps controversially, does not present scenarios of exploitation and violence in the sex industry apart from Stefica falling victim to a scammer who promises to transport her to the US for €6,000, but instead takes her money and leaves her behind.

Ireland's sex industry has been under increasing scrutiny in recent years due particularly to allegations of widespread trafficking of migrant women, including minors. A 2008 study sponsored by the Immigrant Council of Ireland found that 'migrant women are predominant in indoor prostitution', which 'makes up a large segment of the prostitution market in Ireland'.[2] In 2013, the US Department of State named Ireland in its *Trafficking in Persons* report as 'a destination, source, and transit country for women, men and children subjected to sex trafficking and forced labour'.[3] Stefica does not engage in prostitution, nor was she trafficked against her will, and her story finds its way to a positive ending over which she seems to have full personal control. Stefica's decision to become a dancer is her own, and she travels between Croatia, Italy, Japan, and Ireland under her own volition and by her own choice.

Broken Promise Land's narrative arc and (autobiographical) characterisation runs counter to most media and theatrical depictions of the sex industry in Ireland and beyond, such as in Victoria Fradgley's *Never After* (2009), presented by Tabs Theatre Productions in Dublin, which featured an onstage death, violence against women trafficked for the purpose of sexual exploitation, and women confined against their will. *Irish Theatre Magazine* reviewer, Harvey O'Brien, argues that for *Broken Promise Land,* 'there is a constant nagging sense that it stays away from the heart of darkness rather too deliberately for its own good'.[4] Stefica indeed goes so far as to claim of herself and her fellow dancers, 'We are emancipated young women. We are our own bosses', a profession of faith that can scarcely describe the reality of most migrant and non-migrant women working in illegal and legal sectors of the Irish sex industry.

Through provocations such as this, Rendulic's fictionalisation of her own personal experiences in *Broken Promise Land* does not shy away from the centre of debates over not only migrant women and trafficking, but their media and artistic representation. Rendulic's fictional version of herself, Stefica, is decisively not a victim, but she also does not present Stefica as a curiosity or sex object. The set of *Broken Promise Land*'s original production depicted 'a single room in an apartment in Smithfield, Dublin' in drab and realistic detail. Rendulic, as Stefica, was clothed throughout in a simple and non-revealing cotton dress and denim jacket. Despite narrating the choreography of her own dances and revealing other cosmetic tricks of the trade, her physical movements and gestures remained small and non-sexualised.

Broken Promise Land does not allow Mirjana/Stefica's life to be reduced to the circumstances of her temporary occupation. Instead, the frame of the play is the very moment in time when she decides to stop dancing and refuse the offer of a wealthy client from the United States to exchange marriage for her American college dreams. At the beginning of the play, the calendar reads, '3 August 2003', and she attempts to convince herself by saying out loud, 'I can live in New York. I can live in his house, drive his car . . . Go to university'. She then tells us, 'I have to stop hiding', before launching into the full story that brought her to this point. The play's temporal frame of 3 August 2003 is pivotal as we encounter Stefica at a key moment of change in her own biography. She will end the play with a declaration of 'No more hiding' and her plans to get a student visa to stay in Ireland.

Given Rendulic's own positive experiences as represented in *Broken Promise Land*, it is perhaps unclear whether or not she would recommend her course of action to others. But, through this play, she tells her own story on her own terms, literally creating a place for herself on the Irish stage as a migrant actor/playwright. Not only that, Rendulic claims her voice as an Irish one: 'It is an Irish play. The way it's expressed. I've lived here, I've studied here. It's the way an Irish person would say something, even if it's in an accent.'[5] By naming the possibility of an 'Irish' play having an accent, Rendulic models an emerging Irish theatrical interculturalism that will necessarily be reshaped by not only the stories, but the soundscape of its increasingly diverse population.

Female migrant characters and playwrights have been vastly underrepresented in Irish theatre, film and television, relative to their male counterparts. Emerging female artists, including Rendulic, Kasia Lech, Anna Wolf and Alicja Ayres (also interviewed in this collection), among others, have recently begun to reverse this trend. In 2012, Rendulic assisted Alice Coughlan of Wonderland Productions in the development of *Sylvia's Quest*, the story of a Bulgarian domestic worker mediating between the inequitable conditions of her employment, her spiritual relationship to a number of gods with whom she is in constant communication, and her own homesickness.

Brian Singleton argues for the importance of the work of Ugandan–Canadian playwright/actor George Seremba and Adigun's African–Irish Arambe Productions as performances that make use of 'a theatrical agency in the face often of a lack of agency in other spheres of public life'.[6] Rendulic's *Broken Promise Land* does exactly that, as she negotiates her doubly marginalised position as a migrant woman and former sex worker onstage, blurring the line between autobiography and fiction. Her embrace of these experiences and the borderline flippancy with which she narrates her transitions between working in Italy, Japan and Ireland, could certainly be interpreted as irresponsible given the larger social context. But this defiant portrayal of a woman's life remaining whole and moving forward after working in the sex industry by choice also counters the habitually marginalised typecasting of Eastern European actresses in Ireland in secondary or background roles, as 'cleaners or prostitutes'.[7] In the words of Polish Theatre Ireland's Kasia Lech, 'I don't mind playing prostitutes to the end of my life, as long as each of these prostitutes is different: she has her own story, but she is not defined by the fact that, oh yes, she was trafficked, she's here and she's unhappy. End of story'. Rendulic's Stefica views her work as a dancer as only the beginning of her story, a moment in time that propels her forward rather than ending her life. This end is also a beginning.

Notes and References

1 Caomhán Keane, 'New play captures life as a lap dancer in Celtic Tiger Ireland', *Irish Examiner*, 11 March 2013. Read online at http://www.irishexaminer.com/lifestyle/features/humaninterest/new-play-captures-life-as-a-lap-dancer-in-celtic-tiger-ireland-225019.html.

2 The Immigrant Council of Ireland in collaboration with the Women's Health Project (HSE) and Ruhama, *Globalisation, Sex Trafficking and Prostitution: The Experiences of Migrant Women in Ireland* (Dublin: Immigrant Council of Ireland, 2009), p. 13.

3 Cormac O'Keefe, 'Ireland is a source for sex trafficking, says US report,' *Irish Examiner*, 21 June 2013. Read online at http://www.irishexaminer.com/ireland/ireland-is-a-source-for-sex-trafficking-says-us-report-234699.html.

4 Harvey O'Brien, 'Broken Promise Land', *Irish Theatre Magazine*, 7 March 2013. Read online at http://www.irishtheatremagazine.ie/Reviews/Current/Broken-Promise-Land.

5 'Interview with Mirjana Rendulic and Aoife Spillane-Hinks – *Broken Promise Land*', Entertainment.ie, 11 March 2013. Read online at http://entertainment.ie/theatre/feature/Interview-with-Aoife-Spillane-Hinks-and-Mirjana-Rendulic-Broken-Promise-Land/210/4025.htm.

6 Brian Singleton, *Masculinities and the Contemporary Irish Theatre* (Basingstoke: Palgrave Macmillan, 2011), p. 155.

7 Eithne Shortall, 'No More Cleaners or Prostitutes Please', *The Sunday Times*, 18 November 2012, 'Culture' magazine, pp. 6–7.

Broken Promise Land

Mirjana Rendulic

Broken Promise Land was first presented at the Theatre Upstairs, Dublin on 6 March 2013.

Cast

Tea	Mirjana Rendulic

Production Team

Director	Aoife Spillane Hinks
Set & Lighting Design	Zia Holly
Dramaturg	Gavin Kostick
Producers	Stones Throw Theatre & Matthew Smyth

(August 2003. A single room in an apartment in Smithfield, Dublin. The room: A single bed, bedside drawers, a mirror on the wall under which is a chest of drawers. On the opposite side of the room a chair with a few colourful dresses, a suitcase and a rucksack. There is a calendar on the bedside drawer showing today's date: 3 August 2003. Next to it a teacup, a book, fluffy socks. Next to the bedside drawer a hairdryer, a hairbrush and a mobile charger on the floor. A line of shoes on the opposite side of the room. On the chest of drawers: The Adventures of Tom Sawyer, *make-up and other cosmetics, a bottle of water, a cosy white jumper, visa application forms, fluffy blue hot pants hanging on a middle drawer handle. A bottle of baby powder sits on the floor.*

Tea *enters the room dressed up in a blue, summery dress and denim jacket. She leaves her purse on the chest of drawers, takes off her jacket and hangs it on the back of a chair, then takes off her shoes and places them near the long line of shoes. She sees the baby powder on the floor and puts it back on a chest of drawers, then takes off her earrings and a bracelet. She makes a high ponytail and puts on a cosy white jumper. She opens her purse, takes out a mobile phone and starts pacing around the room.)*

I can live in New York. I can live in his house, drive his car . . . Go to university . . .

(*Tea leaves the phone on the top of the bedside drawer, then sits on the bed. She takes out a box of Jaffa Cakes out of the first drawer. She starts eating a Jaffa cake while looking at the phone. After a few moments she leaves a half-eaten cake and hides under the duvet. A few moments pass until she sits up in the bed and addresses the audience.*)

TEA

I have to stop hiding. I've been doing it since I was a child. One of my games was to hide in a toilet, flush away the key and scream: Help! My next hiding place became a field next to our family home. I'd find the furthest spot with the highest grass and then spend all day reading Sidney Sheldon while ignoring my mother's calls. Steficaaaaa! Steficaaaaa! Vragu si iz torbe ispala! That means I fell out of the Devil's bag.

Even now, as a grown up in Ireland, I play my hiding games. My bosses keep asking: Why the hell are you hiding? You are legal, aren't ya? Of course, I am.

And the bosses pretend that they don't have a clue about my fake passport. As far as they are concerned, I'm a seven-foot tall, Italian girl from Milan, with blue eyes and a lot of travelling experience.

Nowadays there is always this voice in my head: If you get caught, you get deported and then you'll have to go back to your Godforsaken country.

I was born in Zagreb, Croatia, one year before Tito died. Tito united all of us Yugoslavians: Catholics, Muslims and Orthodox. We all lived in harmony until the 1990s when the tensions started.

My favourite childhood memory is visiting a bookstore every Saturday with my Dad. He would buy me translated stories like *Gulliver's Travels* and *Grimm's Fairy Tales*. Soon after it was *Little Women, The Adventures of Huckleberry Finn* and also *Conan the Barbarian* comic books!

In the eighties it was good to be in a Communist Party. They sort of sorted you out. But my parents weren't a part of it. We lived in a one-room house that my mother bought with money she inherited. No water. Near the graveyard and the gypsies. The room was built above septic holes and when they had to be emptied we had to take all our belongings out.

The kids in my school used to tease me: You live where those poor houses are!

My father had no inheritance. His mother wanted him to marry an educated woman, a doctor, not a simple woman like my Mum. I only met my grandmother when I was six months old. She didn't like to come to where we lived.

But I had a happy childhood, ice-skating on a nearby lake, playing detectives with my best friend Ivana and watching American TV at her flat. American TV was very popular even during Communism: *Cagney and Lacy*, *Dynasty*, *Moonlighting*, *Sledge Hammer*, and of course, *Beverly Hills 90210*. I so fancied Dylan . . .

Ivana and I invented our own world with the characters from those shows. And we sang to the radio as if we are pop stars . . . I should be so lucky . . . lucky, lucky, lucky. . . .

(*She jumps out of bed and does a twirl.*)

I should be so lucky, love!

Around that time I also changed my name. Tea. You see, Stefica is an old fashioned name that people in villages have. I wanted to have a modern name. The kids in school couldn't stop laughing about it and my parents thought it was just a phase. But even now at twenty-three I call myself Tea.

(*She looks back at the phone on the top of the bedside drawer, then hides it in the first drawer.*)

In 1988, when I was eight, my Dad bought a piece of land in a village and my parents started building our own house. Most of my mother's family were tradesmen so they helped with construction work, but by the time we moved from the city to our new home, the roof hadn't been built. Just a slab of concrete above us that leaked when it rained.

Then, in the early nineties, the war started. My Dad's wage as a school teacher was cut. I was thirteen then. Suddenly my Mum waited in a line to buy brown bread. Sometimes there was none left. I didn't know the times were really bad until one day when my Mum served just a soup, made of flour. As we ate in silence, we watched her tears fall into the plate.

Then my Mum decided to get chickens and rabbits. She also planted all sorts of fruit and vegetables in our garden, but we continued living in this half-built house with no roof. Then the walls started going black.

One day my Dad's childhood friend, a journalist, made an article about us in a newspaper. It was under a title: 'Outrageous conditions for a University Graduate'. As the photographer took my photo I held my cat Mimi, as tight as I could, underneath those dark damp walls.

Around that time my parents started arguing, too. Mostly over money. My Dad wanted to find work abroad so he asked for help from his aunt in Canada. She wrote back: 'It's better if you stay at home and protect your country'.

The war ended. I finished high school and started working at all sorts of jobs: a Kinder Surprise toy filler, door to door sales person, a security guard in a meat factory, a porter, a babysitter. And then, finally, when I was twenty-one, I got a permanent job in a shopping centre in our village.

My mum thought it was a great opportunity. I didn't. Many of my village friends worked there, too. It was like being in school again, but without books. And our tasks were a bit more repetitive: Sliding, Scanning, Typing, Bagging . . . Sliding, Scanning, Typing, Bagging . . . Sliding, Scanning, Typing, Bagging . . . I thought that life is meant to be full of excitements, big things and possibilities, but what I mostly heard were stories of disappointment and helplessness.

I wanted to live in a place where everything is possible, in a place where dreams do come true. Suddenly, I saw myself in sunny California, sitting under a tree at Berkeley University and reading literature. Then there was always Dylan from *90210*, also sitting under a tree and reading literature while giving me little winks!

At weekends, I visited my boyfriend in town. Niko. So handsome. He had a funky hair, played a guitar in a band and lived in a house with four bathrooms and a swimming pool. Niko and I spent three days together, celebrating the millennium at a rave in Dubrovnik. We were there with his mates from an American university.

At the rave, I watched his female friends, they were all dressed up in shiny little tops and silver tights, all confident and free. I wished I was one of them.

But for the next whole year I continued Sliding, Scanning, Typing, Bagging . . . Sliding, Scanning, Typing, Bagging . . . Sliding, Scanning, Typing, Bagging . . . And daydreaming about Dylan, day in and day out. I was almost twenty-two then.

And then, one day, my daydream changed. The sun was shining, I was reading Emily Dickinson and I waited for Dylan to give me a little wink of approval, but he was nowhere to be seen, so I closed the till, walked up to my boss and told her that I need to get some fresh air.

As I walked around the parking lot in front of the Shopping Centre the voice in my head kept saying: You have to get out. You have to!

August 2002. One year ago. I find the ad in the newspaper, looking for girls to work as dancers in Italy. Lots of cash. All safe. I can be a dancer. I know how to move. Niko told me I have prefect timing. And I have been called pretty.

Two days later, I meet Ljubica, the girl from the ad in a cafe in town. She looks so glamorous! She speaks to me in Croatian: the club will take half for each dance, but you will still make lots of money. You can use a bikini for a start, until you get some sexy outfits. Don't worry about not speaking Italian, your English is great! It's simple: You go there, you dance, you make money, you come back.

She lets me smell her perfume at the end and laughs about spending all of her money on perfumes.

That evening I take an old suitcase my mother brought back from Germany when she was my age. I put half of my wardrobe in it, then tell my Mum that I'll be visiting my childhood friend Ivana for the weekend and then I go to the local market and get myself new stilettos and a bikini in a tiger print. The following Friday morning, I board a bus to Italy to earn money wearing them.

The bus is full of people going shopping. Luckily, there is a seat left at the back, next to three bearded men. They are all wearing leather jackets and their hands look so rough!

Four hours later, the bus stops at the Italian border, an immigration officer starts looking through our suitcases and then signals to both me and the bearded men to get off! We receive a stamp in our passports: 'Negare!' 'Entry denied!' And I learn that Italian Border Police strongly disapprove of going 'shopping' with already full suitcase of clothes.

Then I am in a cafe near the border, drinking cappuccinos with the bearded men and plotting our way into Italy. They speak to me as if they've known me for years!

An hour later, a Fiat Punto with Italian plates drives up to the cafe, we all squeeze in and start moving towards the border. We sit in silence as the immigration officer first looks at the car plates, then our faces, then the barrier pole starts raising up. The car starts moving and as soon as the view of the immigration officer diminishes, we all start laughing and high fiving each other: 'Entrata approvato! Entrata approvato!'

They drop me off near Venice. They give me a hug each and then they are off. I see a woman: Autobus? Due? Mestre? Grazie.

I am sitting on the bus number two for less than twenty minutes when I start noticing more trees and fewer buildings. I've missed my stop. I get off on the next stop and start walking along the edge of the road back to town. A jeep pulls up: Tea? Club? Si. I get in and the man drives me to the dancers' accommodation.

I am sharing a room with Sandra, a girl from my country. She has the most gorgeous, long hair I've ever seen! I go to take a shower and she tells me in Croatian: 'Uzas! The water here is disgusting!' I wash very quickly, then throw my new stilettos and the bikini in a rucksack and we are off!

The club is small and the changing room is hot! We are all sweating as we are getting ready.

As I shyly change into my bikini, I watch other girls going through the full procedure: moisturizing, spraying glitter on their bodies, shaving legs on the dry, straightening and curling hair, applying fake nails, sprinkling baby powder in their shoes.

Everyone is trying on and taking off dresses, swapping dresses, buying dresses off other girls, picking out left-over shoes from under the table.

I notice the big breasts most girls have. Mine are the size of strawberries so I take a mental note to get some gel made chicken fillets for my tiger bra next time.

Out on the floor. The manager comes up to me: 'Three rules: Only customers can buy alcohol for you. You cannot take cash from customers, only dance tokens. No touching in the private room.'

Private room? I thought it is only dancing on stage!

Suddenly, I hear the manager shouting: 'American walk' and all the girls start strolling around as if on a cat walk. The manager nods at me and I join them, then men start coming up and picking women from the line. One man approaches me, too. He says to me in English: 'I take you for a private dance!'

The man and I are in a private room. I am standing with my back to him. A song starts playing and I start wiggling around and then I turn: No, no! Not allowed!

The man grabs my arm and I push him away, the bouncer peeks in, the man puts his penis back into his pants and the bouncer pulls him out.

Two hours left 'til closing and I've only had one dance. Suddenly, the bouncer comes up all changed in casual clothes, tells me that his shift is over, then orders me a cocktail and takes me for an hour dance. When we come out, he says to me in English: 'Do you want to go to a beach with me tomorrow?' I have to ask the boss. 'No problem, the Boss and I are friends!' 'Um, maybe, I'll let you know.'

It is about five am when we get back to our apartments. As Sandra and I are lying in our beds discussing the night, Sandra starts telling me how she started working as a dancer. She even worked in a brothel, somewhere in Spain. She got raped by her boss over there. It wasn't anything violent, she says, it's just that he got her very drunk.

I can't imagine something like that happening to me.

That weekend I leave Italy with a smiley face and three hundred Euros in my German suitcase. It would've taken me a whole month to make that back home!

Then I call Ljubica and arrange to come back the following weekend.

When I arrive home on Sunday, I hide in my room to avoid my mother's suspicious looks. And then, I observe myself in the mirror as if I have different eyes. What I see is: a tight stomach, a firm butt, sexy hair, pouty lips . . . I look good!

Suddenly, everyone in the shopping centre is looking at me differently, too. I didn't tell them anything, but it feels as if they know. And my mother's eyes keep following me around.

The following weekend, I only bring a rucksack with me and as soon as I get to the border the car is waiting for me. Ljubica's friend then drives me to a new club, not far from Mestre.

Sandra is also there. She's busy all night so we don't get to talk much. The girls here work much quicker than I do. I don't have the energy. I've just done a long week in the shopping centre.

Then on the second night, while we wait for customers, Sandra teaches me some basic tricks on the pole: bending down, jumping up, swaying, twirling, cat stretches, and then, finally, upside downs. She says: 'You are a born dancer!'

End of the night. I am taking my heavy make-up off when I hear Sandra and another girl talking in English. The other girl saying that she's just come back from an amazing place. Japan. Girls there make lots of money and they can work with a tourist visa. It's just like America, she says.

Just like America . . . In my head I am walking around Berkeley University with books in my hands. I drop my books, Dylan picks them up, looks into my eyes and we fall in love for forever and ever.

Back home, I tell Niko about Japan. He laughs and tells me I am crazy. He also tells me that he is dating a girl from his band now. My mother's eyes keep following me around.

Then one evening after work, I take a bus to an internet cafe in town. I google for hours until I find what I am looking for: exotic dancers from all over the world contact us to dance in Tokyo, Japan.

Click the apply button now, include your best photo, and choose where you want to work!

Click.

That week, I receive three thousand Kuna, my monthly salary from the shopping centre. Then I announce to both my boss and my parents that I am going to England, to work on a strawberry farm. My parents don't say much.

A week later, I am on a plane to Tokyo with my three thousand Kuna converted into Japanese Yen and the *Adventures of Tom Sawyer* in my German suitcase . . . A little TV in front of every seat . . .

Eighteen hours later: Narita airport. An immigration officer smiles at me: 'Tourist?' Tourist! Then gives me a stamp for three months.

I can't believe it! I am in Tokyo! Here I am going to make the money for a student visa in America.

There are twelve million people in Tokyo, I can even get lost in here if I wanted to. I can do whatever I want!

Fifty minutes later, I get off the airport bus. An agent is waiting for me, then drives me to the building where dancers and hostesses from all over the world live, each in their own tiny, little bedsit.

An hour later, I am walking towards the club, following the handwritten instructions the agent gave me. It feels as if thousands of people are walking beside me. I see a cat escaping just before I go inside. No tail? Poor cat.

The club is called Lips. Two floors and red seats all around.

The manager Hiro bows to me and I bow back. He brings me to the second floor and then we stand on the balcony looking down at girls dancing on the raised platform. I also see girls in the VIP area chatting to their customers, sipping from exotic shots and eating grapes and strawberries from the fruit plates.

Hiro then shows me to the changing room and I put a black mini skirt over my tiger bikini. Nobody walks around in just a bikini here!

Then he tells me just one rule: 'Touching only down to waist!' and brings me to the waiting area.

I sit next to Lia from Russia: see through platform shoes, the expensive, comfortable ones. A two-piece outfit that makes her boobs stand out, perfect tan, nails with decorations, big lashes, sparkly dot on her tooth. And when she gets up to dance on stage and takes off her bra, I see she's got glittery stars around her nipples!

I am left to sit for ages in the waiting area. It's almost 1.00 a.m. when Hiro finally brings me to the table that some girls have just left. I introduce myself as Mimi, the two men snigger and then one of them says: 'No more money left.'

Back in the waiting area. Suddenly, Hiro arrives with a phone and Lia starts ringing her regular customers and inviting them to the club. She tells me then that one of her customers brings her shopping every week and shows me a mobile phone she got as a present.

She also tells me that girls who speak Japanese make more. Then teaches me how to say, hai, arigato, hiderly, mosoogo: yes, thank you, left, right in Japanese! And she gives me a bonus word, sukebe: dirty old man or pervert.

2.00 a.m. And after work the bus arrives. Another fifty Japanese men fill up the club. The DJ announces: 'Mimi with very strong legs' and I run up on stage. I see some men snigger, but then I decide to show off what I learned in Italy.

I see the audience in the mirror, so I give them a wink. I do a couple of sexy walks around the pole and when the song gets to its chorus, I grab the pole with both hands and throw my whole body into upside down. The audience claps!

I start moving like a snake and after a few minutes I release one leg into a half split. The audience throws money on stage! Then I slide down into cat stretches. A few more sexy walks and a turn towards the mirror. The song is finishing, so I take off my bra, then I take the bra back and run backstage where I put it back on.

I return on stage to pick up tokens and money left for me. One man calls me up and puts more tokens into my bra and my skirt. Then he takes me for an hour dance and does circular motions on my strawberries until the closing time.

And as I am cashing my tokens at the end of the night, Hiro tells me if I join the man and his friends at the karaoke, I'll get paid more by the club. So half an hour later, I am with Lia and the men at karaoke, eating Korean barbecue and singing: 'Welcome to the Hotel California, such a lovely place, such a lovely place . . .'

Then on my way back home around 6.00 a.m., I ring my Mum from a phone box: 'Ciao, Mama. It's six p.m. I just finished my shift on the farm.'

Very soon, I learn crucial rules for a dancer: Some men prefer boobs covered. Then you are more like a date. Sexy long pants are no good for dancing on the pole. Don't put glitter on your body, men here don't want it on their suits. The most important rule: Don't piss off other girls. Girls share where is good to go next and where you can make money. I keep all my money in my purse because bedsits often get robbed.

Something that bothers me for ages are the little sniggers I hear every time the DJ calls me to dance on stage. Eventually, the perfect Lia explains: 'Mimi means ear in Japanese.'

Lia also tells me about some other, even more glamorous clubs in the city, like the place called Tantra, where all the girls wear long gowns and look like film stars. You have to have a lot of experience to get a job there.

Lia also tells me about a strange club called Deep Kiss Shop, where Japanese men pay ten Yen for a kiss with a tongue!

We are emancipated young women. We are our own bosses. We decide what we are. And if one day we decide to become someone else, we can do that, too, by changing our name, our hair colour, our lips, or cheeks or our nationality.

Some of us are women who used to be men and now we have curvy hips, big breasts, perfect face and a perfect butt. Some of us are amazing acrobats, ex-gymnasts. All of us are great sales people and we can talk any man out of all of his money.

In reality, we always have to follow club rules and we can get fired for silly things: like having three strikes for chewing gum! And the managers are not responsible for our taxes.

But I don't get to think about these things while the times are good. I am just making money for my student visa in America!

As the expiry date on my three-month visa and my twenty-third birthday approach, I decide to visit the American Embassy. I meet a friendly Indian officer. He tells me: 'Because it's your birthday, I will find time for you tomorrow after five.'

I arrive after five. His office smells like cologne my Dad used to wear. I look around admiring pictures of America: universities, monuments, smiley people that got their visas! The Officer comes back with tea and a slice of chocolate cake and says: 'You must try!'

I am almost finished eating when he takes a little wrap out of his pocket. What is it? 'It's a red lipstick I bought especially for your birthday! May I put it on your lips?'

As I am choking on the last piece of cake, I recollect the only other time I received a cake for my birthday. I was fourteen and just as my mother put it on a garden table, we had to run because the civil defence siren announced that the planes are about to bomb us! Then I am running out of his office while the voice in my head keeps shouting: What now?! You can't go home! You have a dream!

I am in a twenty-four-hour internet cafe in Ropongi, ten days before my visa runs out. America: no chance. Canada: no. Australia, New Zealand: I wish! England: no chance ever since NATO bombed Serbia. Ireland? Hmmm. No visitor visa required.

Then I start looking for dancer jobs in Ireland. I, finally, find an ad on Gumtree. Louise, the agent from the ad writes back straight away and says: 'All you need to do is give me a call when you arrive. This is my number. Have a safe trip. Louise.'

November fifteenth. Get off in Dublin, walk up to the immigration desk, pretend it's all normal.

'Stop! Wait!' Out of body experience. Alarm bells in my head. 'Why do you have a one way ticket? Who are you visiting? How did you get three thousand in cash?'

Then I give them Louise's number. I can't hear the phone conversation, but after a few minutes, they give me my passport back with a stamp for twelve days. Out of the interrogation room. One suitcase left circulating around the baggage track. My suitcase.

When I ring Louise, she tells me to get a taxi to the accommodation in Clonsilla. I'll be sharing room number three with Olga from Belarus.

When I arrive to the house, a young woman opens the door and then disappears down the hallway. I bring my suitcase to the room number three. Olga looks asleep, but I can hear her sniffling. I go to the bathroom, and when I come back, my suitcase is sitting outside of the room number three and the door is locked. I go to sleep on a living room sofa.

My dreams are strange that night. I wake up and I see a man's face next to mine. He says: 'Don't worry, you are grand. I am Justin, the manager. You can move into Olga's room.'

Ok!

Justin leaves the room and I go upstairs. Olga is not there. None of her belongings, either.

Later that evening, when a taxi arrives to collect us for work, I sit next to Donna, a big South African girl. We start chatting in English and when I ask her where Olga went, she says Olga went to dance in South America.

'Here we are girls!' says the taxi man. I look up and see the sign: Shooters. When we get inside I can't believe it. Here I am from a glitzy Tokyo stage to a place that smells like Guinness farts and cows. The room is so bare! All there is are tables and chairs made of bamboo and a bowl of popcorn on each bamboo made table. Then I see a lonely pole and an electric shower on a platform in a corner.

I am the last in the changing room. No space left at the mirror. I am standing there, waiting, until an Irish girl arrives and tells me to follow her. She brings me to a bathroom upstairs and introduces herself as Angel. She has the biggest eye-lashes I've ever seen and they are silver!

'You have to come in early to get a spot,' Angel tells me, while fixing her fake eye lashes.

'Fights have happened between girls over mirrors. You can always come up here. We share this bathroom with the pub downstairs. You should see the faces of the pub ladies when they come up to use the bathroom. They just stare at our dresses and shoes, afraid to make a sound. Then they just quickly do their business and leave.'

I decide to do my business quickly, too. I don't want to be seen by the pub ladies.

Midnight. I am almost asleep on a bamboo seat when men finally start coming in. And they are so happy to see me! Most of them have never even met a girl from Eastern Europe before.

In Italy men appreciate athletes, in Japan, dancing is an art form. In Ireland, it is all about the chat. Where are you from? Is that your real name? Are all the girls as gorgeous in your country? Where do you live? How much do you make per night? Are those real?

After a few days, I decide not to speak as much. Of course, I am delighted to be finally using my English, learning strange pronunciations and Irish expressions like: gaff, me ma, bleedin' this and bleedin' tha', but then I get tired of just chatting and going home with hardly any money. I decide to be cheeky and pretend my English 'not so good, but I dance very nice.'

In the changing room you can hear all sorts of conversations. And so many different languages. I always listen to English speaking girls. 'I met Sarah in Guam just before she had a thigh surgery. No way! I used to share accommodation with her best friend Anna who was a hostess in Japan. Do you remember Lisa? She is now dancing in Florida. She says she is pretending to be Eastern European, it helps her make more money.'

In Shooters Irish girls sometimes pretend to be Russian, too. I guess Irish lads prefer us Eastern Europeans. Is it that they are afraid that the Irish girls may know them in real life?

Girls in Ireland love putting on tan. They do their whole bodies backstage! They get some other girl to apply it on their backs with a glove, then they stand there naked waiting for it to dry.

One night I try it. Not only do I ruin my dress, but two hours later, when the tan settles, I can't even recognise myself. I'm black!

Every night, we all have to go home in the same taxi. It's the rule. Justin wants to keep us safe. I always end up sitting next to Kamila. She usually keeps laughing and saying: 'Oh, I am so horny tonight!' All the girls think Kamila is crazy. Maybe she is, but she just bought a second apartment back in Estonia.

One day at work, the big Donna introduces me to Frank, an Albanian man in a stripy suit. He is there with his cousin, also in a stripy suit. As they sit with us, they order a big bottle of champagne and give us girls tokens for free. Frank then tells me that he gets girls over the Mexican border to work in the USA. He gets them a passport and a job in a top club. It costs six thousand. I tell him all about my big dream of an American campus and we agree to meet the next day at the Gresham Hotel.

We meet twice that week in the Gresham. The second time I hand him three thousand Euros and he hands me my new Italian passport. 'Your name is Caterina Adami. She is a bit taller, but they won't notice. Wear heals. The border should be open in a week or two.'

December fifth. Angel is showing me how to put fake eye-lashes on when two new English girls burst into changing room and start shouting at Angel: 'Did you say to Justin that we take cocaine and then show everything to customers in the private room? Did you say that? Did you? Did you?!'

'Please . . . Stop shouting!'

Next, I am on the floor, the two girls pulling my hair and hitting me with their high heels.

It takes the bouncer five minutes to get them off me. When I come out of the changing room, with a ripped dress and blood on my face, Justin looks at me and says: 'You are fired. From tomorrow you'll be working in a different club. In Limerick.'

No way, I am not fucking going! But then I realise: this club is a shit hole, anyway. It can't be any worse in Limerick.

Then the next day on the bus I let Frank know that I'll be working in Limerick, but I am ready to go any time.

The Limerick club is the only club in the whole city, so it's busy, very busy. I am staying again in a semi-detached house with other girls. They are mostly Hungarian with little English, so I have no one to talk to. I am so bored here, but what keeps me going are texts from Frank, telling me that we are going soon. Then I start thinking about Olga and wondering did she ever make it to South America.

Over the next few weeks a few other girls from Shooters are moved to Limerick as well. We all spend the New Year's Eve working. 2003! Woohoo! Then in the morning of January first, I ring my Mum: 'Sretna Nova Mama!' 'Sretna Nova', she says sleepily as I've just woke her up. I tell her that I'll call again soon.

Chinese New Year Celebrations. A group of men jumping around the club, sleeping on tables, none are spending any money. As I try to pass a few of them on my way to the stage, they surround me and start grabbing my bottom. I start throwing them away like Conan. They are flying! Out of body experience. Then fired, again.

Luckily, I know this regular in the club: Seamus. He is a primary school teacher, a quiet sort of guy. He spends his weekends in lap dancing clubs. He tells me that he knows the manager in a Galway club and that he'll ring him to ask if I can go over.

The next day Seamus drives me to the accommodation in Galway. He has all sorts of books in his car. *Grimm's Fairy Tales*! I love them! Then I tell him all about my trips to the bookstore with my Dad.

I am unpacking my suitcase in my new room in Galway. Ne mogu vjerovat! My purse! Where is my purse?! My three thousand for Frank is in it! Then I hear a door bell. It's Seamus, with my purse and the copy of *Grimm's Fairy Tales*. He gives them both to me, then smiles and walks back to his car.

February. We live in a big cottage in Tuam. We get lifts to and back from work.

There is nothing to do during the day so I start jogging in the fields and watching the sheep and cows as I skip forward. I keep texting Frank and he keeps delaying the departure, always for a different reason. It's too late to stop now. I have to continue with it.

March. I finally get a text from Frank. He says that the border security is now very strict due to US invasion of Iraq. We have to wait. He'll let me know when it all clears up.

April. A new text from Frank. He needs the second half of the six thousand Euros asap. We are going in a week! 'What about the US invasion?''All clear.' He'll come to Galway tomorrow to pick up the second half.

I am at the Spanish Arch Hotel sipping Tropical Sky cocktails' when Frank arrives. We spend an hour just chatting and then he explains everything. We'll fly to Cancun and his friend Tony will drive us to the border. It will take two and half days to Miami. The club manager has an apartment organised for me. Then I hand to Frank another three thousand Euros.

Sunday night. My last night. It's a busy night, but mostly short dances. My last customer takes me for an hour dance, orders a bottle of champagne and says that he just wants to talk. When I tell him that I am moving to the USA he tells me that a girl like me will do really well over there. We toast to that!

Back in the cottage, I pack all my dresses, then squeeze money in between them.

Then I go to bed smiling. When I fall asleep, I dream about Olga and I sunbathing in Mexico.

6.15 a.m. I am standing at the Galway Bus Station in my summer shorts, waiting for Frank to arrive.

7.15 a.m. Frank is not answering his phone.

8.15 a.m. I am at the reception of the Spanish Arch Hotel telling the receptionist that his name is Frank, but I don't know his surname.

5.00 p.m. I am sitting on the bus with my German suitcase, on my way to Dublin. Alone. I don't even feel anything.

June 2003. Kamila rents an apartment in Smithfield and I move into her room. We both start working in a newly opened club. I am now in Ireland eight months. One night the manager tells us we have to hand out flyers in Temple Bar. It's the new club rule.

As Kamila and I are standing at the Temple Bar Square, we watch Irish girls going out. Laughing. Free. I wish I was one of them. Suddenly, I see a familiar face crossing the square.

'Donna! Where's Frank?''He's dead. He died in a car accident in Italy.''I gave him six thousand because of you!''I am sorry honey, he stole my money too. He was very good at that. See ya.'

Two days later I am in the Western Union wiring five thousand to my parents. When I call them they tell me they will use the money to finish off the roof on our family house.'You can't live under a roof that leaks one day when we are gone!' My Mum says. Then my Dad tells me that a bank clerk was asking him about the origins of the money from abroad. The clerk said to him:'Sir, may I ask, what kind of work your daughter does?''Djubre jedno!' my Dad swore at him. He also told him to mind his own business. Then my Dad asks me:'Where are you, Stefi?''Ireland.''Irska? Hm. What are you reading now?'

I decide that it's finally time for my strawberries to become melons. Apricots really. I rest for a week, then go back to work.

The work is much easier with the new apricots, but after a while things at the new club start getting strange. Regular customers start telling me that I am very pretty and they love talking to me, but then they take all the new girls for dances. I am not even exotic anymore.

Then one day, as I am walking around the club and watching the new girls in the VIP with their customers and thinking where should I go next, someone touches me on a shoulder. A tall man, about fifty years old, grinning at me with his big white teeth.'Are you free for a dance?'

And there he is! My very very first, American Sugar Daddy. J.F. Kennedy lookalike. That's what he was told when he was younger!

From then on J.F.K. and I drink champagne and talk for hours every night in a private room. Then two weeks later J.F.K. offers me my long lost dream of an American campus, which means I would be living in New York while studying for my bachelor degree. I start filling out the application form for a student visa straight away. J.F.K. is going to be my sponsor!

Then today, J.F.K. and I meet at the lion cage at the Dublin Zoo. He tells me then that he rang the Embassy and they told him that I am not eligible for a student visa, even with his sponsorship. I don't have enough ties to my own country. No house, no husband, no baby.

As I am staring at the lion cage and holding back my tears, J.F.K. tells me that I still can make my dream come true. I can become his fiancée. And then, after three months, we could get married and, after five years, I can get my US citizenship.

Then he says: 'You can meet my children as well.'

I ask him, 'Would you meet my parents, too?'

'Of course', he says.

But I can't hold my tears back at that lion cage at the Dublin Zoo. As I throw my last biscuit to the sleepy lion, I tell J.F.K. that I need to be alone.

(*She takes the mobile phone out of the drawer and starts pacing around the room.*)

I can live in New York. I can live in his house, drive his car . . . go to university.

(*After a few moments she dials a number.*)

Bok, Tata. Dolazim doma. Sutra kupim kartu. Javim sve kad organiziram. Imam. I ja vas. Pozdravi mamu. Dobro. Bok.

(*She speaks to the audience.*)

That was my Dad. I told him that I am coming home. When I get there, I'll check online the requirements and fees for a student visa in Ireland. I want to do American Studies.

I can't believe it's been a year since I got on that bus to Italy. I guess for someone like me, it can take a long time to get to zero. A long time just to get to the starting point. No more hiding. No more Tea. Stefica is starting now.

INTERVIEW
with
Bairbre Ní Chaoimh
former Artistic Director of Calypso Productions

Calypso Productions was founded in 1993 by Donal O'Kelly and Charlie O'Neill. The company sought to utilise theatre as a catalyst for social change. From the beginning, Calypso produced socially engaged work investigating issues such as the effects of structural adjustment programmes on Developing World countries (O'Kelly's *Trickledown Town*) and the marginalisation of the Traveller community (O'Neill's *Rosie and Starwars*). From 1997 onwards, Calypso focused its attention largely on issues of inward-migration to Ireland and the plight of asylum-seekers and refugees in particular. Productions or performance events explicitly addressing these themes included the Féile Fáilte Parade (1997), O'Kelly's *Farawayan* (1998), Roddy Doyle's *Guess Who's Coming for the Dinner* (2001), and Maeve Ingoldsby's *Mixing it on the Mountain* (2003). The dissemination of educational materials and the devising of seminars, debates and workshops around the material presented by Calypso always figured centrally in their mission, but the 2001 formation of Tower of Babel served as a turning point in the company's integration of non-Irish born participants in their work. Tower of Babel delivered drama and music workshops to Irish secondary school students and young asylum-seekers and refugees living in the Dublin area. In addition to mounting original work and producing several short films, many young Tower of Babel actors would also be featured in Calypso's professional productions. We interview Bairbre Ní Chaoimh, who was appointed as Artistic Director in 1998 and served in this position until the company's funding related demise in 2008. A distinguished actor and director who has worked on stage, screen and radio, Ní Chaoimh's founding of Tower of Babel during her tenure garnered a Metro Éireann Media and Multicultural Awards (MAMA) award for her intercultural work with the project.

CHARLOTTE MCIVOR: How did you come to be artistic director of Calypso productions?

BAIRBRE NÍ CHAOIMH: When I started working as an actor in the Abbey in 1980 I was part of Deirdre O'Connell's Stanislavski Studio in Dublin's Focus Theatre. I was primarily interested in acting but gradually became drawn to directing as well. In 1993, with the encouragement of Deirdre O'Connell and Mary Elizabeth Burke Kennedy, I began to direct shows for both Focus and Storytellers Theatre Company. That same year Donal O'Kelly and Charlie O'Neill set up Calypso Productions and they invited me to act in their first ever production, *Hughie on the Wires*. Five years later, they asked me to perform in *Farawayan*, a groundbreaking new play written by Donal. It was a promenade production using a combination of physical theatre, visual images, live music, and soundscapes to convey the experience of what it felt like to be unwelcome in a land far away from home. It was performed on two floors of a ballroom and before being allowed in to see the show, audience members had to queue to have their programmes—which were a replica of Irish passports—checked. This largely non-verbal piece echoed the situation for refugees and asylum-seekers coming to Ireland in the 1990s alongside the experience of Irish emigrants over many years. Before acting in *Farawayan*, I knew very little about asylum-seekers and refugees, nor had I any idea of how the Irish government was dealing with the rise in people seeking refuge here. Donal and Charlie wanted Calypso to be not just another theatre company, but a company that would raise awareness about issues and about the human stories behind them. They printed resource materials to accompany their productions and organised post-show discussions in which the actors would be asked to participate. So, in order to understand the issues in the play and take part in those discussions it became necessary for me to become better informed and this involved talking to and getting to know people for whose lives these issues were having such a huge impact. At that point, Calypso was operating without an artistic director. It was a more like a collective of writers, actors, musicians and visual artists who wanted to effect change. Towards the end of 1998, the Arts Council insisted that Calypso professionalise the structure of the company by bringing in an artistic director. Donal and Charlie asked if I would consider the new post and asked me about any ideas I might have to fulfill the company's vision. While I said I would be interested in the job, I told them I didn't want to give up freelance acting and directing. We finally agreed that I would work as Artistic Director of Calypso for six months of the year alongside a full-time company manager, thus allowing me to continue acting and directing on a freelance basis. That was how I started out working there towards the end of 1999. However, over the next eight to nine years, the work in Calypso on shows and new ancillary projects was to become increasingly absorbing.

CM: From the beginning, Calypso focused on formal experimentation with an attention to social and political issues. How did you make decisions about what to work on or commission from year to year?

BNC: I suppose those decisions were informed by what was happening at the time in Ireland and internationally. Since our remit was to engage with social justice and human rights issues we wanted to focus on the experiences of some of the most vulnerable people in society, people who hadn't a voice or whose voice had been silenced. This led us to look at the perception and treatment of women in Irish prisons [Paula Meehan's *Cell*], people with mental health problems [Gavin Kostick's *The Asylum Ball* and Anthony Neilson's *The Wonderful World of Dissocia*], children in the care system (particularly those abused in industrial schools or in a domestic setting), and asylum-seekers (particularly separated children/unaccompanied minors) seeking refuge in Ireland/Europe [Roddy Doyle's *Guess Who's Coming for the Dinner* and Maeve Ingoldsby's *Mixing it on the Mountain*]. We also explored the obstacles encountered by Irish adoptees trying to find their natural parents [*Stolen Child* by Ní Chaoimh and Yvonne Quinn]. Other plays included *Talking to Terrorists*, which looked at how one man's terrorist can be another man's freedom fighter and two plays exploring South Africa during apartheid and in the present day. Finally, we tried to stage plays involving young performers from some of the new communities that had come to live in Ireland.

One factor that was probably common to all our plays was the exploration of how when one individual or group of people is given power over another group (be it in a prison, a mental health institution, an industrial school or a political system) it seems invariable that there will be abuses, often extreme, and when those abuses come to light, the first instinct always seems to be to protect the organisation or profession rather than the victim, which often leads to a cover up. Our productions aimed to highlight this by presenting the stories of individuals facing all kinds of dilemmas in a humane and provocative way.

In the year 2000 I was looking for a play that would address how Irish people were adapting to the new multicultural Ireland. There were no Irish playwrights engaging with that at the time, but one day as I was reading the *Metro Éireann* newspaper I was delighted to discover the first instalment of a serialised story set in boomtown Dublin that Roddy Doyle had just begun to write. It was called 'Guess Who's Coming for the Dinner' and took a light-hearted look at the different reactions within an Irish family to the arrival for dinner of Ben, a Nigerian asylum-seeker. It focused in particular on the father Larry Linnane, who considered himself a broad-minded liberal until his eldest daughter brought home 'the black fella'. When I first contacted Roddy about turning his short story into a play, he was reluctant to do so, but after a week workshopping the play with him and four actors (three Irish and one Nigerian), he agreed to let us go ahead with it.

The show went on in the 2001 Dublin Theatre Festival and did a national tour in 2002. Because Roddy Doyle is not preachy, or politically correct, he managed to highlight the often contradictory ways people felt about the newly arrived asylum-seekers and to dispel some of the racial misunderstanding that was all too prevalent in Celtic Tiger Ireland. It was accessible and funny, attracting a lot of people who wouldn't have come to see an earnest play about asylum-seekers. (That's one of the problems I found with Calypso—that if people think that they're coming to a play that's 'worthy' in any way or 'telling them what to think', they will avoid it like the plague! I hate that kind of theatre myself and was always having to think outside the box to find plays that would be theatrically stimulating, provocative, and entertaining.)

Apart from Irish audiences we invited asylum-seekers and refugees to come to the show in Dublin and in our touring venues. We provided free tickets for asylum-seekers living on €19 a week and invited them to take part in post-show discussions. We staged the play in two prisons, Mountjoy and Portlaoise. We also performed it for several hundred asylum-seekers in the ballroom of the Mosney Accommodation Centre, having spent three days turning it into a performance venue. Formerly a Butlins Holiday centre, Mosney has accommodated large numbers of asylum seekers since 2001 as part of the government's direct provision scheme. It was established in early 2000 as an emergency response to the growing number of people applying for asylum.

Financially, the show was a success for the company and we decided to use some of the surplus to set up a sustainable programme for the benefit of minority ethnic groups, and particularly, separated children/unaccompanied minors, that would provide an outlet for their creative talent. We needed to make direct contact with young people and to devise a special project for and with them. That was how the Tower of Babel came about.

CM: How did you make the transition to community outreach work in this particular area and bring the Tower of Babel into being?

BNC: The Tower of Babel programme came about as a result of a growing awareness of all the artistic talent within the new minority ethnic communities for which there was no suitable outlet. We were keen to use our imaginative resources as a professional theatre company to devise an integrated cross-cultural arts programme that would develop and showcase the talent and skills of young people from minority ethnic communities living in Dublin side by side with their Irish counterparts. We also wanted to provide recreational opportunities for some vulnerable young people, especially separated children seeking asylum, who were at risk of isolation or exclusion.

Having made contact with Michael Kilbride, a Home School Liaison Officer in the O'Connell Christian Brothers' Secondary School in Dublin's inner city, which had a huge number of newly-arrived foreign students, we started facilitating drama and music workshops with a multicultural group of boys there on a weekly basis. Gradually, however, at the suggestion of the students, we decided to invite some girls from other schools to join the group. We moved the project out of O'Connell's to a more central location in Liberty Hall, where male and female students from various schools around the city could attend. We also invited more separated minors of both genders who were living in hostels around the city to participate. From the point of view of integration, we found it very beneficial to have a number of Irish students with local knowledge and fluent English involved in the group. Accordingly, as the young people were getting to know each other, they began to form relationships and would often meet up outside of the Tower of Babel to socialise together. Some of the participants were very good at music and dance and we arranged sessions for them to capitalise on this, bringing in music and dance teachers and organising drum circles. The students also taught each other songs and dances from their own countries. In addition to having a large number of African students involved, we had participants from Afghanistan and Pakistan and from Eastern Europe as well, from Russia, Poland, Kosovo, Macedonia, Poland and Albania and we had some programme refugees including a boy from Vietnam who had very little English. One of our objectives was to showcase their work. Since some members of the group had very little English we could not stage conventional plays. We also wanted to highlight their musical skills. So, for our Tower of Babel production, we commissioned Maeve Ingoldsby to write a show for them. *Mixing it on the Mountain* had a very simple premise: instead of St Patrick being Welsh and bringing Christianity to Ireland, our actor was Nigerian. The show contained lots of live music and dancing and songs in many languages. The presence of four young professional actors—Lisa Lambe, Fergal Mc Elherron, Emily Nagle and Eva Bartley—anchored the show and raised the bar for everyone. They performed for a week to packed houses in the Samuel Beckett Theatre and it did wonders for their confidence and self-esteem. In the years that followed we teamed up with Phakama in London (who had been doing intercultural work for many years with young people all over the UK) and staged a promenade style multimedia show called *The Museum of Me* in Liberty Hall. Other Tower of Babel shows include *Where Is Home* [staged in response to the attempted deportation of a Leaving Cert student called Kunle Eluhanla], *Suitcases* [Liberty Hall] and *Re-Imagining the World* [Glencree]. We also made a series of short films based on their dreams and fantasies, some of which were shown in the European Parliament in Brussels in 2008 as part of the European Year of Intercultural Dialogue.

CM: You kept the work of the students in Tower of Babel and the professional company fairly integrated. What were some of the other productions in which they collaborated?

BNC: As I mentioned, the Tower of Babel students staged several shows, such as *Mixing it on the Mountain, The Museum of Me, Where is Home,* and *Re-imagining the World.* In addition to this however, we tried, where possible, to include some of the students in supporting roles to professional actors in a few of our mainstream productions for Calypso. Those shows included *Operation Easter, Talking to Terrorists, Bones* and *Fairytaleheart.*

We commissioned Donal O'Kelly's *Operation Easter* because we wanted to look at the 1916 rebellion through the prism of 2006, ninety years on from the Rising. As a starting point, the play is set in Moore Street, which is where the last of the fighting and surrender took place after the rebels had broken out of the post office. Whereas, traditionally, Moore Street was full of exclusively Irish fruit and vegetable traders, ninety years on, it now has lots of restaurants and small businesses run by African and Eastern traders.

There was one member of the Tower of Babel in *Talking to Terrorists.* A girl who formerly lived in Afghanistan and Pakistan played a Palestinian in the play. We had several very talented South African students in the Tower of Babel, so it made sense to cast them in Kay Adshead's *Bones,* a play set in present-day South Africa. We also had a number of very good students from Nigeria and Kenya who were interested in taking part. On paper, the play is a two-hander featuring two women, one black and the other white. However, there are constant references to the crowd outside singing and chanting. So we decided to have that chorus present onstage. We brought in Joe Legwabe, a London-based musician and choreographer from Soweto, who used to play with Ladysmith Black Mambazo, to teach them South African songs and dances, and to teach the non-speakers how to pronounce the various words in the songs, which were in Xhosa, or Zulu, or Sotho. There were about ten Tower of Babel participants in the production, and they sang and danced live every night.

Possibly my favourite production that we did with Calypso was Athol Fugard's superb play, *Master Harold and the Boys,* set during the apartheid era in South Africa. For this show we were able to cast two very fine professional actors living in Dublin—a young South African actor called Conrad Kemp who was a graduate of the Gaiety School and George Seremba, a Ugandan actor studying for his PhD in Trinity. The third actor, Joe Vera, had to be brought over from London as, at that time, there were no suitable actors of his age available to play the part in Ireland. The Tower of Babel students were too young and inexperienced for the demands of the role.

The last production Calypso's Tower of Babel did was Phillip Ridley's two-hander *Fairytaleheart* in 2008. Originally, I had wanted a really talented young actor from Kosovo called Ermal Hyseni to play opposite a young Irish actress. The original script is about two English teenagers, both misfits, who meet up and eventually fall in love. The girl is local and her mother is dead. Her father has recently started seeing another woman and the girl can't cope with it. The boy is an outsider whose stepfather is caretaker of the local hall. My first thoughts were to set the play in Ireland and have the boy play a recent arrival from Kosovo, trying to get to know a local girl. We were in touch with a theatre director in Pristina who wanted us to bring the play to Kosovo. As it happened, however, Ermal was unable to travel because of difficulties around his refugee status. So, instead, I changed the casting and had a young Irish actor play the boy alongside a Polish girl from the Tower of Babel group.

CM: How did the legal status and struggles of participants in Tower of Babel affect the workings of the company?

BNC: Being artistic director of Calypso wasn't just a nine to five job. The majority of our students were from minority ethnic groups, and while not all were separated children, many of them fell into that category. They lived in special hostels for unaccompanied minors in the care of the state. However, once they turned eighteen, if they had not been granted refugee status, they could be deported. So, I spent a lot of time in Calypso—as did some of our very dedicated company managers and administrators like Kerry West, Marguerite Bourke and Selina O'Reilly—lobbying on their behalf with politicians and the Department of Foreign Affairs, talking to solicitors, going with them to different appointments, trying to organise petitions, or demonstrating on their behalf. It was non-stop. I remember when one of our young lads was being deported, and had all of his possessions in black sacks. And we were there with him right up until the last minute saying to the Gardaí, 'Please don't take him, please don't take him.' And out at the airport, his lawyer got a stay of execution and he came back that same night. It was very hands-on. And I remember one of our administrators saying one time, 'I can't do this anymore. I signed up for a theatre company and I thought I could do this, but I don't know if I can keep it up, because emotionally, it's very draining.'

CM: Five years after the end of Calypso, where do you think we are now in regards to immigration and interculturalism in the theatre and beyond?

BNC: Well, I think the situation has changed an awful lot. There are far fewer immigrants coming to Ireland now that the Celtic Tiger era has ended. I think that in terms of the people who are here, some people have integrated very well, but I think that like in any recession, there is a resentment in some quarters and a backlash towards anyone who is not originally from Ireland from the 'They've taken our jobs' brigade. But at the same time, if you look at primary schools, where the norm now is for young children to be in classes with children from all kinds of cultural backgrounds, that gives me great hope. I think it may take until that generation grows up to have a true sense of an integrated society here, and I have great hopes for that.

I also think that the new communities have brought great life and colour to Ireland. When you look around at Dublin now, we have our own little Chinatown in what used to be a fairly depressed area in Parnell Street. Capel Street has also been given a new lease of life, as has Moore Street, where in many cases, previously disused buildings have been revitalised and are being used for a number of small businesses. Our cuisine and the range of foods available in our supermarkets has improved dramatically. People have set up vibrant businesses in formerly disused buildings.

On the cultural front, playwrights like Owen McCafferty, Gary Duggan and Dermot Bolger have begun to write characters of different ethnicities into their plays, and hopefully, in a generation from now we will have people from various cultural minorities who have lived in Ireland all their lives writing new work that highlights their experience. I look forward to that.

INTERVIEW
with
John Scott
founder of the Irish Modern Dance Theatre
(now John Scott Dance)

John Scott is the founding artistic director of the Irish Modern Dance Theatre (1991, now John Scott Dance). Over the last twenty years, he has emerged as one of Ireland's leading figures in avant-garde dance. Born in Dublin and a graduate of University College Dublin, Scott trained at the College of Dance and later performed with Dublin City Ballet. He has studied or worked with many internationally known dancers and companies, including: Andy de Groat, Pablo Vela, the Living Theatre, Anna Sokolow, Yoshiko Chuma, Meredith Monk, Blanca Arrieta Company (Spain), and the Conservatoire Supérieur National pour la Musique et de la Danse (France). In 2003, he was invited to hold dance workshops with individuals who were clients of the Centre for the Care of Survivors of Torture in Dublin. The most notable performances to come out of these workshops are *Fall and Recover* and *The White Piece,* which have been staged multiple times over the last decade, most recently at La MaMa in New York in March 2011 and March 2013, respectively. His work has been produced at the Dublin Dance Festival and throughout Ireland, as well as in Brazil, France, Israel, Palestine and New York. Mr Scott is a founding board member of the Dublin Dance Festival and a guest Lecturer at University College Dublin. In 2004, he was awarded the Cultural prize by the African Refugee Network of Ireland for his pioneering work with survivors of torture.

Matthew Spangler: How would you describe the Irish Modern Dance Theatre, its history, and the kind of work the company has done over the years?

John Scott: I founded the Irish Modern Dance Theatre in 1991 as a contemporary dance company. I have an aesthetic based in avant-garde theatre and dance, in particular, American avant-garde theatre of the sixties, and also some movements that were happening in France in the early eighties. My work is postmodern and non-narrative. In Ireland, it's almost a national crime to not want to tell a story. Of course, there are storytelling elements in my work, but it's not boy-meets-girl, boy-loses-girl, boy-gets-girl. It's not that kind of story. It's more like little fragments of humanity under a microscope. My work is related to the work of Robert Wilson, for example, or Meredith Monk, Trisha Brown, or the Living Theatre, all of whom influenced me greatly. When I was a teenager, the Living Theatre came to the Dublin Theatre Festival, and it blew my mind. I grew up in theatre. My father was the lighting designer at the Abbey, my brother is a director, and I've always been aware of the power of theatre. But when I saw the Living Theatre, I saw the power of dance and the power of theatre magnified, and I could not but embrace that kind of work.

So I founded my company in 1991. Then a few years later, my work expanded to involve non-dancers, older dancers, different levels of people who had something to say for the specific project. I work now with dancers and artists from a variety of backgrounds from the exceptional, highly-trained dancers who can do anything I physically ask them to do—jump, turn, contort their bodies, extend their legs—to people who have no training at all, some of whom have come from far away places, and have lived on the margins of society. But everybody who works in my choreography is virtuosic. If they are not virtuosic in the way of a ballet dancer, they are spiritually or emotionally virtuosic.

MS: In 2003, you were invited to hold dance workshops with clients of the Centre for Survivors of Torture in Dublin. Was this the first time you had worked with this population?

JS: Yes, the Development Manager, Mike Walker, sent me an email, out of the blue, asking if I would host a dance workshop with the Centre's clients. I replied and said I would be delighted. My first workshop was in May 2003. I had many different people in the workshop with different backgrounds. And this Kurdish man told me he had three back operations, and he wanted to be careful, so I thought, I want to do things everybody can do. So we tried simple things. The first thing was lifting our arms over our heads and exhaling, and repeatedly lifting our arms. What immediately struck me was the richness and the power of the intention of what they were doing. I was used to working with dancers who are trained to do *everything* in a movement, which is a delight, of course, but sometimes it's not about the highest jump. And here we were in this big front room—eleven or twelve people lifting their arms up and breathing, and I felt this unexpected emotional connection with them. I didn't feel pity. That's very important: I didn't make *Fall and Recover* out of pity. I didn't do this work to be a good person. I made it because these dancers excited and inspired me as artists and as collaborators. And that first day, I felt something very powerful and artistically beautiful, very rich.

Now, Mike had told me not to ask them what had happened to them because if they start talking, they might suffer flashbacks. The simple movement of lying on the cold floor, for example, might remind you of something painful from your past. One of the dancers told me, she could not stand on stage for very long, because, as she said, 'When "it" happened, I had to stand still for a very long time and don't ever ask me to stand still'. Another dancer, he was young and a very talented mover, but he wasn't articulating his feet, and I said, you have to articulate your feet, and he said, 'I have trouble with this, John', and I said, 'Well, okay, keep doing the exercises, you'll get better with it', and he came up to me after the workshop and lifted up his trouser leg, and from his ankle to just below his knee was just bone and burnt skin—all of his tissue had worn away. I had known that people with these kinds of things lived in Ireland, but until I started doing these workshops, I didn't know any of them personally. I have, unfortunately, come to learn a lot more about it, from seeing people, and also from witnessing the effects.

MS: What exactly did you do in the workshops?

JS: I used techniques like breathing exercises, vocalisation, sound and movement exercises—the usual experimental theatre workshop tools. And I also did trust exercises, weight sharing. One time, I got them to do things like experimenting with their names. I never went in with a fixed idea about what was useful to them. These people were coming voluntarily, and I had to keep them interested, and I had to know that they would come back. I wanted to be in a space where everything was creative. We had a lot of fun. Some of these sessions were like a very interesting rehearsal, or the development phase of a work without the pressure of an opening night ticking like a clock. There was this guy from North Africa. He looked like a professional dancer, and he had an incredible jump. In fact, I had only seen one or two dancers who could jump as high as this guy. So I thought, I'll get him to jump in the show. And there was this woman with incredible arms, and I thought I'll get her to use her arms. So what I wasn't doing was teaching them steps. But I found that if I created situations where maybe there was a musical score, or we were using space in a particular way, and they had the freedom to make work with instructions like, 'move your arms like you're swimming through water, or flying like a bird', then I found the most interesting things happening.

MS: Can you speculate on why some of the participants would have come to your workshops?

JS: One woman, who came from a West African country, said they had tried theatre in one of the groups as therapy, but a lot of theatre exercises are like, 'so tell us something about your childhood, tell us your story.' For some of them, they would start improvising, and then they would come to a part where they just couldn't go on. I think they came to the dance workshops because they felt safer not working with words and because, for some of them, dance is a major part of their culture, and it can help them express something in dance that they can't find words for.

MS: How many participants did you have in a typical workshop?

JS: We were doing well if we had six or seven. Occasionally, fifteen. Sometimes, one. And maybe they would bring a friend and then we'd have another. One time, we were jumping, and some people heard the noise, and they came and said, 'Oh this looks like fun, can I join?' And none of them was ever bothered by the fact that there was not a narrative. They would just get into the thing and live in it. One of the dancers from West Africa said to me, 'When I'm dancing in the studio, it's like when I'm in the bush and you're looking around and you're open to every possibility, be it a snake on the ground, or a chimpanzee jumping off a tree. You're being cautious, but you're also being completely open'. But I have to say, it was not about making 'a piece'. It was about finding ways of living together and experiencing creativity together.

MS: It sounds like you created a close-knit community through these workshops.

JS: Yes. We still get together several times a year. The dancers come around to my house at Christmas, and we go to each other's parties, weddings, these things. We became each other's family. I don't think a day passes when I don't have contact with one or many of them. But what you have to remember is when we created *Fall and Recover* in the spring of 2004, it was a unique time in Ireland. This was the height of the Celtic Tiger, and you noticed more people of colour in the street. And at the same time, there were these fantastic wine bars opening up and people were buying beautiful cars, or lovely clothes, and then there were people who were poor. There was also the Citizenship Referendum going on, and there was a lot of racist talk in the newspapers and among politicians. There was an ugly element to it all. We, Irish, have been refugees and immigrants in so many places, and suddenly when it became our turn, some people would throw out a kind of racism that one wouldn't normally associate with Ireland. After the workshop, I would walk to the bus stop with the participants, or sometimes we'd go for a beer. Occasionally, you'd hear people whispering things, horrible, rude, racist things as we passed them. I was surprised by that.

MS: Because you grew up in Ireland and had never encountered that before?

JS: Well, yes, but I also understood what it meant to be an outsider. I have an Anglo–Irish accent, so as soon as I open my mouth, some people assume I'm British, which is not a good thing to be considered to be in Ireland, so I'd learned to be guarded with my voice and my behaviour, or I could get insulted, or attacked. So I knew what it was like to be in my hometown, or on my street and not feel completely safe, and that's how the people I was working with felt all of the time.

MS: So what was the process for creating a dance performance with this community?

JS: I started by asking them to do a gesture that they do every day: taking a shower, running for the bus, sitting in their computer skills course. Then I asked them to do something from the past. One was a schoolteacher and she mimed being a teacher, and another had been a farmer and she mimed planting things, and this kid who was the fantastic jumper had his turn. I thought, 'Oh, he's going to do something acrobatic', but instead he just stood still and waved. I asked them if they could describe what they were doing. The planter said,

'I'm planting seeds', and the teacher said, 'I'm pretending to teach class', and the jumping boy said his wave was the last gesture he made to his mother before she was killed. He saw her that morning before he went off to the cows, and he waved to her in the distance, and when he came back at sundown, and the village had been raided, and everyone was dead, and his mother had already been buried, according to Islamic practice. So the last time he saw his mother, he had waved. And that was what he did for us. And those gestures made such an impression on me, more of an impression than any incredible virtuosic dance company with these incredible star dancers twirling around and jumping over each other's heads. What I was seeing in the studio that day, it affected me so much, and I thought I have to dare to make a piece with these people. I had this incredibly beautiful and interested group of dancers, of many body types, and they had beautiful gifts, beautiful things they could do, and I asked them if they would make a piece with me and they said, 'Okay'.

MS: But there must have been some difficulties along the way.

JS: There were. Sometimes, I was scared: people don't come to rehearsals all the time, or they come late. And they have many things going on in their lives and maybe asking them to appear in a piece is too much. But even some of these difficulties were, in the end, inspiring. One night, at a practice session, I was alone with this ex-soldier from a country in West Africa, and it was a really wet night and I arrived at the studio and I was soaked, and he was looking very sad, and I said, 'It's such a bad night, will we just have a coffee and call it quits?' And he's this big strong proud man and he stood up and burst into tears. And I said, 'Okay, we'll do the workshop'. So I did the workshop just with him. I got him to do this breathing exercise where you do this exhalation. And he was moving, this big awkward man, in this very heavy way. And I was trying to get him to get lighter, so I said, 'Think you are a bird'. And in front of my eyes, it was like he literally became a bird. And he had been speaking in this halting English, and I said, 'Why don't you speak in a language you are more comfortable with?', so he started speaking with these beautiful, amazing sounds. I never asked him what he was saying. And what he did that night was one of the most extraordinary dances I've seen in my entire life, and I thought, again, I have to make a piece. So I asked two professional dancers who have worked with me for a very long time: Aisling Doyle, who was with me in the very first piece with the company, and Phil Connaughton, who has worked with me for about fifteen years. Both of them are very sympathetic and very special artists. And we started rehearsal. If we had a group, we made a group piece, and if we had just one, we made a solo piece, and if we had two, we made a duet.

MS: A dance production, unlike a spoken-language-based play, is difficult to render in a textual form. Would you describe *Fall and Recover* so we can get something of a mental picture of the production?

JS: The piece starts with a prologue. We cover the stage in white newspaper before it has been printed on. Everybody is wearing white, too. A West African woman is sitting in a chair talking, and an Eastern European woman is sitting beside her, and the Eastern European woman had formerly been a gymnast, and she has this most amazing way of mirroring, so every time the speaker moves her hands, she moves her hands after her, and while this is going on, one by one, the dancers come on stage. In rehearsal, they all had these thick markers, and I had asked them to draw. People drew pictures of their houses in which they had lived in their countries. They drew pictures of their families, little stick pictures. One guy drew a picture of an airplane because he escaped in a plane. Then when the thirteenth person comes on stage, the white paper is torn up and ripped to shreds, and you have this mess of paper, like they've all been torn away from something.

Everyone exits, and the West African woman is alone on stage, talking, and the chair beside her is empty. My mother had died the year before, so I knew the impact of an empty chair, and I knew that they had all lost people in their families, too—the West African woman had lost her husband—and she was sitting next to the chair that was now empty, and she continued to move her arms, and the space is cleared of the paper, and it's an empty space with a black floor. And the dancers enter, one by one, and the next section is all about lines, lines coming together and creating community.

In another section of the performance, we make a kind of Tower of Babel. In this sequence, the dancers speak in their own language, which sounds very beautiful. Then it moves into a section where each of them performs solos based on writing their names—writing their names on the space, writing their names on their bodies, writing their names in the air—making a dance of writing their names. It was something I did at the first workshop, to walk their names across the floor, and the Arab and the English speakers went to different sides of the room because the alphabet goes the other way, and we had an instant choreographic situation with some people going left to right and some people going right to left.

Then the last section of the piece is a kind of coming together. I wanted them to leave a trace. So the dancers lie on the floor with a large package of salt and each of them outlines their body on the floor with the salt and then they leave the stage one by one. What's left is reminiscent of Keith Haring drawings, because the thing is, the salt drawings don't really embody the shape of the person. The head looks so small and the body looks different. Instead, it might be the essence of their soul. And then they leave the stage with thirteen salt ghosts and the lights fade very slowly.

MS: What was the reception to *Fall and Recover* in Dublin?

JS: The reception was phenomenal. The dancers got standing ovations every night. We initially thought we were going to do it for families and friends and clients of the Centre for the Care of Survivors of Torture, and maybe my father and brother and my aunt and uncle might come as well, that sort of thing. But word spread about the piece, and there were lines that wrapped around the block.

MS: And you've presented it several other times since 2004?

JS: Yes, we've performed it in different places in Ireland and in the Dublin Dance Festival in 2009, and then, La MaMa asked if I could bring *Fall and Recover* to New York in 2011. We were still dealing with the fact that some of the dancers were locked into the asylum process. We had some trouble getting visas, at first, but eventually, we worked it out and we went to New York. We ran for three weeks in New York in March/April of 2011. And it was a phenomenal experience because the vision, the dream of America is like this mythological thing. And it's a big, civilised, western country—I think, the *only* big civilised western country—that has a black president, and a black president born of an African father. Performing there meant so much on so many levels. The Statue of Liberty, the whole concept that is America, it was more than just another performance. Opening night, the audience was like a who's who of dance people. I was standing there thinking: this was something that started in a little drawing room of a Georgian house in Dublin in 2003, as a therapy work for torture survivors, and it has turned into a major dance work in New York.

MS: As you do this piece for international audiences, what do you think it has to say about the portrayal of Irishness on stage?

JS: Many of the performers gradually acquired Irish citizenship. Many of them have been living in Ireland for over ten years, or more. Ireland is their country. Some of them have kids in Irish schools. Some have married Irish people. They are Irish. But they kind of turn the image of Irish identity on its head. If you have an image of green fields, and rain, and shamrocks, and tweed skirts, and pints of Guinness, this performance turns the old idea of Irish identity on its head. Alcoholic priests, some incest, a wet day, somebody going crazy with sheep or cows, a kitchen, a kettle, a bottle of whiskey on the table is what people expect to see from Irish art. But life is not really like that; we're not like that. I like to challenge the stereotype of Ireland in my work. But I'd like to think that Ireland can develop, too, that we can grow and expand in more progressive, open, flexible directions.

INTERVIEW
with
DECLAN GORMAN and DECLAN MALLON
Upstate Theatre Project

Upstate Theatre Project was founded in 1997 in Drogheda. As a regional theatre company, Upstate aimed to provide drama opportunities and training at a community level while also producing professional work. Given their situation in the border county of Louth, their early socially engaged work drew on Peace and Reconciliation funding and explored the legacy of the Troubles in community and professional productions. Co-founder Declan Gorman's Border Trilogy (*Hades*, *Epic* and *At Peace*), which was professionally produced by the company, maps the transition in their work from a focus on the legacy of the Troubles to an interrogation of how inward-migration had transformed contemporary Ireland. This strand of inquiry was most developed in their subsequent community projects combining Irish-born and immigrant participants who partnered to devise new works including *Steps* (2002), *Journey from Babel* (2009) and *The Mango Tree* (2012). We interview co-founders Declan Gorman and Declan Mallon. Gorman stayed with the company from 1997 until 2010, while Mallon remains the current Director of Upstate Theatre Project.

CHARLOTTE MCIVOR: How did Upstate Theatre Project begin?

DECLAN GORMAN: The original founding intention was to establish a regional performing arts organisation unlike previous models. Upstate Theatre Project would seek to bridge the perceived gap between high-end, innovative, professional theatre productions for paying audiences, on the one hand, and on the other hand, the area of community engaged practice. Prior to that, you would have had companies based in Dublin and the regions that had excelled in one or other of those areas. For instance, Dublin's City Arts Centre, with which I was very involved at a previous time in my life, was a hub for community-engaged practice in the early 1990s. You had practitioners who had moved beyond bringing touring theatre into disadvantaged communities, and were actually working in an embedded way within communities and working in partnership with community development groups and youth groups to allow the voice of local communities to come through in performance. We were going to do that, but we were also going to have a touring theatre company and the two areas would inform each other. We would seek to create a continuum of practice for a kind of theatre that would very much be rooted and embedded in a community. We set up a structure of four pillars and any work that we would do would have to be tested against those pillars. We had 'Learning' and 'Local' programmes, we had 'Upstate Live' company, which was the touring company, and then we had the 'Laboratory', which is where we would try to bring those different elements together for development of new ideas and we would bring people in from Drogheda or indeed from other parts of the Border area to work together with professionals. Our work was based in Drogheda, but very much centred on a wider border region, which included Louth, Monaghan, Cavan, into County Fermanagh and Tyrone, at times, right up to Donegal, but primarily in the Northeast region.

CM: In the earlier years of the company, you had a fair amount of funding from the EU Peace and Reconciliation Fund. How did this affect your work?

DECLAN MALLON: The EU and Drogheda Partnership were the first ones to fund Upstate Theatre Project. The funding immediately put us down as a regional company, and not just a local company. Although we were based in Drogheda, the irony of the early years is that we actually didn't work much in Drogheda, because south Louth was excluded from the contract with the Peace and Reconciliation Programme, so Monaghan and south Tyrone really became the territory. And, on the question of the EU's reconciliation agenda, how did we respond? We didn't. We allowed the participants to respond. We set up drama workshops, with both adults and young people, and probably the most successful were the young people, because that was one group where the level of funding allowed us to bus participants from the areas that I mentioned into one central spot every second week for a full day of drama. We allowed them to respond because we, ourselves, were never involved, or affected by the

Troubles, insofar as we were south of the border. Whatever happened up North happened up North. It didn't really extend into Drogheda in the same way. One of the things in the early Peace and Reconciliation Programme was that people were suspicious along the border and didn't particularly care to talk about the Troubles that openly. I think our drama workshops gave participants a way of fictionalizing the history, the Troubles themselves, so, at that distance, it allowed for people to think about and share their reflections on the Troubles.

DG: Part of our argument was that it was a leap forward, compared with ten years earlier, to simply have young people from the diverse communities, and particularly across the border, aligned together in a room doing anything creative, or anything constructive together. To try and ram down their throats the imperative that the work would have to concentrate on the grim history from which their parents were emerging, was something that we tended quietly to resist. We preferred to allow the very experience of people being in the room together to be like a foundation stone for a more hopeful future. I think that strategy was particularly effective for the young people's group, because its membership was always drawn from both communities in that time when we were talking about how our world was divided into two communities from either side of the border. It became a little more problematic when we were working with adult groups, which, in spite of our best efforts to recruit from across the religious divides, tended to be strongest south of the border, and to draw participants from one religious faith only, and so that dialogue wasn't particularly happening in the room. In those situations, we had to ensure that the people making the work would provide some insights from their particular perspectives as to what had caused the Troubles, what had brought about the reconciliation and so on. That work was then brought to residential exchanges where they met with people from other communities and it was the sharing of those stories that became quite important.

CM: It strikes me that there are two levels to your work, especially in those areas that are political or politicised. Number one is the level at which you are bringing arts outreach to communities that are underserved, that are not served within a larger arts infrastructure, and then there is the thematic emphasis of your work, that to bring cross-communities together implies that a dialogue will take place, a dialogue that responds to political histories. At this point in Upstate's work, how would you describe your company's relationship to the political itself?

DG: When Declan and I met up in the context of forming Upstate, I was very aware that we were both engaged with politics. We were both informed about politics internationally and within Ireland. What made it possible for us to work so long together was the belief that in its own subtle way that art is part of politics and politics is part of art. In this phase of the work, I think there was a commitment not to reconciliation at any cost, but to a considered and politically aware process of reconciliation that didn't necessarily accord with what official Ireland, or official Northern Ireland, or official America, or official Britain, or official Europe wanted. Rather, it was about trying to listen to what real people who had been through real troubles in the North and on the border area were trying to achieve themselves.

DM: Access to and participation in the arts is, I think, a very political agenda as well. That is something that I think is written into the marrow of Upstate, and that's what we were about. We were about opening up access and encouraging participation, which I think leads to more active citizenship and political participation in the end. So it's that idea of a shared aesthetic space that doesn't belong just to artists alone, doesn't belong to arts organisations, but actually, belongs to citizens in general, or citizen-artists, as we like to call them. Art is not just a commodity; it's rather an activity that people should be involved in.

CM: Taking up the theme, or word, 'citizenship', a thematic shift happened in your work around 2002 when you started incorporating issues around increased immigration to Ireland and multiculturalism, or interculturalism into your work. First came *Steps*, then *At Peace, Journey from Babel,* and finally, most recently, *The Mango Tree*. Can you talk about the shift in your work towards inward-migration to Ireland?

DG: The old bipolar obsession with the Catholic–Protestant or the North–South was being surpassed by the reality that on the streets around us, and in the shops, and in the community centres, there was growing evidence that there were people from other societies and other communities and other nations and other races living among us. And at the time, our work didn't seem to be touching that segment of the society at all. So we started with *Steps*, a collaboration between Upstate and Droichead Youth Theatre, as a group of white Irish people trying to figure out how does our work evolve in order to incorporate the change in the very community in which we claim to embedded. A few miles up the road from Drogheda was Mosney, the local accommodation centre for asylum-seekers. We made contact with the representative of the Department of Justice, and from there, we were put in touch with Jane Spearman, another Irish artist who was working as a resident artist and youth worker in Mosney. Through this, we were ultimately put in contact with a group of fifteen young people who were drawn, literally, from the four other continents of the world, and so we brought them together with fifteen young people from Drogheda for a finite period of time to make an original devised play. The young people who were living in Mosney were mad keen to just meet all the local young people and get involved in this new country that they were living in. It ran really smoothly and the piece of work they chose to make was a comedy. We let them work on what it was they really wanted to talk about. We thought it would be stories about being hidden away on refugee ships and all the rest, but there was none of that. They just made a Christmas comedy that did have a powerful intercultural theme and traced a sexual relationship between a young African man and a young Irish woman. *Steps* was either a parody or a homage, but certainly, it drew from the Christian Joseph and Mary story and was a retelling of the Christmas myth. But when it was over, there was no further funding to continue with that particular programme, and the nature of Mosney was that, even during the course of the programme, they had a dispersal strategy, so the young people were already being moved on, relocated off to Mayo or Sligo, or anywhere in the country. We held on to most of them during the project, but as soon as it was over, they began to disperse, and within eight months, they were all gone. But we had opened a door in terms of our own mission.

CM: After a few more years of research, engagement with local community groups and some short workshops, Declan [Gorman] wrote *At Peace,* a play that would be professionally staged and toured. Significantly, *At Peace* is one of the few plays on immigration to Ireland that has had a multilingual approach to staging. Sections of the script were translated into Latvian, as well as Yoruban. The actors were speaking languages other than English and their lines were projected in translation during the show. Why present the piece as multilingual and who collaborated with you on the translations?

DG: My proposal to perform it in three languages was there from the beginning. If you're standing in the queue of the bank, or if you're in a local shop, you are hearing these languages all the time. It just seemed to me that it made no sense for it to be written and performed exclusively in the dominant language, in the home-country language. This raised exciting artistic challenges, then, about making this work. It also meant that my job, as a writer, was immediately a collaborative process with translators. It wasn't collaborative in the purest sense, in that I wrote the script in English based partly on mythologies I had studied from Yoruban, Latvian and Celtic tradition, partly on stories told to me by people who came along to a series of Upstate workshops prior to the production, and also stories I was researching in the newspapers. It also drew partly from my own experience of being an Irish migrant in Germany in the 1980s in my twenties, arriving without a single word of German. I wrote the play in English and then brought it to Nigerian playwright Bisi Adigun, himself a very well-established theatre practitioner, and also Elita Baltaiskalna, a Latvian translator who was not involved in theatre but had come along as a participant in some of our workshops. We brought in actors from Nigeria, also from the Nigerian community in London, and went over to actually recruit actors from Latvia. The actors took the texts as had been translated and further developed the translations in the workshop, so that they flowed more naturally for them. At the end of the day, the final text owed not only to the translators that were named, but it must also be acknowledged, the actors.

CM: After *At Peace,* the newly formed Louth International Theatre Project (LITP) began to take shape, which was a community-based initiative that resulted in an original devised site-specific performance *Journey from Babel*. How did this group evolve?

DG: Our aspiration was to run the programme in Dundalk and Drogheda and to get a fifty/fifty mix: 50 per cent of people who were indigenous Irish who wanted to commit to this way of working, and 50 per cent of people who were from what was called the 'new communities'. We advertised in the local newspapers, the various unemployment offices, the Citizens Information offices, and the offices where people would go to get documents translated.

DM: The Drogheda end of the project was very successful because of the diversities of the countries that actually came into LITP, and I think it opened people's eyes into how diverse local Irish communities have actually become. The notion of cultural difference in Ireland today is usually reduced to being only between the African and Irish communities, whereas, we had participants in Drogheda who were Irish, French, German, Austrian, Mexican, American and English. Because they were largely white, perhaps some didn't immediately see that they were actually of a different culture than 'Irish'. For audiences and participants, it broadened the base for the notion of cultural difference, of diversity among the new communities that had begun to grow in Drogheda and Dundalk.

DG: But, whereas, in Drogheda, it was working out really well, in Dundalk, where we were not so well embedded or networked, we attracted an overwhelming number of Irish and one or two English people, but almost no participation from outside those communities. So we asked those people to reflect on questions of journeying and migrations as a monocultural group and we then brought their work into a dialogue with the intercultural group that we had formed in Drogheda. The reality of LITP, then, had to be rationalised after the fact to the funders who had wanted to see boxes ticked to say that you had X numbers of Africans, X numbers of Europeans, and all the rest of it.

CM: I'm interested in your use of language around these various projects such as the LITP and, more recently, describing *The Mango Tree* as an intercultural arts participation project. How have you approached naming your projects?

DG: I think it's important to say that we were only learning the difference between terminologies ourselves. I would be perfectly honest and say that I was already working with people from other cultures before I ever stopped to wonder what was the difference between the commonly-used term, 'multiculturalism', and the term, which I suddenly learned was more appropriate to what we were doing, which was 'interculturalism'. And if we, as practitioners and comparatively educated fellows, were struggling with this, then you can imagine that, for the men and women from the community who came to participate in the first ever LITP, such questions of language were not something they were concerned with. But nonetheless, the question of language became quite interesting in the work. That's why I think one of the most successful scenes in *The Journey from Babel* was the scene which involved an Irish café worker who uses unintentionally 'racist' language in the company of two educated young women who are also a couple. This character is representative of the really good-hearted, open, welcoming people in a town like Drogheda, who because they are exposed constantly to a kind of thoughtless racial banter, clumsily use the wrong words. It was a comic and very cutting scene. I think that particular character appealed to people because they felt sorry and felt they could identify with her, because Drogheda people were saying, 'Well, you know, I don't know how to say this, I don't know what words to use, I don't know what language is appropriate anymore. I don't want to hurt people'. So even is it all right to say, 'He's a black?' as the character does? That scene was written following one particular moment in the LITP workshop where the question of language and attitudes came up. There is this wrong-headed idea that there is a homogeneity among cultures that are not the dominant culture in any society. We found that the range in that room, not only of languages, but also of perspectives on what racism might be, and on what is appropriate and what is not appropriate was as diverse as the number of people in the room. Trying to steer through a script based on improvisation in that very situation was very challenging, and it became a fantastic act of interculturalism. And it turns out that interculturalism is the only thing we can really do in that situation.

INTERVIEW
with
Anna Wolf, Kasia Lech and John Currivan
of Polish Theatre Ireland

Polish Theatre Ireland was founded in 2008 with the aim of representing the Polish diaspora in Ireland and creating sites of intercultural exchange between the Polish-in-Ireland and Irish communities. We interview Polish Theatre Ireland's current artistic director, Anna Wolf; actor and literary manager, Kasia Lech; and actor and director, John Currivan, who have been involved with the company since its origins. Polish Theatre Ireland has produced Julia Holewińska's *Foreign Bodies,* original translations of Polish playwright and company member Radosław Paczocha's *Scent of Chocolate* and *Delta Phase,* created an original piece on the work of poet Czeslaw Milosz (*Chesslaugh Mewash*) with an intercultural cast including Slovakian, Lithuanian, Polish and Irish actors, and mounted a series of staged readings called 'Freedom Ltd' of Polish and Lithuanian plays in collaboration with Irish–Lithuanian Theatre Company, Alternatyva Alternatyvai.

Charlotte McIvor: What led to your decision to form Polish Theatre Ireland (PTI)?

Anna Wolf: The first thing we intended was to give a chance to Polish actors, to be a platform for Polish actors to express their thoughts about theatre and use their skills. The second objective was to promote Polish playwriting. We wanted to present Polish texts translated into English and also English texts translated into Polish in order to establish two strands of the audiences: both Irish and Polish. The main goal was to use theatre to depict the coexistence of the two cultures in Ireland, Polish and Irish and to start a collaboration between Polish and Irish actors and artists in general.

Kasia Lech: By extension, to create something new on the stage.

CM: What are the differences and similarities you see between contemporary Polish and Irish theatre?

KL: There is a huge issue of history and the shadow of history in both contemporary Polish and Irish work. There is probably more naturalism in Ireland and possibly more of the grotesque in Poland. To speak very generally, the difference is that there is perhaps more theatre rooted in realist traditions in Ireland, while Polish theatre often embraces symbolism and presentational modes of performance.

AW: The biggest difference is that in Poland, theatre belongs to the director, and in Ireland, theatre belongs to the author, to the writer.

JOHN CURRIVAN: For me, I think, Ireland is moving away from that. People are reminding themselves of the importance of action and not talking about action.

CM: Your production of Radosław Paczocha's *Scent of Chocolate* (translated by Anna Wolf) was the company's premiere and presented in both Polish and Irish on alternating nights. Why start with this play?

AW: This play is the story of a dysfunctional family left by an immigrant mother. This broken hierarchy leads to communication chaos and the main character, Misza, a disabled boy tempted by the scent of chocolate from abroad, is paradoxically the only one who can escape into a different world. It played well because it was the immigration story upside down because we, the company founders, are here, as immigrants, and the audience is watching a story that is actually happening in Poland here in Ireland.

JC: I don't know if this marks a difference between Polish writing and Irish writing, but the drama in *A Scent of Chocolate* never happens, but it's always there. You never meet the mother, but you're always expecting her to come and she doesn't come. It's like *Waiting for Godot,* in that Godot never arrives, in the same way that *Scent of Chocolate* actually boiled down to the choice of Bogusia, the older sister, as to whether or not she would abandon her family and go to America, to join her mother who was never coming back.

CM: John and Kasia, for yourself and the other actors who were playing in both Polish and English in *Scent of Chocolate,* what was it like moving back and forth between those two registers of performance?

KL: I think we rehearsed more in English because it was technical, it was about clarity of speech. Owning your lines in English was harder for us [other Polish actors included Jacek Dusznik, Oscar Mienandi and Alicja Ayres] than owning your lines in Polish. I think the shows were a little bit different from my point of view. The Polish show was maybe more emotional. The English show was more presentational because we were a little bit detached.

CM: John, you are not a Polish speaker, but you acted in Polish. How did you negotiate that challenge?

JC: I found the adjustment easy, not easy, but it was easy enough because I think the other actors had a lot more text. The only barrier was the language. The reason I think that PTI works well in Ireland is that theatre doesn't depend on language. You could have a wordless play in Polish. I was doing a playwriting course in Irish, and the teacher was like, first of all, this is not about Irish, we are not here to talk about the Irish language. We are here to talk about dramatic structure because the Irish language is in a way irrelevant. In the same way, in the way the country that a play is set in, unless there's a civil war on, unless it's set during wartime, it's kind of irrelevant. What's more important is the immediate circumstances and the fact that there's a war on. We could have a war in Poland, Ireland, Syria.

CM: Kasia, was it different to be acting with John when you knew he wasn't understanding you?

KL: John claims that his lines were not much, but his lines were crucial, because very often he was giving the point to what I've said. Usually, it was a matter of yes or no. If he gave me the wrong line, the point was lost.

CM: How did you deal with that as a performer?

KL: I think it was very much the communication between us. Whenever he got the line wrong, he could read from me that this is not the line.

CM: Your second production *Chesslaugh Mewash* had Irish, Lithuanian, English, Polish, Slovakian and French. Why did you choose to work in all these different languages?

JC: Czeslaw Milosz, the poet, was born in Lithuania. He moved to Poland, then he moved to America, and lived the rest of his life there so a lot of his poems deal with: 'Who am I?''Where am I from?''What is my language and what's my origin?'

AW: We wanted to use as many languages as possible and then find one theatrical language. The production of *Chesslaugh Mewash* was a devised performance created by everyone in the crew. We improvised the scenes from the poems that Milosz wrote in 1960 when he was an immigrant himself in Berkeley and we focused on those plots that were describing him as a poet, an artist who struggles to find his own identity, his own language, his own real face in a new foreign world. Using Milosz's poems only, we tried to build new characters, which were actually the masks of Milosz, and through them, tell our personal stories of our times in Dublin 2011.

KL: I don't think we found THE language of *Chesslaugh Mewash*, but the whole idea was that there are so many of them.

AW: There was some negative comments about the mixture of languages in the piece. The idea was that we can understand each other in so many languages but we can't understand each other in English, let's say, on the more emotional level. For example, Oscar [Mienandi] and Cillian [Roche] were playing a scene and they were using the same poem, but Oscar was using Polish and Cillian English. They were trying to find a connection through the same poem in different languages. They couldn't in the beginning, but in the end, there was one word that brought them together.

CM: For your next production, *Delta Phase,* Anna again translated Radosław Paczocha's work into English, but this time, you cast Irish-born actors in three of the main roles, with Kasia playing the fourth, and presented the play only in English. What led to this approach?

KL: It's a tough decision because rehearsing two shows takes more time, by extension, more funding, when it is really hard to get funding in the first place.

AW: *Delta Phase* actually represents another aspect of our goals in producing Polish theatre in Ireland, as it's more of a collaboration between Polish and Irish artists.

CM: Looking at *Scent of Chocolate, Chesslaugh Mewash* and *Delta Phase* together, how does language and dialect function in the company's work?

KL: For *Delta Phase,* the larger decision is that we live in Dublin and we speak English with different accents, like a Polish accent or a Dublin accent. We try to mime the soundscape of the society. We're here and this happens. This society has all those accents.

CM: It seemed to me from watching *Delta Phase* that in your translation, the action of the play, itself, which involves a night out of three young men gone horribly wrong due to drugs and drinking, was transposed to an Irish context.

JC: Yes, it was.

AW: Paczocha came over to see our production and he didn't actually like that we didn't change the Polish names. He said that the actors were struggling with pronouncing the Polish names, but that was the idea: to leave some Polish flavours in the play.

KL: This represented a struggle on different levels, the struggle of this coexistence between Polish and Irish culture.

AW: *Delta Phase* is showing that this production is that coexistence that Irish actors are trying to play in a Polish play.

KL: Irish theatre explores soundscapes, accents and everything, whereas Polish theatre has a fixed stage speech. The dialects were mostly taken out by Communism from the Polish language, so there is a fixed stage speech in most shows. So as a Polish artist or audience member, you're not used to experiencing differences in dialect or pronunciation, so I think that accounted for Paczocha getting annoyed or having problems with the mispronunciation of the names.

AW: He was telling me this from the very beginning—to change the names to English—but I was making my own choice as a translator.

CM: Continuing on the topic of language, would you describe your work as 'multicultural', 'intercultural', or by another term?

KL: In Seamus Heaney's translation of Antigone [*Burial at Thebes*], he uses different rhythms of verse to facilitate the reading of the play in the Irish context, but, without limiting it to this context only. Those different rhythms exist within the world of the play and broaden its context. As Heaney says: 'we all live within language'. I feel that for me is what interculturalism/multiculturalism is in Ireland today, and that's exactly where we fit in. It's about those spaces, about all of us being together and interacting. Hiberno-English: that comes out of interaction. Without interaction from two completely different cultures, English and Irish as well as others, Hiberno-English would never have existed. So this is exactly for me where the Polish Theatre Ireland comes in today.

CM: *The Sunday Times Culture* magazine recently ran a lead article entitled 'No more cleaners and prostitutes please'[1] featuring you, Kasia, as well as fellow PTI member, Alicja Ayres and Robert Zawadski, who was appearing in Owen McCafferty's *Quietly* at the Abbey. How well do you think that the arts are doing at representing the stories of a more diverse Ireland now in 2013?

KL: After this article, some people felt that we were saying that being a cleaner or a prostitute is wrong, and I was thinking about this and how it should have been phrased better. I think what PTI is trying to do for the crowd is draw attention to the problem that the characters that are mostly available for non-Irish actors are defined by the fact that they are Polish and that they are cleaners and that there is nothing else there. You're Polish and you're a cleaner, that's plenty, and we don't need to know anything else. I don't mind playing prostitutes to the end of my life, as long as each of these prostitutes is different: she has her own story, but she is not defined by the fact that, oh yes, she was trafficked, she's here and she's unhappy. End of story. That's, I think, where the constraint is and the problem is that Irish theatre for a long time was very self-focused because it was creating itself. Now, it has to focus on the outside and it's hard because you have to do that without losing yourself and there is obviously the whole postcolonial fear that, if we allow the foreign influence, we're going to get colonised again to some extent.

Notes and References

1 Eithne Shortall, 'No More Cleaners or Prostitutes Please', *The Sunday Times,* 18 November 2012, *Culture* magazine, pp. 6–7.

INTERVIEW
with
Alicja Ayres
Performer

Alicja Ayres moved to Dublin from Poland in 2006. As an actress, she has worked with many companies, including: Polish Theatre Ireland (*Scent of Chocolate* and *Chesslaugh Mewash*) and the Abbey Theatre (*Shibari* at the Peacock Theatre). Her film credits include featured roles in *Sanctuary, The Canal* and *Death Waits*. Alicja is also a singer and art model. She graduated from the Gaiety School of Acting in June 2011.

Charlotte McIvor: How did you get started in theatre?

Alicja Ayres: Before I came here, I remember I really wanted to be involved in performing and acting. But back in Poland, I think I never thought I could actually do it as a way of life, as my job. In Poland, it was more like my hobby, passion. I was studying English and that was supposed to be my main job, earning money and all that, and theatre was just on the side. I didn't do any professional training in Poland and only actually decided here. I just had to give it a try, and do the professional training and give it a try in the professional industry and if it doesn't work, it doesn't work, and at least I'll know, and just leave it at that. I trained at the Gaiety School of Acting in Dublin. First, I did one year of part-time courses because I wasn't sure if I'd just be able to leave my job and do the full-time, because it's like your life is just gone for two years, and then money is another issue as well. After that year, I just decided to give it a try and try to do the full-time training. It's like your life doesn't exist anymore, the life that you had before—your friends, social life—it's like you're just in the school all the time, twenty-four hours, a lot of projects, and people in the group become like your family.

CM How did training at the Gaiety change your own approach to theatre?

AA: We had this manifesto class, which was all about our own work. So suddenly I had to write my own pieces and perform them, my own work, which I had never done before. I discovered that being not from here, I have this kind of background that kind of appeared, it emerged. I'm now thinking about doing some of my own work as well, because it's not that easy to only get acting work when you're not Irish. The options are really limited. It's still much better than it was a few years ago, but this immigration thing is still so fresh that it's not as present in theatre and in film, so it's not that easy to get acting jobs that would just keep me going. I have some ideas for plays, or scripts, or maybe short films, so I'm thinking more and more about doing my own thing as opposed to just waiting for auditions.

CM: Can you tell me about the transition from training into working professionally in theatre, film and television in Ireland?

AA: There is this huge area of independent theatres and filmmakers, in which you usually work for free or expenses covered, and I think everyone goes through that. And I was pretty lucky because right after I graduated, I was doing *Chesslaugh Mewash* for the Dublin Fringe with Polish Theatre Ireland [PTI]. And then, was just trying to find good film projects to get my show reel. Gary Duggan's *Shibari* directed by Tom Creed at the Peacock Theatre was the first fully professional and serious job that I got in a professional theatre. In the time immediately before I got the part, I was in a little crisis, and I was debating taking a break, maybe, and just getting some job to make money and see how it goes, and then I heard about the auditions for *Shibari,* which changed everything again.

CM: In your experience of the film and theatre industry here, is it that if you are non-Irish you are automatically not considered or not sent out for certain roles?

AA: Yes. People were telling me that, but I was still kind of hoping that, I mean, it's natural, I live here, and I have so many friends who are not Irish, and they have normal jobs and normal lives, and they are just like Irish people, and so I thought, surely there will be parts for me. But then, it was really depressing because in the independent industry it's much better, and in theatre as well, that there are more options. But in professional, maybe not theatre, but mainly film, it's almost impossible to get a part, because they would usually contact me for auditions just when they needed an Eastern European girl to play cleaners and prostitutes. The first one was like, 'Yeah, OK'. The second one, 'All right'. But then it keeps repeating and you see that you only get contacted when they need this kind of role. That was the moment when I started to think, 'What should I do now?''Should I maybe go to London and try there?'

CM: *Shibari* was performed at the Peacock in the Abbey, Ireland's national theatre. What was it like getting to perform in that venue?

AA: That was just like living a dream—the whole process of really working on the show starting from rehearsals and then the show. Everyone was just so committed and passionate about the project. Also, it was amazing to be responsible only for your job, which was the character, because usually when you do independent shows, you're responsible for everything, so you have to do a lot of things that you usually wouldn't have to be responsible for, such as promotion and helping with the set, you need to get your own costumes and it's everything around, so it's really just a lot of work. And I love Gary Duggan for writing this play and my character and showing a world where half of the characters are Irish and half of the characters are not Irish. *Shibari* was trying to kind of bring Ireland as it is to the stage and show that we have now a different society and that it should be reflected in film and in theatre.

CM: In the course of your training at the Gaiety, did people mentor you at all about what you might expect as a non Irish-born actor, or was that not addressed at all when you were in training?

AA: They told that I would probably need to work on my accent. In Poland, you have this kind of generic Polish most people use, and you don't really think about the way you are speaking. The accent is not at all an aspect of a character. Only when I came here did I realise that the way you speak and the accent is really important, because it automatically places you somewhere and gives you some identity. I was told it would be important to get at least the most neutral or most common accents like the Received Pronunciation for English, or the generic American or even neutral Irish. But then I was thinking, well, I don't think that I can really sound like 100 per cent Irish. And if they have so many Irish actresses, why would they choose me if they have so many Irish actresses? Ultimately, I was hoping for more opportunities for non-Irish people, for foreign people, or just not from Ireland.

CM: Were there other non-Irish born people in your Gaiety class?

AA: In my group, there was a girl from the UK, two people from the States, and one girl who was kind of Irish–Australian. And the rest of the people were Irish. But all of them, English was their native language, whatever the accent, it was their native language. I was the only one for whom English was a second language.

CM: What is it like training and performing as well in a second language?

AA: I think it's actually paradoxically more natural for me to perform in English because, in Poland, I did a college for English teachers. I'm a qualified teacher of English as a second language. And in Poland, I was actually performing in English because I was doing work at a theatre created within the university. The aim of the theatre was to present the English heritage—plays from Ireland, from the States, from the UK—and also to use the theatre to teach English so you can get a group of students to see an English play in English. I have done one or two shows where I had to perform in Polish and I found it weird, such as when I did *Scent of Chocolate* with PTI.

CM: How have you seen attitudes around immigration change post-Celtic Tiger, and how committed do you think Irish society is to acknowledging where it is now?

AA: In any society, at the beginning, the immigrants come and there's a lot of work, and everything's brilliant and it's great. Once something goes wrong or the economy collapses, people start looking for a scapegoat. So I think it's natural, not just for Irish people, but for everywhere. And it really happens everywhere. That's how the world works. But I don't think it's that bad here. I think we could maybe have more support for the arts for non-Irish artists. It was maybe easier back then to get funding or support from Irish organisations when you were non-Irish.

CM: Those sort of limits would seem to assume that somebody cannot be Irish and Polish at the same time.

AA: When I look for work as an actor, it drives me mad that one of the first things they have to say about me is that I'm Polish. There's so many things about me before I'm Polish. And that automatically puts me into some kind of box, or it defines me in a way. Even when I write my own things, my own scripts or scenes, I never really write about Irish, Polish or people who are very strongly put somewhere in their place on Earth. I write more about just stories, universal stories, and I don't really care who the people are, what accents they have, or where they are from. It's much more just about what's happening between them and the connection, and who they are is just kind of additional background. But even those stereotypical parts, those prostitutes and cleaners, even though they want an Eastern European girl, they really want this kind of Russian, Slavic look and a strong Eastern European accent, more Russian. So even if they would contact me, I'm not what they would be looking for, because I don't look Slavic, I don't look Polish, I don't sound Polish as well. I'm in this kind of Nowhere Land. But also I'm not just an Irish actor that could play any other part. And so Iona in *Shibari* was amazing for me, because I think I actually look much more Romanian than Polish. But she didn't have to have a strong accent, because she's been living here for a while and she even had an Irish boyfriend. *Shibari* was just perfect for me. I would love to have more opportunities like that one, when you can have a character that you can just get your teeth into and just do it.

INTERVIEW
with
José Miguel Jimenéz
Member of The Company

José Miguel Jiménez moved to Ireland in 2004 after studying theatre at the Universidad de Chile for four years and forming two theatre companies currently active in Santiago. He would go on to complete the Bachelor in Acting Studies at Trinity College, Dublin. He is an active professional actor and director and has worked with the Abbey Theatre and Rough Magic Theatre Company, among others. He is a founding member of The Company, a Dublin-based theatre collective also including Brian Bennett, Robert McDermott and Nyree Yergainharsian. Their original devised work includes *Who is Fergus Kilpatrick?* (winner of the Spirit of the Fringe 2009), *As you are now so once were we* (international tour), *Hipsters We Met and Liked* and *Politik* (Dublin Theatre Festival 2012). Projects in development include a work in progress, *Bernardo,* based on the figure of Bernardo O'Higgins, the 'Irish liberator' of Chile, in collaboration with Manuela Infante and Dylan Tighe, first shown at the 2013 Dublin Theatre Festival.

Charlotte McIvor: How did you first get involved in theatre?

José Miguel Jimenéz: I didn't have any connection in terms of family or friends with any sort of an artistic practice. In Chile, I was going to be a vet and I always thought I was going to be a vet. I started a theatre workshop for a month before you apply for college. My first options were vet medicine and microbiology, and then, at the end, was theatre. I didn't get the other ones, and the theatre option was like, 'You can do this in terms of points', and I was like, 'Yeah, let's do it and see what happens.' In Chile, I went to college for four years of training at Universidad de Chile. Then I had a couple of years of professional acting jobs. And I started a theatre company with a group of friends as well, and we started to make productions. I was in one of them and working on the second one, and I was like, 'I have to leave now. I'm twenty-three. I need to go somewhere else. I need to see what else is there.' So I came to Ireland.

CM: What drew you to Ireland?

JJ: I don't know. I had no connection, no family, no friends, didn't speak a word of English. The first year was incredibly difficult, as you can imagine.

CM: Were you familiar with Irish theatre or literature before?

JJ: No, not at all. I think the one thing that was influential was Daniel Day-Lewis. I watched *The Boxer* and *In the Name of the Father*, and I thought that politically Chile and Ireland have similar histories in terms of oppression and revolution, and are both very polarised societies as well. But I always felt that the way in which things got solved in Chile after the dictatorship and with the return of democracy was that we didn't solve things, really. We just masked them with this layer of economic success. A society, a critically divided society was just painted-over with, 'We're okay now, we're over it, we're doing really well.' The bad consequences are coming up now with the student revolution and the incredibly bad education system and the ridiculously unfair distribution of wealth. So I always had that feeling about Chile, that this is the wrong way to do it. Then I saw *The Boxer* and *In the Name of the Father*, and I thought, 'Look at that little island there, divided in two, making it really explicit, really clear where they stand, instead of just going, "I know we're OK".' I know that's not exactly the history, but in a way, it was like, 'This is what it is, this is what we need to do.' And I always felt that walking in the streets of Ireland was a statement of something, a political statement, when you walk on the left footpath, or the right footpath, it means something different. And I always thought it was very exciting. Like, it's clear where you are, it's clear what you're standing for.

CM: So your first year here, you did not speak English, and yet, you were living here. How did you survive?

JJ: I lived in a hostel for three months. I made a few friends there. After three months, we moved into a house and shared a house for a year. I got a job, I worked as a kitchen porter for a while, which is the most difficult job ever. I've done a couple of things, but nothing compares to being a kitchen porter. I was wrecked. And then I was very lucky, I found a job in a small bed and breakfast on the Northside of the city. And the people there were like angels to me. I worked there for four or five years. They were so good to me because I worked there, and then I decided to go to college. I went to Trinity and they accommodated all my shifts, so I could keep working.

CM: That's a big jump, because Trinity College, Dublin's Bachelor in Acting Studies, then, and now, in its new iteration as the Lir, is a very prestigious programme. How did you get involved with the Irish theatre community and what led you to your decision to apply to Trinity?

JJ: At that stage, I was already an actor and a theatre maker, and after six months, or a year, I started to feel, 'What do I want to do?' And I felt it would be very difficult to get into the community because I didn't speak, at that stage, good English at all. And also I was just focusing on acting at that stage, and I was like, 'I'm not going to be able to perform in this country, no one knows me, and I'm not even able to speak it well.' So I thought, 'I need to go to college again. That's a way to get in.' I just asked around about the acting schools, and the Gaiety and Trinity came up, and I think I was told that the best one was Trinity. I went for it, and I auditioned. I think I did well in the audition, as much as I could, and they said, 'It would be interesting to have you here, and it would be an interesting class. We have people in this class from other places as well, but nothing as extreme as "the guy from Chile".' They said, 'We want you in, but you're going to have to learn English, first. So we're going to keep your place for next year. And you go off and learn English for a year and come back.' And I was like, 'No!' because I didn't have the money, I didn't have the time, but I think they were absolutely right in the end. I just kept working that year, trying to solve—that's a whole different story—visas and papers, immigration, a few periods of being illegal, and then finally paying a dodgy English school to get a student certificate and saving money, and then next year, I went to college.

CM: How was the curriculum at Trinity different from what you had done in Chile?

JJ: It was much more practical. It's just practice. Back home, I had studied for four years, so we did have movement and voice, acting and dance. But we also had a much more theoretical side of things as well. The first year was all introduction to acting, which is basically projecting reality onto the stage. So you're first, 'This is me, this is what I'm doing,' and then you go and look at someone on the street and think, literally, 'Oh, I'm going to try to bring that in here.' Once you have that, you go into realism and Chekhov and Russian classics. And you have verse, not Shakespeare obviously, because of the translation, but we used Golden Age Spanish drama. And then, in third year, you have much more contemporary things. You go through an Artaud approach for one term, and then you go through Brecht, which, in theory, divides the year in two. And then you start the last year with what would be the contemporary mix of those two. I always had the feeling that, in Ireland, you're trained much more to become an actor, in the sense of, like, to become an interpreter, another author. I felt the training back home was much more intense, politically. And it was always about questioning. I remember that, and I'm very thankful about that. Everything I do is still informed by that. You think, 'What are you doing?''Why are doing it?''Are you articulating any opinion in what you're doing?''What's your opinion on it?''Where do you stand?'—very politicised. And then you have second-year students, out and writing, making companies, making a makeshift mini-festival, because they want to protest through what they do. And we were always organising festivals for everything. Like taking the university and locking the doors, 'occupying'.

CM: It wasn't like that at Trinity?

JJ: No, it was pretty well-behaved. It was great, though, in technical terms. But there was always something lacking, I felt like, 'Why are we here anyway?' I met more people that just want to be actors, for instance, than back home, where I met many more who were like, 'I want to be a maker of things.'

CM: 'The Company' formed during the Trinity programme. How did the desire to form 'The Company' come about?

JJ: We (Brian Bennett, Robert McDermott, Nyree Yergainharsian and Tanya Wilson) were all in the same class, except for Rob. It's very simple, we thought: 'We don't like what we see.' It was also informed a little bit by my idea that 'We don't need an agent.''What do you want an agent for?' You want to make your own things. Otherwise, why are you going to be waiting to be called and doing things you don't want to do? We need to make a company and be independent of all of that. We had an idea of making a show about reality and illusion; as in, the reality in which we live, it isn't fully real anymore. There's a mix with fiction all over the place, and we can't even get rid of the fiction anymore and get back to the real, because it breaks. The whole thing breaks. But when you try to acknowledge the amount of construction and manufacture in which we live, in systemic terms, in socio-political terms, in terms of history, in terms of where we want to go, how our desires are constructed, and guided to a certain extent, we're lured into a way of living. I think these ideas came about in relation to what were we going to do when we finished at Trinity. Did we want to get into the system of the agent or the 'machine'? Or do we want to stick together and keep this going on among us? In the Trinity programme, you meet people, you become really good friends, you learn from each other, but at the end of it, you're actually in a competition. But we were like, 'That's wrong. That's structurally wrong.'

CM: It sounds like what you have been trying to do is deal both formally, in terms of theatre form, and thematically, in terms of the content of your productions, with these issues within the acting industry. Therefore, reality and illusion is the theme of the work, but also the way in which you create the work is itself the theme.

JJ: We got to the point where we didn't really need to make a theatre piece. We didn't have to make one to be a company. We didn't need to, we didn't have to. Like, 'Let's get rid of all those things, we don't have to make a theatre show.' So we ended up being a band of sorts, but we don't play music, or maybe we do, I don't know. And that became a little bit of a theme of 'The Company.' We never know, we always go, 'We don't know what we're gonna do', and everything we've learned is now out the window, because let's see what we're trying to talk about and whatever we're trying to talk about is going to tell us how it needs to be altered. So we know, for instance, always at the start of that process when we start looking for material to stage, we know, 'Let's look at everything, but not theatre plays. Let's not get involved in theatre plays.' Because if we find a play, we're already going to be working within the theatre structure and we're going to have to break something instead of coming from another angle.

CM: I'm interested in how you made it from the anti-theatrical position to being on the main bill of the 2012 Dublin Theatre Festival with *Politik*. What happened in between?

JJ: When we were working on the first show in 2009, which was called *Who is Fergus Kilpatrick?*, we were thinking about the manufacture of things, and the reality of illusion construction. And we were like, 'Well, then the theatre space is the perfect space to do that.' A theatre in which nothing is really happening, but everything is live. Everything is still a recording, but a live recording with real bodies in action that are not actually reacting to what's really happening in that room and with the constant struggle for credibility or spontaneity, when it's actually the opposite. That's very interesting when it's such a contradiction in itself. That's why that show became a theatre show, though it was really anti-theatrical in many regards. I think that we knew from then on that theatre would be the medium. There's always an impulse to try to leave it. And I love that. I think that you come back with a renewed energy. With *Fergus Kilpatrick,* we got the 'Spirit of the Fringe' in the Absolut Fringe Festival and because of that award, you have to be in the next Festival. At that first Fringe, we were already thinking about James Joyce's *Ulysses,* which resulted in *As you are now so once were we* (which subsequently took Best Production at the Absolut Fringe in 2010). In the end, *Fergus Kilpatrick* was talking about how all of these moments are constructions. You're looking at a construction that we have prepared for you, and you can see we're lying, and then history's lying. And in the end, you see everything's constructed and what are we going to do now? So we thought, 'Jesus, if we say that, if we shake everything, then the next organic question is, "Where are we left then?"' And it's a question about identity. And we're looking at *Ulysses,* and we're like, 'This makes complete sense.' This is the book that defines Irish identity and nationhood from a very interesting point of view, not from a literal point of view, in terms of the story of the Irish nation, but in a common day, in which nothing happens, but Joyce is writing it through literary language. How he speaks about identity is encrypted, structured into the writing. That's what theatre does as well.

CM: You took *As you are now so once were we* on tour internationally to the United States (Los Angeles), Portugal (Portimão), and Germany (Berlin). How does it play abroad?

JJ: It doesn't work as well as it works here. I feel that one of the aims of The Company, as a theatre company, is to always try to dissolve the literal level of the idea, which is a problem for audiences. That's our task, and at this stage, it's very explicit that that's our task. Anything that's literal, we go like, 'No, it cannot be literal', because then it's just so easily consumed that you have actually not said anything. Then we become politicians of the idea, and that enters that cycle of reproduction of the same idea that is consumed. But we always knew that none of those things should be on the stage as an idea. We should never share the idea in those terms. And so I think it was a bit of a problem when we presented it in Portugal and in LA as well. This is a show about *Ulysses*, a show about identity where it was just people playing around with cardboard boxes, basically, and talking about a day in which nothing happened.

CM: You've talked about the perspective of the training in Chile and the theatre scene in Chile being more political. How do you feel that living in Ireland changed your ideas about theatre?

JJ: I always feel that theatre is a very local animal, and I feel that it has to be, and that it inevitably is. Obviously, there is a kind of work that theatre festivals show, there is that aesthetic, and it's almost, not a formula, but it's an aesthetic in a way. You know what shows figure in a festival, and are going to be touring for the next year around Europe or whatever. You have those, and you have, I suppose, more important work, which is local. I think being local makes work more universal as well to a certain extent, but not necessarily in terms of how you can use the work to enter the flow of commercial, touring festivals. It is difficult for me to know how my ideas have changed, because in making theatre, you're always local. You're always reacting to where you are in the end. My feeling is that I am doing the same thing that I was doing back home; but this thing is obviously different because I'm not there, I'm somewhere else. But my relationship with the world, if you want, it's the same. It's still me, still trying to deal with the same problems, which we'll probably never solve anyway. But now, I deal with this language, with these colours, with these corners and streets. But I don't know if living in Ireland has changed my work. I don't know if it has become less political. I don't think that's even possible. How could it? I don't know if I was in Gaza, making theatre in Gaza, if it'd be more political. I don't think so. I think it'd be in reaction to what's going on there. I don't think the theatre in Gaza, again, is more political than the theatre in the States. I don't think it is. I think that would be like saying someone from Gaza is more of a human being than an American citizen. But they are not.

Index